TURNING THE TIDE

OSPREY
PUBLISHING

THOMAS McKELVEY CLEAVER

TURNING THE TIDE

The USAAF in North Africa and Sicily

OSPREY PUBLISHING
Bloomsbury Publishing Plc
Kemp House, Chawley Park, Cumnor Hill, Oxford OX2 9PH, UK
29 Earlsfort Terrace, Dublin 2, D02 AY28, Ireland
Bloomsbury Publishing Inc.
1359 Broadway, 12th Floor, New York, NY 10018, USA
E-mail: info@ospreypublishing.com
www.ospreypublishing.com

OSPREY is a trademark of Osprey Publishing Ltd

First published in Great Britain in 2024

© Thomas McKelvey Cleaver, 2024

Thomas McKelvey Cleaver has asserted his right under the Copyright, Designs and Patents Act, 1988, to be identified as Author of this work.

This paperback edition was published in Great Britain in 2026 by Osprey Publishing

All rights reserved. No part of this publication may be: i) reproduced or transmitted in any form, electronic or mechanical, including photocopying, recording or by means of any information storage or retrieval system without prior permission in writing from the publishers; or ii) used or reproduced in any way for the training, development or operation of artificial intelligence (AI) technologies, including generative AI technologies. The rights holders expressly reserve this publication from the text and data mining exception as per Article 4(3) of the Digital Single Market Directive (EU) 2019/790

A catalog record for this book is available from the British Library.

ISBN: HB 9781472860255; PB 9781472860262; eBook 9781472860279; ePDF 9781472860224; XML 9781472860231; Audio 9781472860248

26 27 28 29 30 10 9 8 7 6 5 4 3 2 1

The quotations on pages 40–41, 48, 57 (Second Lieutenant Bill Mount), 67–68, 224 (Second Lieutenant John E. Teichrow), 229, 235–236, 236–237 (Captain Roy Whittaker), 238, and 240–241 are from Carl Molesworth, *57th Fighter Group: First in the Blue* (Osprey Publishing, 2011).
The quotations on pages 111–115 (Lieutenant (j.g.) Charles Shields, Lieutenant (j.g.) Charles August, Lieutenant G.H. Carter, and Lieutenant Malcolm Wordell) are reproduced from *"Wildcats" Over Casablanca: U.S. Navy Fighters in Operation Torch* by Lieutenant M.T. Wordell and Lieutenant E.N. Seiler, as told to Keith Ayling, by permission of the University of Nebraska Press. Copyright 2006 by Potomac Books, Inc.
The quotation on page 271 is from Thomas G. Ivie, *Aces of the 325th Fighter Group* (Osprey Publishing, 2014).

Maps by www.bounford.com
Index by Fionbar Lyons

Typeset by Deanta Global Publishing Services, Chennai, India
Printed and bound in Great Britain by Clays Ltd, Elcograf S.p.A.

Osprey Publishing supports the Woodland Trust, the UK's leading woodland conservation charity.

To find out more about our authors and books visit www.ospreypublishing.com. Here you will find extracts, author interviews, details of forthcoming events and the option to sign up for our newsletter.

For product safety related questions contact productsafety@bloomsbury.com

CONTENTS

List of Illustrations and Maps   6
Foreword by Richard P. Hallion   10
Author Preface   12

CHAPTER ONE: The Mad Dash   15
CHAPTER TWO: 1942 – The Lowest Year   21
CHAPTER THREE: First in the Blue   38
CHAPTER FOUR: El Alamein   51
CHAPTER FIVE: Opponents   72
CHAPTER SIX: Air War over Casablanca   96
CHAPTER SEVEN: Race to Tunisia   127
CHAPTER EIGHT: Bomber Boys   160
CHAPTER NINE: Kasserine Pass   192
CHAPTER TEN: Tunisgrad   226
CHAPTER ELEVEN: Pantelleria   249
CHAPTER TWELVE: Air War over Sicily   281

Bibliography   307
Glossary   310
Index   312

LIST OF ILLUSTRATIONS AND MAPS

ILLUSTRATIONS

"Regina IV," flown by 57th Fighter Group CO Major Frank H. Mears, was the first plane to take off from USS *Ranger* (CV-4) off the coast of Africa on July 19, 1942. The 57th was the first USAAF unit to enter combat in Europe, flying across Sub-Saharan Africa and up the Nile Valley to reinforce the British WDAF at El Alamein. (USAF Official)

A "Fighting-9" F4F-4 Wildcat prepares to take off from USS *Ranger* (CV-4) on Operation *Torch* D-Day, November 8, 1942. (USN Official)

Brigadier General Jimmy Doolittle, America's most famous aviator, was named commander of Twelfth Air Force following his return from China and the Doolittle Raid on Japan. His fame and acknowledged skill as a pilot kept morale high through the difficult early months of the campaign. (Corbis via Getty Images)

33rd Fighter Group P-40Fs take off from escort carrier USS *Chenango* (ACV-28) off the North African coast on Operation *Torch* D-Day, November 8, 1942. (USN Official)

SBD-4 Dauntless dive bombers and F4F-4 Wildcats of VF-9 and VF-41 on board USS *Ranger* (CV-4) during Operation *Torch*. (USN Official)

Over 100 Spitfire V fighters were assembled at Gibraltar for use by the 31st and 52nd Fighter Groups in Operation *Torch*. (© IWM CM 6699)

LIST OF ILLUSTRATIONS AND MAPS

66th Fighter Squadron P-40F Warhawks take off on a fighter-bomber mission against the Afrika Korps from an advanced landing ground in the Western Desert in the weeks following Erwin Rommel's defeat at El Alamein. (USAF Official)

Following the change of allegiance of French forces in North Africa after the *Torch* invasion, fighter squadron GC II/5 of the Armée de l'Air was re-equipped with ex-USAAF P-40F Warhawks and took part in the Tunisian campaign, flying from Thélepte during the Battle of Kasserine Pass. (Library of Congress)

A pilot of the 31st Fighter Group's 309th Fighter Squadron stands in the cockpit of his Spitfire Vc, named "Steve," at Maison Blanche airfield in Algeria. (USAF Official)

A "Black Scorpions" P-40F loaded with a British 250lb bomb for a fighter-bomber strike. (USAF Official)

Captain Art Exon, commander of the 57th Fighter Group's 64th "Black Scorpions" Fighter Squadron until he was captured in Sicily, was one of the most popular of the group's "Wheels." (USAF Official)

All maintenance was done in the open on the advanced landing grounds in North Africa. The 57th Fighter Group's ground crewmen became so adept they could perform an engine change in 3–4 hours despite the conditions. (USAF Official)

Ground crewmen perform maintenance on a 12th Bomb Group B-25C at an advanced landing ground in Egypt. (USAF Official)

A 309th Squadron Spitfire Vb comes to grief standing on its nose after going off the dirt runway at the advanced landing ground at Thélepte in Tunisia. (USAF Official)

B-25C Mitchell medium bombers of the 12th Bomb Group over the Western Desert in January 1943. (USAF Official)

Douglas A-20B "Havoc" light bombers of the 47th Bomb Group fly at low level over the Tunisian desert in January 1943. (USAF Official)

A wrecked P-48G of the 82nd Fighter Group after a Luftwaffe attack on the group's airfield at Biskra in February 1943. P-38 losses during the initial months of *Torch* forced the USAAF to strip pilots and planes from the 78th Fighter Group in England to make up losses. (USAF Official)

TURNING THE TIDE

A 33rd Fighter Group P-40F at the remote Thélepte advanced landing ground, only 20km from Kasserine Pass in Tunisia, in February 1943 shortly before Rommel's attack against the US Army's II Corps. (USAF Official)

P-38F Lightning "Spud" of the 1st Fighter Group's 96th Fighter Squadron with squadron pilots at Bône airfield in Tunisia, March 1943. (USAF Official)

Ground crew perform an engine change on a P-38G Lightning of the 82nd Fighter Group's 95th Fighter Squadron at an advanced landing ground in Tunisia in March 1943. (USAF Official)

A Ju-52/3m "Tante Ju" trimotor transport in flight over the Mediterranean en route from Sicily to Tunisia to bring supplies to the trapped Afrika Korps and their Italian allies in April 1942. Allied fighters intercepted the large Ju-52 formations and wreaked havoc with the vulnerable transports in battles such as the Palm Sunday Massacre, where the 57th Fighter Group claimed 25 Ju-52s shot down on April 18, 1943. (USAF Official)

Members of the 57th Fighter Group's 64th Fighter Squadron with a P-40K-5 Warhawk at their Tunisian airfield in April 1943. By this time, the Merlin-powered P-40Fs were war weary and out of production, resulting in re-equipment with Allison-powered P-40s. (Stocktrek Images, Inc./Alamy Stock Photo)

P-40Fs of the 64th "Black Scorpions" Fighter Squadron at an advanced airfield in Sicily in July 1943. (USAF Official)

P-40F-15-CU "Carole" of the 65th "Fighting Cocks" Squadron in Sicily, July 1943. (USAF Official)

A veteran P-38F of the 1st Fighter Group's 27th Fighter Squadron during the Sicilian campaign in July 1943. (USAF Official)

The Macchi C.202 Folgore (Lightning) of the 40 Stormo "Baracca." The C.202 was powered by a German DB 601 engine since the Italian aviation industry had failed to develop a reliable high-powered engine, and was the best Regia Aeronautica fighter during the North African and Sicilian campaigns. (USAF Official)

Lieutenant Colonel Benjamin O. Davis, graduate of the West Point class of 1934, was the first commander of the 99th Fighter Squadron, a unit manned by African American pilots trained in the Tuskegee Program, which entered combat during the Pantelleria campaign in June 1943. (USAF Official)

LIST OF ILLUSTRATIONS AND MAPS

Curtiss P-40L Warhawks of the 99th Fighter Squadron taxi for takeoff at an airfield in Tunisia for a mission over Pantelleria in June 1943. (USAF Official)

An A-46 Mustang of the 27th Fighter Bomber Group at Maison Blanche airfield in Algeria, June 1943. (USAF Official)

An A-36 Mustang of the 86th Fighter Bomber Group over Mount Vesuvius near Naples during the Sicilian campaign, August 1943. The Mustang's long range allowed it to cover southern Italy, once it was based on Sicily at the end of July 1943. (USAF Official)

MAPS

Map 1: Casablanca and Oran areas	101
Map 2: Eastern Algeria and Tunisia	129
Map 3: Pantelleria during Operation *Corkscrew*, 1943	255
Map 4: Key AAF Targets in Sicily, Sardinia, and Italy, June 15–July 9, 1943	273
Map 5: Key AAF Targets in Sicily during Operation *Husky*, July 10–August 17, 1943	294

FOREWORD BY RICHARD P. HALLION

With justification – Midway, Guadalcanal, Operation *Torch*, El Alamein, and the Red Army's fatal encirclement of von Paulus' Sixth Army at Stalingrad – historian Henry H. Adams, himself a veteran of the Pacific War, called 1942 "The Year that Doomed the Axis."

But if 1942 doomed the Axis, 1943 was the year in which the Allies put the Axis firmly on the defensive, achieving notable regional successes and setting the stage for the great counter-invasions of 1944 that pushed Nazi Germany back to its borders and confined Imperial Japan to the shores of Asia and Southeast Asia.

While many historians have addressed the great battles of the South and Central Pacific, the titanic Russo–German struggle on the Eastern Front, the arduous and remorseless war to win the Battle of the Atlantic, and the see-saw air war over Europe, few have given any attention to the war in North Africa and the Mediterranean, with Correlli Barnett, Rick Atkinson, and Vic Flintham being notable exceptions.

North Africa, however, was a most important theater, and the Axis powers – Nazi Germany, Fascist Italy, and Vichy France – made strenuous efforts to seize control of it, typified by the campaign to isolate and then invade Malta, and to seize control of the Suez Canal. A significant body of memoirs of leading figures on both sides attests to the importance of the campaign which, by the late winter of 1943, had been decided in the Allies' favor. Next came the landings on Sicily (the first invasive attack on the homeland of an Axis power), followed by the collapse of Italy's government and the Allied invasion of the Italian mainland.

FOREWORD BY RICHARD P. HALLION

The Western Desert campaign is often thought of as a struggle between two great generals, Germany's famed "Desert Fox," Erwin Rommel, and his Afrika Korps, and Britain's Bernard Montgomery and his Eighth Army Desert Rats. But it was much broader than this, characterized by a strenuous air war to control the waters of the Mediterranean and the skies over the Western Desert.

The Western Desert air war was a learning curve for the Allies and Axis alike, and in 1941–43 – but particularly 1943 – the tactics, techniques, and procedures that the RAF and USAAF would employ in the liberation of Europe were first developed, employed, honed and refined, and placed into standard operational doctrine and practice.

No air service had more to learn, more prewar assumptions to change, and more to endure, than the Army Air Forces. Entering the theater in November 1942 with high hopes of rapidly dominating the Luftwaffe and pounding Rommel's tanks, American airmen instead found that they faced some of the finest and most combat-experienced German fighter pilots in Messerschmitt Bf-109 and Focke-Wulf Fw-190 aircraft that were superior to their own Bell P-39, Curtiss P-40, and Supermarine Spitfire Mk V, and at worst equivalent to the best Allied fighter then in the theater, the Lockheed P-38. Over-confidence, inadequate training, and inferior tactics contributed to high losses of fighters, bombers, and light attack aircraft, and poor existing doctrine limited effectiveness of strikes against German land forces.

But over the year 1943, all that changed. By the time the Allies invaded Italy proper, the USAAF, like the RAF before it, was a fit, well-led, highly experienced force with combat-tested and aggressive aircrews supported by magnificent maintainers.

This is a story of high drama and high heroism, told by a master of military aviation history. Once again, Tom Cleaver has given us a work that both informs and entertains, and which makes a substantial and lasting contribution to military aviation historiography.

Richard P. Hallion
Historian of the US Air Force, retired

AUTHOR PREFACE

In August 1942, the Mediterranean Sea was effectively the *Mare Nostrum* ("Our Sea") that Italian dictator Benito Mussolini had set out to create, with Italy the dominant power in the Mediterranean.

Other than the British Eighth Army in Egypt, a small force of British ships and aircraft at besieged Malta, and another small British force at Gibraltar, the southern coast of the Mediterranean was entirely in the hands of either Italian and German forces, or held by the dependent pro-Axis Vichy French. The advance of Field Marshal Erwin Rommel's Afrika Korps had been held at El Alamein, less than 60 miles from Cairo, close enough for the city's residents to hear the sound of artillery.

No one at that moment in mid-August 1942 could have believed that only 11 months later, the entire southern coast and the island of Sicily would be under Allied control; that more than 200,000 highly trained and experienced – and thus irreplaceable – Afrika Korps veterans would be headed to prisoner-of-war camps in the United States; that the armed forces of Vichy France had changed sides to become part of the Allied coalition; that the Italian government was fully engaged in attempting to rid itself of fascism and surrender to the victorious Allies.

Yet that is what had happened over the course of those 11 months.

Adolf Hitler declared war on the United States on December 11, 1941, four days after the Japanese attack on Pearl Harbor, in the belief that the incredible industrial potential of the United States – recognized by all parties as the strongest industrial power on the planet – would not be able to produce an armed force capable of undertaking offensive operations in Europe before the summer of 1943. He expected that – in

AUTHOR PREFACE

that interim – the Axis could defeat the Soviet Union and impose so many continued defeats on the British Empire in Europe and the Far East, that the Churchill government would fall with a dictated peace imposed, all before he would face American forces.

Instead, the first American reinforcements of British forces in Egypt were already in place in August 1942, albeit only in the form of a small force of heavy bombers and a single fighter group, but more were already on the way. Ninety days after Rommel's advance came to a stop at El Alamein, the Eighth Army mounted a counteroffensive sustained by supplies from the United States, while at the other end of the Mediterranean, an American army landed in Morocco, leading to the quick surrender of the Vichy French forces there.

The nine months between the arrival of the US Army and Air Force in North Africa and the end of fighting in Sicily saw some of the most desperate fighting of the war. Rommel's bloodying of the US Army's nose at Kasserine Pass resulted in the longest retreat in the history of that Army. In the air, American pilots flying the P-38 – the most advanced US fighter in North Africa – were so inexperienced regarding use of tactics appropriate for fighting Bf-109s and Fw-190s in a twin-engine fighter that their losses became unsustainable by January 1943; the 78th Fighter Group in England was stripped of P-38s and pilots to make up North African losses.

Yet only six weeks after the Kasserine debacle, by late March 1943, both American ground and air units had changed tactics, and leaders with demonstrated ability were in command. In April 1943, they defeated the Afrika Korps and the Luftwaffe, leading to the first major Axis surrender in May. A month later they began the Sicilian campaign, which saw that strategic island liberated by the end of July. *Mare Nostrum* was now an Allied lake.

As one senior American commander wrote of the North African campaign, "We had to learn to walk before we could run." By the end, the 57th Fighter Group – the first US unit to arrive in Egypt after being launched from the carrier *Ranger* and flying across the African continent to get there – was so good that RAF Western Desert Air Force commander Air Marshal Arthur Tedder, who ranked his fighter pilots as "A" or "B" in skill according to their combat records, listed all the unit's pilots as "A;" they were 40 percent of the DAF's "A" fighter pilots though the unit was only 14 percent of the total.

Sadly, the North African campaign, in which American soldiers and airmen learned the lessons needed to defeat the Wehrmacht in Europe, has been largely forgotten even by those who take an interest in World War II.

It's my hope that *Turning The Tide* will help change that. The record set by these pilots and crews who fought in one of the most difficult combat environments on the planet is one worthy of recall and acclaim.

Thomas McKelvey Cleaver
Encino, California
2024

I

THE MAD DASH

The 48 P-38F Lightnings of the 1st Fighter Group stayed close to the B-26 Marauder in the lead; its crew was responsible for navigation as the fighters cruised at 200 feet over the heaving, white-capped gray water of the Bay of Biscay below, their throttles leaned out to use as little fuel as possible. The pilots had learned on November 8, 1942 that they would depart England the next day. The group had departed from Portreath, Cornwall, in two-flight formations at 0630 hours that morning, November 9. There was a low overcast, but good weather had been forecast all the way to Oran; still, many felt an uneasiness. It was probably best they didn't know the higher-ups who planned the flight expected only half would make it to Gibraltar.

Strict radio silence was observed as they maintained this minimum altitude in hopes the formation would not be picked up on enemy radar; still, each kept an eye out for any long-range Luftwaffe fighters that might pop out of the low overcast above. The pilots were now tired, since they had been woken at 0200 hours to prepare for takeoff. With such a long flight, ground crews in England had made sure to squeeze every drop of gas they could into the P-38s' fuel tanks and the drop tanks that hung below the wings, between the central cockpit nacelle and the engine booms. After several hours in the air, the pilots were straining for the first sign of northern Spain, somewhere off to the left in the hazy sky. They would remain over international waters as they followed the Spanish and Portuguese coast to their destination.

Among the pilots in the 94th "Hat in the Ring" Squadron was First Lieutenant Jack Ilfrey. Destined to become one of the real "characters" of the United States Army Air Forces (USAAF) in World War II, Ilfrey was born and raised in Houston, Texas. In April 1941, he left his studies at the University of Houston and joined the United States Army Air Corps (USAAC) as an aviation cadet. He graduated from flight school at Luke Army airfield in Arizona five days after Pearl Harbor, on December 12, 1941, a member of Class 41-1, and received orders to the 1st Fighter Group along with his commission as a second lieutenant and his silver Army Aviator Wings. He reported to the group on January 11, 1942, almost 11 months before this mission and was assigned to the group's 94th "Hat in the Ring" Squadron, descended from the first American fighter unit to enter combat in France back in 1918; they had been first to equip with the new P-38 in June 1941. With new groups being created from cadres taken from existing groups in the frantic time after the country's surprise entry into World War II, it had taken until March for him to be fully checked out in the big twin-engine fighter. Fortunately, Ilfrey was a quick learner, because that June he and his fellow pilots became the first fighter pilots to go to war by flying the Atlantic. It had taken seven days to fly from Presque Isle, Maine, to Halifax, Nova Scotia, then on to Blue West One airfield in Greenland at the end of a mountainous fjord that meant one landed toward the land and took off toward the water, regardless of the wind, due to the craggy peaks to either side. After two days spent waiting for the weather to clear enough to get airborne, the Lightnings had flown on to Iceland, then reached their destination at Prestwick, Scotland. The mission had been considered so dangerous that every pilot was awarded the Air Medal for the achievement.

Looking back on the flight to North Africa, he later recalled:

Our instructions sounded simple enough when we heard them in the briefing room. We were to fly in groups of eight, with a B-26 leading us. The route kept hammering in my brain: fly across the Bay of Biscay, hit the Spanish and Portuguese coast, continue south then turn left and go through the Straits of Gibraltar. Hit the Spanish Moroccan coast and fly into French Morocco and then into Oran. We were cautioned that Gibraltar should be our first emergency stop. It looked pretty simple, but it turned out otherwise.

Just before reaching the Iberian peninsula, Ilfrey felt a slight jolt. "By the time I realized what had happened, my right engine went out." When the airplane tilted right, out of balance, he realized he had lost the left drop tank. This was soon confirmed when wingman Second Lieutenant Tony Syroi pulled his Lightning alongside, holding a sheet of paper against the cockpit canopy on which he had printed in large letters ONE BELLY TANK. "I switched to another tank and the right engine caught again, but I had just lost 167 gallons of gasoline, and I knew I wasn't going to Oran." Checking his maps, Ilfrey guessed he had enough gas to get to Gibraltar. "I was not going to be separated from the gang, and – to be honest – I have to say that I was not going to miss out on the big adventure ahead – Africa."

Ahead, the B-26 turned to the right – out into the Atlantic – to avoid a squall line off the now-visible Spanish coast on the horizon. If they had to pull out any further, extending the length of the flight, he would be cutting things very close. The formation droned on for an hour, remaining out to sea. Ilfrey's attention flashed from keeping station in the formation to staring obsessively at the gas gauges every few minutes. At the end of the second hour, he had to conclude he wasn't going to be landing at Gibraltar, with the increased fuel consumption of the low-altitude flight and their detour out into the Atlantic. He decided he had to leave the group and head east, hoping to spot the Portuguese coast and an airfield he could land at before he ran out of gas.

Minutes later, he was flying under a partly cloudy sky in sunshine. He strained to see the coast ahead in the haze. Climbing slowly to give himself altitude in case of emergency, he was at 5,000 feet when he finally spotted the coast ahead. A few minutes later, he could make out details of the coastline. Checking his maps, he estimated he was at the Spanish–Portuguese border. Knowing that the Spanish were pro-German, he turned right and flew down the coast deeper into Portugal. The one thing he knew about the country was that it didn't hide pro-German sentiment behind its neutrality, and it might be possible to bribe his way out of the country.

Wavering between thoughts of bailing out before he ran out of gas, or staying with the Lightning to a dead-stick landing in what he hoped would be a field he could find that was big enough, he suddenly saw what the map on his lap told him was the Tagus River. Checking the map, Lisbon was only some 20–30 miles upriver. He turned left and followed the river. Minutes later, he saw what he later described as "the most beautiful airdrome" with long runways, just outside the city. He put his wheels down, circled the field, and put the P-38 down on the main runway.

Ilfrey came to a stop and then saw the welcoming committee: six men on horseback in big plumed hats and red trousers armed with sabers and pistols charged up to where the P-38 was stopped at a taxiway. They gestured for him to taxi the big fighter to what turned out to be the airport administration building. As he did so, Ilfrey tore up and threw out all his maps and papers, letting the propwash scatter the bits and pieces. The guards signaled to him to stop on the apron in front of the building. As he switched off his engines, he saw people converging from all directions. Some flashed the "V for victory" with their hands, but the majority stood there staring at the P-38 as the cavalrymen surrounded the airplane.

Ilfrey climbed out of the plane and stood on the wing, then asked if anyone spoke English. One official did, and Ilfrey explained that he had run out of fuel. He was told he would have to go inside the building and answer questions. As he climbed down, the official told the cavalrymen to protect the airplane from the curious.

Inside, he was provided coffee and cake that he found not to his taste, and other officials arrived to question him. He was told the American legation had been informed of his arrival. A new official asked him if he had been fighting Germans. He responded with his name, rank, and serial number, which made the man angry. He then noticed several German pilots hovering nearby, and out the window he saw the airliners with the swastika on their tails.

After an hour of this, he was informed by yet another newly arrived official that since Portugal was neutral, he would be interned. His airplane would be confiscated, but first it had to be flown to the military airfield on the other side of the city. He was introduced to a Portuguese pilot and told he must instruct the man in what to do to fly the airplane. He later recalled that it was at that moment that the possibility of escape entered his mind.

He agreed to provide the necessary instruction, but also told them the P-38 was nearly out of gas and would have to be refueled, telling them it must be 100 octane. The response was that they had no such gasoline, would 87 octane do? They went back out to the P-38, and while ground crewmen refueled it, he got back in the cockpit while the Portuguese pilot knelt on the wing beside the cockpit.

Once the refueling was complete, Ilfrey explained he would start up and explain what he was doing as he did so. Looking around the cockpit, he realized the parachute and all his personal identification and other items had been removed. The engines were still warm and quickly caught. As the propellers ticked over, he explained things to the other pilot.

At that moment, there was a commotion in the crowd, and Ilfrey looked out to see another P-38 turning to final approach with its gear down. One prop was feathered, the engine shut down. As it touched down, the cavalry galloped off to intercept it. He saw the crowd's attention was now on the new arrival.

Throwing caution to the wind, he advanced the throttles and released the brake. The propwash blew the Portuguese pilot's hat off. As the man tried to find a better hold, Ilfrey advanced the left throttle sufficiently to blow him off the wing. A minute later, seeing others on the field chasing their hats in the propwash, he closed the canopy, pushed the throttle forward, and headed straight toward the runway.

When he arrived on the runway, he stood on the left brake and turned into the wind for takeoff. The crowd was now running across the field after him. He released the brakes and began rolling down the runway. As soon as he reached flying speed he pulled back on the yoke and soared into the air. As he recalled later, he set a course south and hoped they had gassed up the fighter enough to make a 400-mile trip. He stayed at low altitude as he headed south, and in two hours, he saw the unmistakable shape of the Rock of Gibraltar in the distance.

When he landed and reported to the operations office, he found other members of the squadron who were full of questions about how he had managed to get there. He also discovered how much trouble he had created when his storytelling was interrupted, and he was ordered to report to the American officer responsible for USAAF operations on the airfield.

Escorted into the colonel's office, Ilfrey recounted his adventure again. As he later recalled, when he was finished, the colonel wasn't merely mad, he was "hopping mad." For the next 45 minutes, Ilfrey underwent a tongue lashing about how many rules of international diplomacy and the rules of war he had violated. The lecture complete, the colonel told him he personally thought Ilfrey had pulled "a pretty good trick." He was released and told to report back at 0900 the next morning.

After a night of celebrating his escape in the Gibraltar officers' club, a bleary-eyed Lieutenant Ilfrey reported to the colonel's office the next morning as ordered. After another tongue lashing, in which he was informed that the American embassy was prepared to hand him back to the Portuguese authorities, Ilfrey protested that all he wanted to do was go to Africa and fight in the war – couldn't something be done? He was told he would have to wait till the next morning.

The next morning, he was awakened by the colonel's assistant, a captain who told him it was time for him to take off immediately. The captain remained with him while he dressed and had a cup of coffee, then he drove Ilfrey out to his airplane. Once there, Ilfrey was informed that the colonel had told the embassy that the "dumb john" pilot had been sent off to North Africa through some administrative mix-up, and that "he'll probably be dead soon anyway."

"I left that afternoon for Oran, with high hopes and in high spirits," Ilfrey recalled. He landed at Tafaroui airfield at dusk on November 12. The group had already flown their first mission into Tunisia the day before. Their patrol over western Tunisia had been ignored by the enemy.

2

1942 – THE LOWEST YEAR

The time was dire when Winston Churchill and Franklin Roosevelt met in Placentia Bay, Newfoundland, on August 9–10, 1941, to sign what became the Atlantic Charter, the document that set Anglo-American goals for the war. The world situation was frightening. Great Britain – spared from a German invasion in the fall of 1940 and, with the passage of the US Lend-Lease Act in March 1941, assured of US material support – had seen German forces inflict humiliating defeats on British, Greek, and Yugoslav forces in the Balkans; the Afrika Korps had arrived in North Africa at the same time and was threatening to overrun Egypt and close off the Suez Canal, thereby restricting communication with India. The Germans had invaded the Soviet Union on June 22, 1941; few policymakers in Washington or London believed the Soviets could resist the Nazi onslaught for more than six weeks. While Britain focused its efforts on dealing with the Germans in Europe, they were concerned Japan might take advantage of the situation to seize British, French, and Dutch territories in Southeast Asia.

Six months later, in early 1942, events had only become worse. The year 1941 had ended with the Soviets holding off the Nazi onslaught by the skin of their teeth, with a winter offensive that pushed the Germans back from the gates of Moscow sufficiently to give the Red Army the opportunity to catch its breath, the result of German mistakes in the previous months that left their armies unequipped to face one of the coldest Russian winters on record. On December 5, 1941, fresh Soviet Siberian troops, prepared for winter warfare, attacked the German forces in front of Moscow; by late January 1942, the Wehrmacht had been driven back 60–150 miles, ending the immediate threat to Moscow that marked the closest point that Axis forces ever got to capturing the Soviet capital.

Two days after the Soviet offensive began, the United States was plunged into the war by the surprise Japanese attack on Pearl Harbor. The attack shocked the country as had no other event in its history. With the battleships of the Pacific Fleet lying on the mud in Pearl Harbor, the US Navy was unable to mount any relief to American forces in the Philippines, attacked at the same time, while the British Empire reeled from an attack against Malaya launched from Japanese bases in occupied French Indochina.

When the United States declared war on Japan on December 8, the country was not at war with the enemy American military and political leaders had been preparing to face over the previous year. They were at war with Japan only. The problem was solved three days later when Adolf Hitler, for the only time in his career, honored a promise made to an ally when he declared war on the United States in accordance with the terms of the Tripartite Alliance Treaty signed with Italy and Japan in November 1940, in which Germany had promised to come to the aid of either of its allies should they become involved in war with a third country. Hitler's advisors argued strongly against this move, with Hermann Göring pointing out that Hitler was "playing Churchill's game," as he told his interrogators in 1945; his argument – that the United States would not unilaterally declare war on Germany and that its involvement in a war in the Pacific would deny Britain increased military supplies without which they could do no more than maintain their defensive actions against Germany, at a time when the country was committed to a fight to the death with the Soviet Union – fell on deaf ears.

The German declaration of war was followed by an American reply on December 12, and the country that had the greatest potential power was now fully involved in World War II. That Mussolini had followed Hitler's act within hours, putting all three Axis powers into battle with the United States, was seen in both Berlin and Washington as an afterthought.

While both Britain and the United States reeled before the Japanese offensive in the Far East, the Soviet offensive slowed as the skies cleared after January 4, and the Luftwaffe was able to provide air support to beleaguered Wehrmacht units. As Soviet reserves ran low, the offensive ground to a halt on January 7, having pushed the exhausted and freezing German armies back from Moscow. Despite orders from Stalin for more offensives in order to trap and destroy the German Army Group Centre before Moscow, the Red Army was exhausted and overstretched. The attempted offensives failed. The winter counteroffensive had driven the Wehrmacht from the gates of Moscow, but the city was still threatened, with the front lines close.

The year before, Hitler had been reluctantly forced to dispatch a German army to North Africa to stiffen his Italian ally in the battle with the British forces defending Egypt and the Suez Canal. Generalleutnant (Lieutenant General) Erwin Rommel's Afrika Korps outperformed its British opponents due to the superiority of German armor. British success with Operation *Crusader* in November 1941 saw the front line in the Western Desert re-established at El Agheila. The Japanese attack in Southeast Asia made it even more important that Britain hold India and the Suez Canal while the enemy in Asia advanced toward India.

Despite President Roosevelt's enthusiasm for an American offensive operation in Europe by the end of 1942, both he and Prime Minister Winston Churchill realized that logistics were the primary obstacle. After Pearl Harbor, the United States faced significant logistical challenges in mobilizing for war. It had a small standing army that had only begun to expand following the introduction of conscription in 1940. Production capacity was still ramping up, though the president had called on the aviation industry to produce 50,000 combat aircraft by 1943. The United States was having trouble training men quickly enough to meet the growing needs in both theaters and did not have enough ships to transport what men and supplies it did produce. To address shortages, Democratic majorities in Congress quickly implemented a series of rules regarding factory conversions, and began to debate implementing price controls to curb inflation.

With the fall of the Philippines on April 18, 1942, after months of sacrifice with few military victories to show for it, Americans began to question Roosevelt's ability to lead the country in wartime. The news of the Doolittle Raid on Tokyo the same day that General Wainwright surrendered on the Philippine island of Corregidor gave public morale a jolt, but more was needed. Republicans, looking forward to the November off-year elections, were campaigning on economic policies that would significantly reduce rationing and mandatory service; Democrats were concerned this would hinder the country's ability to meet wartime production demands. Democrats also worried that should Republicans win back Congress, they would attempt to roll back President Roosevelt's New Deal reforms they had opposed since 1932.

Democratic leaders believed the key to winning public support was to show that American soldiers were taking the fight to the Germans. George B. Wolf, a confidante of the president and a senior power broker in the Democratic Party, predicted in an April 17 letter to Roosevelt, "Democrats will lose control of Congress at the coming election, barring a military victory by the United States or United Nations." White House officials took note of a radio broadcast from Rome that "The ill wind that blows for the Democrats is due to the fact that Roosevelt has brought the nation into war... Struggles will continue until there shall be military victories."

Since the US had entered the war, the United States and Great Britain had attempted to come up with a mutually acceptable strategy for confronting the Nazis. The US Joint Chiefs pressed for Operation *Roundup*, an invasion of northern France by four divisions of Anglo-American troops, to take and hold the Cotentin peninsula. The British were absolutely determined not to face the Germans in northwestern Europe until there was as much of an overwhelming advantage as could be gained; Churchill could not politically withstand another bloodletting in France on the scale of World War I, and knew that if the invasion was not successful the first time, there would be no political or military ability to mount it a second time.

In the meantime, a new offensive by Rommel's Afrika Korps in the Western Desert of Libya and Cyrenaica pushed the British and Commonwealth forces back, beginning in early June. This would continue through the month of July, until the Eighth Army held its position at a small rail station in western Egypt called El Alamein.

To this point, General Marshall and the Joint Chiefs had been focused since Pearl Harbor on putting resources into Britain for a decisive air and amphibious action in western Europe in 1943. The British situation in the summer of 1942 presented a dilemma: loss of the Middle East meant loss of the southern supply routes to the USSR through the Persian Gulf and Iran, as well as the main air ferry route to India. Loss of the ability to resupply India would make it impossible to defend the lifeline to China. The loss of the oil fields in Saudi Arabia, Iraq, and Iran would result in cessation of Allied air and naval activity in the Indian Ocean. The strategic loss to the Allies could cost them the war. The key to the Middle East was Egypt. In the face of this, the Americans had to face the fact they could not mount action in northwestern Europe while this crisis was unresolved.

The German offensive had, as a side effect, brought the first American military force in the Middle East into action. What was known as HALPRO, the Halverson Provisional Detachment – named for its commander, USAAF aviation pioneer Colonel Henry Halverson – had begun life in the United States in January 1942 as a desperate attempt to provide long-range airpower in the Far East after the destruction of nearly the whole of the Far East Air Force in the Philippines with the Japanese invasion in December 1941. The goal of HALPRO was to launch air raids on the Japanese Home Islands from China, for which they trained in February and March. The 24 B-24Es then flew the southern route across the South Atlantic and along the air route across Sub-Saharan Africa, headed for India, and then onward to their destiny in China; they were completely lacking in the ability to create sustained air operations, and their purpose was to stage one or perhaps two bombing missions against Japan as "morale-building operations." The bombers were in Sudan when the Doolittle Raid on April 18, 1942, accomplished that morale-building mission, leaving the B-24s without a purpose.

Air Marshal Sir Arthur Tedder, commander of British air forces in the Middle East, had requested an American heavy bomber unit be committed to the Middle East back in January at the Arcadia Conference, for use in attacking Axis ports in Italy and Greece that were supplying the Afrika Korps, but the request had been refused by USAAF commander General Henry "Hap" Arnold as a diversion of forces he did not have to spare. With the 23 B-24s now in Sudan without a mission, Tedder renewed his request with more urgency this time, and HALPRO was diverted north to the Middle East in May 1942. The USAAF agreed to do this since the leadership saw the opportunity of using the force to mount a strategic bombing strike against the sole Axis oil field in Europe at Ploesti, Romania. The bombers were now based at Fayid in Palestine, which put Ploesti just barely within their range. General Arnold ordered Colonel Halverson to mount an attack with every available plane in his unit.

On June 13, 1942, 13 B-24s took off from Fayid headed for Ploesti, the first USAAF bombing raid against Axis targets in Europe. The range was such that they would not be able to return by the same course over the Mediterranean, and the decision was made that they would overfly Turkey, violating that nation's neutrality, to land at Habbaniyah, Iraq. Unfortunately, without an accurate weather forecast, they arrived over Romania to find the country largely covered by clouds, which particularly obscured their target at Ploesti. The B-24s dropped their bombs to little effect, inflicting only minimal damage. The Luftwaffe had taken over the defense of Ploesti, and the force was intercepted by Bf-109s of I./JG 53 that were stationed near the target. In fierce individual battles, five of the bombers were shot down and several others were damaged to varying degrees.

Four returning aircraft were forced down in Turkey – three near the capital at Ankara and one at Izmir – due to fuel shortage and battle damage. Two managed to reach Aleppo, Syria, which had recently come under Allied control with the invasion of that French possession, where they crash-landed. Three others got as far as Mosul in northern Iraq, where one crashed and the other two were heavily damaged in their landings following their damage over the target. In the end, only four B-24s of the 13 managed to make it to Habbaniyah and finally return to Fayid. The damaged aircraft in Syria and Iraq were eventually repaired and flown back to Palestine over the next two months. Following this near disaster, no more long-range strategic missions were planned.

On June 16, HALPRO entered combat in support of the British. Seven B-24s were sent to intercept the Italian fleet, which had put to sea to stop a convoy from Alexandria headed to Malta. The bombers found the Italian warships and claimed five hits on a Littorio-class battleship and one hit and a near-miss on a Cavour-class battleship. The Italians reported a hit on one of the forward armored turrets of the battleship *Littorio*, though the 500lb bomb had little effect. The Italians continued on, and the Allied convoy was forced to turn back to Alexandria, though search planes later confirmed the Italians had called off their attack and recalled the force.

Following the mission to Ploesti and the attack on the Italian fleet, HALPRO flew nightly missions against the port facilities at Benghazi and Tobruk, where supplies for the Afrika Korps were landed; these strikes were important since Benghazi was beyond the range of the RAF bombers that were available. On June 21, nine bombers started fires in Benghazi's port. The Regia Aeronautica's 150° Gruppo Autonomo was assigned to the defense of Benghazi and claimed one B-24 shot down, but all nine returned safely. Three days later, ten B-24s badly damaged the railroad sidings, greatly reducing the supplies that could be loaded for transport on to the forces at the El Alamein front. Four bombers hit Tobruk on June 25, following up with further strikes against the port on June 26 and 28; the B-24 shot down over Tobruk on June 28 was the first USAAF loss to enemy action since the Ploesti raid. The raids against Tobruk in July were effective enough to deny Rommel sufficient supplies to break the British position at El Alamein as their forward units retreated from Mersa Matruh in the first battle fought there; had the Eighth Army not held at this time, it is likely Rommel could have taken Cairo and the Suez Canal. In these raids, the Italian aerial defenders discovered that the two 12.7mm machine guns that each of their C.200 and C.202 fighters carried were inadequate to attack and destroy the American four-engine bombers.

HALPRO was joined in July by the nine surviving B-17s of the Far East Air Force's 7th Bomb Group that had retreated from the Philippines to the Dutch East Indies and thence to India. These survivors were combined with the surviving B-24s into the 1st Provisional Bomb Group, under Halverson's command. The B-17s flew their first mission against Tobruk on July 2. Four days later, six B-24s found an Axis convoy and hit two, including a crucial fuel tanker that was left on fire. On July 7, 11 B-24s, in the biggest mission flown since Ploesti, blew up an ammunition ship in Benghazi harbor. The bombers flew almost-daily missions against Benghazi and Tobruk through July while the British held the Afrika Korps in front of El Alamein; the losses of supplies were specifically mentioned by Rommel as the reason why his force was unable to prevail in the First Battle of El Alamein. The bombers ended the month with a raid on Souda Bay, Crete, where Axis supply convoys formed up for the run to Benghazi, on July 28; two ships were set on fire along with several warehouses.

Five days before the Crete mission, the four squadrons of the USAAF's 98th Bomb Group arrived in Egypt on July 23, bringing 48 B-24s to the theater; they flew their first mission on August 1. The 1st Provisional Group flew its most successful mission on August 6, when seven B-24s carrying 1,000lb bombs struck Tobruk, setting one ship on fire and badly damaging the pier it was moored to. The American attacks over the previous 30 days had reduced Tobruk's handling capacity from 2,000 tons per day to 600, and it never recovered to more than 1,000 tons per day during the remainder of the Western Desert campaign.

While this was happening, Roosevelt had made it clear in May that he wanted to take some decisive action in 1942, preferably before the election. Churchill responded by presenting Roosevelt with a plan for the US to take control of western North Africa from Vichy France, relieving German pressure on the British in Egypt, and creating a longer-term opportunity for further offensives in southern Europe. The US military leaders were absolutely against the idea, seeing it as a diversion from the main front in northern Europe. However, Roosevelt was concerned about the domestic political implications of not taking some action before the November congressional elections. Later statements by Secretary of War Henry Stimson and Army Chief of Staff George Marshall clearly showed that domestic political priorities shaped President Roosevelt's decision-making about military operations in 1942.

Even as late as June 1942, a decision to land in North Africa was anything but assured. It was one of several potential operations debated by the Anglo-American Combined Chiefs of Staff. US military planners were almost universally against the North Africa landings, believing the United States was being drawn into a peripheral war theater to protect British colonial interests. They continued to favor the cross-Channel invasion plan known as *Roundup* because it took a direct approach and would draw additional German units away from the Eastern Front. Churchill and the British chiefs of staff were unanimous in their refusal to support a cross-Channel invasion until American troops had been battle-tested. Despite the apparent impasse, Roosevelt remained adamant that an offensive action would take place in 1942, going so far as to promise Soviet leader Joseph Stalin a second front before the new year.

Each time American military planners thought they had dissuaded Roosevelt and the British from a North African invasion, the operation, known initially as *Gymnast*, would resurface in discussions whenever Roosevelt pushed for an offensive before the year's end. Secretary of War Henry Stimson disparagingly called *Gymnast* "Roosevelt's secret baby." By July, Roosevelt's military advisors presented radical alternatives out of protest, suggesting the United States abandon the European theater to focus on General Douglas MacArthur's Pacific campaign. Roosevelt, less than impressed, angrily dismissed the idea.

Viewed in hindsight, the desire of American military leaders to mount a cross-Channel invasion of France in 1943 was unduly optimistic. British objections that there would not be enough landing craft produced by the time of the invasion proved correct; in fact, several versions of important landing craft were only chosen for development in 1943, as a result of experience gained in the North African invasion. The requirement of the Allied air forces to create conditions of air superiority if not supremacy for the invasion proved impossible in 1943, simply due to the nonexistence of aircraft in sufficient numbers and capability to defeat what was still a very strong Luftwaffe organization on the Channel Front. In fact, air superiority would not be established over western Europe until late April 1944, mere weeks before the Normandy invasion occurred. An invasion limited to taking the Cotentin peninsula as originally suggested would have meant the Allied force on the continent would have been bottled up by Wehrmacht forces without having to touch any of the units on the Eastern Front. Additionally, had US Army ground units landed on the Cotentin peninsula in a 1942 or even 1943 cross-Channel invasion performed as poorly as did many US Army units during the initial phase of operations in North Africa, it is more than likely that the experienced Wehrmacht units opposing them in France would have defeated them. It is unlikely that the Allies could have performed a second successful Dunkirk evacuation with the Germans as fully in control of western Europe as they were in 1942–43. The end result would have been that in the face of the first defeat, a second invasion could not have been mounted. European "liberation" from the Nazis would have come in the form of the Red Army battering its way through to the English Channel at some unspecified date, and even that would only have been a possibility if the Western Allies had been defeated in France in 1942–43.

Additionally, had there been a landing in 1943, the Soviets were not yet strong enough to mount a large offensive to prevent the Germans from transferring any significant force to western Europe. The Battle of Kursk, from which the beginning of Soviet superiority in numbers can be dated, only happened in the summer of 1943 and was very close-run. There could have been no thought of a front-wide offensive like that which came in June 1944 two weeks after the Normandy invasion, which saved the Allies in the Battle of Normandy by preventing any significant Wehrmacht reinforcements of the units in northern France.

At the end of July 1942, in one of the few direct orders he would give during the war, President Roosevelt ordered the North Africa landings to occur in the fall of 1942. The other similar major presidential action was his decision to support General MacArthur's plan to invade the Philippines in 1944, which was made for its effect on the 1944 presidential election. Though planning and logistics for the Mediterranean operation were challenging, the president was insistent, begging General George C. Marshall, "Please make it before Election Day!" The invasion date was set for September 30, 1942 and the operation renamed *Torch*.

This ambitious timeline allowed planners only two months to prepare for the first major offensive against the German army. On August 30, Roosevelt told Churchill that he wanted the operation to be a purely American affair: "It is my earnest desire to start the attack at the earliest possible moment... I feel very strongly that the initial attacks must be made by an exclusively American ground force supported by your naval and transport and air units." Churchill went along with the decision, primarily because the French in North Africa were openly hostile to British forces and were less likely to fight against Americans.

The US Army ground forces were not the only part of that organization that opposed the idea of a campaign in North Africa. The leadership of the USAAF was in the midst of its first buildup of forces for what would become the Eighth Air Force in Britain for the strategic bombing of Germany. A diversion of forces to North Africa at that point was rightly seen as a setback for the main strategic bombing campaign. As it was, when the commitment was made to send forces to the Twelfth Air Force, the result was the escort force was stripped of the one fighter in the USAAF inventory capable of providing long-range escort in the European combat environment, and was forced to start over in 1943 with the P-47, a fighter that took until the following November to acquire the capability of providing long-range fighter escort to major German targets in central Germany.

Interestingly, Eighth Air Force itself had originally been formed in early 1942 to support Operation *Gymnast*. When this was dropped,

Eighth Air Force was transferred to Britain in the spring of 1942 where it became the force for which it is best known. In the end, the units taken from Eighth Air Force and transferred to Seventh Air Force that participated in combat had a more immediate effect on the goal of defeating the Luftwaffe in that campaign than they would have had operating from Britain over Germany. The fact that the fighters were still short-ranged was not a concern in North Africa where they flew from airfields close to the front. In the end, the USAAF and Commonwealth chewed up 40 percent of the Luftwaffe in the summer of 1942, which made the Eighth Air Force's campaign over Germany – as difficult as it was – much easier since a significant number of experienced German airmen had been removed from the battle over western Europe before it really got going.

Logistics proved to be the challenge even Roosevelt could not overcome. Disorganization within the newly established supply line meant American convoys could not move enough supplies to match Roosevelt's timeframe. So much was dispersed, lost, and sunk while crossing the Atlantic the projected landing date had to be revised several times. The target D-Day of September 30 quickly became October 15, then October 30. In September, US military planners insisted upon a third landing site at Casablanca to protect the Strait of Gibraltar and supply lines going in and out of the Mediterranean. On October 10, Marshall gave Roosevelt the bad news: *Torch* would have to be delayed until November 8 – five days after Election Day. As it was, the main American invasion convoy was not able to leave the United States until October 23, 1942.

Marshall made it clear that acting sooner risked sending an under-equipped and under-manned force onto the beaches with little or no backup. Roosevelt understood defeat in the landings would be far worse than no action at all, and resigned himself to facing public discontent in the elections. Notably, he did not make an effort to move up the landing date. Marshall later recalled, "The president was very courageous about that."

Roosevelt did make one final request of his military commanders. When he heard British General Bernard Montgomery planned to start his counteroffensive at El Alamein on October 26, he pleaded with Marshall, "Please delay it. The British always get licked." Even Marshall was unable to accomplish such a task; the offensive proceeded on schedule for a resounding British victory.

TURNING THE TIDE

On November 3, 1942, the Democrats took heavy losses in both houses of Congress. In the Senate, they lost nine seats and their supermajority; in the House their majority slipped from over 100 to just 13. When Roosevelt's press secretary Stephen Early was informed of the North Africa invasion only hours before it happened, the missed political opportunity was obvious. He lashed out at Marshall, yelling, "You almost lost us control of Congress!" He was not the only one who believed this. A December 9 election post-mortem by the Democratic Party reported: "Opinions given by voters very generally indicated dissatisfaction with the conduct of the war. Had the North Africa campaign opened one week earlier, it might have made a substantial difference in this election." What was lost was the ability to pass the planned Second New Deal, which would have included the implementation of a national health care system and provided all citizens with the programs that were finally passed as the GI Bill in 1944: government-supported programs to promote affordable home ownership, start a business, or take part in higher education.

On November 8, 1942, over 100,000 American and British forces landed on the beaches of Morocco and Algeria. They were commanded by General George S. Patton, Jr., under the overall leadership of Supreme Allied Commander, General Dwight D. Eisenhower. Major French opposition to the landing was confined to Oran; within days a bargain had been struck with French commanders for cooperation between the two armies. Allied forces quickly consolidated gains in Morocco and Algeria.

The decision not to land at Tunis due to fear of German attack from Sicily and Sardinia quickly led to the action by the Germans – spooked by the "neutral" Vichy government's deal with the Allies – to immediately occupy Vichy France and take control of defensive positions in Tunisia. The fact the Axis won the "race for Tunis" allowed them to delay opening the Mediterranean by the Allies for six months.

General Patton later wrote that Roosevelt's decision to overrule his military advisors and push forward with *Torch* was "about as desperate a venture as has ever been undertaken." In the end, it proved to be an enormously successful gamble. American military leaders were correct that *Torch* would delay a cross-Channel invasion by up to a year, but the campaign gave the Americans necessary combat experience, secured routes of transit through the Mediterranean, and provided the launch point for the Sicilian invasion.

Eighty-odd years later, the landings remain a remarkable feat of coordination, cooperation, and logistical resolve that was unprecedented for the time. The strategic significance and success of Operation *Torch* are no less important when the operation is placed in its political context. Even so, it is important to recall that the landings were anything but assured. Domestic politics continue to influence military strategy decisions more than three-quarters of a century after Roosevelt issued his orders. So long as democratic institutions allow the public to hold the commander-in-chief accountable, leaders will fight wars with domestic political considerations an important part of their decision-making calculus.

The aircraft operated by the USAAF in North Africa were a mixed bunch. The most advanced fighter was the P-38, which was still far from the fully developed fighter it would become. The P-38F, which initially equipped the three fighter groups that saw combat, was the first production sub-type that was really combat capable. Still, the fighter had a reputation for being dangerous, particularly in a dive. As one of the first aircraft capable of approaching Mach 1, it experienced compressibility, which led to control difficulty in a dive. As speed built up in a dive from high altitude, the ability of the pilot to operate the controls was restricted by high-speed airflow over the control surfaces. The longer the airplane was held in a dive, the steeper the dive became; wind tunnel tests in 1941 had revealed that at Mach 0.74, the center of pressure under the wing began to move aft, which allowed the nose to "tuck under" and steepen the dive. Thus, by the time the P-38 reached a lower altitude where the air was thicker and control could be regained, if the airplane had tucked beyond the vertical there was no hope of recovery, and if the tuck was close to vertical, the distance necessary to pull through on a dive recovery would be greater than the altitude above ground level. The result in either case was a fatal crash with the pilot unable to open the cockpit canopy and bail out. Since this phenomenon did not have a solution, other than not to enter a maximum-performance dive, this meant that pilots did not fly the airplane to its limits in combat. This problem would be unresolved until dive flaps were installed on the lower surface of the wing outboard of the engine nacelles beginning at the factory with the P-38J-25 sub-type in the summer of 1944; dive-flap kits arrived in P-38 groups to be fitted to earlier fighters, but this would have no bearing on the use of the airplane in North Africa.

There was an additional problem with the twin-engine fighter regarding recovery from an engine loss on takeoff. Loss of one engine in a twin-engine, non-centerline-thrust aircraft on takeoff creates sudden drag, which yaws the nose toward the dead engine while the wing on the side of the dead engine rolls down. Normal engine-out training for engine loss on takeoff has the pilot apply full power to the remaining engine to maintain airspeed. If that was done in the P-38, regardless of which engine failed, the engine torque and p-factor force resulting would produce a sudden, uncontrollable yawing roll; the aircraft would then flip inverted and hit the ground. Eventually, pilots were taught to reduce power on the running engine while feathering the prop on the failed engine, then increasing power gradually until the P-38 was in stable flight. With the dirt and dust on a North African airfield, losing an engine on takeoff was a common event; until pilots arrived who had been properly trained, the result of an engine loss was almost always loss of the pilot in the resulting crash.

The cooling system for the engines involved circulating air from the radiators into the leading edge of the outer wing. Because the radiator was too small for adequate cooling in desert conditions, and because this system for cooling the air turned out to be inadequate, the problem of engines overheating and failing was a common one for a pilot to deal with in 1942–43 in North Africa.

The result of all this was a fatal accident rate that outstripped the air force's ability to replace fighters. Of the four P-38 groups that had been sent to Britain to provide an escort force for the bombers of Eighth Air Force in the summer of 1942, two were transferred to Twelfth Air Force in October for the Moroccan invasion, with the third group to arrive in Britain a month after Operation *Torch* being sent immediately to North Africa to make up for the high loss rate. In February 1943, the fourth VIII Fighter Command Group lost all its airplanes and pilots other than flight and squadron leaders, with the planes and pilots sent to North Africa as replacements. The loss rate was so bad during the fighting in Tunisia in early 1943 that the 14th Fighter Group was taken off operations in February, just when the group was needed the most during the fighting at Kasserine Pass and immediately after.

When the P-38 went up against the Bf-109 and Fw-190 in combat, pilots initially tried to fight in the P-38 using traditional high-g maneuvering. However, the airplane was too heavy to fight the lighter single-engine fighters that way; coupled with the P-38 pilots being unwilling to throw their airplane around in combat, their more experienced German opponents had the advantage, which showed up in the loss rates. Toward the end of the campaign, the P-38 groups finally began taking the advice of the Lockheed technical representatives attached to the units – to fight the airplane in the vertical plane. This allowed the pilots to use the P-38's dive and zoom superiority over the two German fighters; the combat loss rate went down, and scoring went up.

The P-39, which equipped several fighter groups, proved a disappointment, due to its loss of performance above 10,000 feet since the turbo-supercharger the fighter had originally been designed with had been removed in early development. However, the fighter's heavy armament of a 37mm cannon firing through the propeller hub, with two heavy .50-caliber machine guns also mounted in the nose, made the P-39 very useful in ground attack, and the P-39 fighter groups eventually became fighter-bomber units.

The P-40F used by the USAAF in North Africa differed from previous P-40 sub-types in being powered by a Merlin engine, rather than the Allison V-1710. Unfortunately, this was the first Packard-built Merlin V-1650, which was a Merlin XX series engine which did not have a high-altitude rating. Thus, the P-40F still had the problem experienced by the Allison-powered P-40s used by the RAF as the Kittyhawk, in that its best altitude was 18,000–20,000 feet, which meant the fighter was almost always at an altitude disadvantage when attacked by enemy pilots in either Bf-109s or Italian C.202 fighters powered by the DB 601 engine, which had a much higher altitude rating that allowed the enemy pilots to initiate the fight with a diving attack on the USAAF fighters. Nevertheless, the P-40F and later P-40L established good records in North Africa. The P-40 could out-roll the Bf-109, and its stronger construction allowed it to be thrown around in combat in ways a 109 pilot could not equal for fear of shedding a wing.

The RAF Spitfire Vb and Vc fighters used under "reverse Lend-Lease" by the 31st and 52nd Fighter Groups could hold their own against the Bf-109F and Bf-109G fighters used by the *Jagdgruppen* in North Africa, though the 109s had better altitude performance. However, the Spitfire V was completely outperformed by the Fw-190A that equipped II./JG 2, bettering the German fighter only in the ability to turn tight. Eventually, German losses were not replaced, and II./JG 2 was withdrawn from North African combat in March 1943, when the unit was no longer combat effective due to losses. That month saw both groups receive limited numbers of Spitfire IX fighters powered by the Merlin 61 that improved overall performance, particularly at altitude. The fact there were only a small number of these advanced Spitfires available meant that both groups could only provide a four-plane flight of these in each squadron, and they were used to give high cover for the Spitfire Vs that remained in use.

The Luftwaffe the USAAF fought in North Africa was not yet the spent force it would become over northern Europe in the following year. Each of its *Geschwadern* (wings) and *Gruppen* (groups) were led by experienced high-scoring aces – called *Experte* – and each *Staffel* (squadron) often had experienced *Experte* leaders who had been flying combat since the Battle of Britain two years earlier. Almost all German pilots the Americans encountered in North Africa had received extensive prewar training, and initially these pilots were man-for-man superior in training and experience to their American opponents. The air war in North Africa was a tough classroom with a steep learning curve for the USAAF units. In the end, the Americans prevailed because of numbers; their losses could be replaced, if not exactly quickly then certainly more rapidly than their opponents. By the spring of 1943 after the Battle of Kasserine Pass, the *Jagdflieger* ('fighter pilots') always found themselves outnumbered by their USAAF and Commonwealth opponents.

The B-25 Mitchell and B-26 Marauder bombers proved themselves in combat, as did the B-17 Flying Fortress and the B-24 Liberator. The need of fighter escorts for the bombers was clearly demonstrated though. By the end of the campaign, the concept of close escort of bombers by fighters had been abandoned in favor of a more offensive strategy that allowed fighters to go after the enemy before they could attack a bomber formation. The strategy Twelfth Air Force Commander

Jimmy Doolittle had approved following his experience in North Africa was later applied to the operations of Eighth Air Force in Britain when he assumed leadership of the major US air command; the change in escort tactics transformed the air war over northern Europe. This allowed Eighth Air Force to achieve its assigned goal of defeating the Luftwaffe and establishing air superiority that allowed the Normandy invasion to take place.

Prior to entry into the war, most of the USAAF's air combat plans and proposed operations were based primarily on theories of airpower that had been developed during the interwar period. Given the small size and limited resources of American armed forces in that period, there was little opportunity to put any theories to practical work in training operations. The result was that much of the strategic and tactical plans and policies had to be thrown out and revised "on the run" during operations in North Africa.

Overall, the invasion of North Africa provided the American military with the chance to test their operational theories, discover what did not work, and hone both their amphibious forces and their army and air force to provide the ability to take on the still-powerful German Wehrmacht. This first successful Allied amphibious operation was soon dwarfed by those that followed. But in the words of Air Force historians W.F. Craven and J.L. Cate, "not in complexity, in daring – and the prominence of hazard involved."

Even the US defeat at Kasserine Pass was paradoxically advantageous to the US Army both for its ground and air units. Rommel and the Axis leadership were lulled into a false impression of US capabilities, while the Americans learned valuable lessons, and made positive changes in their command structure and tactics both in the air and on the ground.

While the USAAF went from strength to strength following the North African campaign, the Luftwaffe's loss of 40 percent of its strength over the course of the campaign – and more importantly, the loss of tested combat leaders and front-line pilots – would never be made up, and would have a dramatic effect on that air force's conduct of operations through the remainder of the war and particularly over the next 12 months following the Axis surrender in North Africa in May 1943.

3

FIRST IN THE BLUE

The South Atlantic morning sky was clear 150 miles off the African Gold Coast on July 19, 1942, as USS *Ranger* (CV-4) swung into the wind and increased speed to 30 knots, her structure straining as the turbines reached maximum revs. *Ranger*, the first US purpose-designed carrier built as such from the keel up, had joined the US Navy on June 4, 1934, three years after her keel was laid and nine years after design began in 1925. Unfortunately, the construction delay meant she arrived in the Navy several years late, the product of by then outdated thinking regarding the role of an aircraft carrier. Relatively small in comparison to the other American fleet carriers at an overall length of only 730 feet, she was closer in concept to the Navy's first carrier, USS *Langley*. Her small size, lack of speed, and lack of armor meant she could not participate in a fleet action, which kept her from joining the Pacific War. However, she was now the only large carrier left in the Atlantic Fleet, with USS *Wasp* (CV-7) having departed for the Pacific a month earlier, despite the fact that – like *Ranger* – she lacked the necessary armor to successfully survive a carrier battle. Such actions had revealed their deadly nature during the previous 70 days at Coral Sea and Midway; the loss of two of the Navy's small fleet of combat-capable carriers in those battles meant *Wasp* would have to take her chances.

But *Ranger* was perfectly capable of performing her assignment that morning.

On her bridge, Captain C.T. Durgin watched the activity on the flight deck as the ship turned into the wind and prepared to launch aircraft. Flight deck crews busied themselves assisting pilots into their cockpits, and the air was filled with the sound of coughing Merlin engines as the props began spinning and exhaust smoke flowed over the deck with its acrid odor.

Rather than the blue and gray F4F Wildcat fighters, SB2U Vindicator dive bombers, and TBD Devastator torpedo bombers of *Ranger*'s own Air Group Four, there were 36 Curtiss P-40F "Warhawk" fighters, painted in Army Air Force olive drab and gray. Below on the hangar deck were 36 more Army fighters, waiting for the flight deck to clear after the successful takeoff of the first group. The P-40s were manned by pilots of the 64th, 65th, and 66th Fighter Squadrons of the 57th Fighter Group, the first USAAF fighter unit to deploy to the European Theater since the United States had joined the war seven months earlier. This was the second time *Ranger* had ferried Army fighters to Africa, having sent off the P-40Es of the 51st Fighter Group on May 10 on the first leg of their long flight to India.

The 57th Group was en route to Egypt as reinforcement for the RAF, the first of seven USAAF fighter and bomber groups promised to the British by President Roosevelt in May, their departure sped up by the fall of Tobruk a month before on June 21.

Soon the propellers of the first 18 fighters were spinning, dissipating the exhaust smoke.

Strapped into the cockpit of the first P-40F with the white number "01" on her flank ahead of the white star insignia, the name "Regina IV" beneath the windscreen, group commander Major Frank H. Mears stood on his rudder pedals and pressed his toes forward, holding the now-vibrating fighter with the brakes as he watched the launch officer's spinning hand. In moments, the Merlin engine was screaming at full power. Looking out to either side of the fighter's long nose, Mears thought the 300 feet of flight deck ahead did not look like enough for takeoff. Like the rest of his pilots, Mears had never been on an aircraft carrier before the day they were loaded aboard *Ranger* in New York Harbor a week earlier, and his knowledge of a carrier takeoff was limited to the lectures given by the naval aviators on board. He recalled that the 51st Group had lost three P-40s that stalled and spun in on takeoff the first time this had been done.

And then the launch officer's arm shot forward. Mears released his brakes, and the Warhawk – lightly loaded with only 110 gallons of fuel and only 300 rounds of .50-caliber bullets in the wing gun bays – shot forward with enough acceleration to push him back in his seat. The tail came up, and he could clearly see the end of the deck. It seemed too soon that he reached the moment of fly or crash, but the Warhawk soared into the air. He remembered the instruction to push the nose down and gain flying speed before climbing away; a stall and crash now would put him directly in front of the oncoming ship. Mere feet above the waves, the airspeed indicator read the necessary 100mph and he pulled back on the stick, soaring into the sky as he turned left and circled the ship, waiting for the other five Warhawks in his flight to take off and join up.

On the flight deck, the remaining 17 pilots followed Mears' climbing turn against the backdrop of the deep blue sky and took heart with his success.

First Lieutenant Roy E. Whittaker, aged 23, taxied into takeoff position. The pilot had joined the USAAC in the spring of 1941 and had earned his wings in the same class as future stars George Preddy and John Landers, five days after Pearl Harbor. Following duty as a flight instructor in early 1942, he joined the 65th Squadron – then based in New England – that May. Whittaker stood on the brakes while he pushed the throttle to full power. The launch officer again shot his arm forward and Whittaker released the brakes, making his signature "zigzag" takeoff. Lifting off, the Warhawk dropped below the bow before reappearing as it climbed after Mears. None of the observers were ever sure whether this was accidental or not, but Whittaker's reputation in the group as a "hot pilot" was solidly established.

The next four Warhawks took off one at a time, joining Mears and Whittaker. Mears then banked east and led the flight to Accra airport. Launching the next two six-plane flights took 30 minutes. With the first group of 18 P-40s on their way to Accra, the second group started up and took off with no problems. The first Warhawk of the third group was airborne two hours after Mears' departure. The pilots had all observed the first two groups get airborne, which allowed them to take off more efficiently; the last left the deck 40 minutes after the first of the group.

Once the deck was clear, it took another hour for the last group to be ranged for takeoff. Second Lieutenant Bill Mount of the 64th Squadron recalled his departure from *Ranger*:

> We had tried practice take-offs at Mitchell Field and had gotten off in between 1150–1300 feet into a 20-knot wind. The US Navy told

us the deck was 750 feet long, and heading into the wind made a big difference. It was only after we were aboard and learned that the aft half of the deck was full of P-40s that we were told we would only be allowed to use the front half of the flightdeck, about 350 feet. That's when we got a little worried. I took off between 30th and 40th… We had been required to run all our trim tab controls to both extreme positions every day during the voyage in order to avoid corrosion. As a result, when I went to take-off, I had forgotten to reset the tabs. The aeroplane was trimmed full tail heavy and full left rudder. I spent the take-off roll trying to adjust the tabs and fighting the controls. We had also covered the canopies with some stuff to eliminate sun reflections. In the damp climate off the Nigerian coast, condensation mixed with the goop so it was impossible to see out with the canopy closed, so I left it open.

Eventually, Captain Archie J. Knight's P-40 was the last still on board. Four hours after the launch began, Knight applied full throttle and his Warhawk accelerated down the deck and lifted off to join the five overhead. The sailors on deck watched the final formation become small in the distance as they flew toward Africa. Captain Durgin gave the order to reduce speed to cruising, and the carrier and her escorting destroyers turned north to return to the United States.

On January 15, 1941, The 57th Pursuit Group was activated at Mitchell Field, New York, part of the Northeast Defense Sector, assigned to I Fighter Command. With the war in Europe already in its 17th month, the group was the product of the expansion of the US Army Air Corps, still nine months from becoming the US Army Air Forces, and struggling to organize the air force all the leaders knew would be needed in the coming war. American military forces were badly neglected during the Depression, with the United States Army's 180,000 men ranking it 19th in the world, smaller than that of Portugal.

The new group was made up of a headquarters unit and three squadrons – the 64th, 65th and 66th Pursuit Squadrons – each with an authorized strength of 24 aircraft and around 360 personnel. At the time of activation, the group consisted of ten airplanes and fewer than 100 officers and men, all "hived off" from other Air Corps groups. Over the rest of 1941, growth came in fits and starts with men assigned directly from training schools, then just as rapidly transferred out after gaining a little experience, to form the cadre of other new combat units.

Captain John E. Barr, the first group commander, transferred in April 1941 to the 51st Pursuit Group at Hamilton Field north of San Francisco, replaced by Major Reuben Moffat, previously the commander of the 33rd Pursuit Group. Moffat, a highly accomplished pilot, had been the first USAAC pilot to take off from an aircraft carrier on October 14, 1940, when he flew a P-40B off USS *Wasp* in a test of deployment procedures off the Virginia coast. In August, Moffat was replaced by Major Clayton Hughes, a West Pointer and former cavalry officer.

The group was equipped with varying numbers of P-40C fighters, with the first P-40E Kittyhawks arriving that fall. Pilots were able to build flight hours as the number of available fighters increased. Though the group's mission was air defense for New England, in reality it was a training unit during 1941, with responsibility for turning the group's fledglings into fighter pilots falling to a cadre of experienced aviators who included Lieutenants Romulus W. Puryear, CO of the 64th Pursuit Squadron, and Philip G. Cochran, commander of the 65th. Lieutenants John Alison, Harry Pike, and Robert Brouk would later make their reputations in China, while Captain Peter McGoldrick and Lieutenants Leonard Lydon and Edward Carey would all rise to command the 57th in combat, all future fighter group commanders. When Puryear was transferred in July, First Lieutenant Frank H. Mears took command of the 64th Squadron.

In October 1941, the 57th was considered to have sufficient experience to participate in a cross-country exercise. Led by Major Hughes, it flew via the southern route to McChord Field, Washington. Plagued by bad weather and mechanical problems, 12 of the 25 P-40s were lost, with four pilots killed in the crashes. Thirteen pilots reported to Second Interceptor Command at McChord on October 28. After flying one mission from McChord, the 57th were ordered to March Field in southern California, where an official inquiry into the disastrous flight would be convened. Further problems saw only ten P-40s reach March by November 4. While many pilots felt that Major Hughes bore responsibility for the group's problems due to a series of bad decisions, Hughes emerged from the hearing with his professional reputation intact. However, days after the Pearl Harbor attack, Hughes was relieved of his command.

Following the US entry into the war, 1942 saw the 57th take on a steady schedule of air defense patrols and practice missions as pilots and ground crew honed their skills to be ready for deployment to a combat zone; most thought they would end up in the Pacific. At various times during these first months of war, squadrons were dispersed to airfields at Groton, Connecticut; Quonset Point, Rhode Island; Mitchell Field on Long Island; and East Boston, Massachusetts.

While the 65th Squadron was at Groton, their colorful CO, Captain Phil Cochran, asked his old college roommate, cartoonist Milton Caniff, to design a badge for the squadron. The result was a feisty-looking Rhode Island Red rooster in a pilot's helmet with a chip on his shoulder. The squadron was christened the "Fighting Cocks," double-entendre intended. In late May, Cochran acquired a handsome Rhode Island Red rooster to serve as the squadron mascot, naming him "Uncle Bud;" he would travel the Atlantic, North Africa, Sicily, and Italy with the group during its many moves over the next two years before being accidentally killed at Grosseto, Italy, in 1944. Cochran was reluctantly transferred to take over the 33rd Pursuit Group in June, replaced by Captain Art Salisbury, though the spirit he had brought to the squadron would remain. He would later found the Air Commandos in India with his friend and fellow 57th Group alumnus John Alison, while his friend Caniff turned him into the character Flip Corkin in his comic strip *Terry and the Pirates*, which became wildly successful during the war and into the 1950s. Salisbury would also appear in the strip as "Art Solitary."

On June 28, 1942, Major Frank H. Mears, who had been with the group since its founding, moved up from command of the 64th Squadron to take charge of the group, which had changed its designation from "Pursuit" to "Fighter Group" the previous month. Four days earlier, Air Force Special Order No. 168 had arrived at group HQ at Quonset Point airfield, announcing, "The officers on the attached roster will proceed without delay to Mitchell Field, New York, reporting to the commanding general, I Fighter Command. Upon completion of this temporary duty they will proceed to station outside limits of Continental United States. This is a permanent change of station. Dependents will not accompany any of these officers."

Mears at the time had 27 pilots in the group, whose training was considered sufficiently advanced for them to head off to war. The group had already been allowed to take pilots from the nearby 33rd and 56th Groups to bring them to authorized strength, and pilots had been arriving over the previous week. Among those who soon reported to the group was Second Lieutenant Edward "Duke" Ellington, who came from the 56th Group and was sent to the "Fighting Cocks." Ellington, who had graduated from flying school and pinned on his pilot's wings five days after Pearl Harbor on December 12, 1941, later recalled:

> Ten of us in the 61st Squadron of the 56th group were ordered to the 57th, which we were told was soon to be under orders to deploy to the war zone. We were told we had been selected because of our experience, since each of us had 100 flying hours since we had joined the group after graduation from flying school! Those hours couldn't be considered very selective, since in that time we had flown the P-36, the P-40, and the P-43, along with building time in T-6s. Nobody knew where we were going, but Art found out the three of us who were assigned to the squadron had no gunnery training, so he organized a tow plane and we got four flights over a weekend, which introduced me to the business end of being a fighter pilot.

The pilots began arriving at Mitchell Field by June 30 and got a good hint about their destination when they saw the 72 brand-new P-40F Warhawks on the flight line were all painted in a pinkish tan applied over their olive drab upper surfaces. The P-40F differed from the P-40Es they had been flying by having the Allison V-1710 engine of the P-40E replaced by the Packard-built V-1650-1 Merlin – equivalent to the Rolls-Royce Merlin XX and designated Packard-Merlin 28 by the RAF – with a single-stage two-speed supercharger that produced full power at higher altitudes than the Allison engine could reach, as it lacked a supercharger.

Confusion reigned when the group was informed they would be deploying to the Middle East on board an aircraft carrier, which they would have to fly off of when they got to their destination. Second Lieutenant Dale Deniston remembered, "When we arrived at the base, the airfield contained about 75 brand new P-40Fs painted a pink color, which we guessed might be desert camouflage… All aircraft were all brand new, with only four hours total engine and flight time."

The pilots received instruction on how to make carrier takeoffs by the naval aviators of *Ranger*'s air group. Deniston remembered, "They painted lines on the runway to indicate about a thousand feet. We were to set flaps, set trim tabs to compensate for torque, run the engine up to full power, hold the stick back and then release brakes. Into the wind, I think the least distance we were able to get airborne was twelve hundred feet!" A few days later, the 57th flew to NAS Quonset Point. Deniston recalled spotting a carrier in port as he landed:

> After landing, sailors along the runway directed me to taxi off down a road right to the dock. I taxied up to the dock next to the carrier and was given the sign to cut the engine. As I sat in the cockpit filling out my Form I report, sailors were climbing all over my aircraft and removing my engine cowling… The hoist came down, was attached to the engine mount and my bird was taken up to the flight deck of USS *Ranger*. Soon all the aircraft and pilots were aboard, and we were at sea, destination unknown.

Ellington recalled that the P-40s were stored in many different ways on board the carrier: "Many were stored in the hangar deck. Room was critical. Many were hoisted by cable and hung from the ceiling. The rest were on the flight deck. Once we were at sea, they told us we were headed to Africa, and that we would then fly across the continent to join the British in Egypt. We young fellows were impressed that they thought we could do this."

When *Ranger* got to sea, she was joined by the light cruiser USS *Juneau* (CL-52) and seven destroyers. The task force stopped in Trinidad to refuel before heading across the Atlantic. On July 4, the on board holiday celebration was interrupted by one of the destroyers spotting a German U-boat and depth-charging it. Ellington remembered that "The next day, Axis Sally said on the radio that the *Ranger* had been sunk."

Ellington remembered, "Landing at Accra was no problem, as the runway was long and wide. We did damage a few with ground loops, but not me. Buck Bilby, who was a great pilot, landed short and trashed his plane. We had loaded a few rounds of ammunition because some of the territory we were to fly over was Vichy French and not friendly. The rest of the ammunition boxes were filled with cigarettes." The P-40s only stayed at Accra long enough to refuel. The earlier arrivals were already off that afternoon, led by RAF Hudsons. Pressing on eastward in smaller flights, the first ones reached Lagos that evening.

Ellington's flight was memorable, as he recalled, "The 65th took off the next day. The flight was hairy for me because we were flying in and out of cloud cover, and at one point I got vertigo. The only thing I could do was hang on my element leader's wingtip. After only a few minutes, which seemed like an eternity to me, we broke out into clear skies and things got better. But that happened three times to me before we got to Lagos."

Lagos was a primitive field with no taxiway. Ellington's flight leader led the formation off the runway onto a road that ran parallel. After carefully S-turning, he started to close on the fighter ahead. "I touched the brakes and the next thing I knew my wheels were in soft ground and the tail came up and I got the prop." With a bent tip on two blades, it looked like Ellington's trip was over since there were not any spare props and he was left behind when the flight headed on. "This innovative sergeant, Skeets Gallagher, just sawed off all three tips and hammered things straight. I tested the prop and things seemed okay."

Ellington hooked up with a group of American-flown Hudsons that were heading on. He recalled:

> The field was still under construction, and there were hundreds of native workers out on the runway with tamping rods hardening the surface. When the planes were ready to take off, they all got off the runway and climbed up on a row of 50-gallon fuel drums to watch the airplanes. The first Hudson gunned down the strip, but he got a flat just before liftoff, and the plane rolled over and went into the fuel drums, which exploded. Nobody got out of the crash and many of the workers were killed or injured. It was one of the most gruesome incidents I saw in the war, and we had to take off past it while they were still fighting the fire if we were going to get to Kano before dark.

Ellington's difficulties continued. At Kano, his battery died. The rest of the flight went on without him. Finally, a replacement was found, but now he was alone again. "A Pan Am DC-3 landed, and the pilot learned my problem, and said he'd take me on to Khartoum. I flew 300 miles on the wing of that DC-3. It wasn't the most comfortable way of flying, but I was glad to have someone to lead the way." He was able to rejoin his flight, which had been delayed at Khartoum due to dust storms in the Nile Valley ahead.

The adventure continued, as Ellington recalled:

> We partied a couple nights then left flying along the Nile to Cairo. We had to land at Wadi Halfa. The desert heat was intense. We were landing against a sand background, with no differentiation between the landing ground and the surrounding country. It was impossible to judge distance on landing and there wasn't one of us who didn't level off high, stall, and drop the plane in on landing. Fortunately, none of us banged up our airplane there. We had a few more stops and then there we were at Cairo. We flew over the pyramids, which was quite something for a boy from Spearfish, South Dakota.

In the week and a half after taking off from *Ranger*, the three squadrons had made their way across the continent in stretches of 100 to 300 miles. By August 1, they had reached Muqeible in Palestine. The 64th and 66th Squadrons remained there, spending several weeks training with the RAF. The 65th flew on for a sojourn on Cyprus that Ellington remembered as one of the best times of the war. "I loved the brief time we were there. Swimming in the Mediterranean, and the night clubs were open. The flying was great, but our introduction to British food was something I never forgot. We lived on soup, bully beef, and biscuits and bread, which were wormy. We soon learned to 'preflight' those, remove the worms and go on from there."

After a few weeks, the "Fighting Cocks" received orders back to Palestine. Ellington had a final misadventure when he tried to show he was "one of the hottest pilots in the squadron" by making a tight landing pattern from an overhead-360 approach:

> I managed to ding my wingtip on landing, so there I was waiting for repairs while the others left. Two came back two days later to escort me across the water, but my engine acted up and I had to make a forced landing that ended with a group of Cypriots thinking I was a German who had "bombed" them when I released my drop tank before landing. Fortunately, a British major showed up and rescued me. I was glad to get rid of that airplane, it had been nothing but

trouble. I finally got to Palestine and Art Salisbury welcomed me saying that with all my troubles "I hope you get the first Me-109."

In preparation, an advance group of 42 senior technical personnel were flown directly to Palestine from Miami, arriving on July 14. Before they climbed on board the waiting C-47, Corporals Bill Hahn and Herb Jorissh were pulled aside and given a strange assignment. Hahn remembers:

> [We] were instructed to report to Lieutenant Silks, the squadron intelligence officer. He handed us "Uncle Bud," and told us we were to chaperone this bird to Cairo. Herb and I could have wrung "Bud's" neck many times during the flights. He went among the men pecking at their legs, and when airborne he would flap his wings and try to crow, but over 10,000 feet he lost his crow. What a frustrated bird he was. We delivered "Bud" to our final destination in good health and in one piece. He lived a good life among men of the squadron, being occasionally allowed an Egyptian hen to play with.

With combat-experienced RAF pilots from the Western Desert Air Force as instructors, the 57th flew practice missions and learned their new role as fighter-bombers. The P-40 was particularly well suited for this role since it had a heavy armament and could withstand amazing amounts of battle damage to bring a pilot home safely. Although the P-40F's climb performance was sluggish and it was combat limited to altitudes below 20,000 feet, it was more maneuverable than either the German Bf-109 or Italian C.202 fighters that it would face.

Among the pilots who had flown to Palestine with the 57th were four from the next group to come, who were expected to gain combat experience with the 57th and pass it on to the newcomers when they arrived.

The third USAAF unit sent to the Middle East was the 79th Fighter Group, which was activated on February 9, 1942, as the 81st Pursuit Group; on April 28, 1942, it was officially redesignated as the 79th Fighter Group with its three squadrons: the 85th, 86th, and 87th Fighter Squadrons. Much of the original cadre personnel came from the 57th Fighter Group.

After some initial training in North Carolina, the group moved to New England, where headquarters was established in an old barn "cleared of cattle and swallows, but not of cobwebs," as group commander 30-year-old West Pointer Lieutenant Colonel Peter McGoldrick recalled. The 85th Squadron operated from the nearby airfield in Bedford, Massachusetts, while the 86th went to Theodore Green Field in Hillsgrove, Rhode Island, and the 87th settled at Rentschler Field near Hartford, Connecticut. Personnel from bases and training depots along the east coast began arriving to flesh out the units. A summer of intensive training saw the pilots begin learning to use the P-40 as a fighter-bomber. Just as the group was beginning to feel like things were taking firm shape, the War Department transferred a number of pilots and ground personnel from all three squadrons to become cadre for the 325th Fighter Group, which was activated in early August.

On September 27, Lieutenant Colonel McGoldrick announced that orders had been received to prepare for overseas movement. The P-40Es that had been inherited from the 57th Group were turned over to the 325th. Leaves were canceled and bags were packed. The next evening, the ground personnel of group headquarters left "secretly" by rail, joining the ground personnel of the three squadrons at the National Guard armory in Indiantown, Pennsylvania, where they received shots and final issues of equipment over what was remembered as six hectic days. The next move took them to the naval base at Newport News, Virginia, where they went aboard a troopship, the new Cunard liner *Mauretania*, successor to the original *Mauretania* that was sistership of the *Lusitania* of World War I fame.

The group's pilots were sent by rail from Connecticut to Miami, Florida, where they began flying out of the 36th Street Airport in C-54s on October 23. The route took them across the South Atlantic along the route developed by the United States in collaboration with Caribbean and South American nations, stopping at Trinidad, then on to Natal, Brazil, site of what was the largest airfield in South America. From there the C-54s flew direct to Monrovia, Liberia, with a fuel stop in the mid-South Atlantic at remote Wideawake airfield on Ascension Island, halfway between Natal and Monrovia. The island was small, and with World War II navigation, a ditty had sprung up among the fliers making use of the field: "If we don't hit Ascension, my wife will get a pension."

The transport flew on to Monrovia, then Accra. At Accra, the USAAF and RAF had established a P-40 assembly depot over the summer. Here, the pilots met their planes – 72 P-40Fs recently repainted in "Desert Tan" that was already taking on the pinkish tone under the equatorial sun. Flying over Nigeria, French Equatorial Africa, and the Sudan with A-20s providing navigational guidance for the P-40 formations, they stopped at Kano, Fort Lamy, and Khartoum before flying up the Nile Valley to land at the airfield in Heliopolis, Egypt.

As the pilots went through their aerial adventure, the group's ground echelon on board *Mauretania* traveled alone to Rio de Janeiro, depending on the liner's speed to avoid U-boats. After a day in port refueling, she departed on October 20, headed into the South Atlantic. The 7,000 Allied personnel on board got a rough introduction to life at sea when she dipped far into the "Roaring Forties" to avoid a U-boat wolf pack and round the Cape of Good Hope, arriving in Durban on October 30, where everyone was overjoyed to be given 48 hours ashore. Raising anchor on November 1, *Mauretania* made a run up the east African coast and arrived at Port Tewfik, Egypt, on November 12, at which time the troops learned the war in North Africa had heated up with the American invasion of French Morocco four days earlier.

The 79th's men were sent on to Kasfareet, near the Great Bitter Lake, where they were lodged in brick barracks. The squadron historian wrote:

> These were far from luxurious. Everyone slept on hard concrete floors. We froze at night, sweated during the day, and fought hordes of pernicious flies throughout. We almost perished on the British rations, some of the offerings in the mess being beyond reasonable description. At night we watched two-year old movies under the stars and during the day there was swimming in the Suez Canal, if you liked ice water. We had our first contact with the British, beginning a relationship first characterized by prejudice on both sides; but later one of mutual confidence and trust.

The night of November 17, they were put aboard an ancient train that took them through Cairo and up to Alexandria, where they climbed aboard trucks and drove through a stinging sandstorm that blocked all visibility until shortly before they arrived at Landing Ground 174, 30 miles west of Alexandria.

There they learned of the death of Lieutenant Colonel McGoldrick and the disaster on the night of November 6.

4

EL ALAMEIN

In the year following the German intervention in North Africa, British commanders had been dumbfounded by the way in which Rommel seemed to know their every weakness, to make countermoves to actions they had only recently decided on. During the fighting in the first week of July 1942, the Australian 9th Division solved the mystery when they captured the German 621st Signal Battalion. The unit's records revealed that Rommel had been receiving detailed information about the strength and movement of British forces from Berlin. Reports that were sent to Washington by the US military attaché in Cairo, Colonel Bonner Frank Fellers, were intercepted and decoded following the theft of American code in a covert operation by Italian military intelligence at the American embassy in Rome shortly before Rommel's appearance in North Africa. Following this discovery, use of the code immediately ceased, meaning Rommel's seemingly "extrasensory perception" on the battlefield ended. This intelligence coup was crucial to the ability of the British to hold at El Alamein.

Geography played a role in stopping the Axis forces 50 miles from Alexandria in early July at El Alamein, an otherwise-inconsequential railroad station on the coast that constituted the last good defensive position in the Western Desert. The steep slopes of the enormous Qattara Depression – a veritable sea of sand impassable by military vehicles – were 40 miles south of El Alamein; they effectively contained the area of battle and forced any attacker to mount a frontal assault. The First Battle of El Alamein, which commenced on July 1, lasted most of the month, ending on July 27 with 13,000 Allied casualties. The back-and-forth seesaw of action resulted in defeat for the Axis attackers when they were unable to crack the British defenses. The front lines were so close to both Alexandria and Cairo that when the wind was from the west the sound of artillery fire could be clearly heard in the Egyptian capital.

Despite his successful defense at El Alamein, General Claude Auchinleck was relieved as Commander-in-Chief Middle East Command and commander of Eighth Army in early August when Prime Minister Churchill and General Sir Alan Brooke, the Chief of the Imperial General Staff (CIGS), visited Cairo. Auchinleck was replaced as Commander-in-Chief Middle East by General Harold Alexander, who had a good relationship with the prime minister. Eighth Army command was assigned to Lieutenant General William Gott, who was killed when his transport aircraft was shot down by Luftwaffe fighters over the Mediterranean while en route from Malta to Egypt. Lieutenant General Bernard Montgomery, who was flown from Britain to replace him, arrived on August 13. He would command the coming Eighth Army offensive.

El Alamein became the first campaign in which Britain's ability to decode German communications became the winning edge. "Ultra," as it was known to those privileged few who knew of its existence, was able to provide the location, routing, and cargoes of the supply ship convoys sailing from Italy for North Africa. Torpedo bombers based on Malta, as well as submarines operating from the island, were able to attack these convoys, which by the beginning of September put the Afrika Korps on short rations of everything from food to artillery shells to spare tires and gasoline. Interestingly, in his reports, Rommel blamed the shortages on the Italians' failure to support him. There were never any questions from anyone on the German side about the Allied success at intercepting convoys headed to North Africa.

Attacks by Egypt-based units of the Western Desert Air Force (WDAF) on the Axis supply lines that extended from Tripoli and Tobruk 350 miles along the coastal road were crucial to the Allied success. Derna and Matruh, which were even smaller than Tobruk, though closer, were unable to handle the amount of traffic needed to keep Rommel's force adequately supplied. The WDAF was a truly international organization, composed of units of the RAF, Royal Australian Air Force (RAAF), and

South African Air Force (SAAF). At this point, the WDAF constituted the most experienced tactical air units in any Allied air force.

While the Germans were dealing with shortages, the Allies in Egypt were finally receiving replacements and new supplies. Of particular note was the arrival of Sherman tanks from the United States. The Sherman was considerably superior to any British tank, and finally gave the 7th Armored Division and other armored units a tank that could meet the German Panzer IV on an equal footing. Supplies from the United States continued to arrive in ever-increasing numbers through September and October, providing the material necessary for the planned British offensive.

The American air units arrived shortly before the outbreak of the Battle of Alam el Halfa, fought between August 30 and September 5 south of El Alamein, when Rommel attempted to defeat the Eighth Army before it became too strong. The British learned of the German plans through Ultra. General Montgomery deliberately left a gap in the front's southern sector, knowing the Germans planned to attack there, deploying armor and artillery around Alam el Halfa Ridge, 20 miles behind the front. When the enemy attacked, tanks remained in their defensive positions on the ridge, acting as antitank guns to support the infantry. Short on supplies, Rommel was unable to maintain the attack on the ridge, which therefore failed. Montgomery did not exploit the defensive victory at this time, continuing the methodical buildup of strength for his planned offensive. Rommel later claimed that British air superiority determined the result, being unaware of Ultra. After the failure at Alam el Halfa, Rommel's forces lost the initiative, which became known to the Allies through Ultra. The crisis of the summer was over, with Axis strategic aims in Africa no longer possible.

Following their arrival in Palestine, the 57th's unit commanders and flight leaders were sent to WDAF squadrons to gain experience flying as wingmen to the combat veterans, who called the Western Desert "The Blue." The Americans were at first surprised to come face to face with the physical conditions of the Western Desert, which was nothing like they had imagined a desert to be. The landing grounds the RAF were using were west of the Nile and east of El Alamein, only a few miles behind the front lines. The first mission flown by the Americans was on August 9, a patrol with 260 Squadron RAF that included four Americans as wingmen.

The coastal plain was featureless and hard, with little sand and many rocks. A landing ground was created by clearing rocks, marking the boundaries of the runway with two 55-gallon drums to either end and placing a wind sock on a pole to the side at the halfway point. Tent villages where pilots and ground crew lived and worked were created off to the side. Water was scarce while the flies were plentiful. Veterans later recalled that the best way to determine how long a man had been at the front was to watch and see if he could swallow a morsel without swallowing the fly that was always found on the food. Those who had been in "The Blue" longer than a month became experts at this.

These conditions hardened the Americans rapidly. Group personnel became highly irregular with regard to uniforms and military bearing. This was the result of the lack of water, which made bathing, shaving, and washing clothes a luxury. There was nowhere to hide on a desert landing ground when enemy air forces attacked. The slit trenches hacked out of the rocky soil were not deep and offered little protection from flying bullets and shrapnel. Additionally, they discovered that while the desert could be hot and dry during the day, it could become quite cold and damp at night, since there were few clouds to hold in the heat. Dust storms could develop quickly, with the dust rising several thousand feet in the air and obscuring visibility for a hundred miles. With zero visibility and flying sand everywhere stinging like a swarm of bees, men could only crawl into their tents and wait out the storm. After the first bad storm on September 4, 1942, 66th Squadron crew chief Tech Sergeant Herb Gluckman wrote in his diary, "We have to take all precautions to keep the dust from getting in the engines. It gets all over." "Duke" Ellington later praised the ground crews for their work. "Getting the sand out of every nook and cranny in the engine, radiator and supercharger was hard, dirty work in the conditions we found ourselves in at the landing ground. We pilots owed our lives to their diligence."

Five days after the first orientation mission, six 57th Group pilots took off on August 14 as part of a 260 Squadron formation escorting 12 Boston III attack bombers, the British version of the A-20, flown by SAAF pilots to attack Fuka Station. As the Kittyhawks crossed the lines just north of El Alamein, they were hit by 14 Bf-109Fs that attacked from out of the sun. In the whirling dogfight that ensued, First Lieutenant William W. O'Neill, Jr. of the 65th Squadron, who was flying wing for Flight Sergeant Ron Cundy, spotted a Bf-109 below to the right. Breaking flight discipline, he dove to attack and was quickly overwhelmed by five more Bf-109s. The fight was brief but fierce and resulted in O'Neill's fighter being shot up and catching fire. He managed to bail out over the Mediterranean. Landing close to shore, he inflated his dingy and paddled to the beach, which turned out to be Allied-held territory. When he returned to 260's landing ground, he reported he had shot down two Bf-109s, for which his claims were never credited. He and the other Americans, who had also violated flight discipline, received what they recalled as a "real ass-chewing" about how they had not only endangered themselves but the entire flight. This lesson would be taken back to the 57th, where air discipline became the measure by which a man was reckoned worthy of being awarded a leadership position in the air.

As the 65th Squadron's Michael Murphy later recounted, rank had no bearing in the 57th as to whether a man was assigned a leadership position when it came to flying. "There were a few majors who spent their entire tours as wingmen, led by first lieutenants who had demonstrated the necessary skill and ability."

Twenty-one days later, on September 4, 1942, the 66th Squadron's Second Lieutenant Thomas T. Williams was credited with probable destruction of a Bf-109, the first official American fighter claim in the Mediterranean Theater of Operations (MTO). Assigned as wingman in the top cover flight flying P-40F "77" on a morning escort mission near El Alamein, Williams got his chance when several Bf-109s and C.202s appeared out of the north and attacked the middle cover flight. When a 109 flew in front of him, Williams opened fire and saw his bullets hit home before being forced to break off when another enemy fighter got on his tail. One of the RAF pilots nailed a C.202, before the enemy departed as quickly as they had appeared. Back at the landing ground, Williams reported his fight but could not say for certain what the result was. Several days later, a gunner in one of the Bostons they had been escorting claimed he had seen Williams' fight and that he could confirm the enemy fighter had gone down. When 66th Squadron intelligence officer Major Porter R. Chandler called the squadron to get further information for confirmation, the field telephone line went dead and stayed dead. Williams was left with an official "probable."

"Duke" Ellington had experienced a rough start when he was first assigned to fly with the South Africans in September. He later recalled:

> My first mission with them wasn't a howling success. When we got the signal to start up, my plane wouldn't start. The squadron took off minus one Yank. Finally, I got her started and took off, but I was so inexperienced I couldn't find them and returned to the landing ground. When they returned and debriefed, the squadron commander asked me what happened. When I told him I took off on my own and tried to catch up to them, I caught holy hell. The idea I would scamper off by myself into enemy territory was too foolhardy to understand. I learned my lesson and managed not to screw up any more while I was with them.

September 13 saw the 57th declared fit for operations after the group's pilots had flown 158 missions with the RAF and SAAF squadrons they had been assigned to. Three days later, the three squadrons reunited at their own landing ground, LG 174. On September 16, the 57th began independent operations as a reserve unit, under operational control of 211 Group. On September 29, Warhawks of the 66th Squadron attacked a German airfield and got involved in a fight with defending Bf-109s. Major Charles Fairlamb in "91" got the opportunity to prove to the rest that the P-40 could indeed "take it" when he was hit in his left outer wing by 20mm fire from a Bf-109 that put a big hole in the wing. Fairlamb flew back to LG 174, where everyone was impressed that the hole was big enough for him to stand upright in.

On October 7, the group began flying operations as an integral part of 211 Group and was soon busy escorting bombers, and flying fighter-bomber raids to hit enemy airdromes behind the lines to eliminate the Luftwaffe as a threat to Commonwealth ground troops.

Looking to create additional morale in the group as they entered combat, the 64th and 66th Squadrons were encouraged to take up names and adopt symbolic insignia, as the 65th had already done with "Uncle Bud," their rooster mascot, and naming themselves "The Fighting Cocks." 64th Squadron took inspiration from one of the most persistent and dangerous pests to be found in "The Blue" – black scorpions, predatory arthropods with a nasty sting that invaded their tents at night and made shaking out one's boots in the morning to avoid being stung by a new resident therein "standard operating procedure." It was decided "Black Scorpions" was a good squadron nickname, and soon their P-40Fs were sporting a painting of the nasty pest on their radiator cowlings, the work of the squadron artists. The 66th Squadron finally took inspiration from being called "Squadron X" by a war correspondent's report on their activities. Adopting "X" as part of their insignia, they became the "Exterminators." The group as a whole adopted the motto "First in the Blue" for being the first Americans to operate in the desert and honoring the term for it used by their Commonwealth allies.

Intelligence reports in early October revealed that Regia Aeronautica and Luftwaffe units at the landing grounds near El Daba (LG 105) and Qattafa (LG 104) were now trapped by heavy rains and unable to fly. The 12th Bomb Group and RAF units attacked the airfields on October 9, destroying ten enemy aircraft and damaging an additional 22. The 57th's first official mission saw Major Clermont "Pudge" Wheeler lead six 64th Squadron P-40Fs to escort bombers attacking El Daba. First Lieutenant Bill Mount remembered getting the group's first aerial victory:

> I was flying on Bob Barnum's wing. We were high cover to fend off any Germans who got airborne. There had been light rain the night before, which left their field muddy. Barnum saw something and did a quick half-roll and split-S that I could not follow. About that time, I saw this lone Bf 109 fly across in front of me heading out to sea. I was above him and he was climbing. I tacked onto his tail, diving slightly and caught up with him, gave him a long burst and saw the aeroplane disintegrate, breaking in two behind the cockpit. It fell into the ocean. By then I was on my own and, as I recall, proceeded to return to base.

First Lieutenant George D. Mobbs later wrote in his diary about the mission:

> We got mixed up and got to the landing ground ahead of the bombers, but went in to strafe anyway. That is, most of us did. I was on the outside, and just as we started to go down, four or five '109s started to attack me. I turned into them and got a short burst at one, but it was a 90-degree deflection shot. Three of them kept attacking me,

and I kept evading them, and occasionally getting a shot. Meanwhile, the rest of our airplanes had gone in to strafe and then flown out to sea, but I couldn't join them because the three German fighters kept on attacking me.

I was running the engine at 55 to 65 inches of mercury and 3,000rpm, so I could pretty well stay with them. They would keep alternating the attacks between them. After a few minutes I got on one of their tails and was overtaking him. I didn't open fire until I was about 100 yards from him. I gave him a squirt and nothing happened. I moved over a little and changed my sighting, and on about the third burst his airplane burst into flames and fell off to one side. I was going to watch him go down so I would have a chance of getting credit for one destroyed, but one of the other jokers attacked so I was busy evading him. However, I spotted the first one moments later a few thousand feet below me, still spiraling down, but I never got another look at him after that.

I was still in a hole. The other two kept attacking, one after the other. Later, I got a few shots at one from directly behind and slightly above as we were diving. I could see the airplane jerk each time I pulled the trigger but saw no debris or fire from it, and I was drawn away by the other one attacking. I must have hit the Jerry, because I never saw him again. Now I just had one to worry about, but on his next attack I finished my ammunition. He kept following and attacking, but with just him to worry about, I was making pretty good time back toward our lines. On another attack we met head-on, and I don't think he fired his guns. I didn't see them, anyway, and I was already out of ammunition.

We were down pretty low by then – 1,000 feet – and the German ack-ack had opened up at me. But I was going so fast that they were shooting behind me. I had everything forward. I was running awfully hard, and the ack-ack was getting pretty close to the Jerry pilot behind me. It was kind of amusing, because it looked as if I was going to make it back if my engine didn't quit. We were so low that I could see the ack-ack gun emplacements below.

Fortunately, the Merlin held together and the enemy pilot finally turned away, allowing Mobbs to return to base. He was awarded one Bf-109 probably destroyed.

On October 13, the 65th Squadron had its baptism of air combat when it got into a fight with 20 Bf-109s over El Alamein. First Lieutenant Arnold D. Jaquan in P-40F "47," named "Sally," made the squadron's first claims for one Bf-109 destroyed and a second damaged. The 64th's Lieutenant Mobbs, who had survived his baptism of fire four days earlier, scored his first confirmed victory.

Montgomery's offensive began with concentrated air strikes on October 20. The air forces marshaled were the greatest assembled for close support of a single army up to then. There was a two-fold objective. The first was to gain complete air superiority, allowing the bombers and attack aircraft to soften up the enemy by harassing supply lines. This was the first real use of fighter-bombers. During this part of the battle, the 57th Group flew 10 percent of the Western Desert Air Force's total sorties.

The 64th and 65th Squadrons operated with fellow 211 Group units 6 Squadron RAF and 7 Squadron SAAF, both of which flew the Hurricane IID, an aerial tank-hunter armed with two 40mm cannon underwing that was particularly effective against German armor, while the 66th Squadron was transferred to 239 Wing, where the pilots of the Kittyhawk-equipped 3 and 450 Squadrons RAAF, and 112 and 250 Squadrons RAF were flying in the fighter-bomber role. They were glad to welcome the Americans with their Merlin-powered P-40Fs, which had better high-altitude performance than the Allison-powered Kittyhawk I, II, and III and were used as escorts for the fighter-bombers. The 57th operated through the Second Battle of El Alamein with the group divided this way.

The second phase of the battle began the night of October 23/24, when the Eighth Army's heavy artillery opened fire against German positions along the 40-mile front, which stretched from the beaches of the Mediterranean Sea to the impassable Qattara Depression. At first light on October 24, 230,000 Commonwealth troops began moving forward in three distinct assaults against the 107,000 Italian and German troops facing them. The 57th's Warhawks performed close air support, bombing and strafing army targets. Their first missions were flown at dawn and then continuously through the day; planes returning from a mission were serviced as rapidly as possible and soon took off on another. During the first and second phases of the battle, the Americans were credited with approximately 40 percent of the aerial victories of the entire Western Desert Air Force. During this second phase, most of the Luftwaffe units supporting Rommel were put out of action on the ground.

On October 24, the 57th flew three escort missions for Douglas Boston attack bombers. The Warhawks had only one encounter with enemy fighters that day, with no claims made. The next day, the 64th Squadron's midday mission to attack the Bf-109 base at LG 20 saw the first victory scored by First Lieutenant Lyman Middleditch, Jr. Captain Glade "Buck" Bilby saw dust rising from the airstrip when the eight Warhawks arrived over the target. With no aircraft on the field, it was obvious the enemy fighters had just taken off. Bilby led the P-40s in an attack on a group of trucks parked at the field's edge. Just after they dropped their bombs, five Bf-109s attacked. Middleditch – in P-40F "No. 17" – spotted two Bf-109s on Lieutenant Ernest D. Hartman's tail. Turning right onto the tail of the leader, he fired a burst that sent the enemy fighter into the sea. Middleditch's victory was confirmed by three other pilots.

The 57th Group initiated what came to be called the pre-dawn fighter-bomber attack. The first of these was remembered later as the "Fuka Show," flown in the early morning of October 27. The P-40s took off before dawn; trucks lined up along the side of the runway flipped on their lights at a signal, allowing a flight of 12 to take off abreast, followed quickly by two more flights. The fighters stayed on the deck as they flew out to sea, to a point west of the target, then turned back from the north, over the coastal ridge, and attacked Fuka in the dawn's first light. The enemy was so surprised that there was little flak, and the destruction of aircraft on the airfields was phenomenal, with the Warhawks claiming most of the aircraft on the field destroyed from bombing and strafing.

On October 28, eight 65th Squadron P-40s carrying bombs, covered by eight 64th Squadron fighters, had just dropped their bombs on an enemy airfield near El Daba when they sighted 20 Regia Aeronautica Fiat CR.42 biplane fighters and 20 Stukas escorted by Bf-109s. Though heavily outnumbered, they attacked, turning into the enemy formation.

Middleditch's top cover flight attacked one of the two Bf-109 formations. He hit one of the flight of four that smoked on his first pass and then dove after another, but missed it due to excessive speed. As he attempted to regain control of his fighter, he spotted the crash of his first victim a moment before three more Bf-109s attacked him as he crossed the coastline. They pursued him and he turned into each as they attacked him, firing when he had a chance. The first Bf-109 splashed into the sea and he also managed to hit another solidly in its fuselage. It managed a half roll before catching a wingtip in a wave, cart-wheeling into the water. Middleditch had only had two working guns as he engaged the last Bf-109 in a turning battle until the enemy pilot lost his nerve and broke off, allowing him to return safely to LG 174. Overall, the Warhawks claimed seven destroyed, three probably destroyed, and three damaged, without loss. The next day they claimed four more enemy fighters.

On October 30, the 64th Squadron flew an attack mission against the enemy landing ground at El Daba. Second Lieutenant Rocky Byrne, a former professional basketball player who had joined the squadron ten days earlier after arriving as a replacement, remembered his first mission:

> Twelve P-40s from the 64th Squadron took off under the leadership of Major Clermont "Pudge" Wheeler. It was dark when we took off and formed up over our landing field. I was flying the fourth P-40 in Major Wheeler's flight. I joined up on the wing of a Lieutenant Lancaster, and, in the pitch dark, I stayed there by sticking close to the blue flame from the other P-40's engine exhaust stacks.
>
> After we formed up, Wheeler led the three four-plane flights out over the Mediterranean at less than 100 feet over the water. This was to evade the German radar. We quickly lost sight of the coast and continued on in a very tight formation.
>
> We flew along over the water like this for about forty minutes, and then, just as it was getting light, I heard Major Wheeler say, "Turn the guns on." Then I sighted the coastline. Since we had flown out over the Mediterranean from our base, there had been no landmarks and no guides even for direction. I was thinking, there was no way we could be close to El Daba, but we hit the landing ground right on the button.
>
> We caught the Germans by complete surprise. They were in their chow lines, for breakfast. As we came in, I saw that their landing ground was pretty much the same as ours – desert sand and tents. It was temporary and mobile, just like ours.

We were through the base in less than ten seconds. That's all we were supposed to do; one strafing pass at whatever targets we felt like hitting. We spread out and hit them from less than 100 feet. I shot up some planes on the ground and hit some other equipment and, probably, some people, too. There was no antiaircraft fire – no time for them to man any guns – but they must have been throwing their helmets up at us as we passed right over their heads. I was so low that I'd have flown into the ground if I had depressed my gunsight any farther.

It turned out that the Luftwaffe wasn't completely asleep. They had a gaggle of Me-109s in the air, even at that early hour.

Major Wheeler's flight was the last one off the target, and I was the last man in it. By the time we got over the German landing ground, I sensed that the rest of the squadron had already climbed out and was heading east across the desert, toward home.

When we came off the strafing run and started to climb to clear the landing ground and re-form, the 109s were at one o'clock high. I saw them first and called them in over the radio. I was just lining up on Lieutenant Lancaster, getting ready to rejoin on his wing, when I saw the 109s. Lancaster tried to pull his plane in to avoid the fire from one of the 109s, but he pulled it in too tight. His P-40 stalled out and, at that low altitude, it crashed and burned. Maybe it was hit by German bullets, too. Lancaster was killed in the crash.

The 109 that had opened fire on Lancaster had me on a platter. He was coming up at an angle, from about my one o'clock. I was dodging tracers the size of golf balls – 20mm. I flipped over on my back because my airspeed was so low, and he flashed into my sights almost at once. I blasted him to pieces as he soared up past me, only a second or two after he had opened fire on Lancaster.

The only thing I had going for me was the six .50-caliber machine guns in my wings. I turned them on whatever 109s I could reach as they made repeated passes at me. As I climbed to get away from them, however, I used up all my ammo, and I still wasn't free of them. I was at about 2,000 feet when I happened to remember that the Qattara Depression was only a little farther south of El Daba. The depression was a wide, deep valley in the desert, 300 to 400 feet below sea level, much like California's Death Valley. It was my only out. I dove to the deck and, at full throttle, headed south.

Sure enough, I found what I was looking for. I dove right over the edge, straight into one of the ravines, and flew straight down to the floor of the depression. Somehow the Germans lost me. When I leveled out on the floor of the Qattara Depression, I headed due east at full power, with the throttle bent over the firewall. I was going flat out on the deck when I glanced up one of the ravines to my north and spotted a column of troops wending its way in single file over an outcropping on the side of a canyon. I wheeled around in a 180-degree turn and came back. There were about 120 of them waving their weapons and jumping up and down. They were Italians. I had no ammunition left, so I just waggled my wings in salute and headed back on course to the east.

When I hit the other side of the Qattara Depression, I flew up to the desert floor and turned on a heading for our own landing ground. It was a long way home, but I got there in one piece without further incident. I reported my sighting of the Italian troops as soon as I landed.

I was amazed to find out that other members of the squadron had tangled with the German fighters. Pudge Wheeler had damaged a 109, the leader of one of the other flights was given credit for a probable, and two lieutenants damaged a total of three other 109s.

Between October 19 and 31, the 57th flew 743 sorties, claiming 27 enemy aircraft destroyed, six probably destroyed, and 15 damaged.

The squadrons repeated their pre-dawn attacks on other German landing grounds on November 2. The result of the battle was a tactical defeat for the Luftwaffe, which never again seriously contended for control of the air in the rest of the breakthrough at El Alamein and the ensuing Libyan campaign. Throughout the campaign, the Allied air units were opposed by the three *Gruppen* of JG 27 and one of JG 53, flying Bf-109Fs and Gs, plus seven Italian *gruppi* equipped with Macchi C.202s.

First Lieutenant Roy E. Whittaker was one of the future group aces who began their scores during the Battle of El Alamein. He was among the 57th's pilots assigned temporarily to the RAF's 250 Squadron, flying his first combat mission – bombing and strafing tents and trucks south of El Alamein – on August 28.

On the morning of October 26, Whittaker completed his 13th mission flying escort for bombers. At 1425 hours the same day, the 65th Squadron, led by Captain Thomas W. Clark, was scrambled to intercept an incoming air raid after a formation of Italian C.202 Folgores south of El Daba were spotted. In the ensuing fight, Clark emerged with two claims and Whittaker and First Lieutenant Robert Metcalf claimed one each. In another fight near El Daba with Italian CR.42 biplane fighters the next day, Whittaker shot down one confirmed, one probable, and one damaged. These victories put him on his way to becoming the 57th's leading ace by the end of the campaign.

On the morning of October 28, the 66th Squadron was assigned to duty with 233 Wing at LG 91. While flying a bomber escort mission that day, the squadron was jumped by Bf-109s when it became separated from the rest of the escorts. The only claim was made by Second Lieutenant R.J. "Jay" Overcash for the first of five victories he scored in the North Africa fighting. On a second afternoon mission, the "Exterminators" attracted further attention from roving Bf-109s. In the battle that developed, Captain Raymond A. Llewellyn, First Lieutenant Robert M. Adams, and Second Lieutenant Thomas M. Boulware each scored one.

The 64th Squadron's Robert J. "Rocky" Byrne was the last of the group's future aces to claim his first victory at this time. Byrne, flying the same P-40F – "13" – that Lieutenant Middleditch had flown when he scored his three victories on October 27, was a wingman in one of two flights flying a dive-bombing mission on October 30. While 12 65th Squadron Warhawks flew top cover, Major Clermont Wheeler led the fighters ten miles out to sea before he turned southeast to approach the target at 13,000 feet. On reaching the coast, Wheeler spotted the targeted building and banked into his bomb run, with the seven P-40s close behind. They released their bombs at 8,000 feet with none hitting the target. As they pulled up, six Bf-109s attacked them head-on.

Wheeler and second flight leader Captain Richard E. Ryan managed snap shots at enemy fighters as they passed, with Wheeler credited for one damaged and Ryan one probably destroyed. Byrne also fired at a passing 109 but saw no hits. Spotting three others below, he dove on them, closing in behind one and opening fire; when the enemy fighter hit the ground, one wing came off as the rest caught fire. The other two fled.

Not everyone was so lucky. First Lieutenant Gordon Ryerson damaged one before he was attacked by two others that hit him in his engine, cockpit, and tail section. With the controls damaged and wounded, Ryerson could only turn left but somehow managed to return to base where he flipped over on landing. The P-40 was written off, but Ryerson survived to return to combat flying, only to be killed in action a few weeks later.

Reconnaissance flights reported that the coast road from El Daba to Fuka was black with traffic headed west on the morning of November 3. The Western Desert Air Force sent every unit to attack the retreating enemy. The 57th flew multiple attacks that afternoon, shuttling between its base and the battlefield as quickly as the Warhawks could be rearmed and refueled. By November 4, the Afrika Korps' collapse forced Rommel to disengage and order his entire force to retreat west to avoid destruction and re-establish itself on a line south from Ghazal, despite Adolf Hitler's strong disagreement.

Dawn on November 5 saw the aerial assault continue; the havoc, confusion, and destruction meant the enemy was unable to hold the new line. A retreat to Fuka was similarly defeated. On November 6, the German retreat became a rout as the smoke from destroyed vehicles drifted over Sidi Barrani, Sollum, and the Halfaya Pass. An attempt to hold against the British advance by German forces was quickly broken at Jedabya.

Now it was the turn of the Eighth Army to experience delays as its supply lines stretched west from Egypt. The Western Desert campaign became a 1,400-mile chase across Libya and Tunisia that would continue for the next six months. For all his tactical brilliance as a field commander, Rommel had simply not been able to overcome the sheer weight of numbers put on the field by Montgomery.

In the air, JG 27, which had dominated the air over the desert since its arrival in the theater in April 1941, collapsed under the pressure of Allied aerial attacks. The *Geschwader* was already depleted in both aircraft and experienced pilots at the outset of the battle. III./JG 53 had moved to North Africa to reinforce the "Afrika" Geschwader at the end of July. In mid-October, in the face of increased RAF air opposition leading up to the Battle of El Alamein, I./JG 27 and I./JG 77 moved from Sicily, where they had been engaged in the final campaign against Malta, while II./JG 53 and the *Jabos* of I./Sch.G 2 also flew in for reinforcement. In late October, a decision was made that war-weary JG 27 would be entirely replaced by JG 77, which was still operating II. and III.Gruppen on the Eastern Front under the leadership of famed *Experte* Joachim Müncheberg. III./JG 77 arrived in North Africa on October 29, followed by II./JG 77 in early December. JG 27 departed North Africa for Italy in late November.

The *Jagdgeschwadern* were just receiving the Bf-109G-4 at this time. Developed from the nearly identical-looking Bf-109F, the new "Gustav," as it was called, was powered by a Daimler-Benz DB 605 engine that increased its power by having larger pistons than the DB 601 used by the "Friedrich." The displacement and compression ratio were increased as well as other detail improvements to ease large-scale mass production. Takeoff and emergency power of 1,455hp was achieved with 42.5 inches of manifold pressure at 2,800rpm. The DB 605 suffered from reliability problems during the first year of operation, and Luftwaffe units were ordered to limit maximum power output to 1,292hp at 2,600rpm and 38.9 inches of manifold pressure.

The Gustav was not an aerodynamic improvement on its predecessor. Ace Heinz Knoke recalled in his postwar memoir *I Flew for the Führer* that in the landing pattern with gear and flaps down, the fighter had to be flown at full power. The one good thing about the new fighter was that it had even more high-altitude capability than the Bf-109F, with an operational ceiling of over 30,000 feet. In late November, the *Jagdgruppen* started receiving the "definitive" Bf-109G-6 as replacement aircraft; this sub-type replaced the two fuselage-mounted 7.65mm machine guns with two 13mm weapons, which improved firepower.

JG 77's *Kommodore*, Major Joachim Müncheberg, was two months short of his 24th birthday when he led the *Geschwader* to North Africa in October. On arrival, he had 100 victories to his credit; by the time he met his death in combat over Tunisia on March 27, 1943, he would be victorious in 135 combats in the Battles of France and Britain, on the Eastern Front, and in the Mediterranean. In 1941, as *Staffelkapitän* of JG 26's 7.Staffel, he took the unit to Sicily in early February 1941; the 12 Bf-109E-7s transformed the air war over Malta, establishing absolute air superiority over the island between their arrival on February 9, 1941 and their departure for Greece at the end of May, during which time they claimed 38 victories, including 20 by Müncheberg, while losing neither pilots nor aircraft. He was a leader his men respected.

The pilots of JG 77 were all combat-experienced, but air combat over the Eastern Front was different from that in the West and North Africa. With the size of Allied units, the tactic of four-plane patrols used in the East had to be changed. Patrols were generally flown in at least a *Staffel* strength of 10–12 fighters. Despite being outnumbered by their Allied opponents, they would give a good account of themselves by the time the survivors were evacuated to Sicily in May 1943.

One of the more interesting German pilots the 57th would confront was Leutnant Heinz-Edgar Berres, *Staffelkapitän* of 1.Staffel of JG 77's I.Gruppe, which arrived in North Africa just before the Battle of El Alamein. Berres had shot down a B-24D of the "Halverson project" during the first Allied attack on the Romanian oil fields at Ploesti on June 12, 1943, atop six victories he scored previously on the Eastern Front that spring. The *Gruppe* then engaged in combat over Malta that summer, where Berres shot down a Spitfire. His score increased in combat over Egypt and Libya, with the first an RAF Kittyhawk on November 1 over Bir-el-Abd, another on November 3 northwest of Quotaifiya, and an American P-40 from the 57th on November 11. On December 14, he shot down a Spitfire over El Agheila for his 25th victory. With a score that would have made him the envy of any Allied fighter pilot, Berres was finally accorded the accolade *Experte* by Müncheberg.

During the El Alamein battle, the 57th Fighter Group scored 27 confirmed victories, five probables, and 12 damaged while losing eight P-40s. More importantly, the group was now a mature combat team, the masters of the WDAF's fighter-bomber tactics.

The most difficult part of the air campaign at that point was moving squadrons forward to new landing grounds. Following the experience of the RAF, the 57th divided each squadron into A and B Groups, with enough ground support personnel in each to keep the aircraft operational. While A Group continued servicing the P-40s, B Group moved forward to the next base to prepare for operations. When the fighters moved to that location, A Group would move farther forward. In the process, the group's well-organized "scroungers" performed miracles in getting damaged enemy equipment left behind in the retreat working again, cannibalizing parts from vehicles that were beyond restoring. Soon, it became impossible to determine the national origin of the ground formation, as it used American, British, German, and Italian vehicles and equipment. German BMW motorcycles were particularly prized.

On November 9, 64th Squadron armorer Sergeant Lyle Custer, wrote of the campaign:

> Today we went on another 100 miles closer to the front. There were a lot of wrecked German tanks and trucks, and a few dead bodies,

along the road. Saw a lot of wrecked airplanes on aerodromes, most of them German but a few British too. There are a lot of minefields. Some of the towns we went through were Bir-El Arab and Daba. Most of the towns are only piles of stones. We saw lots of enemy prisoners, mostly Italians but some Germans. As we came near our field they said there were snipers, so we had to have our rifles ready. We reached our field in the afternoon… Two enemy airplanes flew over. The ground is so hard that we cannot dig a fox hole – there are large stones under the ground.

The Libyan desert was even more hostile than the conditions they had experienced in western Egypt. Radio technician Sergeant Thomas Tackett of the 64th Squadron remembered, "I got caught in a sudden and vicious sand storm on my way to the mess tent. I probably wouldn't be here today had I not stumbled into one of our fighters, hopped on a wing, climbed into the cockpit, pulled the canopy shut and waited out the storm."

The group's landing grounds were so close to the front that at one, LG 75, 40 miles southeast of Sidi Barrani, the advance ground echelon had to wait while an enemy armored force was driven off the field. At another landing ground 35 miles southwest of Sirte, the group underwent three days of concentrated bombing and strafing attacks.

The 79th Fighter Group, which had followed the 57th to the Middle East, was close to being declared operational in early November. Group commander Colonel Peter McGoldrick had assigned himself to fly operations with the 57th in order to gain combat experience to pass on to his pilots. On November 6, the flight he was with attacked a German convoy on the coastal road near Charing Cross, Egypt. As McGoldrick banked around for a second strafing pass, his Warhawk was hit by ground fire; attempting a wheels-up landing, the P-40 skidded into a minefield, and he was killed in the subsequent explosion. With the enemy falling back, the emergency that had brought the American units to the theater was no longer so desperate, and the 79th's introduction to combat was delayed. Through late November and December, pilots flew with the 57th in order to create a cadre of combat veterans when the group became operational.

The 66th Squadron returned to the group on November 19, the same day that the famous RAF 112 "Shark" Squadron joined it for the rest of the advance through Libya. The desert conditions meant that the P-40Fs, which had only been in the theater for three months, were becoming rapidly worn out. The Merlin-powered Warhawks were in demand in every USAAF fighter group in the theater; due to production shortages, the 64th and 66th Squadrons received P-40Ks as replacements in late November, since they were arriving in Egypt as Kittyhawk IIIs for the RAF. The P-40K was Allison-powered, and distinguishable from the P-40F by an enlarged vertical fin that was the first response to the directional stability problem that had plagued the P-40 since it first appeared. The P-40K was faster at low level than the Merlin-powered Warhawk, but power rapidly fell off over 15,000 feet since it had only a single-stage supercharger. The P-40Fs of the 65th, which could operate at 20,000 feet, carried on as high cover for the new fighters.

A mission flown on December 8 to bomb an enemy airfield near Mussolini's famed Marble Arch memorial on the border of Cyrenaica and Tripolitania saw the P-40Ks prove they could hold their own. Twelve bomb-carrying P-40Ks of the 64th Squadron, with three flown by pilots from the newly arrived 85th Fighter Squadron of the 79th Fighter Group that would soon reinforce the 57th, were assigned as attackers with top cover by three flights of 65th Squadron P-40Fs.

Captain Richard E. Ryan, in P-40K "20," led the attack, with the Warhawks approaching at 5,500 feet under an overcast sky. Several Bf-109s were seen to take off minutes before the attack, and they made an aggressive attack as soon as they reached sufficient altitude while the Americans recovered from their attack dives. Ryan got a shot at one on the first pass, claiming it as damaged. First Lieutenant George Mobbs and Second Lieutenant Steven Merena of the 64th claimed two each, as did the 65th's First Lieutenant Arnold Jaqua, while the 64th's First Lieutenant William S. Barnes got one. First Lieutenant Sammy Say of the 79th Group's 85th Fighter Squadron, who was attached to the 64th to gain combat experience, was credited with a Bf-109 damaged for the 79th's first credit. Say's wingman, Second Lieutenant Bill Abbott, was hit and wounded in the fight.

Mobbs recalled that he got good shots at two different 109s during the fight:

> Because of the intensity of the fight I hadn't observed the final results of the first one. The second one was in a downward spiral, and I

tried to watch it go down. This lack of caution led to my problem. Suddenly, holes appeared in my left wing. It seemed to take a long time for me to realize what was happening. I started a tight turn and moved into a position to retaliate, but when I pulled the trigger nothing happened. My guns wouldn't fire. I also realized I was now alone. I started trying to make headway toward our lines, hoping to get to friendly territory in case I had to go down. It was difficult to make progress. As soon as I would head toward home I was attacked. I then saw there were two above, two on my left and two above to my right. Two from one side would make a pass and I would turn into them, and then the two from the other side would make a pass. In an attempt to make better progress I thought I would turn into them only to the point that I could see the cannon hole in the Me 109's nose spinner – maybe then they wouldn't be leading me enough, and I could make more progress toward home. Somewhere in here I took a hit in the left fuselage and a fragment in my left thigh.

Although I have a clear recollection of the thoughts I had as to how to thwart their efforts to shoot me down, the sequence of those efforts is vague in my memory. I know that somewhere in there I thought my chances were so slim that when turning into them I contemplated trying to ram one. I felt that the German anti-aircraft helped me in my plight because in shooting at me they were also getting close to the Me 109s. Eventually they broke off, either because they were out of ammunition or low on fuel, or both. I made it back to our strip and belly-landed – a very rough belly landing. My trim tabs were ineffective, probably damaged by gunfire, and I was exhausted. If you look closely at the Me 109 you will note that there is a hole in the spinner for the cannon. There is also a protrusion on the left side of the engine cowling about the size of an old-fashioned stovepipe. These are two images that I saw frequently in my dreams after that day.

Two days after this fight, Major Tarleton "Jack" Watkins, CO of the 79th's 86th Squadron, was credited with a Bf-109 damaged. Squadron mate Captain Fred Borsodi was credited with another Bf-109 damaged on December 13, and scored the group's first aerial victory when he shot down a Bf-109 on December 15.

With Tripoli captured on January 23, 1943, the Eighth Army paused to regroup and replenish. Ahead in southern Tunisia stood the Mareth

Line, constructed before the war by the French to protect the Tunisian colony from Italian Libya; consisting of steel and concrete fortifications and an underground communications system, it resembled the Maginot Line in France. The Afrika Korps had arrived there in January; with the respite given by the Eighth Army to replenish and reorganize, Rommel had taken the time to add tank traps, minefields, gun emplacements, and miles of barbed wire to turn the line into a heavily defended defensive position running from the Gulf of Gabes to the Dahar and Matmata hills to the west, beyond which lay the barren wastes of Darfur and the Grand Erg sand desert. The fighters of JG 77 were stationed close behind the line at Zuara, Bir Toual, Gabes, and El Hamma.

The 57th's advance party set up a base at Ben Gerdane, where the group settled in for what would prove to be their longest time at one airfield in the campaign since the breakthrough at El Alamein. The 57th could look back at a record of having flown nearly one-fourth of the fighter-bomber sorties by the Western Desert Air Force, in the process being credited with 62 enemy aircraft destroyed, 12 probably destroyed, and 42 damaged for a loss of 26 P-40s, the majority by strafing, with 15 pilots lost, eight of whom were confirmed as POWs.

Back in Egypt, the 324th Fighter Group, which had followed the 57th and 79th Groups in organization and training back in the States, had arrived in Egypt in early December and was undergoing rapid training to bring them up to combat standard as soon as possible.

On the morning of January 20, 1943, the 79th Group's "A" detachment departed the group's base at LG 174 for the long trip across Egypt and Libya, arriving at their new operating base at El Gazala, a few miles west of Tobruk, on January 24. The P-40s flew up the next day, and the "B" echelon arrived at the end of the month. On February 2, they broke camp again and moved to a new landing ground, Darraugh North, 60 miles from Misurata; the field was a dusty, miserable hellhole where the aircraft were frequently grounded by sandstorms.

The coming frontal assault on the Mareth Line was bound to be a costly, bloody affair.

5

OPPONENTS

The North African campaign would be the first real confrontation between the USAAF and the Luftwaffe. At this time, though it was soon to be stretched to its limits, the Luftwaffe still had many highly experienced pilots, men who had kept the RAF at bay for two years on the Channel Front and who had decimated the Red Air Force when Hitler turned east in Operation *Barbarossa* the summer before the United States entered the war; it was truly a force to be reckoned with, equipped with fighters that were the equal if not the superior of those flown by their opponents. The school of combat run by the Luftwaffe's *Experten* over the Tunisian desert forced American pilots through a steep learning curve. In the early months, American inexperience led to losses so severe that replacing them led to the near-dismemberment of the Eighth Air Force in England, which lost all four fighter groups intended to provide the escort force the command's leaders knew they needed, later mythology about their belief in the "self-defending bomber" notwithstanding.

From the entry of the German Afrika Korps into combat in North Africa in May 1941 until August 1942, the only fighter unit permanently assigned to the North African campaign was JG 27, the "Afrika" Geschwader. In the face of growing Allied strength as supplies of aircraft, armor, and other military equipment from the United States began to reach the British Commonwealth forces in Egypt, III./JG 53 moved from Sicily where the *Gruppe* had been committed to the Malta campaign to North Africa to reinforce the "Afrika" Geschwader in

December 1941. The *Gruppe* would only remain in North Africa for a few weeks but would return on May 25, 1942, to support the Afrika Korps' drive on Egypt that came to a halt in July at El Alamein.

The *Gruppe*'s first success came on May 27 when the unit's current top scorer, 9.Staffel's Oberfeldwebel Werner Stumpf, shot down an RAF Kittyhawk. On May 31, an air battle saw the *Gruppe*'s pilots down six Kittyhawks. Between June 1 and 15, a further 18 Kittyhawks were added to the *Gruppe*'s score during the battle at Ein el Gazala. On June 14, as the Commonwealth forces began the retreat from Gazala, the *Gruppe* escorted Stukas in an attack on a Malta-bound convoy from Alexandria; during the attack, they shot down five of the RAF fighters flying cover over the ships. The *Gruppe*'s most successful day of its entire time in North Africa occurred the next day. The other British convoy headed to Malta in Operation *Pedestal* had been discovered, and III./JG 53 was ordered back to Sicily to meet this challenge. Its route was via Greece to Sicily from Libya, which took them across the eastern Mediterranean. The *Gruppe* formation was 80 miles north of Derna over the sea when it spotted a large formation of twin-engine aircraft, which turned out to be a strike force of Beaufort torpedo bombers escorted by Beaufighters, searching for elements of the Italian fleet at sea. In a series of confused fights, eight Beauforts and two Beaufighters were shot down. Now short of fuel, they landed at Maleme on Crete.

Following the short time spent in Sicily opposing Operation *Pedestal*, III./JG 53 returned to North Africa on July 1. Over the next several weeks, it would move its bases east four times as the Afrika Korps continued its advance, until the Eighth Army was able to hold at El Alamein against a series of German attacks during July that finally ended on July 25. Between then and the opening of the Eighth Army's offensive in late October, air battles over the front involved small formations on both sides, with concomitant low scores; the *Gruppe*'s pilots only scored a total of three on eight different days during this period, with only ten victories scored in the entire month of September.

This came to an end on October 9; following rainstorms that flooded the Luftwaffe's forward airfields on the El Alamein front, the RAF mounted a short offensive to attack the bases and destroy as much of the Luftwaffe as possible while the weather limited enemy flight operations. In appalling conditions that day, II./JG 53 managed to get a few *Staffeln* airborne and scored nine Kittyhawks shot down over several different missions. However, it also lost 13 fighters on the ground to the bombing raids. Oberfeldwebel Stumpf, the *Gruppe*'s leading ace, was shot down and killed by flak on October 13. Its last score during this tour in North Afrika, a Kittyhawk shot down on October 23, gave the *Gruppe* a score of 107 over the five months. The British offensive began that day, and the *Gruppe*'s tired pilots were evacuated to Sicily on October 27, leaving their fighters for the newly arrived JG 77. In late October, a decision was made that the war-weary JG 27 would be replaced entirely by JG 77, whose II. and III.Gruppen were still operating on the southern Eastern Front under the leadership of famed *Experte* Joachim Müncheberg.

III./JG 77 duly arrived in North Africa on October 29, followed by II./JG 77 in early December, while JG 27 departed North Africa for Italy in late November. The pilots of the *Geschwader*, known as the "Ace of Hearts" *Geschwader* for its unit symbol, had served in all the theaters of war, from initial involvement in the invasion of Poland and then Norway, to the Battle of Britain, the Balkans campaign, and the Eastern Front, with their most recent combat in the Malta campaign; they numbered among their ranks many high-scoring *Experten*. However, the pilots of III./JG 77 quickly learned that North Africa was unpredictable and far more dangerous then than the Eastern Front, when 40-victory *Experte* Hauptmann Wolf-Dietrich Huy, 7.Staffel *Staffelkapitän*, was lost in combat with Spitfires on October 29, shot down to become a POW.

The Luftwaffe policy of placing top-scoring aces in command of fighter units did lead to higher morale in the *Geschwadern*, but often these men did not have the skill to manage such an organization effectively. The two men who led the *Geschwader* in North Africa were able to combine the skills of the high-scoring ace leading from the front in the air with the ability to manage what it took organizationally to support that effort. Major Joachim Müncheberg was just short of 22 when he brought the *Geschwader* to North Africa, but his experience in the Battle of Britain, the Malta campaign in 1941 – where the 12 Bf-109s of his 7.Staffel from JG 26 transformed the air war – and on the Eastern Front later that year and through 1942, belied his age. Charismatic and talented, he inspired loyalty among all who served with him.

Following Müncheberg's death in combat in March 1943, his place was taken by Major Johannes "Macky" Steinhoff. Seven years

Müncheberg's senior, Steinhoff had an equally impressive combat pedigree and experience, arriving in North Africa as a 150-victory *Experte*. The additional experience age gave him meant he was the man who could hold the *Geschwader* together through the defeat in North Africa, the Sicilian campaign, and the initial battles in Italy following the Salerno invasion.

The quality of German aerial leadership in JG 77 extended into the *Geschwader*'s component *Gruppen*. *Gruppenkommandeur* Hauptmann Heinz "Pritzl" Bär, 29, had started as a mechanic in the newly created Luftwaffe in 1935, then became an enlisted pilot in JG 51 after completing the service's thorough prewar flight training; he entered combat the first week of the war on the Western Front, then worked his way into a commission and further promotion from demonstrated ability during the Battle of Britain. He had come from JG 51, where he commanded IV.Gruppe to lead I./JG 77 at Malta in May 1942. When he arrived with his *Gruppe* in North Africa in late October, his personal score stood at 99, and he had been awarded the Ritterkreuz des Eisernen Kreuzes mit Eichenlaub und Schwertern (Knight's Cross of the Iron Cross with Oak Leaves and Swords), the highest award for combat that existed in the Wehrmacht. He would increase his score by 80 by the end of the North African campaign in May 1943. His keen sense of humor and attitude of disrespect to higher authority made him popular with his men.

II./JG 77's *Kommandeur* was Hauptmann Anton Mader, a 29-year-old Austrian who had joined the Austrian Air Force in 1933; he was transferred as an *Oberleutnant* to the Luftwaffe following the 1938 Anschluss. Flying with I./JG 76, he opened his score in the Polish campaign. During the Battle of Britain, he became *Staffelkapitän* of I./JG 2 in September 1940. Following the death of II./JG 77 *Kommandeur* Hauptmann Helmut Henz in May 1941, Mader took command of the unit and took it to the Eastern Front in June, where he scored 73 victories before bringing the unit to North Africa in December 1942. He left in March 1943, succeeded by Major Siegfried Freytag, another JG 77 *Experte* who was a veteran of the Balkan campaign and the Eastern Front before coming to the Mediterranean in the spring of 1942, where he became known among his Luftwaffe comrades as the "Star of Malta" for his victories over Spitfires there. He had 85 victories at the time he took command.

III./JG 77's *Kommandeur* was Major Kurt Ubben, who turned 33 the month he brought the *Gruppe* to North Africa, making him the oldest and longest-serving of the *Geschwader*'s *Gruppekommandeuren*. Ubben had joined the Reichsmarine (the Weimar Republic's navy) at 20 in 1931, and transferred to the Luftwaffe in 1935, where he trained as a naval aviator. Assigned to JG 136 – the *Trägerjagdgruppe* (Carrier Fighter Group) intended to serve on the carrier *Graf Zeppelin* – out of flight training in 1938, he flew combat missions in the Polish campaign and the Norwegian campaign, remaining in the unit when it became III./JG 77 in 1940; he took part in the Battle of Britain, the Balkans campaign and the Eastern Front, where he took command of the *Gruppe* in September 1941 following award of the Ritterkreuz des Eisernen Kreuzes. By the time he arrived in North Africa, Ubben had received the Eichenlaub to his Ritterkreuz the previous July for 80 victories.

JG 77 included in its ranks two outstanding pilots – Leutnant Heinz-Edgar Berres, *Staffelkapitän* of 3.Staffel, I./JG 77, and Leutnant Ernst Wilhelm Reinert of 4.Staffel, II./JG 77. Berres began his combat career with Lehrgeschwader 2 in Operation *Barbarossa* in the summer of 1941. His unit became 3.I/JG 77 when LG 2 became I./JG 77 on January 6, 1942. He scored his first victory against the USAAF after I./JG 77 was transferred to Romania in late March; on June 12, 1942, when 13 B-24D Liberators of the "Halverson project" flew the USAAF's first attack on Ploesti, Berres claimed one B-24D shot down. Prior to arrival in North Africa, he had flown in the Malta campaign from July to October, shooting down 11 Spitfires.

Operation *Torch*, following quickly after the opening of the Second Battle of El Alamein, put the Afrika Korps and the Italian armies in a vice-like situation, squeezed from east and west. Forced to respond to the Allied landings in the French North African colonies, the Wehrmacht enacted Case Anton, the occupation of the demilitarized zone known as Vichy France, to forestall an expected Anglo-American landing on the Côte d'Azur. Hitler ordered the movement of substantial reinforcements to Tunisia to prevent an Axis collapse in the region. The Allied decision not to land at Tunis, due to the potential exposure of the invaders to German air attack from Sardinia and Sicily, guaranteed German success in the race for Tunis, which allowed the Axis to retain a foothold in Africa. The subsequent Battle of Tunisia prolonged the Axis presence for a further six months.

The Allied landings in Morocco and Algeria saw *Kommodore* von Maltzahn lead the *Geschwader* Stab. II. and III./JG 53 to Tunis on November 9, the day after the landings. I./JG 53 followed two weeks later. At the time the *Geschwader* first arrived, the situation was alarming but not critical. Their first assignment was to cover the all-important sea and air supply routes from Italy to Tunisia.

The American First Army in Algeria posed the greater threat. Three days after its arrival, JG 53 claimed its first success of the new campaign, a Spitfire shot down over the port of Bône on November 12. On November 14, the tables were turned when 7.Staffel again engaged Spitfires over Bône and Leutnant Dietrich Hirsch was lost. On November 21, III.Gruppe moved south from Tunis to Djedeida, where the *Gruppe* was joined by I./JG 53 on November 25.

Ost Front *Experte* Hauptmann Franz Götz, hitherto *Staffelkapitän* of 9.Staffel, had taken over III./JG 53 from the departing Major Erich Gerlitz shortly after its arrival in Tunisia. The afternoon of the day I./JG 53 flew in to join III.Gruppe at Djedeida, 17 American M3 Grant tanks suddenly appeared out of the hills to the west. Opening fire on the airfield at a range of 875 yards, they first circled the base, probing for nonexistent antitank defenses. Finding none, they promptly charged across the field, shooting at everything. Fortunately, their initial fire had been inaccurate, and those Bf-109s not already airborne were able to escape in a mad, free-for-all scramble. Unfortunately, the Stukas of II./StG 3 were unable to get away, and the *Gruppe* lost an estimated 15–24 dive bombers, either shot full of holes or mangled beneath the tracks of the Grants. I./JG 53 headed to Bizerte, on the coast, while III./JG 53 returned to Tunis.

On November 28, I. and II.Gruppen responded to an American attack on Bizerte and shot down five P-38 Lightning escorts and a Spitfire. On November 30, III./JG 53 was ordered to return to Sicily to provide cover for the Tunisia-bound convoys from ports in Sicily and also defending airfields and ports in southern Italy as XII Bomber Command began flying bombing raids. In Tunisia, I. and II./JG 53, accompanied by Oberleutnant Julius Meimberg's high-altitude *Staffel*, 11./JG 2, moved forward to Mateur. The headlong Allied advance was now losing momentum as the winter rains arrived, and by the year's end was bogged down entirely in the snowy mountains west of Bizerte and Tunis.

I. and II./JG 53 began a punishing assignment of flying escort missions for Ju-88 bombers and Ju-87 Stukas attacking Allied positions, as well as flying ground-attack sorties to support the Afrika Korps and *Freie Jagd* (free hunt) patrols to defend their airfields. The *Gruppen* had their most successful day of the campaign to date on December 4, when they were scrambled to intercept a formation of Bristol Bisley Vs, a variant of the Blenheim V, that they mistakenly identified as Douglas Bostons as the bombers flew close by Mateur. They submitted claims for and were credited with shooting down all 12 of the unescorted British bombers, including three by Oberleutnant Meimberg, and two to 4.Staffel *Staffelkapitän* Leutnant Fritz Dinger, and a bomber and a Spitfire to Oberfeldwebel Stefan Litjens. The final score was 18 destroyed, a total JG 53 would never equal in the remaining months of the North African campaign. On December 18, *Geschwader Kommodore* von Maltzahn shot down the first B-17, one of 40 attacking Bizerte harbor. The scores of the three leading I.Gruppe *Experten* – Wilhelm Crinius, Friedrich-Karl Müller, and Wolfgang Tonne – stood at 107, 103, and 102 respectively at the end of the year.

The retreat out of Egypt into Cyrenaica and the continuing withdrawal westward as the Afrika Korps fell back to the Mareth Line in Tunisia brought losses to JG 77 that had nothing to do with air combat, when each hasty evacuation westward forced it to abandon aircraft that might have been repaired and returned to service had there been time for the ground crews to work on them. The overwhelming number of the Bf-109G-2s that had been the main *Geschwader* equipment when they first arrived in North Africa had been lost by the end of the year through air combat and abandonment. Fortunately, sufficient replacements of the more heavily armed Bf-109G-6 sub-type arrived in the theater to return the units to strength by the time they settled into Tunisian airfields in early 1943.

In January 1943, I./JG 77 moved into southern Tunisia to confront the Americans. Berres, by then *Gruppe* adjutant, claimed an American-flown Spitfire on January 8 and a B-25 Mitchell on January 14, then two P-38s on February 4 and two more P-38s and a B-25 four days later, ending the month with a claim for two P-40s on February 26. The Battle of the Mareth Line began in March, and on March 7 Berres engaged Spitfires over the front line and claimed one shot down for his 33rd victory.

Taking command of 1.Staffel on March 24, the day after the loss of Joachim Müncheberg, Berres led 13 Bf-109s of I./JG 77 to intercept 18 B-25 Mitchells of the 321st Bomb Group, escorted by P-40s of the 57th Fighter Group; he claimed a P-40, a B-25, and a second P-40 in 11 minutes for his 37th–39th victories. After claiming his 40th victory over a P-40 on April 2, Berres was shot down near Oudref but escaped back to German lines. He claimed his 44th victory over Cap Bon on May 5 before I./JG 77 escaped to Sicily.

Leutnant Ernst-Wilhelm Reinert joined II./JG 77 as a *Feldwebel* after completing flight training, and was assigned to 4.Staffel on June 14, 1941, just before Operation *Barbarossa*. Claiming his first victory on August 8, 1941, he received the Ritterkreuz after his 53rd victory in the spring of 1942, and had 103 victories by October 3. He was personally decorated with the Eichenlaub by Adolf Hitler on November 4, the second *Feldwebel* in the Luftwaffe so honored. II./JG 77 arrived in Libya on November 10, 1942. During the Tunisian campaign, Reinert gained 53 additional victories. He was promoted to *Leutnant* on April 1, 1943, in recognition of his prowess; that day he became "an ace in a day," scoring three Spitfires from the 31st Fighter Group in the morning and two from the 52nd Fighter Group in an afternoon mission. His 153rd victory, a Spitfire shot down at 1055 hours on May 6, 1943, was the final Luftwaffe aerial victory in Tunisia. On May 8, when JG 77 evacuated its headquarters from Korobus airfield, Reinert flew a Bf-109 sitting on the lap of Leutnant Zeno Bäumel in the tiny cockpit, with 4.Staffel's chief mechanic Oberfeldwebel Walter in the rear fuselage. En route to Sicily with this load, he spotted and shot down a Royal Navy Fleet Air Arm Martlet fighter, which crashed into the sea.

In November 1942, II./JG 51 was transferred from the Eastern Front to North Africa, fighting over Tunisia before being transferred to Sardinia on April 19, 1943 due to losses. The *Gruppe* handed over its remaining Bf-109s to JG 77, having lost 26 pilots killed, almost a 100 percent loss rate since their arrival five months earlier.

II./JG 2, commanded by Oberleutnant Alfred Dickfeld, took their Fw-190A fighters, which had dominated the RAF's Fighter Command since their introduction to combat on the Channel Front a year earlier, to North Africa as part of the Luftwaffe reinforcements sent to Tunisia, arriving from Santo Pietro, Sicily, on November 18, 1942. Their 36 Fw-190s were superior to all Allied fighters then operational in North Africa. *Gruppenkommandeur* Dickfeld, 32, was a Battle of Britain and Eastern Front veteran and Ritterkreuz des Eisernen Kreuzes mit Eichenlaub winner, who had scored his 100th victory on the Eastern Front the previous May, including 11 in one day. Other leading *Experten* in the *Gruppe* included Kurt Bühligen and Erich Rudorffer. The 25-year-old *Leutnant* Bühligen was 4.Staffel *Staffelkapitän* and a Channel Front veteran since the Battle of Britain, who had been awarded the Ritterkreuz des Eisernen Kreuzes a year before arriving in North Africa. Oberleutnant Erich Rudorffer, also 25 and a two-year veteran of the Channel Front since entering combat in the Battle of Britain, had been *Staffelkapitän* of 6.Staffel for a year by the time JG 2 arrived in North Africa, and was also a *Ritterkreuz Flieger*, awarded the Ritterkreuz des Eisernen Kreuzes in May 1941; at the time JG 2 moved to North Africa, he was still in hospital recovering from wounds received in a battle on the Channel Front and would only rejoin the unit in December on his recovery. These three would cut a wide swath through their Allied opponents over the next six months, scoring over half the victories the unit would be credited with.

Upon arrival, II./JG 2 was placed under the control of Oberleutnant Günther Freiherr von Maltzahn, *Kommodore* of JG 53, and was based at Bizerte. The *Gruppe* flew its first North African mission on November 19, covering the arrival of German seaborne reinforcements at Tunis; the appearance of Fw-190s over Tunis was as nasty a surprise for RAF pilots in Spitfire Vs as had been their appearance over the Channel Front the previous November.

Kurt Bühligen scored the first JG 2 victory in North Africa during the *Gruppe*'s first major action in combat with the Spitfires of the Western Desert Air Force's 81 Squadron on November 21, 1942, leading to his promotion to *Oberleutnant* on December 5. The *Gruppe* was credited with its first P-38 Lightning on December 1, shooting down four more two days later on December 3, the work of 30-year-old Feldwebel Kurt Golsch, one of the *Gruppe*'s *Alter Hasen* (old hares) NCOs, who would become the *Gruppe*'s fourth-ranked *Experte* in the campaign. The next day, the Fw-190s intercepted a formation of obsolescent Bristol Bisleys over Tunis along with the Bf-109Gs of newly arrived II./JG 53, claiming all 12 bombers from 18 and 614 Squadrons shot down in a five-minute battle. That same day, they claimed four P-38s, including

Erich Rudorffer's first claim for a Lightning, two days after he arrived from France.

Initially, the German pilots found their USAAF opponents were overconfident and inexperienced, with P-38 pilots willing to try to dogfight the more maneuverable German fighters. Bühligen, who scored two P-38s on December 26 that were escorting B-17s bombing Bizerte, later claimed the P-38 was easy to fight since a pilot could recognize its unmistakable silhouette at a distance and be prepared early for the fight. He demonstrated his prowess against the Lightnings on January 7, when he was credited with three more, and another on January 14. On February 2, Bühligen became an "ace in a day," claiming three P-40s, a Spitfire, and a P-39 Airacobra in combat near II./JG 2's new base at Kairouan. Ten P-40s of the 33rd Fighter Group were lost, eight from the 59th Squadron and two from the 60th Squadron, with five pilots killed in action and one captured. The JG 2 pilots claimed a total of 13 Allied fighters, of which 11 were reported lost.

On February 9, 1943, six Fw-190s led by Rudorffer – who had two days earlier become acting *Gruppenkommandeur* after Dickfeld was injured in an accident and evacuated – claimed 16 aircraft in a fight in which Rudorffer made his first large multi-victory score, claiming eight Spitfires in the 32-minute battle, the first time he became an "ace in a day." After the war, Rudorffer recalled the tactics he used in the battle:

> I had come to see that Marseille's strategy of remaining in the vertical as much as possible when fighting the British was a good strategy with the P-38s, whose pilots were foolish enough to think they could engage in close combat in that heavy fighter. This way, you could come in above or below at speed, combining timing with marksmanship. The secret was to do the job in one pass. It could be from the side or behind, and I usually tried to open fire at 50 meters. I practiced swooping in and out of defensive formations with my comrades. In Africa, Allied fighter pilots often used the "Lufbery," and in this circle it was often possible to slip in and out and shoot many of them down.
>
> On February 9, we were south of Tunis about 180 kilometers. We got word at Kairouan that *dicke autos und indianer* (bombers and fighters) were on the way. One Staffel was already sitting in their aircraft and I ordered them off. I was always last to take off and waited

to get the latest information on the enemy's course and speed. I took off with my *schwarm* and headed toward the enemy. They came from the west, about 24 B-17s, 18 P-40s, 20 P-38s and a similar number of Spitfires. We were at about 7,000 meters and the bombers were below us with the P-40s above.

When we started for the bombers, the P-40s came down on us and that's when the dogfight began. After a time, the P-40s went into a "Lufbery" circle and I began to slip from low to high and shoot them down. I managed to shoot down six in about seven minutes. As I recall my combat report, I got the first at 1359 hours and the last at 1406 hours. By that time the fight had broken up and everyone had scattered. Then I saw some P-38s strafing below me, and though I only had my *schwarm* with me at the time, I went down on them and surprised them. I got one coming from above and then went up again and came down on another and shot him down. That gave me eight for the day – I remember it because it was one of the best days I ever had.

American records for this are lacking, but the war diary of the Armée de l'Air, Groupe de Chasse II/5 recorded that nine P-40s escorting P-39 Airacobras of the US 81st Fighter Group engaged Fw-190s near Djebel Bou Dabouss. The P-38s of the 1st Fighter Group's 94th Squadron may have also been involved in the engagement. Six days later, on February 15, II./JG 2 engaged Spitfires of the 31st Fighter Group and Lightnings of the 82nd Fighter Group. Rudorffer claimed four P-38s and three Spitfires in the fight. He would become known for such multi-victory fights during the remainder of his wartime career, leading the Luftwaffe in such claims.

II./JG 2 ended its North African assignment on March 12, with only ten Fw-190s left serviceable. That day, Bühligen made his final North African claims for two P-38s and a B-17 shot down. The *Gruppe* was evacuated to Sicily on March 22, for transfer back to the Channel Front. Erich Rudorffer was promoted to official *Gruppenkommandeur* of II./JG 2 on April 1. During the four months it was in North Africa, II./JG 2 claimed 150 enemy aircraft shot down for eight pilots killed, a truly astounding performance. Allied loss records support nearly all of these claims. Kurt Bühligen led the victory list with 40, followed by Dickfeld with 36, and Rudorffer with 34, including ten bombers; Feldwebel Golsch scored 25.

OPPONENTS

Major Heinz Bär's I./JG 77 had arrived in North Africa in December. It had primarily faced RAF and RAAF units, and did not enter combat with USAAF units until January 25, 1943, when Bär scored his 149th and 150th victories, both 57th Group P-40Fs, with the first from 66th Squadron and the second from the 65th in a fight that included RAF Kittyhawks from 112 Squadron and 450 Squadron RAAF. The P-40 squadrons admitted the loss of ten, as claimed by the *Jagdfliegern*, including three from the 65th and two from the 66th. After achieving his 149th aerial victory, General Hans-Jürgen von Arnim submitted Bär for the Ritterkreuz mit Brillanten (Knight's Cross of the Iron Cross with Oak Leaves, Swords and Diamonds), but von Arnim's submission was ignored by Göring, who disliked Bär for his insubordinate character and Saxon accent, which the Reichsmarschall detested.

On January 27, Bär shot down two P-40s from the 33rd Group, following this on February 4 with his first B-17 victory – a B-17F of the 97th Bomb Group that was part of a mission flown by the 97th and 301st Bomb Groups, escorted by P-38s from the 1st Fighter Group. On February 15, he shot two 31st Group Spitfires flown by Lieutenants Joe Reed and H.E. Huntingdon, whom the group recorded as lost that day.

In early March, I./JG 77 transferred to Fatnassah airfield in southeastern Tunisia. By early April, Bär had increased his tally to 179; by the end of April, he was suffering severe mental and physical exhaustion, leading to a loss of fighting spirit as the *Gruppe* fought a losing battle against ever-increasing Allied air superiority. After several arguments with Göring and Colonel Johannes Steinhoff, JG 77's new commander, Bär was transferred to France "for cowardice before the enemy" following JG 77's evacuation from Tunisia and demoted to *Hauptmann*. There, he took command of Jagdgruppe Süd, an operational training unit.

Jagdgeschwader 53, better known, the "Pik As" (Ace of Spades) Geschwader, was one of the oldest German fighter units of World War II, its origins going back to 1937. At the outset of the war, the *Geschwader* contained a high proportion of ex-Condor Legion pilots, including Werner Mölders, among its experienced personnel. The Battle of France thus saw the *Geschwader* score heavily during May and June 1940, with some 275 claims against Armée de l'Air and Royal Air Force forces. While JG 53 was making a reputation for itself during the Battle of Britain, Reichsmarschall Hermann Göring learned that

Geschwaderkommodore Major Hans-Jürgen von Cramon-Taubadel's wife was Jewish. As punishment, he ordered the Stab./JG 53 to remove the "Pik As" emblem and replace it with a red stripe around the engine cowling. While all Stab./JG 53's Bf-109s were stripped of their "Pik As" insignia, soon after the whole of JG 53 stripped the swastikas off their fighters' vertical fins in protest.

III./JG 53 was transferred to North Africa in December 1941, while the other two *Gruppen* moved to Comiso airfield in Sicily for operations against Malta. The *Geschwader* was broken up late that summer, with II./JG 53 operating from the island of Pantelleria for operations over Malta and to participate in attacks on British supply convoys. I./JG 53 deployed to the Eastern Front in Luftflotte 4's 8th Air Corps to support Operation *Blau*. By September 1942, I./JG 53 claimed 918 victories, losing 34 Bf-109s, with 18 pilots killed in action and nine wounded. On November 1, 1942, Hauptmann "Tutti" Müller became I./JG 53 *Gruppenkommandeur* and led the unit back to the Mediterranean, where the *Geschwader*, based on Sicily for an abortive and short-lived blitz against Malta, was defeated by the defenders. During its 1942 operations over North Africa, Sicily, and Malta, JG 53 claimed a total of 388 aircraft shot down, with Hauptmann Gerhard Michalski the leading scorer with 25 claimed over Malta.

With the British offensive at El Alamein and the Allied invasion of French North Africa in November, the *Geschwader* again found its components separated. By early November, after the British breakthrough at El Alamein, III./JG 53, which had been in combat in North Africa since the previous December and was seriously battle-weary, was withdrawn to Sicily when I./JG 77 arrived in Egypt on October 27.

Following the Morocco landings, JG 77 *Kommodore* Oberst Günther Freiherr von Maltzahn led I. and II./JG 53 to Tunisia, where they opposed the Allies until the end of April 1943.

While the Luftwaffe *Jagdflieger* was man for man more experienced than its American opponents at the outset of the North African campaign, the American pilots turned out to be fast learners, changing their incorrect tactics and adopting combat-tested tactics from their RAF allies, and quickly disabusing themselves of the overconfidence with which many had entered combat in the weeks after *Torch*. Additionally, the Allies had more airplanes available and were able to make good losses more quickly than the Germans could. By the final battles in the weeks after mid-March 1943, the *Geschwadern* were operating at half-strength and less, with replacements virtually impossible to obtain.

Between the landings in North Africa in November 1942, and the withdrawal of the final units from Tunisia in early May 1943 before the Axis surrender, the Luftwaffe lost 2,422 aircraft of all types, a figure that represents 40.5 percent of the force's total strength on November 1, 1942. The long-term impact of the Tunisian campaign on the Luftwaffe far outweighed the value to the Axis of denying the Mediterranean to the Allies for an additional six months. Pilot losses, including those killed and those taken prisoner, amounted to approximately 15 percent of total aircrew strength. These losses would never be made good, and the shortage of trained and experienced aircrew they represented would exacerbate the effect of the losses the Luftwaffe would experience over northern Europe seven months later fighting the rejuvenated Eighth Air Force. The North African campaign was the first major step toward total defeat of the Wehrmacht.

Too often in histories of World War II, the participation of Italian forces is either overlooked, undervalued, or actively ridiculed; in part, this is the result of Allied propaganda at the time, which when combined with some retrograde attitudes that persisted in the United States until the 1950s regarding those of Italian ancestry, has led to a view of the Italian armed forces and their contributions to the battle in North Africa that does not fit with the actual facts of the matter. These views were also held by many of their German allies at the time, since the Italian armed forces were of little strategic importance, combined with the fact that the Afrika Korps was originally sent to North Africa in 1941 to save the Italians from defeat at the hands of the British. The Regia Aeronautica in particular has come in for this less-than-accurate perception.

In fact, the pilots of the Regia Aeronautica were worthy opponents, and their aircraft – while not produced in sufficient numbers due to the lack of a modern industrial base in Italy at the time – were first class in design and performance when compared with their Allied opponents. As with Italian cars, they needed more care than a similar product from either Britain, Germany, or the United States, but when cared for they achieved first-class individual results. One can look at the designs of Mario Castoldi, famed as was R.J. Mitchell for his interwar Schneider

Cup Trophy racers, who created the C.200 Saetta ("Lightning"), the C.202 Folgore ("Thunderbolt"), and the C-205 Veltro ("Greyhound") and notice something unlike any other products of any other designer: the left wing is slightly longer than the right. This was Castoldi's answer to the aerodynamic phenomenon of torque created by the spinning propeller that powered the airplane. Unlike other similar aircraft, this meant that the pilot did not have to constantly trim the aircraft to correct for torque as power was increased or decreased; it also allowed turns to either left or right without having to be concerned about controllability, which was the case with all British, German, and American fighters other than the P-38, which canceled torque through the fact that the propellers of each of its two engines turned in the opposite direction to the other. The result with the Castoldi fighters was what was reported as "finger light control" by Allied pilots who tested captured examples of all three. Prior to the C.202, Castoldi's Saetta – like all other Italian fighters – suffered in consequence of the Italian aviation industry's failure to create high-powered piston engines in the class of the Merlin, the DB 601 and 605, and the Allison liquid-cooled engines or the Pratt and Whitney R-2800 radial. When the airframe of the C.200 was mated with the German Daimler-Benz DB 601 engine to create the C.202, the result was a fighter with equal performance to the Spitfire; the C.205 powered by the DB 605 created a fighter that could take on the P-51 Mustang successfully. The only complaint Italian fighter pilots had was the comparatively light armament of their fighters, which was solved in the C.205 through the provision of 20mm cannon mounted in the wings like the Spitfire.

Castoldi's fighters were not the only good performers in the Regia Aeronautica's fighter force. Fiat's G.55 Centauro ("Centaur"), also powered by the DB 605, could outperform both the Spitfire IX and the P-51D in fighter-vs-fighter combat. The Reggiane Re. 2001 Falco II ("Falcon"), powered by the DB 601, had similar performance to the Spitfire V, and the DB 605-powered Re. 2005 Saggitario ("Archer") was in the same class as the Spitfire IX and P-51B. The failure of the Germans to provide sufficient engines, and the Italian aviation industry to produce license-built copies of Daimler-Benz engines that met original performance specifications, limited the introduction of the fighters using these powerplants. Italian fighter pilots who transitioned to the Bf-109G considered the airplane a step down from what they had been flying, and Allied pilots were glad they only met these Italian opponents in small numbers.

As regards pilot skill, Italian pilots were graduates of flight training that equaled that of the Luftwaffe, the RAF, and the USAAF. The percentage of Italian fighter pilots who became aces was similar to the overall fighter-pilot population percentage of their German allies and the Allied opponents they faced. These men fought well despite being completely outnumbered in the air and lacking logistical support on the ground. Despite being held in high regard by the Italian public for victorious campaigns in Ethiopia and Spain, and setting many flight records in the interwar years, the Regia Aeronautica was unready when committed to World War II. The problem for the fighter force was that the tactical views of the fighter pilots – as was the case with JAAF and IJNAF pilots in the Pacific – had not changed since World War I, favoring close-in high-G combat maneuvering that was increasingly out of place with modern fighters, which led to a preference for obsolete types like the CR.32 and CR.42 Falco biplane fighters that were completely outclassed by their opponents; indeed the CR.42 was ordered into production two years after the Hurricane, Spitfire, and Bf-109 entered mass production, the last biplane fighter to enter production anywhere. The first two "modern" monoplane fighters, the C.200 Saetta and Fiat G.50 Freccia ("Arrow"), suffered from being underpowered from the lack of suitable high-power engines and a too-light armament; in addition, they featured open cockpits because the pilots claimed enclosed canopies restricted their vision in combat. It was not only tactics and equipment that were outdated, but serious shortcomings in the operational capability of the fighter pilots were exposed, the result of prewar training's failure to consider training in modern aerial gunnery and instrument flying. There was a lack of technical development regarding ground-to-air and air-to-air radio communication, with the fighters not even carrying radios at the outset.

The Regia Aeronautica's shortcomings were first revealed in the Spanish Civil War when the CR.32 came up against the Soviet-supplied I-15 Chato biplane and the I-16 Mosca monoplane fighters used by its Spanish Republican opponents. The CR.32 held its own because of the superior training of the pilots, but this provided a false sense of superiority in the obsolescent design of the fighter. The SM.79

trimotor bomber was also seen as better than it was because none were shot down by opposing fighters during the conflict. These successes delayed the introduction of more modern types, while Italian designers and builders were proud of their "artisan" efforts, which delayed modernization of production capability. The result was that on the day Italy entered World War II, the main fighter was the obsolete CR.42, while the C.200 and G.50 were never produced in large numbers and were disliked by their pilots, who refused to adopt tactics better suited to these aircraft. The superb C.202 was produced in such small numbers after it finally entered production in 1941 that it had almost no impact on the fighting in North Africa, while front-line units like the 8° Gruppo were still flying the outmatched and thoroughly obsolete C.200 at the time of the Italian surrender in 1943.

Mussolini took Italy into the war in June 1940 despite entreaties from his military commanders who knew the army, navy, and air force were unready for such participation in the kind of war World War II had already become, since Il Duce believed German victory was imminent and he wanted to be sure that Italy got a share of the spoils. Events proved the dictator wrong and his military advisors right.

The Regia Aeronautica saw the majority of its wartime service in North Africa, beginning with the Italian offensive against Egypt launched from the Italian colony of Cyrenaica (Libya) in September 1940. The British counteroffensive that began in December pushed the Italians back and took nearly all of Cyrenaica by January 1941, an action that saw the destruction of much of the African-based Italian air force units. The Italian situation was so fraught that the German X Fliegerkorps left Sicily at the end of January to enter combat in North Africa, followed in February by the commitment of the Afrika Korps. Over the spring and summer of 1941, Italian fighter units provided escort for Luftwaffe Stuka dive bombers, and cooperation between German and Italian units grew stronger at the unit level.

C.200 Saettas finally appeared in North Africa in July when the 153° Gruppo arrived with their Saettas at Castel Benito, Libya, joined shortly after by the G.50-equipped 20° Gruppo. The Germans reached the point where their supply lines could no longer support an offensive in September, forcing them to halt their advance against the British. In September, the British counteroffensive took them back into Libya. David Stirling's Long Range Desert Group was now operational and struck at Axis-held airfields, destroying most of the 20° Gruppo's G.50s at Sidi Rezegh.

The British had regained territory as far west as El Agheila by January 1942, when Rommel opened an offensive at the end of the month that saw the Axis armies reoccupy Benghazi at the end of January. By this time the C.202-equipped 150° Gruppo was active in Libya.

The Afrika Korps and the Italian Army attacked the Gazala–Bir Hachim line beginning on the morning of May 26, when 59 C.202s of the 150° and 3° Gruppi made a surprise dawn attack on the Allied airfield at Gambut where the 24 Kittyhawks of 250 Squadron RAF were found parked wing-to-wing on the landing ground. The Italians claimed to have "wiped out" the British fighters by strafing, but 250 Squadron's records recorded only two Kittyhawks destroyed, though several had varying degrees of damage. When the Axis armies attacked that afternoon, Italian fighters provided the majority of the close air support, strafing British units ahead of the attackers. That night 800 German and Italian aircraft attacked the port of Tobruk, which had withstood a siege of 241 days during the German offensive of 1941; under this punishment, Tobruk surrendered the next day. Fortunately for the Commonwealth forces, the Luftwaffe and Regia Aeronautica units were not able to advance as quickly as the ground forces during the retreat that finally ended at El Alamein, allowing the troops to retreat without enduring air attacks. While the Eighth Army and the Desert Air Force had developed close communication which provided good air support, neither the Luftwaffe nor Regia Aeronautica units ever developed such coordination with their ground forces. This would prove critical when the Axis air forces were not able to provide such support when the Second Battle of El Alamein commenced at the end of October. Of the 700 Axis aircraft present in Egypt at that time, only 150 were fighters, while only 180 Stuka dive bombers and German and Italian fighter-bombers were available. They faced over 1,000 British aircraft, supported by the newly arrived USAAF 57th Fighter Group.

The Allied landings in Morocco were a complete surprise to the Italians, even more so than the Germans. The first Regia Aeronautica mission against the Anglo-American forces – a bombing attack against the port of Bône on November 12 flown by ten SM.84 Pipistrello ("Bat") bombers of the 32° Gruppo from Sardinia – failed to rendezvous with their 150° Gruppo C.202 escorts from Sicily due to the poor weather delaying the bombers' arrival at the rendezvous point; and a lack of radio that prevented the two groups finding each other resulted in the bombers proceeding without escort. Three were shot down over the port by defending American fighters, and three more damaged bombers were destroyed attempting to land, while the remaining four were also damaged in combat with several wounded aircrewmen.

Initially on entry into the war, the Regia Aeronautica did not award individual victory credits to pilots. Instead, all pilots involved in a combat were recognized for any enemy aircraft shot down. This changed over time, but it was not until March 1942 that the State Maggiore finally decided that the publicity of awarding individual victory credits to pilots was good for civilian morale when reported in the press and radio. As a result, the Regia Aeronautica went so far as to award cash prizes to pilots for victory claims, and the requirement of two witnesses along with the claiming pilot to award a victory was changed to taking the pilot's word for the claimed victory. Italian pilots were no more likely to make insincere claims for victories than were their Luftwaffe allies or RAF and USAAF opponents, but all pilots overclaimed due to the general inability of a flier engaged in air combat to witness the final result of a fighter he had taken a shot at. The RAF, USAAF, and Luftwaffe maintained the requirement of at least one witness to confirm a claim.

Sergente Teresio Martinoli is considered by most Italian air force researchers to be the Regia Aeronautica's top ace of the war. Exhibiting an enthusiasm for flying at an early age, he obtained a glider pilot's license in 1937 and was drafted into the Regia Aeronautica in 1939, where he received flight training. Beginning his wartime career with 384ª Squadriglia of the 157° Gruppo, then transferred in August 1940 to the 78ª Squadriglia of the 13° Gruppo in 2° Stormo in Libya, he flew combat during the Italian advance into Egypt, scoring a Gladiator of 112 Squadron RAF on October 13, 1940. Transferred to 4° Stormo in January 1941, he then was sent to 9° Gruppo, which was the first unit to fly the C.202 Folgore. In action over Malta in the spring of 1941, he claimed three Hurricanes and a Blenheim. After withdrawal from Sicily to Italy, the unit returned to the Malta campaign in early 1942, where the C.202s first faced the Spitfire V. During combats in May he was credited with three Spitfires shot down and a Spitfire probable. At the end of the month the unit transferred to Libya. Between May 29 and October 9,

Martinoli was credited with six Kittyhawks and two Spitfires. He shot down a further Kittyhawk on October 23, just before the Second Battle of El Alamein, after which he was transferred back to Italy.

During the invasion of Sicily in July–August 1943, Martinoli shot down a P-38 and a B-17 while flying the new C.205 Veltro. Following the Italian surrender, he joined the Aeronautica Co-Belligerante (Co-Belligerent Air Force, the pro-Allied Italian air force). His final victory of the war was a Ju-52 shot down over Podgorica, Yugoslavia. Teresio Martinoli was killed in a flying accident on August 25, 1944, during conversion training to the P-39 Airacobra that had just been provided to the pro-Allied air force. Giulio Reiner, his fellow ace and commander when he was in the 73ª Squadriglia, remembered Martinoli thus: "Behind his discreet and closed character was a fighter pilot who possessed exceptional eyesight, making him an unfailing marksman. In fact, it seemed as if Martinoli had a sixth sense when it came to detecting the enemy's presence, for he would usually spot his position in the sky well before any of us could."

Franco Lucchini enrolled in the Regia Aeronautica's pilot officers' course for 1935 at age 21 and was awarded his pilot's "wings" a year later. He volunteered for duty in Spain in 1937, serving with the famous Asso di Bastoni (Ace of Clubs) XXIII Gruppo under the name Lunigiano. He scored one personal victory while serving with the Aviazione Legionaria, and shared in two more. Shot down twice, he evaded capture the first time but was captured on July 22, 1938, the second time, and spent six months as a Republican prisoner in Valencia.

Returning to Italy in 1939, Lucchini was assigned to 4° Stormo outside Tobruk. Shortly after the outbreak of war on June 14, 1940, he scored his first victory of World War II when he shot down an RAF Sunderland flying boat on June 21, forcing it down in the port of Bardia, where the crew was captured. By the end of 1940, he had shot down a Gladiator and a Hurricane. In early 1941, 4° Stormo re-equipped with C.200s and transferred to Sicily where it took part in the Malta campaign, during which he added four Hurricanes to his score in June and September, when he was injured in a crash-landing on the small island of Ustica.

That October of 1941 4° Stormo re-equipped with the C.202, and on December 1 Lucchini became commander of 84ª Squadriglia. In April 1942 4° Stormo was back in Sicily escorting bombers to Malta;

he shot down two Spitfires on May 5 and 15, after which 4° Stormo was sent to North Africa at the end of the month, participating in Rommel's summer offensive, during which Lucchini personally claimed four Kittyhawks, two Spitfires, two Hurricanes, and a Boston between June 4 and September 3, sharing in over a dozen other victories. His final North African victory was a Kittyhawk shot down on October 20; shot down and wounded on October 24, he was evacuated to Italy, followed by his war-weary unit that December.

In May 1943, Lucchini and 4° Stormo were back in Sicily. That June he took command of 10° Gruppo, based at Catania. The unit was outnumbered every time it took off to fight. He claimed his final victory on July 5 when he shot down an American-flown Spitfire fighter escort for USAAF B-17s of the 99th Bomb Group over Gerbini. Moments later, Lucchini was caught in the deadly crossfire of the Flying Fortresses and his C.202 fell to the ground, out of control. His body was found two days later, still in the remains of his fighter.

In an amazing coincidence, minutes after Lucchini was shot down, fellow Aviazione Legionaria veteran Sottotenente Leonardo Ferrulli – the 21-victory leading ace of 4° Stormo ranked behind Lucchini as the Regia Aeronautica's third-ranking ace – was also shot down by the same bomber formation.

Lucchini's wingman, Amleto Monterumici, remembered his leader years later: "He was always ready to fight, and courageously sought out the enemy at every opportunity. As with a great number of fighter pilots, he was blessed with extraordinary eyesight, which meant that he could spot his enemy and anticipate an attack. Although he was serious, withdrawn and occasionally timid when on the ground, in the air he transformed himself into a frightening, and aggressive, fighter." The top-scoring Italian ace to survive the war was Franco Bordoni Bisleri, scion of a Milan family business that was famous throughout Italy for its Ferro-China Bisleri liqueur. He saw a career in the Regia Aeronautica as a way to promote his aspirations as a race car driver; he had already shown he was a talented racing driver by the time he graduated from the exclusive San Carlo College in the city. Initially failing to join the Regia Aeronautica because of a minor nasal problem, he obtained a private pilot's license and entered the air force in 1937 as a temporary *Sottotenente Pilota* (second lieutenant pilot). Returning to civilian life in 1939, Bisleri rejoined the air force when Italy entered the war. Assigned to the 18° Gruppo's 95ª Squadriglia, he flew in the Corpo Aereo Italiano in Belgium during the Battle of Britain.

Upon its return to Italy in January 1941, 18° Gruppo was sent to North Africa. With his nickname "Robur" – a name connected with the advertising campaign for his family's liqueur – painted on his CR.42, he shot down a Blenheim on March 10, 1941, east of Benghazi. On April 14 he shot down a Hurricane and another Blenheim on the 17th, shooting down two more Blenheims on June 2, after which he was promoted to *Tenente* (second lieutenant). Returning to Italy, the *Gruppo* re-equipped first with G.50s, then C.200s in the fall of 1941 when they were sent to Greece, where the unit did not encounter any enemy aircraft.

18° Gruppo returned to North Africa in July 1942 as part of 3° Stormo, flying ground attack missions on the El Alamein front. Despite this, Bisleri managed to shoot down six Kittyhawks and a Boston between October 20 and November 7, an amazing accomplishment for a pilot flying the obsolescent C.200. Ironically, he was injured in a car accident on November 19 and evacuated to Italy on a hospital ship.

Following a long convalescence, Bisleri returned to 3° Stormo, now based at Cerveteri airfield outside Rome, in June 1943. Equipped with the new C.205 Veltro, the unit was tasked with the air defense of the Eternal City. Bisleri and his flying mate "Gigi" Gorrini became press favorites in the battles against American bombers in the Regia Aeronautica's final campaign, during which he added six B-17s and a B-26 to his score between July 30 and September 5, demonstrating what a properly armed Italian fighter plane was capable of.

Bisleri's career ended with the Armistice on September 8, which found him tied with his friend Gorrini at 19 victories, making both the top-scoring surviving Italian aces of the Regia Aeronautica. After the war, he returned to his family business and dedicated his life to sports car racing, winning several titles, including the Italian Championship in 1953 after taking first place in the famed Mille Miglia.

Giorgio Solaroli, Marchese di Brioni, who was a squadron mate of Franco Bisleri in the 95ª Squadriglia of the 18° Gruppo in the Corpo Aerea Italiano, was the grandson of General Paolo Solaroli, one of the heroes of the *Risorgimento* (the unification of Italy) who had been a friend of Garibaldi. Raised with the rich military tradition in his family, he had applied to the Accademia Aeronautica as soon as he had finished college. Graduating in July 1940, he was made a *Sottotenente Pilota* and underwent fighter training at Castiglione del Lago before arriving in Belgium to join the Corpo Aerea Italiano. Returning to Italy, the 3° Stormo became part of the Malta campaign. On July 21, 1941, a convoy codenamed "Substance" sailed for Malta. On the afternoon of July 23, the convoy came within range of aircraft from Sicily and Malta. Solari's CR.42-equipped unit was assigned to escort S.79 Aerosiluranti torpedo bombers of the 278ª Squadriglia in an attack that included S.79s from the 10° and 30° Stormi, Ju-87s of the 101° Gruppo Tuff, and 27 C.200 escorts from the 54° Stormo. The attackers gained one hit that damaged the destroyer HMS *Firedrake* before they were attacked by 272 Squadron Beaufighters covering the convoy. One was claimed by Solaroli and Sottotenente Carlo Brigante Colonna. This was the Beaufighter flown by 26-year-old Sergeant William Matthew Deakin and 24-year-old Sergeant Clifford Franklyn Jenkins, which failed to return to Malta from the mission.

Following this, Solaroli was promoted to command the 377ª Squadriglia Autonoma, which was combat-testing the new Re.2000 fighter, which failed to live up to the high expectations that surrounded its development.

Transferred to the 74ª Squadriglia just before the unit converted on to the C.202 Folgore in May 1942, he arrived in North Africa that summer, flying from Abu Haggag, in Libya. Solaroli scored his first victory, a Kittyhawk of 450 Squadron RAAF, on July 25. He had a memorable mission on September 4, when his flight encountered a formation of Bostons with a heavy escort of Kittyhawks. Solaroli later wrote about the battle in his diary:

> My wingman, Sergente Maggiore (Sergeant Major) Mantelli, and I swept down onto the left flank of the escort. I immediately began to fire at a Kittyhawk which filled my gunsight. There was absolutely no reaction from the English pilot, so much so that I got to within a few meters before I saw him explode, turn on his back and crash into the ground. I pulled up vigorously, for I had to avoid other enemy fighters which were snapping at my heels. With the speed I had gained in the dive I soon found myself at a favorable altitude to attack another formation. This time I again managed to machine-gun a Kittyhawk at close quarters. I hit the aircraft and observed that it caught fire.

As he opened fire on the second Kittyhawk, Solaroli was in turn attacked by 260 Squadron's Flight Sergeant N.D. Stebbings, who set the Folgore on fire and wounded Solaroli in his head and leg. He chose to stick with his fighter and managed to regain friendly territory, where he crash-landed. Extricating himself from his fighter, he limped off westwards in search of help. He wrote, "Finally, I saw three men waving their hands at me, telling me not to move as they carefully made their way towards me. They explained that I had landed in a minefield – it must have been pure luck that I had not blown the whole place up!"

After a month in hospital, Solaroli rejoined his unit and on October 20 engaged in another fight with 260 Squadron's Kittyhawks, sharing in the destruction of two with Sergente Mandolesi and Capitano Pinna. One of the 260 Squadron pilots reported missing after the fight was Flight Sergeant Stebbings.

Promoted to *Capitano* in November, Solaroli returned to 18° Gruppo's 95ª Squadriglia as commanding officer on December 3. The unit fought through the Battle of Tunisia in the spring of 1943 in a rearguard action that saw it shift bases five times in just seven weeks. Between January 8 and March 23, Solaroli claimed two Spitfires, a P-38, and a B-26. With only a few fighters left, 3° Stormo was evacuated to Italy to re-equip in anticipation of the invasion.

The 95ª Squadriglia was one of the units responsible for defending Rome. During battles over the city in August and September, Solaroli claimed four P-38s shot down, the last on September 3, five days prior to the Armistice; he was credited with a total of 12 victories.

The Regia Aeronautica had been unready for the conflict in which it found itself in mid-June 1940. The losses suffered over Malta and in North Africa in the next three years ensured the early defeat of Mussolini's Italy.

6

AIR WAR OVER CASABLANCA

James E. Reed fell in love with airplanes as a teenager watching P-26s fly over his family home in Memphis, Tennessee. After the Reeds moved to a Mississippi farm outside Ripley in the Mississippi Delta of Sunflower County in 1935, he graduated from high school in 1939. His family's straitened financial condition left him with only the option of attending Sunflower Junior College in Moorehead, Mississippi, where he cleaned classrooms, worked in the fields, and worked for a local laundry to pay his way; by picking up fellow students' clothing and bringing it to the laundry, his own was done free. During his sophomore year in 1940–41, he enrolled in the Civilian Pilot Training program at the school, where his instructor was a former crop duster, and obtained a private pilot's license by the end of the school year.

Graduating in June 1941, he applied to the Army Air Corps for flight training. He recalled that he managed to keep his bad left leg and ankle – the result of childhood polio – from being spotted by the doctors during his medical exam. Returning home to work for the summer, he received notification from the Army that his application had been accepted and he was to commence flight school at Stamford, Texas, in September. Having just turned 20, he had to get parental permission, which involved long discussions with his reluctant mother before she finally assented.

The train he traveled on to Texas was so old the passenger cars had potbellied stoves in them for heating. At Stamford, he became part of Flight Training Class 42-D. Shortly after Pearl Harbor, he graduated from primary flight training and reported to Randolph Field, Texas, for basic flight training. He was surprised on graduating from basic flight school to receive an assignment to fighters, which he had requested; as he recalled, he was one of the few who got the assignment they requested. At Foster Field on the Texas Gulf coast, he flew the T-6 Texan and finally the P-35, the first close to high-performance airplane he had flown; he found he liked that kind of flying a lot.

Graduating and receiving his Army Aviator's wings on April 29, 1942, new Second Lieutenant Reed received orders to join the 59th Pursuit Squadron of the 33rd Pursuit Group, at the time based on the Glenn L. Martin Company's airfield in Baltimore, Maryland. There, he was introduced to the P-40F Warhawk, the fighter he would eventually fly in combat in North Africa.

The group was first activated in January 1941 as the 33rd Pursuit Group, with cadre taken from the 57th Group, and began training in fighter operations at Mitchell Field, New York. Following the Pearl Harbor attack, the 33rd moved to Philadelphia, where the motley collection of P-36s, P-43s and P-40Bs they were issued were used in an air defense role while the pilots trained for combat. A few weeks after Reed's arrival, the group was redesignated the 33rd Fighter Group as the USAAF changed its organizational nomenclature. The 59th Squadron soon moved to Philadelphia, Pennsylvania, and then to Millville, New Jersey, outside Atlantic City, where the men lived in tents beside the runway while they went through gunnery training.

On August 25, 1942, the three squadrons flew from Philadelphia back to Mitchell Field. In early September, the group was alerted to move to Fort Dix for overseas transfer, with rumors flying around it would go to Egypt like the 57th Fighter Group. Before it could make the move, the orders were canceled and the group returned to Philadelphia, where it became one of the fighter groups assigned to the Twelfth Air Force for the coming invasion of North Africa. A week was spent practising short field takeoffs; eventually it learned this was because it would be taking off from an aircraft carrier that would carry it to North Africa.

In early October, after receiving brand-new P-40Fs, the 33rd flew to the Philadelphia Navy Yard, where hooks were welded onto the fighters, since they would have to be catapulted off the carrier that was transporting them. Reed celebrated his 22nd birthday on October 20, when the group was confined to base prior to departure. On October 21, it flew to East Field at the Norfolk Navy Base, through a bad storm in which several of the fighters landed on a highway. Once the airplanes had all arrived at the Navy field, the pilots taxied their P-40s to the docks on October 22 to be loaded aboard the new escort carrier *Chenango* (ACV-28). *Chenango* had originally been built as a T3 oil tanker, launched on April 1, 1939, as *Esso New Orleans* by the Sun Shipbuilding and Dry Dock Company, in Chester, Pennsylvania. Acquired by the United States Navy on May 31, 1941, she was commissioned a fleet oiler with the name *Chenango* on June 10, 1941, as AO-31. After limited service with the Atlantic Fleet, she was decommissioned at the Brooklyn Navy Yard on March 16, 1942 for conversion to an escort carrier. She had only completed her conversion and been recommissioned as ACV-28 on September 19, 1942, a month before the 33rd Group went to war.

Reed wrote in his diary (that everyone was ordered not to keep but fortunately for history many did) that the food on board *Chenango* was the best he had eaten since joining the Army. As the convoy *Chenango* was part of headed east across the Atlantic, the pilots spent their days working on the airplanes and giving them names. Three days out from the invasion, the fleet ran into a storm. *Chenango* came within two degrees of her tipping point to capsize three times. Reed had watch duty that night and had to constantly check the aircraft tiedowns, that they were not too tight or too loose.

Operation *Torch*, the Anglo-American landings in the French North African colonies, was at the time the most ambitious amphibious operation ever launched; the fact that all US ships came from bases in the United States made it the only inter-continental invasion ever mounted. That it was accomplished at the same time the US Navy was going "all in" in commitment of ships and other forces to the climactic battles that led to victory at Guadalcanal was the first indication of how US power would become global during the war.

General George Marshall and Admiral Ernest King continued to oppose the landings after the Allied Combined Chiefs of Staff (CCS) met in London on July 30, 1942 at the Arcadia Conference, as they had throughout the spring, advocating a cross-Channel invasion of France as soon as possible despite British opposition to such a move. Marshall went so far as to suggest to President Roosevelt that the US abandon the "Germany first" strategy and give the Pacific War priority. Roosevelt replied that doing so would do nothing to help the Russians, which he was adamant must be a US objective. He then ordered Marshall and King to give *Torch* precedence over other operations and that it was to take place at the earliest possible date; this was one of only two direct orders he gave his commanders during the war, the other being his decision to adopt General MacArthur's planned invasion of the Philippines over the objections of Admiral Nimitz in 1944. Both decisions were made with US domestic politics considered equal in the president's mind with military needs; he faced a difficult mid-term election in November 1942, and American public opinion had taken a beating in the months since the Pearl Harbor attack with the Axis forces seemingly victorious everywhere. As it was, Marshall's opposition delayed the invasion by a month, and in the event, Operation *Torch* would come a weekend too late to affect the 1942 mid-terms, with the result that the congressional New Deal coalition was defeated by conservative Republicans and southern Democrats who took control in Congress.

The invasion's purpose was to provide a base in western North Africa for a pincer movement against the Afrika Korps, which began to retreat from Egypt the week before the invasion following the British Eighth Army's breakthrough in the Second Battle of El Alamein. Lieutenant General Dwight Eisenhower was placed in overall command of ground forces, after General Joseph Stilwell, the commander originally proposed, revealed himself as a vitriolic Anglophobe during the Arcadia Conference. Initially, the invasion planners identified Oran, Algiers, and Casablanca as key targets and added a landing at Tunis to secure Tunisia and position the Allies to rapidly interdict supplies for the Afrika Korps in Libya. Unfortunately, Tunis was within range of Axis airfields in Sicily and Sardinia, and the Axis powers were determined to make such an operation too dangerous. A proposed alternative was a landing at Bône in eastern Algeria, 300 miles closer to Tunis than Algiers. However, the limited resources available meant the Allies could only land at three places. Eisenhower believed landings at Oran and Algiers were crucial. He thus faced two options: the western option involved landings at Casablanca, Oran, and Algiers, with ground forces moving as rapidly as possible to Tunis as soon as any Vichy opposition was ended; the eastern option involved landings at Oran, Algiers, and Bône, followed by an overland advance to Casablanca, 500 miles west of Oran. He came down in favor of the eastern option since it included the opportunity of an early capture of Tunis; additionally, it was believed the Atlantic swells at Casablanca made a landing there considerably riskier.

Eisenhower's choice was opposed by the Combined Chiefs of Staff, who were concerned about the possibility that the invasion might result in Spain abandoning its neutrality and joining the Axis, which would result in the loss of Gibraltar and the closing of the Strait of Gibraltar, thus cutting off the Allied lines of communication. The decision was made to take the western option as being less risky, since Allied forces in Algeria and Tunisia could be supplied overland from Casablanca should the Spanish close the strait.

Marshall's opposition to *Torch* overall, and his opposition to landing in Algeria, resulted in British military leaders questioning his strategic ability; they pointed out that the Royal Navy controlled the Strait of Gibraltar, and that it was unlikely Spain would intervene since General Franco was still recovering from the destruction of the Spanish Civil War. Landing in Morocco ruled out an early occupation of Tunisia and would provide extra time that would allow the Germans to reinforce the Afrika Korps and take control of Tunisia. By the time the invasion plans were finally approved, Eisenhower told General George S. Patton, Jr., who would command the front-line forces, that the six weeks it had taken to come to a conclusion were the most trying of his life.

The Allies believed the Vichy French Armistice Army would not oppose the invasion, because of information supplied by the American Consul Robert D. Murphy in Algiers. Thus, plans were made to secure their cooperation. The US had recognized Marshal Pétain's Vichy government in 1940, while the British had recognized General Charles de Gaulle's French National Committee as a government-in-exile. North Africa was part of France's colonial African empire and nominally a part of Vichy, but support for the collaborationist regime was far from universal.

Pre-invasion dealings with the Vichy forces in North Africa were facilitated by "Agency Africa," an informal intelligence group established in July 1941 by Mieczysław Słowikowski and fellow Poles Lieutenant Colonel Gwido Langer and Major Maksymilian Ciężki. In little over a year of operation, "Agency Africa" had become one of the war's most successful intelligence organizations. The extensive contacts the organization had made among senior Vichy commanders resulted

CASABLANCA AND ORAN AREAS

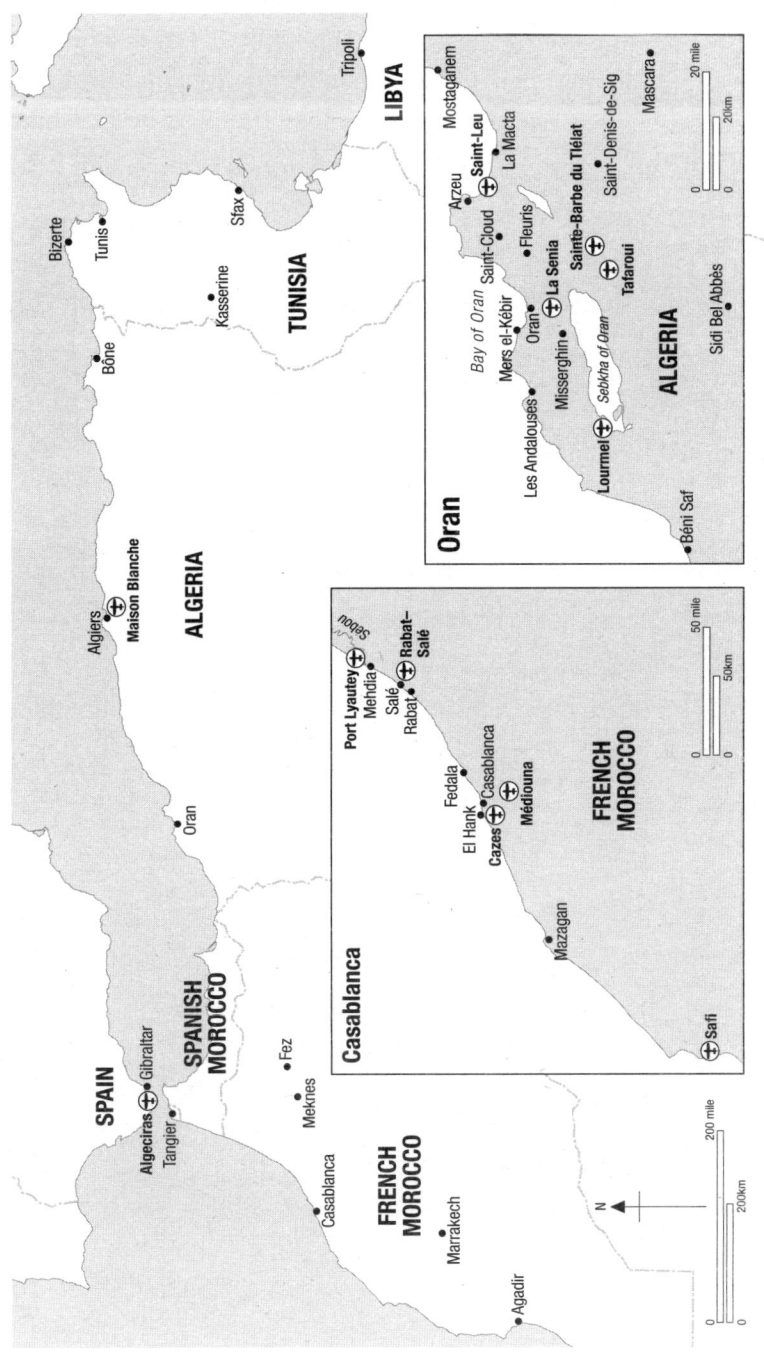

in information the Americans and British put to good use in planning the invasion and their dealings with the French.

The French forces were deeply divided, with Vichyites and Gaullists each considering the other to be traitors to France. General de Gaulle was desperate to be recognized by the Americans as he had been by the British as the leader of French forces, though the Americans were actively opposed to him and his movement. Admiral William Leahy, who had been the American ambassador to Vichy and was now President Roosevelt's personal naval advisor, informed the president that de Gaulle was, in his view, "an apprentice dictator." Churchill had also become "irked" by the general's pretensions. The Americans supported French General Henri Giraud; he and de Gaulle had a long history of disagreement before the war over the employment of armored forces in the event of German invasion, and both had come to dislike each other, particularly since de Gaulle had been proven right.

Giraud had been captured by the Germans during the 1940 blitzkrieg campaign but made a sensational escape from a prison camp in April 1942. Returning to Vichy, he tried to convince Marshal Pétain that Germany would lose, and that France must rejoin the Allies. While he failed to convince Pétain, the government refused to return him to the Germans. Giraud in return remained loyal to Vichy but refused to cooperate with the Germans and voluntarily return to prison. Heinrich Himmler retaliated by ordering the Gestapo to assassinate him and arrest and hold hostage any family members to discourage him from cooperating with the Allies; 17 members of Giraud's extended family were tracked down and arrested.

As plans for the North African operation advanced, S. Pinkney Tuck – *chargé d'affaires* at the American embassy in Vichy – contacted Giraud secretly on orders from Washington. The American decision to work with Giraud was due to his service before and between the two world wars having been in North Africa, where he had extensive contacts with military, political, and social leaders throughout the region who respected him. He was given the code name "Kingpin." Giraud was already planning for the day American troops landed in France and agreed to support a landing in French North Africa, but only if American troops were used exclusively and either he or another French officer commanded the operation, a condition he considered essential to maintaining French sovereignty over the North African colonies.

De Gaulle fumed when Giraud designated General Charles Mast – an anti-Gaullist – as his representative in Algeria. On October 23, Mast met with US General Mark W. Clark, who landed at Algiers secretly from the British submarine HMS *Seraph*, and American Consul Robert D. Murphy, who revealed to him that the invasion was on; however, the Americans only promised that Giraud would take command "as soon as possible." When this was communicated to Giraud, who was still in France, he demanded a written commitment that he would take command within 48 hours of the landing, and that there would also be landings in Unoccupied France. He insisted he could not leave France before November 20.

Murphy managed to persuade Giraud that he had to leave earlier than that. When the general requested an airplane be sent for him, he was told he would be taken to Gibraltar in an American submarine. Since there were no US submarines in the region, he was picked up with his two sons near Toulon on November 5 by HMS *Seraph*, masquerading as "USS *Seraph*" with US Navy Captain Jerauld Wright in "command" of her actual captain, Lieutenant Commander N.L.A. Jewell and crew, and taken to Gibraltar to meet Eisenhower. He arrived at Gibraltar on November 7, hours before the landings were set to begin, and met with Eisenhower, who asked him to take command of French troops in North Africa and order them to join the Allies. Giraud had expected to command the whole operation and refused to participate in any other role, stating "his honor would be tarnished" since he would only be a spectator.

The next morning, with news of the landings, Giraud relented. Refusing to leave immediately for Algiers, he stayed in Gibraltar another day and then went to Algiers. Asked by a correspondent on his arrival why he did not come to Algiers immediately, he replied, "You may have seen something of the large Gaullist demonstration that was held here last Sunday [November 8, the day of the invasion]. Some of the demonstrators sang 'The Marseillaise.' I entirely approve of that! Others sang the 'Chant du Départ.' Quite satisfactory! Others again shouted 'Vive de Gaulle!' No objection. But some of them cried 'Death to Giraud!' I don't approve of that at all."

American forces took the leading role in the invasion due to the bad feelings on the part of the French toward the British for events such as the Royal Navy's attack on the French fleet in the naval anchorage at Mers el-Kébir immediately after the 1940 Armistice as part of an attempt by the British to prevent the French Navy being handed over to the Germans, which killed over 1,300 French sailors. This had been followed by the unsuccessful attempted invasion of Dakar in Senegal that September to overthrow the Vichy government of the colony and establish a pro-Allied government of de Gaulle's Free French forces. In June 1941, British forces had invaded the French colony of Syria after the Vichy government allowed Luftwaffe aircraft to use Syrian airfields for attacks on British forces in Iraq during the Iraqi national uprising that spring, to ensure German forces would not be based there for attacks on Egypt. The British invasion of Madagascar had only concluded with the expulsion of the Vichy government there the month before the North African invasion. Because of this, all the Fleet Air Arm aircraft based on British carriers that provided support for the invasion had their British markings covered over with the US white star insignia.

Since the nearest land base was Gibraltar, USAAF fighters could not provide cover for the invasion until French Air Force airfields were seized by the invaders. Thus, air cover for the invasion was provided by four British carriers from "Force H" covering the landing at Algiers and three from "Force O" covering Oran, while four American carriers covered the landings at Casablanca.

Task Force 34 – the Western Task Force – would carry out landings at Casablanca, Port Lyautey, and Safi. Troopship convoy UGF-1 departed the Norfolk, Virginia, naval base that was naval headquarters for the invasion on October 23, bound for North Africa. The convoy was joined on October 26 by Task Force 34, a covering force of battleships and cruisers that sailed from Casco Bay, Maine, and on October 28 by the aircraft carriers as the fleet passed Bermuda. The fleet was screened by 38 destroyers because German U-boats were operating in the Atlantic and represented a significant danger to the transports; the fleet stretched 25 miles long and 25 miles wide.

The Moroccan invasion was covered by a carrier air group that included all four of the newly commissioned Sangamon-class auxiliary aircraft carriers (ACV) converted from oil tankers. Their conversions had been rushed to completion, along with crew training, in order to support the invasion; they were the first of what would become known later as escort carriers (CVE). The air group was led by USS *Ranger* (CV-4).

TG 34.9, the Center Group that would land at Casablanca, was supported by *Ranger*, carrying VF-9's 27 F4F-4s and VF-41's 27, along with VS-41's 18 SBD-4s, accompanied by USS *Suwannee* (ACV-27), carrying 29 F4F-4s of VGF-27/28/30 with nine TFB-1s of VGS-27. TG-34.8, the Northern Attack Group that would land at Port Lyautey, was supported by USS *Sangamon* (ACV-26) with 12 F4F-4s of VGF-26, along with nine SBD-4s and nine TBF-1s of VGS-26, with *Chenango* (ACV-28) carrying the 77 P-40Fs of the 33rd Fighter Group that were scheduled to be flown ashore once an airfield was captured. Task Group 34.10, the Southern Attack Group that would land at Safi, was supported by USS *Santee* (ACV-29), carrying 14 F4F-4s of VGF-29 and VGS-29's nine SBD-4s and eight TBF-1s. *Ranger* carried 72 aircraft, while the three auxiliary carriers had 99 aircraft in total. The 109 Wildcats were primarily responsible for opposing the French Armée de l'Air units, assigned to take on what would soon be known as escort carriers (CVE). The other three auxiliary carriers had a total of 99 aircraft ready for combat. With *Ranger*'s 72 planes, the Air Group's total was 171 combat-ready aircraft: 109 Grumman F4F Wildcat fighters, 36 Douglas SBD Dauntless dive bombers, and 26 Grumman TBF Avenger torpedo bombers.

To oppose these forces, the Vichy Armée de l'Air de l'Armistice had 205 aircraft in Morocco. The defensive fighter force included 78 fighters – 38 Dewoitine D.520s in Aéronavale Flotille 3F and 40 Curtiss Hawk H-75s shared between GC I/5 and GC II/5 of the Armée de l'Air. There were 160 aircraft in Algeria, including 76 D.520s with GC II/3, GC III/3, and GC III/6. The units in Tunisia were the weakest with only 69 aircraft, with only 24 D.520s of GC II/7.

In the event, the units of the Aéronavale and the Armée de l'Air resisted the invasion strongly at all three locations. Most of the combat at Algiers and Oran involved squadrons of the British Fleet Air Arm, but during the afternoon of the first day, USAAF Spitfires of the 31st Fighter Group flying to the newly captured airfield at Tafaroui did engage the D.520s of GC III/3. Other than that combat, the air battles of the invasion involved only the US Navy and Fleet Air Arm.

The landings at Casablanca provoked the strongest French response. Allied military planners had anticipated an all-American force might be greeted as liberators. After all of France's Atlantic coast had been occupied by the Germans in 1940, Casablanca was the main Vichy-controlled

Atlantic port and the most important Vichy-controlled naval base after Toulon. The base was defended by the El Hank coastal artillery battery of four 194mm (7.6in) guns and four 138mm (5.4in) guns. Additionally, the forward quadruple 380mm/45 Modèle 1935 gun turret on the modern battleship *Jean Bart* was operational; the ship itself had been under construction when the Germans attacked in 1940 and had managed to escape from the Saint-Nazaire shipyards during the invasion and sail to Casablanca, where she remained incomplete and moored to the mole in Casablanca harbor two years later.

The night of November 7, pro-Allied General Antoine Béthouart attempted a *coup d'état* against the French command in Morocco with the goal of surrendering to the Allies the next day. His forces surrounded the headquarters of General Charles Noguès, the Vichy-loyal High Commissioner for North Africa. Noguès was able to telephone loyal forces, who stopped the coup. The attempt alerted Noguès to the Allied invasion, and he immediately ordered French forces to resist.

French naval forces in the port of Casablanca the morning of November 8 were the light cruiser *Primauguet*, two flotilla leaders, seven destroyers, eight sloops, 11 minesweepers, and 11 submarines. Commander Vice Admiral Michelier knew nothing of the coming invasion because he was not trusted by the French Army officers who were in contact with the Americans, due to his having been a member of the Armistice Commission responsible for enforcing the terms of the surrender to the Germans until he had taken command at Casablanca three weeks earlier.

Despite Allied attempts to maintain secrecy, the Algiers invasion fleet had been detected by the French when it passed through the Strait of Gibraltar, though it was not identified. French naval forces went on high alert at this point.

Task Force 34 broke into its three component task groups on November 7, which moved to their respective targets overnight. Task Group 34.8, composed of six troopships and two cargo ships escorted by the battleship USS *Texas* (BB-35), the light cruiser USS *Savannah* (CL-42), and six destroyers, was to land 9,000 troops of the 60th Infantry Regiment to seize the Port Lyautey airfield. Task Group 34.10, with four troopships and two cargo ships escorted by the battleship USS *New York* (BB-34), the light cruiser USS *Philadelphia* (CL-41), and six destroyers, would land 6,500 troops of the 47th Infantry Regiment near the phosphate port of Safi to cover the southern approaches to Casablanca. Task Group 34.9 would land the 19,500 troops of the 3rd Infantry Division near Fedala, 15 miles northeast of Casablanca.

In the early hours of November 8, the French Resistance fighters of the Géo Gras Group staged a coup in Algiers. Commanded by Henri d'Astier de la Vigerie and José Aboulker, they seized the telephone exchange, radio station, governor's house, and the headquarters of the 19th Corps. American consul Robert Murphy took some men with him and drove to the villa of General Alphonse Juin, the senior French Army officer in North Africa. Surrounding the villa, Murphy tried to persuade him to side with the Allies. Murphy was surprised to learn that Admiral François Darlan, commander-in-chief of all Vichy French armed forces, was in Algiers on a private visit. Murphy was unable to persuade either Juin or Darlan to side with the Allies. Later that morning, the local Gendarmerie arrived and released Juin and Darlan.

The invasion fleet approached the Moroccan coast undetected under cover of darkness on Sunday, November 8, 1942. There was no extensive pre-invasion bombardment, in order to preserve secrecy to the last moment due to fear that Spain would allow Luftwaffe aircraft to use Spanish airfields to respond to the invasion if there was an extended bombardment, and also out of concern not to cause large numbers of French casualties.

The 15 transports of the Center Force anchored eight miles off the Fedala beach at midnight, and the troops soon began manning the landing craft in the darkness. They arrived at the Line of Departure at 0600 hours. Alerted by the noise of landing craft engines, the Pont Blondin coast defense batteries switched on their searchlights and illuminated the beach approaches, but they were extinguished when the landing craft support boats opened fire with machine guns. By 0700 hours, 3,500 troops were ashore despite the destroyer *Wilkes* (DD-441) and a scout boat tasked with marking Red Beach 2 having gotten out of position when they maneuvered to avoid an unidentified boat thought to be hostile. This resulted in landing craft running onto rocks at full speed, with the loss of 21 of the 32 landing craft from USS *Leonard Wood*. Unfortunately, though all troops went ashore quickly, their inexperience led them to remain on the beaches long enough so that French forces were able to organize resistance to advances from all the invasion beaches during the course of the day.

At 0720 hours, four destroyers of Destroyer Squadron (DesRon) 26 opened fire on the French shore batteries. In return, French gunners damaged USS *Ludlow* (DD-438) and *Murphy* (DD-403). In return, the US flagship USS *Augusta* (CA-31), opened fire on the Fedala beaches. The shock wave from the first salvo blew out the bottom of a boat in a davit about to be lowered that was loaded with the gear of Major General George S. Patton, Jr., commander of the invading troops; the boat dropped from its davits into the sea, where it quickly disappeared from sight. *Augusta* was joined in firing on the French batteries by USS *Brooklyn* (CL-40).

Thus began the Naval Battle of Casablanca, the largest surface action in the Atlantic since the Napoleonic Wars.

Wichita and *Tuscaloosa* initially engaged the coastal defense batteries on El Hank and the French submarine pens. At 0704 hours, the battleship USS *Massachusetts* (BB-59) opened fire at the incomplete battleship *Jean Bart*. Only commissioned in May 1942, *Massachusetts* – soon known to her crew as "Big Mamie" – had completed her shakedown cruise just in time to participate in the invasion. SBD Dauntlesses of VS-41, which had arrived over the port just before *Massachusetts* commenced firing, dive-bombed the ships in the harbor.

At 0718 hours, *Jean Bart* was hit by two 500-pound bombs in quick succession. The first damaged the port aircraft catapult, started a fire, and flooded the manual steering compartment, while the second hit the quay the battleship was moored to and exploded; the blast deformed the hull plating on her starboard side. Between 0708 and 0719 hours, *Jean Bart* fired four two-gun salvos at *Massachusetts*. Firing then ceased when the smoke screen laid by *Primauguet* and the destroyers when they attempted to sortie from the harbor drifted between *Jean Bart* and the US ships. *Ranger*'s VS-41 SBD Dauntless dive bombers, with TBF-1 Avenger torpedo bombers from *Suwannee*'s VGS-27, arrived overhead and attacked *Primauguet* and then the submarine base in Casablanca harbor.

At 0725 hours, *Massachusetts* opened fire on *Jean Bart*, scoring a hit that penetrated both armor decks and exploded in the empty magazines for the missing 152mm secondary armament. At 0735 hours, another salvo exploded close to *Jean Bart*'s bow, deforming the hull plating. With this hull damage and the damage from the bomb that hit the quay, *Jean Bart*'s hull was opened and the ship began taking on water.

At 0736 hours, another shell struck the quay; the explosion hurled concrete fragments that injured nearby antiaircraft gunners and caused additional flooding. A minute later, a 16-inch shell passed through the funnel and struck the edge of the armor deck. Another shell from the same salvo struck the edge of the quay and was then deflected down by the armor belt, passing through the bottom of the hull, and buried itself in the sea floor, failing to explode. At 0806 hours, *Jean Bart* was hit by two shells from another salvo; the first hit the main battery turret, pushing the front glacis down and jamming the turret. The second hit the barbette and broke up on impact, though fragments damaged the armor deck. A final hit was scored at 0810 hours, when a shell hit the quarterdeck, penetrating the sloped armor deck to explode in the ballast compartment, which caused additional flooding in the steering compartment.

While "Big Mamie" had become the first US battleship to engage an enemy battleship since the Spanish–American War, the shells she fired had problems similar to those that plagued American torpedoes, with several failing to explode. Only the 16-inch hit that exploded in the 152mm magazine could have threatened the ship's survival, had the magazine been full of propellant charges. *Jean Bart* – which should have been knocked out – was sunk at the pier, where there was only some 15 feet of water beneath her keel; she went on to be completed in 1951.

With *Jean Bart* now out of action, *Massachusetts* and the other US warships shifted fire and destroyed the El Hank coastal artillery batteries, an ammunition dump, and sunk the merchant ships in the harbor. One 16-inch shell also hit the floating dry dock holding the submarine *Le Conquérant*; while the dry dock sank, *Le Conquérant* was able to get underway before the sinking, but was sunk on November 13 by two VP-92 PBY Catalinas off Villa Cisneros.

Unknown to the Americans, *Jean Bart* had not been put out of action. During the day, workers quickly cut away the deformed steel that jammed the main battery turret and restored operation at 1724 hours. The next day, the ship's 90mm guns fired on advancing infantry, and *Jean Bart* was able to engage the heavy cruiser *Augusta* on November 10, nearly hitting the American flagship with the second salvo; three of her nine two-gun salvos straddled *Augusta*; the cruiser withdrew at high speed, and *Ranger* had to launch a second air strike.

TURNING THE TIDE

Nine SBDs, armed with 1,000lb bombs, escorted by eight Wildcats, attacked *Jean Bart* at 1500 hours on November 10, with the fighters strafing the battleship's antiaircraft batteries. Two bombs were solid hits: the first extensively damaged the forecastle, while the second destroyed part of the hull toward the stern. The bombs started fires that were not suppressed until shortly after 2000 hours. The extensive flooding led *Jean Bart* to settle by the stern and submerged the turbo generator room; the main diesel generators were disabled by shock from the bomb explosions leaving the backup diesels as the only electrical power.

Over the course of her engagements with American forces, 22 of *Jean Bart*'s crew had been killed, with the same number wounded. She had only fired 25 shells from her main battery, but despite significant damage by the bomb hits on November 10, her turret was still operational, in addition to the 90mm guns, but both batteries lacked power.

By the time the naval battle was over, *Jean Bart* was sunk at the pier, the light cruiser *Primauguet* was grounded and burned out, the two destroyer leaders had been grounded while the four destroyers were sunk, along with seven submarines either sunk at the submarine base or when they attempted to sortie and attack the invasion fleet. Additionally, numerous merchant vessels were sunk. The French Navy had fought valiantly against great odds; no ship surrendered until ordered to do so by Vice Admiral Michelier and only after he was ordered to do so by his superiors. More than 460 French sailors were killed and at least 200 wounded.

There was considerable air action over Casablanca. *Ranger* launched nine Wildcats of VF-9 led by squadron commander Lieutenant Commander Jack Raby at 0610 hours to attack Cazes airfield. They hit the field with three strafing passes that left many aircraft on the ground on fire. Another eight VF-9 F4F-4s were launched to strike Sale airfield, where they arrived just in time to catch several Martin 167 twin-engine bombers warming up to take off and attack the fleet, setting them afire.

The French air defenses were provided by the Curtiss Hawk 75s of Groupe Chasse II/5 "Lafayette," the descendants of the American-manned Lafayette Escadrille in World War I. The first French Hawks to make it into the air over Casablanca – six fighters of GC II/5 led by Lieutenant Pierre Villacèque – encountered American floatplanes over the harbor calling gunfire for the fleet. Sergeant Lavie shot down the OS2U Kingfisher flown by Lieutenant Thomas "Tommy" Dougherty and observer Lieutenant Clyde Etheridge, who were spotting fire for their ship, the battleship USS *Massachusetts*. The other floatplanes fled while Dougherty and Etheridge were captured.

After VF-9's Wildcats departed, *Ranger* launched 18 F4F-4s for a strike against Cazes. At Cazes, six Hawk 75s led by Commandant Georges Tricaud were just taking off when the Wildcats appeared overhead. Observers on the ground saw Tricaud and Battle of France ace Capitaine Robert Huvane shoot down two Wildcats before Tricaud's fighter was hit and caught fire, blowing up over the field and killing him. Minutes later, Huvane was shot down and killed after shooting down two Wildcats for his seventh and eighth victories. He was soon joined by Lieutenant de Montgolfier, who attacked one Wildcat but was shot down and killed by the wingman. Six more Hawks from GC II/5 managed to get airborne and join the battle; Lieutenants Legrand and Villacèque each claimed a Wildcat before they were shot down and forced to crash-land.

VF-41's Lieutenant (j.g.) Charles "Windy" Shields recalled the two Hawks were so close that he could see their insignia. He went after one and in his eagerness overshot his target, later recalling:

> As I went past I saw he was coming round on my tail. I pulled up and came back over in a quick turn that brought me with my nose toward him. I was too far away and much too anxious. I gave him a burst from long range. Those .50-calibers got him. I could see him, standing still in the air as if something had jerked him up by the tail. He looked as though he was going to stall to take evasive action, and he fell over to starboard, his wing fluttering.

Shields remembered how the Hawk "hit the ground, bounced, and with his motor still running ricocheted across the field until he came to stop in a water hole... There was no sign of the pilot." Suddenly, Shields realized he was separated from the other Americans:

> I remembered about our keeping together. I knew I was plumb crazy to be down there all alone. Presently I saw a Wildcat coming in across the airfield very fast with two P-36s on his tail. The French pilots were scissoring round behind him and giving him alternate bursts... Chuck [Lieutenant (j.g.) Charles August] called me over the radio, "Windy! Windy! Get those bastards off my tail quick!" I went down

then with my throttle wide open. One of the French planes saw me and broke away. I got on his tail but he slipped away. Those P-36s are extremely maneuverable.

Shields remembered seeing August make a steep chandelle that let him get on his opponent's tail and shoot him down. He continued, "I got my man in the sights, lost him, got him again, gave him a burst, then another. He went up into a climbing turn, a darn silly thing to do. I only had to pull up my nose and take a simple shot at him. He staggered and rolled over, then righted himself. A streak of orange flame came from his starboard side, and he went down spinning and burning."

Shields was then caught by two Hawks whose bullets tore into his fuel lines, opening his wing while smoke filled his cockpit. An incendiary bullet had caused a fire:

A great lick of flame came up at my face and I knew it was the end. I pushed back the hood and tried to turn the plane on her back, but she wouldn't have it... I decided to stall her, and at the moment when she lost flying speed, I braced my knees and jumped... The parachute opened, and I floated down feeling angry and frustrated. A French plane came at me. I thought he was going to shoot me but he just flew past me, wagging his wing tips and waving his hands and laughing like hell.

Another antiaircraft hit caused the right landing gear of August's Wildcat to droop. Other Wildcats rescued him as he tried to outfly the fighters chasing him over the airfield. Shaking them off, he turned on another Hawk. "My position was just right and I made a high attack from the beam and gave him a long burst. The .50-caliber bullets hitting at about 60 per second seemed to rip him open like a can opener. He stopped in his line of flight, turned turtle and went down in flames."

August spotted another Hawk and a Dewoitine 520 and pulled in on their tail, opening fire on the Hawk:

The P-36 shuddered. The weight of metal you put into them with the 50-calibers seems to jar them off their line of flight. I got in to 50 yards, feeling strangely elated. I was sure of hitting him now as I gave him a burst with all guns and pulled up over him while he was hanging in the air and rolling about with a convulsive movement, rather like an animal in pain.

August described the resulting crash. "The red-and-yellow-nosed plane turned over in a slow roll with its engine running and began to fly on its back. It was like watching a beginner crash in a training flight… It went down quite slowly. A plume of dark smoke spurted from the ground where it hit." Climbing for better altitude, August could see fires burning all over the airfield.

> I made one run over some parked aircraft… [One of them] subsided gently to the ground as if a giant had suddenly sat on it… I suddenly found I was losing speed… I cussed and stuck the nose down and checked the instruments. I had about 60 gallons of fuel but oil pressure was zero… Underneath was what looked like the world's worst terrain for a forced landing – hills, rocks and gullies. I was at about 1,100 feet when my motor let out a noise that was like a cracked bell sounding over a radio at full blast. Then came a terrible vibration.

August hit the stabilizer and injured his leg when he bailed out. Grabbing the D-ring and pulling it, the parachute opened a moment before he hit the ground. He recalled, "Hit is hardly the term. I crashed very heavily and painfully because I was swinging like a pendulum. When I got my breath, I found myself on my back being dragged along by the parachute."

Under fire, the French managed to take off in ones and twos and soon outnumbered the attackers. Lieutenant G.H. Carter expressed grudging respect for them:

> I got separated from the gang and three Vichy pilots came from nowhere on my tail. I did everything I knew to get them off, but they kept on… I got a shot at one and turned him off with smoke coming from his motor. Then the other got me at close range. He hit my plane behind somewhere, and the control became difficult. The best thing to do seemed to be to head for the sea and try to make the carrier. That Vichyman on my tail was smart and exceedingly aggressive… His second burst shot away my oil cooler lines.

Carter began to lose height quickly. "A bunch of bullets hit the back armor. I couldn't do anything about it so I stuck her nose down. A plane showed up on my right then. I saw it was the French pilot who had shot me down. He was grinning like mad and waving his hand... He was still overhead when I made a crash landing on the water. Quite a chivalrous guy."

GC II/5 had 13 D.520s on strength, which the Americans reported seeing, but none engaged in combat since the unit had no ammunition for their 20 mm guns.

GC II/5's combat journal described the air battle:

> The Grummans are very tenacious, provided with invincible weapons, they are three times as numerous as us and soon gain superiority over our unfortunate Curtiss planes. Our pilots, in spite of their lack of training and decrepitude of their planes, fight a fierce battle and clearly defend their lives, downing numerous enemies. Commandant Georges Tricaud is killed after having downed a Grumman above the runway. Captain Robert Huvet, one of our most brilliant pilots, with six confirmed victories [over Germans], is killed at his post. Adjutants (Warrant Officers) François LaChaux and Paul de Montgolfier and Sergeant Lucien Heme, all superior pilots, also fall on the Field of Honor. Several other pilots are defeated and wounded, some seriously: Captain Elie Reyné received a bullet in the right thigh; Lieutenant Georges Ruchoux, after overcoming one enemy plane is wounded in one leg, burned and parachutes; Lieutenant Fabre is seriously wounded by three bullets in his left arm; Lieutenant Villacèque, heavily engaged against several enemy planes, defeats one of them, after which he is wounded in the face by plexiglass splinters and landed roughly. While these battles are going on, other formations are machine gunning the field, burning one after the other, nearly all of the Douglas (DB-7) twin-engine craft [11 out of 13] of GB (Groupe de Bombardement) I/32.

VF-41 claimed 13 destroyed and one probable in the air, and six destroyed and eight damaged on the ground. French losses were recorded as six GC II/5 pilots shot down and killed, two wounded, one forced to bail out and another killed in a takeoff accident. Several

Hawks returned so badly damaged they were junked. Seven Wildcats were claimed destroyed and three probables. American losses were six F4Fs and pilots failed to return to *Ranger*, and Shields and August became POWs.

The fight over Cazes was a battle of near equals. The Wildcats and Hawks had top speeds of just over 300mph and both were highly maneuverable, though the six .50-caliber machine guns in the Wildcats were heavier than the six 7.62mm weapons carried in the Hawks. The French were more experienced in combat, though they had been limited to the number of hours they could fly before the invasion, so the Americans had more recent flight time.

Eight Wildcats from VF-9 and another eight from VF-41, led on a second patrol by VF-41's executive officer, Lieutenant Malcolm "Mac" Wordell, spotted five French destroyers headed toward the transports and landing craft. Wordell led a strafing run on them. "I started firing at about 4,000 feet as my sights began to travel down the center line of the last ship in column. I could see the tracers were squirting on the decks and bouncing off. I almost felt that I was running into my own ricochets. Actually, I was seeing the red pencils of their tracer fire coming up at me."

The attack, accompanied by the American fleet opening fire on them, stopped the destroyers, but antiaircraft fire damaged Wordell's Wildcat. He later recalled, "It wasn't until after I was over the leading ship that I almost subconsciously heard a noise, the same kind of noise you hear when you jam a screwdriver into the top of a can of milk." As oil streamed from his engine and the cockpit filled with smoke, he crash-landed in a field and was taken prisoner.

The untried Navy fighter pilots had received a rough initiation to combat, losing seven F4Fs to enemy fighters and flak. Their inexperience also resulted in four VF-9 pilots shooting down an RAF Hudson off Fedala they identified as a LeO 45. The next day, pilots from VF-41 made a similar mistake by shooting down an RAF photo-reconnaissance Spitfire.

Additionally, the Navy fliers suffered several more casualties due to flak or mechanical failure. *Santee*'s air group bore the brunt of the trouble, losing three aircraft in landing crashes. VGF-29's pilots were ensigns just out of advanced fighter training at NAS Miami, who had impressed new squadron commander Lieutenant Commander John

T. "Tommy" Blackburn, who had been their senior instructor before taking command of the squadron. The only other experienced aviator in the squadron was executive officer Lieutenant (j.g.) Harry "Brink" Bass who had won the Navy Cross for his attack on the Japanese aircraft carrier *Shōhō* at the Battle of the Coral Sea.

VGF-29's first combat mission on November 8 was a disaster when they could not find their target, while poor weather and damaged homing equipment on board *Santee* forced them to ditch or force-land their Wildcats. Four pilots landed at Safi airfield, where they were temporarily imprisoned by the French. Blackburn was forced to ditch his Wildcat in the Atlantic when his landing gear wouldn't come down. He was adrift in his life raft for three days before he was fortuitously spotted by a destroyer and rescued. Believing he had failed in his first combat command, Blackburn later recorded in his memoir, *The Jolly Rogers*, that he was amazed to return to Norfolk and find he was being assigned as commander of VF-17, the second Navy fighter squadron to equip with the F4U Corsair. His second combat command would write an epic history in the South Pacific.

At Rabat-Salé airfield, GC I/5 "Champagne," commanded by Capitaine Edmond Marin la Meslée – the French ace of aces in the Battle of France in 1940 – in the absence of commanding officer Commandant Montraisse, led 12 Hawks that took off without orders mere minutes before the arrival of eight Wildcats from *Sangamon*'s VGF-26. Intent on strafing the field, they destroyed two Hawks and nine LeO 451 bombers of GB I/22, on their first pass. Marin la Meslée's Hawks were unable to find and engage the Wildcats in the overcast skies, so they soon departed.

By November 9, the US Army was firmly established in Morocco. Despite this, French army and air force units continued to resist the invasion. Dawn saw GC II/5's five surviving Hawk 75s take off on patrol.

Ranger received a report from Allied troops at Fedala that they had been strafed by the five Hawks, which were supporting the advance of enemy troops and tanks from Casablanca. *Ranger* launched nine VF-41 Wildcats as ground support, covered by eight VF-9 F4Fs. Lieutenant Commander Tom Booth, VF-41's skipper, led his Wildcats in repeated strafing runs against the column. At 0730 hours, 15 Douglas DB-7, LeO-451, and Martin 167 bombers were spotted by the VF-9 Wildcats approaching the beachhead. GC I/5's 16 Hawk 75s, led by Capitaine Marin la Meslée, provided escort. The French bombers managed to drop their loads on Allied landing barges in the Oued-Nefifik wadi, but they inflicted little damage. The eight VF-9 F4Fs, led by squadron commander Lieutenant Commander Raby, dove through the clouds and attacked the escorting Hawk 75s.

In the melee that followed, five Hawk 75s were shot down; two French pilots were killed, including five-victory ace Lieutenant Maurice Le Blanc. Ace Adjutant Chef (Chief Warrant Officer) Georges Tesseraud was badly wounded, though he managed to get back to Rabat and land safely, while Lieutenant Camille Plubeau force-landed uninjured. Sergeant Chef (Master Sergeant) Jérémie Bressieux managed to score his ninth victory flying the Hawk 75 when he damaged the only Wildcat lost in the fight; Ensign C.W. Gerhardt was forced to ditch his F4F at sea. This was the last victory scored by a pilot of the Vichy French Air Force.

When one Hawk dodged an attack by overeager Ensign Marvin Franger, the pilot made a tight turn and stayed with the Frenchman. He related, "I was able to slide in on his tail and that was the end. He started smoking and I saw fire as he went down. I didn't see him go in but our section leader, Al Martin, saw the crash."

At midday, Marin la Meslée led GC I/5's five remaining Hawks on a strafing mission. GC II/5 at Cazes received reinforcements when five Hawks were flown in from Meknes, but minutes later 13 VF-9 Wildcats arrived overhead and strafed the field, destroying the five newly arrived Hawks as well as six Dewoitine D.520s and six DB-7s. The attack put GC II/5 out of the battle, as they had no more operational aircraft.

The pilots of the 33rd Group had expected to be launched from *Chenango* on the first day of the invasion. Their orders were to fly to Casablanca, then on to Port Lyautey and land there after the airfield was captured by paratroopers. As it turned out, the Port Lyautey field was not taken until the evening of November 9. The little carrier's flight deck was not long enough for the P-40s to take off under their own power, so the fighters were catapulted individually, a very slow process. The 33rd Group was the first P-40-equipped fighter group to enter combat in Operation *Torch*. When some 35 P-40s had been launched – which appeared to Lieutenant Reed to be even more dangerous than they had been told when almost every plane dipped below flight deck level, nearly touching the water before reappearing in a climb – the launch was stopped for the day. The problem was that the P-40s had a higher takeoff speed than the F4F Wildcats the carrier had been designed to carry, and there was not sufficient wind across the deck.

The morning of November 10 saw the Vichy French units in Morocco with only 37 operational fighters and 40 bombers. By noon VF-9 was airborne, scouting for enemy planes. Leading 13 Wildcats at 10,000 feet, Raby spotted many aircraft on the ground at Médiouna airfield. The F4Fs concentrated on rows of fighters and half a dozen DB-7 bombers. After five strafing passes, all the bombers and most of the fighters were burning. During one low strafing run a DB-7 exploded just as Lieutenant Ed Micka passed over; damaged by the explosion, the Wildcat crashed. A French officer later wrote, "We buried him on the spot with full military honors. Over the grave we put a white cross, to which we affixed the identification tag of the brave flier." Micka was not the only loss. Defending French flak gunners hit several F4Fs, including Lieutenant (j.g.) Mayo A. Hadden's. Despite heavy damage from 12 hits and a shrapnel wound in his leg, Hadden managed to bring his Wildcat back to *Ranger*.

Two Potez-630 reconnaissance aircraft were lost over the airfield at Chichaoua, one shot down by an F4F and the other by a Dauntless, with four more of the aircraft destroyed in a later strafing attack. The French Air Force was nowhere to be seen for the rest of the day, and the Navy fliers spent the time scouring the roads ahead of advancing US forces.

On November 11, Reed and the rest were finally catapulted off the carrier. When they eventually arrived at Port Lyautey airfield, they found it full of wrecked aircraft. The single short concrete runway had three bomb craters in it, one near each end and one in the middle. The craters at the north end and in the center had been filled with dirt, but the one at the south end, which was where the P-40s were supposed to land, was still open. Reed had to go around and make a second attempt. In the end, 17 of the 75 P-40s that had made it off *Chenango* successfully – two had crashed on takeoff – were wrecked trying to land at Port Lyautey. Reed was told by those who had flown in on November 10 that group commander Lieutenant Colonel William Momyer had set the tone of the landings by wrecking his airplane first, and then ordering radio silence be maintained so that the second group did not learn of the problem until they arrived overhead. Once on the ground, they found that the concrete runway was surrounded by so much mud that a P-40 sank into it so deep that the main wheels disappeared up to their axles. Two days were spent repairing the less-damaged fighters, and the 33rd finally arrived at Casablanca on November 13.

The 33rd's ground echelon had traveled by ship and landed on the invasion beaches after the first waves of troops had cleared them on November 8. Sergeant Ed Newfield recalled that its first night in North Africa was spent digging foxholes because there were still French snipers in the vicinity as it bedded down near the beaches. It was not until November 14 that the ground and air echelons were reunited at Casablanca.

The evening of November 11, GC's I/5 and II/5 received a message from General Noguès that the fighting was over, and an armistice was proclaimed. Vichy fighter squadrons based at Marrakech, Meknes, Agadir, Casablanca, and Rabat had some 86 fighters available at the time of the landings. Over the first 48 hours of battle around Casablanca, the *Armée de l'Air* units in Morocco had lost 13 Hawk 75s shot down with 11 destroyed on the ground. Four ace pilots had been killed and two badly wounded.

Honor served, the former Vichy French fliers quickly joined the Free French. Re-equipped with American aircraft, the units fought valiantly through the rest of the North African campaign.

VF-9's Lieutenant (j.g.) Chick Smith summed up the feelings of most Navy pilots: "We thought of the French as traditional allies, and it was disappointing they resisted us as much as they did."

Supported by the Royal Navy, American and British troops were able to take Oran with little opposition, with the port under Allied control by November 9.

Air combat over Oran and Algiers had been limited to the first day, though fighting on the ground continued for two more days until Darlan had agreed to the ceasefire. The Fleet Air Arm suffered the loss of 53 aircraft, most of which involved non-combat operational losses on board the carriers, due to the inexperience of the pilots in deck operations.

The Spitfire-equipped 31st and 52nd Fighter Groups were the first USAAF units to arrive in North Africa. Both had been originally assigned to Eighth Air Force. The 31st's first combat operation had been the Dieppe Raid on August 19, where it had scored its first victories. On October 7, it loaded its gear onto lorries that headed out of the gate, destinations unknown. It was declared "non-operational" on October 13. Between October 19 and 23, the 31st departed Westhampnett airfield in Britain in separate groups; overnight trains delivered it back to where it had started; it boarded transports in the Firth of Forth on October 22, and the convoy departed on October 25. The group learned it was about to take part in the invasion of North Africa. The voyage on board the small transport HMS *Leinster* was remembered as a battle with seasickness due to the ship's almost-constant pitching and rolling until it was off the Portuguese coast a day before its arrival at Gibraltar on November 6. The 52nd Fighter Group, which had yet to see combat, traveled on board a different ship in the convoy.

Both groups had assigned a handful of pilots and ground crews to "Squadron X," which had been flown to Gibraltar to assemble the Spitfires they would take into combat. Once arrived at Algeciras airfield, they found there were only 44 Spitfires available for each, and they only had ten days to get the fighters ready. On November 7, the morning after the pilots arrived, Twelfth Air Force commander Brigadier General Jimmy Doolittle informed them the 31st would cover the landing at Casablanca while the 52nd would cover the landing at Oran.

The ground echelons of both the 31st and 52nd Groups were on board transports in the invasion fleets. Disembarkation drills had been held all day on November 6. That night, the fleet "ran the straits" at Gibraltar, staying to the south near the African shore – "the Malta Route" – in imitation of a Malta convoy. Once through the strait, the fleet broke up into the individual attack forces. With the coming of dawn, the ground crewmen donned their packs and climbed down the cargo netting hung over the transport's sides; dropping into the bouncing landing craft, they headed toward shore. The assault troops had already landed and taken the beaches. Once ashore, the ground crews gathered and then were put to work helping to unload following landing craft.

Back on Gibraltar, dawn brought a change in plans. At 0500 hours, the 88 Spitfires of both groups were lined up on the side of the 3,400-foot

Algeciras airfield. The 31st was in the lead, ready to take off first and head to Casablanca to provide air cover for General Patton's troops. The 52nd would follow, flying to Oran. As the pilots sat in their cockpits, information received from the landings changed their orders. French resistance at Algiers and Casablanca was not what had been expected. However, French forces at Oran were engaged in major resistance to the landing. The order was passed to delay takeoff.

Doolittle asked the 52nd's CO, Colonel Allison, how long it would take him to get off and get to Oran. The general was shocked by Allison's reply: "About a day and a half." He gestured to the 31st's airplanes ahead, and to 31st's CO Colonel John R. Hawkins. "Shorty Hawkins' planes are all in front of us!" Doolittle turned to Hawkins and asked the same question. "About twenty minutes," the colonel replied. Doolittle changed the plans on the fly: fly to Oran and land at Tafaroui airfield. By now it was 1530 hours, and the pilots, who had been roused at 0300 hours, were scattered on the field.

Hawkins climbed into his Spitfire and started up; within minutes the rest had gained their fighters and started up. Eighteen minutes later, Hawkins led the 31st's Spitfires in a low pass over the airfield and turned southeast, headed to North Africa. Doolittle, who that morning had watched an RAF wing take an hour to assemble and head off, was impressed.

The group arrived over Tafaroui at 1700 hours. Looking down on the field, they saw numerous bomb craters. Hawkins made a low pass over the field, looking for a safe area to land. He radioed, "If I land right side up, land where I land. If not, find another place." Hawkins landed, the 308th's Spitfires dropping in immediately behind him while the 309th's fighters stayed high to give cover. Just as the last of the 308th's airplanes landed, a French artillery battery opened up on the field. A flight of four 309th Spitfires made a strafing run on the French, which silenced further fire. The 309th's Lieutenant Byrd turned onto final approach and was just at touchdown when a Vichy French Dewoitine D.520 fighter suddenly dove out of the sun and opened fire; Byrd was shot down and killed. The attacker was one of four D.520s the Americans had misidentified as Hurricanes. Major Harrison Thyng and First Lieutenants Carl Payne and Paul Kenworthy raised gear and flaps and took off after the attackers; each shot down one. These victories set Thyng and Payne to join the very few USAAF pilots who would claim kills over German, Italian, Japanese, and Vichy French aircraft during their wartime careers.

Payne reported:

> I had made my final turn with wheels and flaps down, and I heard over the radio that enemy airplanes were beating up our field. I immediately pulled up my flaps and wheels and started circling. I had made almost one complete circuit of the field when I saw three French Dewoitines diving upon the field with guns blazing. I then immediately attacked them, taking snap shots at them. I was then following two of the fighters. One of them broke away, and as he left, I gave him a good long deflection shot and saw no results. I then started climbing after the first Dewoitine, which was above me and out of my range. As I closed within range, I gave him a good three-second burst, seeing an explosive shell strike his wing. He half rolled and did an aileron turn downward. I followed, and he pulled up into a steep climb, or Immelman. I closed fast upon him, and at close range my machine guns peppered his fuselage and wings. I was out of cannon shells by this time. His right wing exploded and caught fire. The pilot baled out at 5,000ft. I watched both he and his airplane go down. The air was clear of enemy fighters by then, and we landed unmolested.

An hour later, three C-47s carrying paratroopers of the 82nd Airborne Division landed. They were part of a force that originally numbered six that was supposed to drop on Tafaroui that morning. They had become lost and ended up landing on the Sebkra D'Oran dry lakebed, where they came under French artillery fire. The paratroopers on board had jumped out to try to silence the French guns, but then French fighters appeared overhead. As the paratroops sprinted for the planes under fire, the C-47s taxied across the lakebed, picking up troops, and managed to take off. Three were shot down. The three survivors had found Tafaroui in the midst of the 31st's fight with the Dewoitines.

As it turned out, though the ground forces had reported taking Tafaroui, they were only half right. The Americans held the middle of the field, while French forces still held either end. French snipers opened up on the airplanes, and the pilots hurriedly took cover in a long trench on the east side of the field. Hawkins borrowed two machine guns from the seven tanks that had been left to hold the field and set them up for defense. Hay bales were broken open, and the pilots took turns standing guard overnight while the others tried to sleep on the hay in the trench. The surviving paratroopers dug foxholes and settled in.

On White Beach, the ground echelon of the two groups had spent the day unloading supplies from landing craft that beached some 30 yards off the beach. Exhausted, the men fell asleep in a line of French foxholes. At 2200 hours they were awakened by the arrival of trucks to take them to Tafaroui. They then learned that the field was still "contested" and that the pilots were "under fire." The leaders of the ground echelon quickly decided to push on through the night to get to Tafaroui as quickly as possible. They were told that if the French attacked the truck convoy, they should jump out and hide in the darkness, then try to make their way back to the beach. Six antitank M3 halftracks, each armed with a 75mm cannon and two machine guns, escorted the trucks.

Setting off at midnight, the little convoy bumped through the darkness for three hours through enemy-held territory. At 0300 hours, they came upon a group of three tanks. They managed to convince the tankers to escort them on to Tafaroui once the sun came up.

Dawn on November 9 at Tafaroui found the pilots crouched in the trench. Neither the pilots nor the paratroopers could take any action to clear the field, since to raise one's head over the top of a trench or foxhole was to invite a shot from the French snipers, who were already awake and on the job. The 308th's CO, Major Avery, looked across the runway at the remains of Byrd's Spitfire, with his corpse visible in the cockpit. He led five men across the airdrome to retrieve Byrd, but halfway there they heard the sound of an airplane and looked up to see a French bomber zoom overhead and drop a solitary bomb. It exploded in the middle of the runway, leaving a large crater. For now, the 31st Fighter Group was not going anywhere.

An hour later, the ground echelon with its three escorting tanks and six halftracks appeared. The field was quickly retaken as the French retreated. As if there had not been enough trouble already, they then received a warning that a French Foreign Legion unit was headed toward the airdrome.

The fighters had no gas or ammo. A store of French gas in five-gallon cans was found in the surviving hangar, while Technical Sergeant Hanson of the 309th found French 20mm ammunition that could be used, and Technical Sergeant Nast and squadron engineering officer Lieutenant Elliot found they could use the French 7.62mm ammunition in the fighters' .303-caliber machine guns. The big crater in the middle of the runway was filled, and operations could commence. At 0700 hours, Lieutenant Colonel Dean led Lieutenants Corrigan and Waltner for a recce flight to find the French Foreign Legion. They soon spotted the French – the column was ten miles long. They immediately attacked, strafing the French and setting three tanks on fire and destroying four trucks. Landing back at Tafaroui, Corrigan was too close behind Dean and chewed his tail off with the prop. Both Spitfires were now sources of spare parts for the others.

At 0800 hours, Dean and Avery took off and attacked the French again, setting fire to three more tanks. While they were up, the remaining Spitfires got off from Tafaroui. The 308th went looking afield for more targets while the 309th went after the Foreign Legion column. The hapless Legionnaires were soon routed and dispersed, leaving their burnt-out equipment behind. By noon, the threat of counterattack was over. The 307th Squadron flew in from Gibraltar soon after.

In mid-afternoon, the field was suddenly subjected to an 18-minute shelling from French artillery in the nearby hills. Dean and Avery, as well as Captains Davis, Fleming, and Hill, and Lieutenants Wooten, Ramer, and Waltner, managed to get airborne during the attack. As they searched for the enemy artillery, they spotted tanks below and made an attack; fortunately, after only two had opened fire, they discovered they were attacking their own armor and broke off. Minutes later, they spotted the French position and strafed it thoroughly. Fifteen minutes later, the American tanks arrived and finished the job.

By the time the 31st had left Gibraltar on November 8, it was too late for the 52nd Group's three squadrons to fly into Oran before darkness fell. The next day, the 4th Squadron flew a mission to cover the beaches at Oran and then went on to land at La Senia. The 2nd Squadron escorted the B-17 that carried General Doolittle. The weather was bad, and in the severe conditions several of the squadron's fighters and Doolittle's B-17 were forced to land at Tafaroui. The 31st's ground echelon was able to refuel the Spitfires from the French supplies it had discovered, and after the weather cleared sufficiently, they and the general flew on to La Senia. The weather was poor over the next four days, but the two squadrons flew armed recce missions over the battlefield in search of French units.

On November 10, the 5th Squadron left Gibraltar for North Africa, but Lieutenants Lee Trowbridge, Edwin Smithers, and Edward Scott were forced off course in the difficult weather and force landed in Spanish Morocco, where they were interned by the Francoist forces. Squadron CO Captain George Deaton and the other 11 pilots made it to Tafaroui before the weather closed in.

General Giraud had flown to Algiers on November 9; he was rebuffed when he attempted to assume command of French forces, and his broadcast directing French troops to join the Allies was ignored. Eisenhower, supported by Roosevelt and Churchill, made an agreement with Darlan in which the admiral ordered all French forces in North Africa to cease resistance and cooperate instead.

On November 11, the French forces in North Africa surrendered, and the Americans immediately began the move into Tunisia. Soon after, General Eisenhower ordered that the port of Bône in extreme northeastern Algeria be defended against attacks by Luftwaffe units stationed across the Sicilian strait, the waters between Sicily and Cap Bon. There was only room at the Bône airfield for one of the 52nd Group's squadrons; a coin toss determined that the 2nd Squadron would make the move.

When Adolf Hitler learned of Admiral Darlan's agreement with the Allies, he immediately ordered the occupation of Vichy France and ordered German forces be sent to Tunisia. German forces took control of Unoccupied France on November 11. The French fleet at Toulon scuttled itself to avoid being taken by the Germans. Admiral Jean-Pierre, commander of French forces in Tunisia, obeyed orders from Vichy not to resist the German troops arriving by air. The Germans seized the airfields and brought in more troops before any Allied units could intervene.

While General de Gaulle had no official power in Vichy North Africa, most of the population publicly declared Free French allegiance. Following the Armistice, Darlan was installed in power on November 22, when General Clark signed an agreement recognizing him as High Commissioner of French North Africa and West Africa, while Giraud was appointed commander of all French forces under him. The American press protested, dubbing Eisenhower's decision the

"Darlan Deal" and blaming President Roosevelt for allowing a brazen bargain with Hitler's Vichy French puppets. On December 24, 1942, Darlan drove to his offices at the Palais d'Été, where he was shot by Gaullist resistance fighter Bonnier de la Chapelle, a monarchist; he was tried by court martial under Giraud's orders and executed on December 26. With the strong backing of General Eisenhower, Giraud was then appointed to succeed Darlan. When he ordered the arrest of those who had participated in the Algiers coup, with no opposition from the Americans, public opinion began to turn against the Allies.

The Eisenhower agreement meant the US would allow officials appointed by Vichy to remain in power in North Africa. There was no recognition of the Free French, which Britain recognized as France's government-in-exile and had supported them taking charge in other French colonies. The decision offended British and American public opinion; the Vichy French were seen as Nazi collaborators. However, Eisenhower insisted he had no real choice if his forces were to move into Tunisia to deal with the Axis forces which had taken control, rather than fight the French in Algeria and Morocco.

Following the decision by the government of French West Africa to join the Gaullist Free French in January 1943, British Minister Resident in Algiers Harold Macmillan brought de Gaulle and Giraud together; despite their personal hostilities, he convinced them to serve as co-chairmen of the Committee of National Liberation (CFLN) in June. Finally admitted to power, de Gaulle built a strong political base, but Giraud failed to do so. In November 1943, de Gaulle became head of the CFLN and *de jure* head of the French government and was finally recognized as such.

7

RACE TO TUNISIA

It was soon apparent in the week after the Moroccan landings that the Allies had miscalculated in their fear of an immediate Axis response to a landing at Tunis, which had led to the adoption of the "Eastern strategy" in the invasion. The Germans and Italians *were* surprised by the Allied invasion of French North Africa and had no immediate plans for a riposte to such an action. General Doolittle thus put every effort into moving units of the newly arrived Twelfth Air Force as far east as possible in Algeria, to maximize their ability to cover the coming battlefield in Tunisia. This was complicated by the fact there were very few airfields in the country, and what were there were not very modern. They quickly became crowded with bomber, fighter, and other units using a base, with all the difficulties involved in operating aircraft with very different performance parameters from the same field. Additionally, the rainy season in North Africa lasted from November to March. Only Port Lyautey, Tafaroui, Maison Blanche, and Bône had any paved runways and there was only one at each. The forward bases the Allies used were quickly turned into quagmires of mud by the rain.

Paratroop operations were conducted to capture airfields nearer the front lines, with Youks-les-Bains taken on November 15 by paratroopers of the 2nd Battalion, 509th Parachute Infantry, dropped from 20 C-47s of the 60th Troop Carrier Group flying from Maison Blanche; there was no air or ground opposition, and the field was operational for Allied units by November 17. The Allies were in a race with the Germans to control the airfields.

The Vichy government had informed the Germans on November 9 that French air bases in Tunisia and the Department of Constantine in eastern Algeria were available to the Luftwaffe, qualified only by the condition that no Italian forces be involved. By dark, Luftwaffe aircraft were landing at El Alouina airdrome near Tunis. Over the course of November, 1,200 Ju-52s would land at Bizerte. JG 51 completed its transfer from Sicily to Tunisia on November 11. A week later, the first Fw-190As from II./JG 2 flew from Sicily to El Alouina. The Germans had an advantage in the geography of Tunisia, which was rocky and thus allowed good drainage of the airfields in the country during the rainy season, unlike the situation in the majority of the Algerian airfields used by the Allies.

The Allied buildup was equally rapid. The problem was that Tafaroui was in west-central Algeria, too far from the front. Additionally, most ground echelons, which had been sent by sea from England, had not yet arrived, with those that were there undermanned, which dramatically slowed operations. Oran, the main port of entry for the region, was a scene of congestion as ships arrived and spent days at anchor before they could be brought alongside a pier and unloaded; to make things worse, there was no prioritization of cargoes to get the most needed items ashore as soon as possible. There was a shortage of trucks, and the French rail system was totally inadequate for the needs of the Allies to move men and equipment forward quickly. The Allies set to taking control of the airfields in eastern Tunisia as rapidly as possible to bring their fighter forces closer to the battlefield.

The 1st Fighter Group had flown from England to Gibraltar on November 7, flying on to Oran on November 9 to base at Tafaroui airfield outside the city. Operations began on November 11. The 14th Fighter Group was a week behind the 1st in making the trip to North Africa. The group's 48th Fighter Squadron left Portreath on November 14, with the 49th Squadron following four days later, on November 18. When the 48th flew to Oran's Le Senia airfield the next day, it found it was supposed to have gone to Tafaroui. There it found the base crowded with Lightnings from the 1st Group and Spitfires from the 31st Group. First Lieutenant Bill Schottelkorb, a dedicated diarist, recorded that the pilots started to look for a place to live among the old French buildings. Once they did, they made a fireplace in the rear yard from stones, where they heated C-rations for meals. The biggest

EASTERN ALGERIA AND TUNISIA

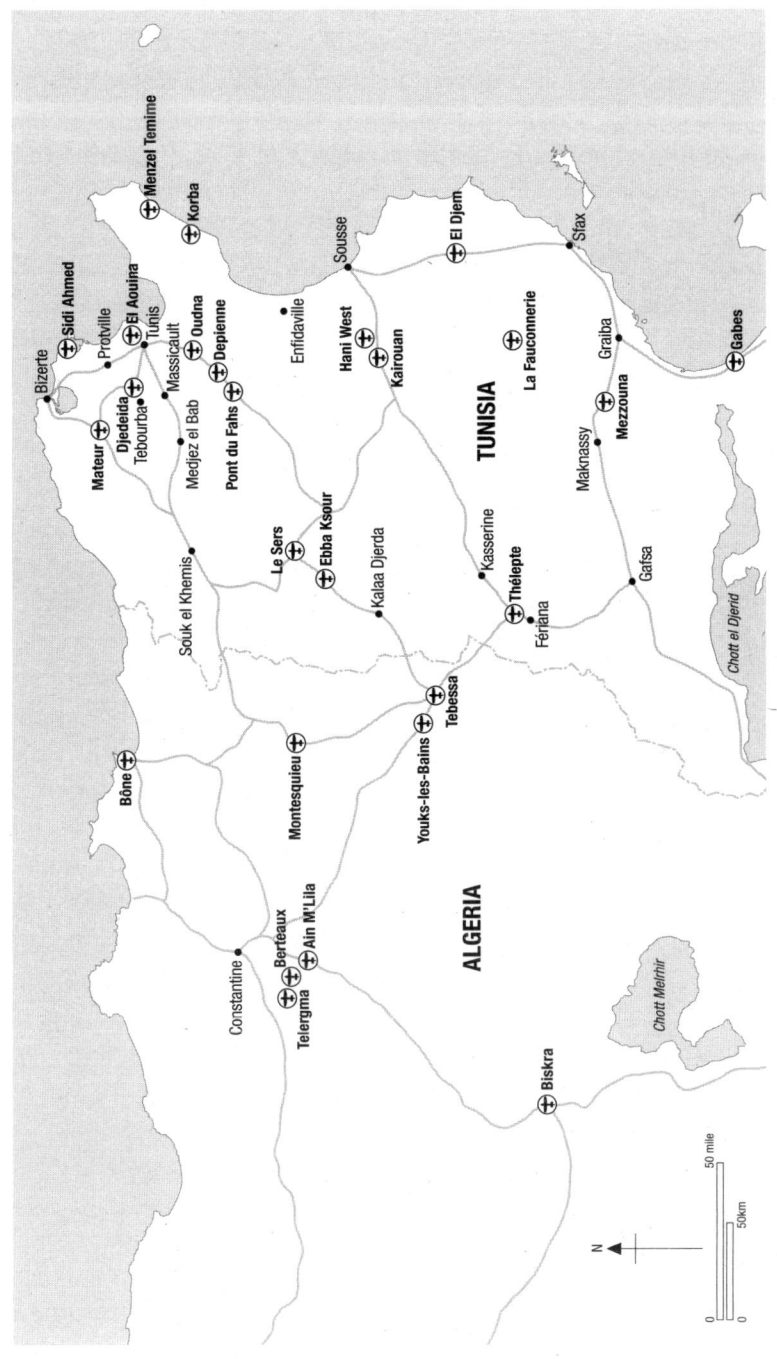

problem on the field was getting sufficient good water. After drawing water from one of the wells, they had to use purification tablets to avoid cholera.

On November 22, First Lieutenant Mark Shipman from the 1st Group's 94th Squadron shot down an unidentified twin-engined Italian aircraft for the P-38's first victory in North Africa. Though he never "made ace," Shipman subsequently claimed a six-engined Messerschmitt Me 323 Gigant transport and a Bf-109 by the time he completed his tour at the end of 1943. Jack Ilfrey, who was also on the mission, remembered that before Shipman shot the bomber down, "We had our first casualty when Everett Umphrey closed on that bomber to identify it and got too close; the top gunner opened fire and hit him in his cockpit. It struck me how unnecessary his death was; that's the part you think about."

Bône was close enough to enemy air bases in Sicily that the port was subject to air raids from the arrival of Allied troops on November 12. The port and airfield were of crucial importance, since the port could handle 22 ships and the airfield was in range of Bizerte. By noon the day after the Allied arrival, five C-47s carrying antiaircraft guns, crews, and ammo, escorted by P-38s of the 1st Fighter Group, arrived to provide the port's defenses. Youks-les-Bains was taken on November 15 by the 2nd Battalion, 509th Parachute Infantry, of the new 82nd Airborne Division without opposition; the next day the paratroopers took nearby Tebessa airdrome.

In the meantime, the 31st Group, which remained at La Senia, was charged with maintaining air defense over Oran harbor following the French surrender. After ten days of boredom as the rainy season began, the harbor was raided by Ju-88s on the night of November 21. By November 25, continuous rain had turned the airfield into soft mud. On November 27, after two days of clearing weather, the skies opened up and the men learned that it really could rain in North Africa despite its reputation as a desert. As the pilots and ground crew heard of the mounting successes of the 52nd at Bône, the feeling began to spread that the 31st might miss out on all the action.

On November 29, the airfields of Depienne, Pont du Fahs, and Oudna southwest of Tunis were taken by paratroops, to establish the first Allied presence inside Tunisia. These landings had been made in preparation of an immediate attack on Tunis. When this was canceled, the paratroopers returned to Algeria by land, suffering 19 killed, four wounded, and 266 missing in their retreat.

The B-17s were forced to depart Maison Blanche after an attack on the airfield on November 20 by Ju-87 Stukas and Ju-88 bombers flying from Sardinia that lasted two hours and resulted in the loss of two B-17s, two P-38s, six Beaufighters, and four photo-recon Spitfires. A follow-up raid the next night saw 16 aircraft on the field damaged. On November 22, the B-17s returned to Tafaroui. An indication of just how hard the first 60 days in North Africa were is shown by USAAF claims for 109 enemy aircraft destroyed and 26 probables, for a loss of 70. The Luftwaffe managed to stage more than one raid on each of the major Allied airfields in Algeria during this time, despite bad weather. Over the Tunisian battlefields, German fighter units often had numerical superiority over their Allied opponents.

Publicity around the P-38 Lightning during World War II made the claim that the Germans were so fearful of the fighter that they had named it "Der Gabelschwanz Teufel" (The Fork-Tailed Devil). In fact, nothing could have been further from the truth. In North Africa – the first air campaign in which large numbers of P-38s took part – many German *Experten* thought of the fighter as a juicy target, due to the fact its one-of-a-kind shape made its identification easy at a much further distance than any other Allied fighter, allowing an opponent to prepare himself for the coming combat. Additionally, P-38 pilots initially used tactics that did not utilize the fighter's best strengths and apply them against enemy weakness. The willingness of P-38 pilots to engage in a traditional dogfight led to losses that were nothing short of disastrous during the opening months of the North African campaign, to the extent that after two of the first four P-38 groups originally assigned to the Eighth Air Force in England for long-range-escort support of the bombers were diverted to North Africa, a third group had to be sent to make up losses. Then all the airplanes and all of the pilots except flight and Squadron leaders of the fourth and last Group to arrive in England were taken away and sent to North Africa, forcing VIII Fighter Command to start over as an organization. By the spring of 1943, as the P-38 pilots finally learned the best tactics to use, the tables were turned and the Lightning saw its best wartime service, other than in the Southwest Pacific, in the Mediterranean theater through the remainder of the war. But the myth of "The Fork-Tailed Devil" was never born over drinks in a forward base officers' club; it was purely a product of the Publicity Department at the Lockheed factory in Burbank.

For the P-38 pilots, the airplane's known proclivity to end up in a terminal velocity dive that a pilot could not get out of successfully kept many of them from flying the airplane to its limits. The problem was that the Lightning was one of the first airplanes capable of getting into "compressibility" as speed approached Mach 1. Very little was known by anyone at the time about this phenomenon. The problem had been apparent since the 1st Group had received the first YP-38s in the summer of 1941. The 94th Squadron's Captain Newell Roberts recalled his own close encounter with death in his first flight in one of the YP-38s:

> In September 1941, a group of us was sent to the Lockheed Corporation's Burbank, California, plant to be taught to fly the new YP-38, a pre-production training and in-service test model of the twin-engine Lightning fighter. After a brief transition course, we flew this batch of YP-38s back to Michigan.
>
> During our period of testing the YP-38s, several of the airplanes buried themselves in the earth while doing combat or acrobatic maneuvers from high altitudes. On one occasion, I had a YP-38 up to 20,000 feet and was doing acrobatics. When I did a slow roll, the airplane would not come out of the dive. The Lockheed technical representative who had been assigned to the 1st Pursuit Group had told me earlier that, if I ever got the airplane into a dive and it would not come out, I should quickly roll back the trim tab and, if I was lucky and had enough altitude, it would come out of the dive. I quickly rolled the trim tab back and the airplane came out of the dive at about 100 feet off the ground. I immediately brought the airplane back to Selfridge Field and landed. The technical staff went over that airplane from stem to stern. They found that the wings were buckled and it wouldn't be able to fly anymore. They then took the airplane apart and discovered the problem. On the counterbalance shaft controlling the back horizontal rudder were two stop bolts that kept the shaft within a certain arc. When the airplane vibrated, the bolts worked loose and turned downward in such a way that it became

impossible to get the airplane out of a dive at high speeds without using the trim tabs. This aeronautical engineering monstrosity was corrected at the Lockheed factory and we had no more difficulty bringing the airplane out of a dive.

By the time the correction was made, most of the YP-38s had either buried themselves in the ground or were unable to fly any longer. Of course, when several of the YP-38s had buried themselves in the ground following uncontrolled dives, they had also buried the pilots.

With its outstanding climb capability, Lockheed stressed to both the USAAF and new P-38 pilots that the prime combat tactic to evade the enemy was to climb away when attacked by hostile aircraft. Unlike other twins, the Lightning could easily out-climb all single-engined fighters in 1942. German opponents came to respect the P-38's ability to pursue them after a bounce even when they were using the boost achieved from a "dive-and-zoom" maneuver. Unfortunately, neither the USAAF leadership nor the pilots initially accepted Lockheed's advice; initial losses were high during early combat in North Africa until pilots learned the value of what they had been told by the Lockheed tech reps in their units. By 1943, many an Axis fighter pilot in North Africa was astonished to look back and see the P-38 he had just attacked closing in on him in a climb.

Once the Lightning's best performance characteristics were understood, P-38 pilots fought in the vertical plane, which negated the advantage in horizontal plane maneuverability held by their single-engine opponents. At the outset, most pilots were afraid to use this capability to its maximum advantage because of the known danger of diving a P-38; the dive flaps that would solve this, and the hydraulically boosted controls that made the Lightning more maneuverable than nearly every opponent, would not appear until the final year of the war, long after the battles over Tunisia were memories in the minds of those who survived.

The main P-38 attribute most feared by German opponents was its armament. German pilots were warned to avoid taking on a Lightning head-on. The P-38's nose-mounted battery on the aircraft centerline meant a Lightning could effectively hit any enemy in range, without the pilot having to worry about convergence of fire, as was the case for fighters that carried their weapons in their wings. Even in a tight high-G turn the P-38's guns would still function, producing a weight of fire that could penetrate the hull of a destroyer.

What P-38 pilots liked most about the airplane was its range. Any target within a radius of 400–500 miles could be reached in a Lightning. Commanders in North Africa and the Pacific came to rely on the P-38 for long-range interceptions such as that on April 18, 1943, when P-38s from Guadalcanal flew outside the island chain a distance of 600 miles to surprise Admiral Yamamoto as he arrived at Bougainville, a mission that could not have been performed by any other Allied fighter. The Lightning also had an impressive ordnance load for the period, soon demonstrating that it was able to carry up to a 1,000lb bomb on the underwing shackles.

Many World War II fighters had mechanical quirks that led their opponent to think they had shot down an airplane that in fact got away. When the Bf-109 pushed over into a negative-G dive, it emitted smoke through the exhausts that frequently led a pilot that had been shooting at it to claim it shot down since it "emitted smoke, then fell away." Both the P-38 and the P-47, due to their turbosuperchargers, would spew clouds of dark smoke from the turbocharger exhaust when a pilot opened the throttles quickly in an emergency, which gave the impression the aircraft had been hit and was crippled, particularly since pilots were still diving away when attacked; seeing a Lightning heading down gave the impression of a shoot-down. It is likely this is why *Experten* Kurt Bühligen and Franz Schiess stated that the P-38 was the easiest Allied fighter in the North African theater to shoot down. Schiess claimed 17 Lightnings shot down before he fell victim to one. Bühligen received official credit under the strict German victory accreditation system for 13 P-38 victories.

A major problem for the P-38 groups was that they were created in a period of massive organizational expansion in late 1941, and particularly in early 1942 following Pearl Harbor. This led to difficulty in maintaining group leadership and cohesion, as a flight leader in one squadron became the squadron commander in the next after the first unit was divided and a second unit created, with those personnel as "cadre" expected to train the newcomers assigned. Thus, when the P-38 groups went to war in the fall of 1942, they were still working themselves out organizationally.

All the technical and personnel difficulties would come to a head following Operation *Torch*, since the Lightning was the USAAF fighter given the most responsibilities during the campaign in Tunisia. Newell Roberts recalled, "Our early losses in pilots and aircraft were unbelievable, both from enemy action and from maintenance problems caused by lack of spare parts and the wearing effects of dust and sand on machinery. In two instances during our first months in North Africa, the total number of aircraft in our three squadrons ran from the usual total strength of 80 aircraft down to approximately only 30 aircraft. And in most instances, this involved the loss of the pilots as well."

By the end of 1942, the Lightning units were sustaining severe losses, though they had demonstrated their value as the best USAAF fighter in theater. In part this was due to the incorrect combat tactics used, which did not exploit the airplane's strong points, and also to the lack of combat experience on the part of American pilots. Because of the high attrition rate, there was soon a shortage of P-38s.

The 82nd was unlike all other USAAF fighter groups. Personnel originally came from the 1st Pursuit Group, the first unit to equip with the P-38 in the summer of 1941. The group was founded at the Muroc Bombing and Gunnery Range – today's Edwards AFB – which the original members of the group would always remember as the worst place to ever start a fighter group, and the best possible place for the 82nd Pursuit Group to train, since it prepared them for what they found when they arrived in North Africa. Radio technician Sergeant Tom Abberberger remembered Muroc in a letter home as "The last outpost of civilization. The sand and wind are miserable. The numerous hard, flat expanses of dry lake bed make the area one huge landing ground. There are no trees, just sand, sagebrush and jack rabbits."

Most of the pilots who filled out the original ranks were staff sergeant pilots from USAAF Class 42-C; their existence was the result of congressional authorization of an expansion of enlisted pilots after the last class had closed in 1932. Originally expected to fill non-combat flying roles, the needs of the service in the post-Pearl Harbor expansion of the USAAF had changed. Difficulties in integrating enlisted pilots into the USAAF resulted in the program being phased out at the end of 1942, by which time some 2,000 staff sergeant pilots had been graduated and awarded their wings. Fred Wolfe recalled that life for the enlisted pilots at Muroc included being outranked by the men who took care of the airplanes. Group commander Lieutenant Colonel William Covington had been doubtful about the flying sergeants when he learned they were to be assigned to the group, but he later became their foremost advocate, telling anyone that because of their dedication, they were the best pilots in the group and established the spirit of the group that would prevail throughout the war. Several of these men received commissions as flight officers, a warrant officer rank, before the group went overseas, and by the summer of 1943 all those still in the group became flight officers. Some would become commissioned officers, and Staff Sergeant "Dixie" Sloan eventually finished his combat tour in the fall of 1943 as the top-scoring Twelfth Air Force ace; by that time, he was a full captain.

The P-38 units didn't merely face the disadvantage of limited numbers during the initial fighting. While there were enough fighters to supply five squadrons – the 27th, 71st, and 94th Squadrons of the 1st Fighter Group, and the 48th and 49th Squadrons of the 14th Fighter Group – their combat-experienced Luftwaffe opponents soon had the measure of the inexperienced Americans. The P-38's distinctive configuration was identifiable at a great distance, which allowed enemy pilots to prepare for combat with the Lightnings. Initially, P-38s were employed in close escort, which meant they could not take offensive action against enemy interceptors prior to an attack. The Lightning pilots had to watch the dust rise from enemy airfields as German and Italian interceptors climbed to superior heights without disruption. Aside from the policy of sticking close to the bombers, the P-38 pilots employed escort tactics that left them at a disadvantage. As the Lightnings weaved in great arcs to stay with the slower bombers, they were easy to attack; German pilots reported this tactic not only ineffective but dangerous to the American pilots themselves. By the spring of 1943, the Americans had learned their lesson the hard way through painful losses. By that summer, General Doolittle authorized more offensive escort policies, while the pilots had learned to stay in the vertical plane in combat.

The 49th Squadron was the first in the 14th Group to experience enemy action, when Luftwaffe Ju-88s bombed Maison Blanche airfield at Algiers the night they arrived from England. Eight of their P-38s were damaged in the bombing. The next day they moved on and joined the 48th at Tafaroui.

The 14th Group's first combat mission came on November 20, a long-range strafing mission in Tunisia. After taking off from Tafaroui, the six P-38s stopped at Tebessa, another small field in eastern Algeria, to top off their tanks, which was accomplished laboriously with five-gallon Jerry cans brought in by a C-47. They were finally able to take off in the late afternoon but experienced bad weather and found little to shoot at. Antiaircraft fire caught Second Lieutenant Virgil Smith's Lightning, knocking out an engine. He and Second Lieutenant Leo Yates fell behind the others and were eventually forced down by the bad weather. The other four got lost and ended up bellying in at the Arab village of Negrine, just across the border in Algeria. Losing all six P-38s for no score against the enemy was a hard way to begin operations.

The next day, following their inauspicious first mission, the 14th engaged the Luftwaffe for the first time. Escorting B-17s on a mission to Tunis, the 48th Squadron intercepted Bf-109s intent on attacking the bombers. Second Lieutenant Paul Ziegler got one in his sights, then managed to press the microphone button instead of the trigger. His wingman, Second Lieutenant Carl Williams, Jr., shot the Messerschmitt fighter down for the group's first victory.

With the Germans pouring troops into Tunisia, both P-38 groups were pressed into ground attack missions since they had longer range than the P-39 and P-40 fighter-bombers. On November 24, on a flight near Kairouan, the 48th Squadron's First Lieutenant Bill Schottelkorb and his wingman Second Lieutenant Jim Tollen spotted a large German motorized column in the distance. They turned and shot up the vehicles. Pulling off their strafing run, they spotted what Schottelkorb identified as a Ju-88 3,000 feet above them. He later wrote in his diary:

> We did a steep climbing turn... I pulled 3,000 rpm and 42 inches of mercury for about five minutes, gaining height and airspeed. The Ju-88 was throwing out clouds of black smoke in an effort to escape. At about 500 yards, the rear gunner fired at me. At 300 yards, I started firing and held everything down in a steady burst. At 100 yards I was bouncing around in the prop wash and thought I was

going to run into him, so I pulled straight up. Jim closed in and put a burst into the left engine and fuselage.

Schottelkorb describes how the rear gunner bailed out as the Ju-88 lost altitude. "The right main gear was hanging down as it skimmed the ground. It plowed a path over fairly level ground and skidded to a halt. The right motor was torn completely loose. Jim and I returned victorious."

While Schottelkorb and Tollen were shooting down their bomber, a flight from the 49th Squadron patrolling between Gabes and Sfax spotted a large formation of Italian and German transports. The pilots returned to Tafaroui claiming eight Savoia-Marchetti SM.81 Pipistrello transports, five Ju-52 transports, and a Ju-88 bomber for no loss.

November 29 saw all of the 52nd Group finally together in North Africa when nine 2nd Fighter Squadron Spitfires arrived at Bône; the squadron was quickly engaged in fighter sweeps and bomber escorts, as well as local defensive patrols. On November 30, during a sweep over Tebourba, the squadron claimed the 52nd Group's first victories, 2nd Squadron CO Major James Coward and Captain Harold "Ray" Warren each destroying a Bf-109G. Coward, who later rose to command the 52nd, reported, "We were put on to two Me-109Gs by ground radio. We spotted them at 0900 hours at about 3,500 feet. We turned into them as they came towards us, went under us and dove for the deck. My Number Four, Lieutenant Aitken, called the break for my section, and I broke right and down and got onto the tail of one of the two. After two short bursts it caught fire and crashed in flames." The next day, December 1, group executive officer Lieutenant Colonel Graham West and First Lieutenant McDonald each damaged a Bf-109 over Tebourba.

Over the next week, the 52nd's Spitfires fought several engagements. On December 2, one of the group's future aces opened his account. Captain "Vince" Vinson later described how he downed an Fw-190 west of Mateur, Tunisia: "I gave the enemy aircraft a one-second burst. Strikes were seen as it weaved through a valley, and I closed to 50 yards, striking the engine – it smoked and stopped operating. The prop began windmilling. My next burst hit the wings and the left wing then exploded, probably due to HE cannon ammunition, and the 190 went into a steep spiral. I stayed with it down to 100 feet from the ground." Vinson continued his run the following day, when he joined with Squadron Leader "Razz" Berry and Flight Sergeant LeHardy to shoot down an Fw-190, one of three spotted north of the airfield; the day after, December 4, he waded into the Messerschmitts escorting a formation of Ju-88s near Tebourba and shot down another Bf-109G. Several other pilots made claims during this fight; Captain Jimmie Peck, who had claimed 3.5 enemy aircraft destroyed over Malta earlier in the year flying with the Spitfire Vb-equipped 126 Squadron, was credited with damaging one of the Ju-88s. The squadron suffered its first combat loss when Lieutenant Walter A. Karl was shot down and killed in the engagement.

Lieutenant Colonel Fred Dean took command of the 31st Group on December 5; it was still ground-bound by the rains, which had the field knee-deep in mud with no break in sight. Finally, on December 21, the field had dried enough for the Spitfires to get off the ground, so the group was transferred to Maison Blanche, where it was alarmed to discover the mud was as bad as that at Le Senia, while there were none of the "luxuries" of indoor living they had found at the old base.

Two days later, on December 6, 12 2nd Squadron Spitfires met 12 Bf-109s over Tebourba; while one enemy fighter was destroyed, Lieutenants Jack M. Shuck and Stephen Freel were lost. In the aerial battles that broke out during the first week of December, the 2nd Squadron pilots gained credit for six destroyed, two probables, and six damaged, while losing three. The winter rainy season had begun a few weeks earlier, and heavy rains that developed on December 7 brought air action to a stop for two weeks. The squadron resumed operations on December 19, when Jimmie Peck, on a mid-morning patrol near the airfield at Bône, spotted three Fw-190s and chased after them, eventually catching them at low altitude. When one pulled up into a climb, he opened fire at near-maximum range, knocking off part of the 190's right wing. Before he could witness its crash, he came under fire from another Fw-190 and was forced to break off, thus only credited with a damaged.

Twelfth Air Force command realized Tafaroui was too far from the front lines and that Tebessa was too small for safe operations with P-38s. The 1st and 14th Groups were transferred to recently captured Youks-les-Bains airfield, south of Constantine, on November 26. Life on the new field was difficult. Jack Ilfrey recalled that their personal equipment did not arrive for a week, and they slept on the wood floor of a building he thought would collapse on them at any moment. "It was heaven when our bedrolls arrived!" He also remembered the rain. "I thought it rained hard back home in Houston, but that was just a little shower compared to the rain we got at Youks." They had just enough fresh water available to brush their teeth but none for any other washing. Shaving became irregular, and only when they could heat water in their steel pot helmets. "Now and then, we managed to go into the town of Youks for a wash-off at the old Roman baths. As a rule, we stayed in the bath a longtime, knowing it would be uncertain when we would be able to return."

On November 28, eight P-38s – one four-plane flight each from both 14th Group squadrons – set out to Bizerte from Youks on a tactical reconnaissance mission to confirm the number of German aircraft on the field. Two Lightnings were forced to abort when their drop tanks would not feed; the other six continued on. Approaching Bizerte airfield as low as possible, the P-38s popped over a hill just west of the runway. There, over a lake, were what Second Lieutenant Ervin Ethell identified as 20 Ju-52 transports on crosswind turning final to land on the airfield ahead. There was also a Ju-88, which First Lieutenant Virgil Smith of the 48th Squadron was seen to shoot down. The P-38s ripped into the formation. Ethell – the only pilot in his squadron to have undergone RAF gunnery training in England – shot down four of the Ju-52s, while Lieutenants James Butler and Virgil Lusk got two each and shared a fifth. As Ethell lined up Ju-52 number five for the victory that would make him an "ace in a day," he saw Butler and Lusk being chased by 109s and turned in on the tail of one. He saw pieces fly off before tracers flashed over his head and he realized he was under attack. Ethell managed to out-turn the enemy fighters by using the fact the P-38 did not experience torque to make sharp right turns into the attackers at minimum altitude, a maneuver the Fw-190 pilots dared not follow for fear of entering a high-speed stall followed by a low-altitude crash. After outmaneuvering several attackers, Ethell found himself alone in the air and turned away back to the west, returning to Youks.

While the P-38 groups fought the mud at Youks-les-Bains, 52nd Group executive officer Lieutenant Colonel West led four 2nd Fighter Squadron Spitfires to Bône on November 27. Lieutenant

John F. Pope later recalled that the four were the only airplanes that were able to take off from the very muddy La Senia airfield. At Bône, the squadron reinforced 81 Squadron RAF, whose Spitfires had arrived at the port on November 15, and became part of RAF 322 Wing, commanded by Petrus H. "Dutch" Hugo. Lieutenant Miles Ryan recalled that they quickly learned the port and the airfield were under near-constant German attack – "bombs at night and strafing by day." The small airdrome had two short runways, only one of which was operational. It was 1,800 feet long and surrounded by bomb craters. The rains soon turned everything but the PSP matting of the runway into sticky, glutinous mud; the front lines were only 30 miles to the east. The four Spitfires immediately took off with the RAF fighters to meet an incoming German raid. Wing Commander Hugo shot down a Bf-109 and Squadron Leader Ronald "Razz" Berry and Flight Officer Rigby shared another. That night, seven Ju-88s bombed Bône airdrome, leaving 11 aircraft unserviceable and destroying five Hurricane fighter-bombers while damaging the runway.

The rains that announced the arrival of the winter of 1942–43 in North Africa came early in November and were the worst in many years, with extended periods of rain turning the entire region into a muddy quagmire. It was said that there had been no major military operation in the area during winter since the Third Punic War. December was so rainy that it was clear there could be no major offensive to take Tunis before the spring. Due to the relatively short ranges of the majority of Allied fighters – Spitfires had only a 90-mile range, while the P-40s were good for 300 miles if they were carrying a bomb in place of the drop tank – it was crucial that airfields be taken that were close enough to the battlefield for these aircraft to engage the enemy. Although the Luftwaffe units in Tunisia that had arrived beginning in mid-November after the Allied invasion were no stronger than their Allied opponents, the ubiquitous Ju-88 bombers that seemed to attack everywhere could operate from the relative safety of Sicily and Sardinia. One of the French fields captured for use by the Allies was Thélepte, situated in the mountains just north of the Sahara Desert, on a plateau at an altitude of 2,500 feet, surrounded on all sides by mountains. The field had a 6,000-foot gravel-based runway that was all-weather, a big change from the muddy bogs of La Senia, Bône, and Maison Blanche. There were no trees and no buildings. The field was the closest Allied airfield to the front and was only some 20 minutes' flying time from airfields the Luftwaffe was using. Being surrounded by hills meant that low-flying raiders could be virtually on top of the field before they were spotted.

Youks-les-Bains was soon a sea of mud. There was no way of keeping things dry, and soon beds, clothing and everything else was damp and moldy. Heat was provided by "stoves" made from five-gallon Jerry cans burning 100-octane aviation fuel. Heat for living quarters and for water used in very basic laundry was possible, but there was no way to heat enough water for bathing and shaving, which became things of the past for the duration of the season.

Moving the aircraft on the field became progressively more difficult. The 14th Group's Lieutenant Ervin Ethell once tried to move his P-38 and found it impossible to drag the airplane out of the bog even with the engines running at 75 inches of manifold pressure. Finally, with men on the tail bouncing the airplane to get the nose wheel out of the mud, Ethell managed to get loose and taxi to the airstrip. He later recalled that there was a 1,700-foot ridge of stony ground that drained well, just off to the side of the field. Pilots found it possible to land downhill and take off uphill on the ridge safely when the airfield itself was a morass of mud. "That strip was really too short for a P-38," he wrote, "but we managed to pull them off the ground with full flaps and then milk them up as we made a shallow climb." The Luftwaffe was aggressive during this time, with night raids mounted by Ju-88s against Youks-les-Bains and Tebessa.

On November 29, the 1st Group's 94th Squadron flew another strafing mission. Ilfrey later recalled, "We took off before dawn and were on our way to strafe the airdrome at Gabes just after sunrise. We got initiated to concentrated ground fire. It separated us and when I came across Captain Newell Roberts, we proceeded to fly back across the desert to the mountains. About halfway there, Roberts saw two planes in the distance headed toward us." Roberts banked toward them, calling to Ilfrey, "Let's go see what they are."

> As we turned toward the planes, we recognized them as enemy because they gunned their engines, which caused black smoke to come out of the exhaust. We got closer and recognized them as Me-110s. I said to Roberts "Let's go after them." His voice was shaking with excitement

as he replied, "Roger. I'll take the one on the right and you take the one on the left."

These were the first German planes we had seen in the air and at first it was hard to realize we were going to shoot them down. We closed in behind and I must have opened up at 5,000 yards' distance – about five times too far behind. I pulled in closer, got him squarely in my sight and let go again. This time the bullets had effect. Then I realized that there was something red coming out the back of the cockpit. It took what seemed like a long time to realize the "something red" was the rear gunner firing tracer bullets at me!

Roberts closed on the lead plane and opened fire, hitting an engine that caught fire before the 110 fell off and headed down to crash and explode. "The plane I shot down hit the ground and crash landed. The two crewmen jumped out and it was a funny sight to see them running on the ground as it was flat desert and there was no place to hide. Roberts made a run, giving them a few squirts, not actually trying to hit them, just scaring hell out of them."

The two P-38s turned away and headed back to Youks. "We had made our first contact with the enemy. Roberts and I were the first in the outfit to get an enemy plane."

On November 30, the 1st Fighter Group's 27th Fighter Squadron flew a mission to Bizerte, escorting B-17s of the 97th Bomb Group. It was the group's first combat mission, flown by 16 27th Squadron P-38Fs. "A" Flight commander was 22-year-old Captain Joe Owens; his element leader was First Lieutenant Harold "Mendy" Mendenhall. The two had been in flight class 41-D and had flown together since June 1941. Mendenhall was considered the best aerobatic pilot in the squadron. Owens' wingman was Second Lieutenant Marcus "Junior" Linn, 19, a former "Yank in the RAF" who had joined the 27th in England just before the group moved to North Africa. Mendenhall's wingman was 21-year-old Second Lieutenant Henry "Smitty" Smith, who had joined the squadron when they were based at Mines Field in Los Angeles the previous April; "Smitty" was an avid poker player, known for trying to run horrendous bluffs on his game partners. "A" flight was assigned as top cover for the mission.

Owens recalled that the weather deteriorated as they approached Bizerte, with the cloud deck below the formation solid after they passed

Algiers. "Fortunately, as we came over the target, there was a hole in the clouds through which the bombers could visually bomb."

The bombers made their drop without opposition from ground fire or airplane and turned to head for him.

Owens recalled:

> The other P-38 flights were close to the bombers as the entire formation passed below us. We were making a wide right turn to clear the area behind the withdrawal. At that moment, I saw a single-engine fighter climb up through the hole in the clouds. I started down after it by making a steep spiral dive. I had the presence of mind to check and make sure the guns were hot and all the switches were on.
>
> We started our dive at about 26,000 feet and had to lose about 9,000 feet. As the speed built up, the plane became nose-heavy and the controls started getting squirrelly as it approached the edge of compressibility. As I neared the enemy plane, I identified it as an Me-109. I was closing much too fast to make a good attack, and I was pulling a lot of Gs as I started to fire from 150 yards at an angle of around 60 degrees above and behind him. I fired a short burst, and, wonder of wonders, I managed to hit him in the left wing and the aft part of the fuselage. The pilot did a half-roll to the left and popped down into the clouds. I pulled up into a steep climbing turn to the left and headed west to rejoin the formation.

Owens could only find Mendenhall. When he asked over the radio where the rest were, Junior made an unintelligible reply, then Smitty reported he and Junior were together, but Junior had an oil-pressure gauge that was bothering him. They were just above the cloud deck, heading for home.

> At that moment, I saw another Me-109 about a quarter of a mile to our left and slightly below us. He was climbing on a southwesterly heading that would put him in position for an attack on our bombers. I put the balls to the wall, and Mendy and I started after him. I managed to get directly behind and slightly below the Me-109 as we closed to a range of 100 yards. My pulse rate matched my airspeed as we passed through 25,000 feet at 220 miles

per hour indicated. I was getting extremely nervous, apprehensive, and just plain scared as I recalled the words of an RAF pilot who had told us, "The most dangerous time, chaps, is when you've got your pipper on the bloke."

I closed to about 200 feet when the 109 banked slightly to the right. I thought, Oh, oh. This is it. You had better do what you are going to and right now! I fired a short burst. When I saw that I had him boresighted, I clamped down on the gun button until there was an explosion in the Me-109's fuselage and the tail blew off. It started tumbling, and a great deal of smoke was coming from the midsection. Mendy hollered, "You got him! You got him!" I replied, "Yeah, I got him!" Then I uttered the immortal words used by fighter pilots, "Let's get the hell out of here!"

Owens and Mendenhall found the two wingmen flying just above the clouds.

For some reason, Junior had feathered an engine. We flew cover above them and we headed for home.

The rest of the squadron returned to base about thirty-five minutes ahead of us. They were not aware of what had happened, since in all of our radio talk there had been no mention of enemy aircraft, no talk of "bogies" or "bandits." No one associated Mendy's "You got him!" with enemy activity. Junior landed first. Then, after Mendy and Smitty landed, I proceeded to give the base a buzz job, followed by a victory roll.

Owens taxied to his parking spot on the desert strip and shut down while his crew chief and other ground crewmen pointed excitedly at the nose of the Lightning, with its gunfire stains. "I could hardly wait to tell the world of my astounding feat. I was doing my best 'There I Was' story when the staff car arrived." A grim-looking group CO, Lieutenant Colonel Ralph Garman, accompanied by a downright angry-looking squadron CO, Major Willie Weltman, got out and headed toward Owens' fighter. "I thought, maybe I shouldn't have done the slow roll, as my mind flashed back to Bangor, Maine, where Weltman had placed me under house arrest awaiting a court martial for blowing over a sailboat as I was doing a low-level navigation mission. I had escaped the hangman at Bangor because a senior officer interceded in my behalf, but now I was thinking that I was in real trouble."

The 1st Fighter Group had a policy against low flying and other dumb stunts that had been implemented shortly after they had arrived in England. Weltman's first words were, "You dumb SOB! What the hell are you trying to do?" Owens recalled, "Colonel Garman was a bit more restrained, but he wasn't smiling as he spoke. 'Joe,' he said, 'you know the policy. What's the idea?' I was searching for some way to extricate myself when, luckily, I remembered Garman's closing remarks in the speech he had made when we first arrived in England. So I said, 'Why, Colonel, sir, don't you remember? You told us the rule didn't apply if we shot somebody down.'"

Colonel Garman was suddenly all smiles and demanded to hear Owens' account. "So I repeated my 'There I Was' story. Weltman also cooled off and offered his congratulations. I was off the hook. In the end, I was officially credited with the second Me-109 destroyed and the first Me-109 damaged. For the moment, I was the top-scoring pilot in the 1st Fighter Group."

Luftwaffe records confirmed that Owens did score a "probable" and a "victory." Unteroffizier Otto Reuss, of III./JG 53, made a test flight of a recently repaired Bf-109G from their base at Bizerte and was wounded when he was attacked by a P-38 while on a routine test flight over Bizerte. Leutnant Horst Wunderlich, of II./JG 51, failed to return to Bizerte after taking off to intercept B-17s approaching the field.

Owens recalled that, after this fight, he was initially of the opinion that air combat was easier than he had been told. However:

> It never happened to me like that again. The few additional victories that I was able to gain came as a result of reacting rather than acting. In a matter of weeks, our fighters were to cede the initiative to the Luftwaffe because we became committed to the role of close bomber escort. In fact, we never seemed to get close enough to suit the bomber crews. At times, we put a flight in line-abreast formation directly beneath the lead box of bombers. The idea was to compensate for the lack of firepower that an early-model B-17 could project forward. It became our job to deter the enemy fighters from making sustained head-on attacks against

the bombers. We experimented with new formations and tactics almost daily in an effort to increase our effectiveness as escorts.

We eventually settled on a loose, finger-four formation for the individual flights, with the entire squadron right down on top of the bomber formation. Within the flight, if it was operating alone, the two elements would fly abreast and space themselves widely enough apart to allow either element to turn inside and protect the other. The key word was "protect" – we were on the defensive.

The 1st Group's strength quickly fell due to the incorrect strategy of close escort, which put the Lightnings at an initial disadvantage when enemy fighters attacked a formation, leading to German pilots scoring easy victories over P-38s that were unable to throttle up to full power quickly enough, to the point that on December 15, 1942, two P-38s wound up escorting 18 B-17s on a mission to Tunis. The two pilots shot down four Me-109s and two Fw-190s on that particular mission, but no claims were made due to lack of corroboration since the group rules precluded claiming pilots from confirming each other's victories.

Newell Roberts and Jack Ilfrey got a chance to increase their scores on December 2, when Roberts led a flight to strafe Faid airdrome. Roberts recalled:

On December 1, our group commander called me back to his headquarters, which was still at Nouvion, and asked me if I would volunteer for a mission. Colonel Garman was a very fair individual and would oftentimes ask for a volunteer for a hazardous mission. He never at any point in time ordered any of his men to do anything; he always asked them to do it.

The mission, due to be flown on December 2, was to be an armed reconnaissance to the Tunisian coast by four P-38s from our squadron. On the way out, we were to strafe enemy positions at Faid Pass, which was ninety miles from Youks-les-Bains. Faid Pass was a target because, during that period, German tanks, troops, and supplies were all passing through it on their way to fight our troops elsewhere in Tunisia. The Germans had built pillboxes there and emplaced artillery to protect the pass.

After strafing the German positions at Faid Pass, my flight was to continue on to the Tunisian port of Sfax, 60 miles beyond the pass. We were to reconnoiter the harbor and the town and then turn southwest another 80 miles to the Tunisian port of Gabes. As at Sfax, we were to reconnoiter the area and then turn inland for the 155-mile return leg to Youks-les-Bains. As far as everyone was concerned, this appeared to be a suicide mission, but when Colonel Garman had finished explaining it to me, I accepted.

I asked three other pilots to accompany me, and they all accepted. Flying in the number three slot as element leader would be Jack Ilfrey, who had been my wingman and had shared in my first combat victory on November 29. My wingman would be 2nd Lieutenant Robert Lovell, and Ilfrey's wingman would be 1st Lieutenant Richard McWherter. Naturally, when I went into combat, I wanted to choose the most competent combat pilots that we had. I chose McWherter and Lovell to fly with Ilfrey and myself on that particular day because they were among the top-notch combat pilots in the squadron.

After attacking Faid, the four P-38s got involved with several Bf-109s over the Gabes airfield. Roberts later reported:

> We shot up three gun posts at Faid from 0720 to 0735 hours and then headed for Sfax. We flew along the coast at between zero feet to 500 feet. It took us only ten minutes to cover the 60 miles at our flying speed of 360 miles per hour. The weather at that time was excellent – blue skies, no rain, and unlimited visibility. We continuously scanned the beautiful sky for enemy aircraft, but we saw nothing. I could see Sfax some ten to fifteen miles before we reached the coast. The town looked peaceful and quiet, but there was a huge battleship in the harbor, about a half-mile offshore in the beautiful blue waters of the Gulf of Gabes.
>
> I flew down along Sfax's wide main street with my wingman, Lieutenant Lovell, following in trail. The street ran north to south, parallel to the beach. I am sure we were flying all of three feet off the stone-paved street, which fortunately had no obstructions along its entire length. The props were just barely missing the ground. We had plenty of room on each side of our wingtips since the street was about half again as wide as a P-38. The buildings were for the most part white. They were small and mostly two or three stories high. As I glanced to the right and left, I saw that the fronts of the buildings

facing the main street had been removed. The buildings looked just like aircraft hangars. In fact, much to my amazement, I saw that Me-109 fighters and other German military airplanes were parked inside buildings on both sides of the street. All any of the aircraft had to do was taxi out into the street and take off. There was absolutely nobody shooting at us. Our arrival had come as a complete surprise to the Germans.

Ilfrey later recalled that they stopped strafing at 0735 hours, just before the American ground troops attacked.

Our strafing had silenced the German guns, permitting the troops below to encircle the enemy.

After that, we turned south-southwest to parallel the coastline of the Gulf of Gabes. Our next objective was the port of Gabes, some 80 miles from Sfax. We flew as low to the ground as we possibly could, usually no higher than treetop level. About 15 minutes later, as we were approaching Gabes from the northwest side of a forest, I saw four Me-109s taking off from an airdrome to our southeast. The airdrome itself was about a half mile south of the town.

The lead Me-109 was at treetop level, about 50 feet in the air. I opened the throttles of both my engines past the red stop, thus activating the water injection and giving myself a considerable temporary boost in power and speed. I would have no problem catching up with the 109s because they were still taking off and thus going quite slowly. By the time I turned in to line up on the lead Me-109, he was only about 100 feet in the air. He did not turn to meet me or even try to evade; he simply continued his takeoff to the northeast. I doubt if he knew I was there. I banked to the left of the lead Me-109 and came around right on his tail. The whole body of the airplane appeared in my gunsight. I was not more than 50 yards away and gaining on him. My aiming point was dead on the entire stern section of the Me-109. He was a sitting duck and I was right on him. I was so close to him when I opened fire that, when his airplane exploded in front of me, pieces of the wings and other parts hit my plane.

I followed through on my sharp turn to the left and came directly up on the tail of another Me-109. In the brief portion of a second, this Me-109 pilot tried to evade, but there was no escape. Again, I was not more than 50 yards – or maybe only 50 feet – from him when I fired. I was something like 20–50 feet away when he also blew up in midair. This airplane just disintegrated. The battle was on. After I shot down two of the Me-109s, two of the others tried to attack me head-on. As I took snap shots at these and at other Me-109s that were pulling around in front of me, I noticed that one Me-109 had climbed up to about 1,000 to 2,000 feet above us and was just circling.

Before I could go up to get him, however, the flak batteries at the airdrome opened fire. They cut loose with everything they had, firing at all of us, including the Me-109s. The bursting flak filled the air with a huge cloud of smoke, so extreme that it became necessary for me to fly on instruments when going through it, which I did two or three times while looking for more enemy airplanes. I hit the third one, giving it a long burst that caused it to blow up in the air. I hit another Me-109 at about 200 feet and saw thick black smoke pouring from it. Lieutenant McWherter saw this plane crash to the ground.

Ilfrey remembered:

Roberts yelled over the radio "There's four of them taking off! I'll take the first one!" Bill Lovell yelled he was taking the second one and I took the third while McWherter went for the fourth. The Messerschmitt I was shooting at had barely left the ground. He had just got his wheels up and banked over, and he seemed to stay in the bank as I shot at him. Finally, his wingtip hit the ground and he cartwheeled into a flaming explosion.

At that moment Ilfrey heard someone call that six others had taken off. "I turned around sharply and there was another ME spitting lead. I cut loose and then we whizzed by each other. He'd made a direct hit on the oil line in my right engine and it didn't take but a few seconds for the engine to freeze up." Ilfrey turned away and hoped he could make it the 60 miles back to base. "The P-38 on one engine is no match for a 109 for combat or speed. I could make a maximum 275 miles an hour and I was right down on the ground ducking in and out of the sand dunes."

Two Bf-109s chased him, taking turns shooting at the P-38. Ilfrey called for help. "Bill Lovell called he was close behind and Roberts said he saw me and was coming."

Roberts recalled:

Jack flew out of the cloud of bursting flak and headed in the direction of Youks with only one engine running. He'd been hit in the right engine, and the propeller was feathered, but he had full power on the left engine. I went down to escort him home, flying approximately three feet off his right wingtip and matching his speed of about 275 miles per hour. We were just three to four feet off the ground, with the propellers not quite hitting the vegetation.

To us, flying low was not a bad risk. In fact, it was the only maneuver in a case like this. Our being so low made it difficult for an enemy fighter to come down and shoot at us because the attacker would be in danger of running his own nose into the ground while he was trying to get his sights on one of us. Flying low for Jack Ilfrey and myself had never been a problem. We could strafe targets accurately with our props clicking over only a few feet off the ground. At that point in time, Jack Ilfrey was one of the Army Air Forces's best combat pilots.

I was keeping my eye on the Me-109 that I had spotted circling alone above the airdrome. As Jack and I began our race toward home, I glanced toward the German again, just in time to see him execute a half roll. He pulled his nose through, and, when he rolled out, he was right on Jack's tail. I wanted to get a deflection shot at the Me-109, which was flying some ten to twenty feet to my left. From my position off Jack's right wing, I eased off my throttle and turned slightly to my left. I ended up about twenty feet in back of the Me-109. I wanted to shoot the pilot. I had the Me-109's nose in my sight, but when I pressed the firing solenoid nothing happened. I was out of ammunition! I was helpless. I could see the German's bullets going into Jack's airplane, peeling the metal up as they penetrated. I could also see the German sitting in his Me-109. He looked around at me and laughed! I was so close that I could see his eyes were blue, he had blondish hair, and he had a light complexion.

You do things in combat on the spur of the moment, without thinking. You act instinctively. You don't wait, or concentrate, or try and make up your mind. It is instilled in a combat pilot to act automatically to save a comrade's life. In combat, you have a devotion to comradeship that very few people ever achieve at any other time in their lives. What I did was start to ram the German airplane with my left propeller. When the German saw me coming, he immediately turned to the left. As he did, his tail hit my left wingtip. The collision demolished the Me-109's tail assembly, the pilot lost control, and the Me-109 dived into the ground. I looked around, but there were no more Me-109s in the air. As Jack and I continued on to Youks-les-Bains, I flew close formation with him.

Ilfrey recalled, "When I was able to lift myself out of the cockpit, I realized I was scared, shaking and weak." Ground crewmen counted 268 bullet holes in the P-38. "A cannon shell had gone through my radio and lodged in the armor behind my seat. Another cannon shell hit a blade of my propeller on the left engine, and another shell had hit the hydraulic reservoir under my seat, which left me ankle deep in fluid. When I learned all of this, I was good and scared."

Roberts later wrote:

It is my belief that twelve Me-109s were destroyed in the air on that particular mission, but only seven were officially credited as destroyed. By my count, however, nine Me-109s were shot down in air combat, one was destroyed when I cut off its tail, and the remaining two were shot down by the enemy flak batteries. Officially, I was given credit for two Me-109s, Jack Ilfrey was given credit for two, Lovell was given credit for one destroyed and one damaged, and McWherter was given credit for two. Ilfrey and Lovell each also received unofficial credit for one Me-109 destroyed on the ground.

Ilfrey's P-38 never flew again. He later wrote in his memoir *Happy Jack's Go-Buggy*, "It's funny how during the actual dogfighting and shooting you don't get really scared. You seem to only be fighting for your life. It's before the combat takes place, the suspense, the waiting and wondering where the enemy is that gets you keyed up. The actual combat doesn't last more than a few seconds, even though it does seem like a lifetime."

Unteroffizier Forster of 5./JG 53 claimed to have shot down a P-38 at an altitude of about 400 feet 25 miles west of Gabes at around the time of this action; he thought he had downed Ilfrey.

In mid-December, the 1st Group moved from Youks-les-Bains to Biskra, a flat field of hard sand with better drainage than Youks, allowing the P-38s to operate without getting bogged down on the field when it did rain, which was much less frequent than at Youks. Before the war, Biskra had been a winter resort for Europeans and was located on the southern side of the mountains on the edge of the Sahara Desert. Ilfrey remembered that while the base was hot and dusty during the day, the nights were cold, with as much as a 60–70-degree temperature swing between maximum daylight temperature and the minimum nighttime reading. The group's pilots were very happy when the "Transatlantique" hotel, which had been the primary resort hotel before the war, was taken over and turned into aircrew quarters. Ilfrey was now flying P-38F 41-7587, which carried the name "Texas Terror" on the left boom in honor of his home state, and "The Mad Dash" on the right, memorializing both his escape from Portugal and outrunning the German fighters on December 2. "Each day, we escorted the heavy bombers to bomb targets in Tunis, Bizerte, Cagliari and Sardinia. We fought the Germans on just about every mission. We were lucky they couldn't put a lot of fighters up because we didn't have very many either."

The third mission flown from Biskra on December 20 stood out in Ilfrey's memory. "While we were escorting the bombers near the target, I spotted a lone B-17 far below us that had dropped out of formation and was trying to head for home. Three or four Focke-wulfs were making passes at him, doing their best to knock him down." Ilfrey called in the enemy, and the mission leader told him to try to help the B-17. Ilfrey recalled:

> Having the advantage of 8–10,000 feet on the Germans, we were able to dive on them and I told the flight to each pick out one each. I caught the one I picked out unaware and made a good hit on him and he burst into flame. I saw my wingman get one and then I saw

the other two Germans turn in on him, shooting. They disappeared in a cloud bank and I never saw him again.

Bob Neale yelled there were two coming in on me. I evaded the attack and in the ensuing dogfight our P-38s outperformed the two Focke-Wulfs and we were each able to confirm the other's victory. We then got the hell out of there because there were many more Germans than we had anticipated. We saw two P-38s below and dived to join them; they turned out to be McWherter and Murdock, and it appeared we were in for another dogfight even though we were low on gas and ammo.

The four had been flying together since they first joined the group back in the States. Ilfrey described the flight: "We knew we could depend on each other. Ten Focke-Wulfs dove on the Lightnings. We were able to weave in front of each other, and after several attacks we were able to outdistance them. It would have been futile to have remained since they had everything on us — altitude, speed and numbers."

On arrival back at base Ilfrey learned the bombers and fighters had claimed 20 victories. "For several weeks thereafter we were not bothered with the enemy, just annoyed." However, the Luftwaffe discovered where the Lightnings were based. "The enemy started coming over in groups of five or six at night. One night about 30-plus Ju 88s came over and really beat up our field. One 500-pounder hit right in the middle of our tent area, knocking down most of the tents and scattering the squadron kitchen. Shrapnel from the bombs literally threw beans all over the place." The next morning, before putting their tents back up, everyone dug themselves "a foxhole to end all foxholes."

On December 26, 1942, Ilfrey led a flight on an escort mission to Bizerte. The target was protected by the experienced *Kanal Jagdfliegern* of II./JG 2 "Richthofen," the most-experienced Luftwaffe fighter group other than JG 26 after over two years of front-line combat over the English Channel. The *Gruppe*'s new Fw-190A-4s they had just re-equipped with were led during this mission by 4.Staffel's Leutnant Kurt Bühligen, a 40-victory *Experte* already credited with two P-38s since the *Gruppe* had arrived in North Africa on November 19.

Over the target, Ilfrey again spotted a damaged B-17 under attack by German fighters. He led his four down on the enemy and quickly shot down one Fw-190. With that, Jack Ilfrey had a score of five and a half under the Twelfth Air Force's shared victory scoring system and was the first P-38 ace in North Africa. Shortly after, the command changed the scoring system to get rid of shared victories, and Ilfrey had six. The 14th's Virgil Smith, who had a score of 3.85 under the old system, became an ace with five. The eight P-38 escorts lost five of their number in combat with the Würger pilots, including two claimed by Bühligen.

On December 28 Smith claimed a Bf-109 and was tied with Ilfrey. That day, General Doolittle came to Youks-les-Bains to visit the units there. Coincidentally, the Luftwaffe managed to pay their respects to the general with a bombing raid that left several Lightnings damaged, for no losses for the Germans.

Smith's position only lasted 48 hours; on December 30, Smith was one of eight 14th Group pilots who escorted the A-20C Havoc light bombers of the 15th Bomb Squadron on a mission to Gabes airdrome. There, the Lightnings were jumped by Bf-109s of JG 53. While one enemy fighter was claimed by Captain Wade Walles, Smith and his wingman Second Lieutenant Richard Carroll got in another fight with the 109s and became separated from the rest of the group. Carroll was shot down in the wild fight, while Smith's P-38 was badly damaged before he could break off and head for American lines. Just as he crossed the front lines, the P-38's "good" engine began to falter, and he set up to land wheels down in an open area. Unfortunately, he hit an unseen fence just before touchdown and was killed when the Lightning flipped over.

It is possible Smith was the 35th victim of 85-victory *Experte* Oberfeldwebel Herbert Rollwage of 5./JG 53, who had claimed his first P-38 victory 19 miles northwest of Gabes at approximately the time Smith was lost. Ilfrey was now the leading P-38 ace of the entire USAAF. Famed war correspondent Ernie Pyle, who was visiting with the group at the time, wrote about Ilfrey as the leading ace in North Africa; the story was later included in his book, *Here Is Your War*. For this achievement, Ilfrey was awarded the Distinguished Flying Cross.

Reinforcements for the P-38 groups in North Africa arrived just before Christmas in the form of the 82nd Fighter Group. Of all the groups that flew to North Africa from England, the transfer flight of the 82nd was the most hair raising.

The first formation of 82nd Group Lightnings began taking off from RAF St Eval in Cornwall at 0400 hours on December 23, 1942. Like the 1st and 14th Groups, pilots were briefed to fly no higher than 200 feet above the Atlantic to avoid radar detection and interception by the enemy. As was done previously, each of the four formations were led by a B-26 Marauder that provided navigational guidance. As with the other groups, the ground support personnel were sent to North Africa by ship, which meant the pilots would be on their own for at least a week after their arrival in North Africa. The pilots stuffed as much as they could carry into every available space in the P-38s. Many pilots reduced the .50-caliber ammunition they carried to make space in the nose.

The flight path was far out in the Bay of Biscay, so the possibility of interception by the enemy was not seriously considered. But as the leading formation of the 95th Fighter Squadron reached a point halfway to the Spanish peninsula, four Ju-88C fighters of 14./KG 40 popped out of the clouds, taking the Lightnings by surprise and shooting down an A-20C Havoc that was "tagging along." The "Tail-end Charlie" P-38 was shot down and the pilot killed when his fighter struck the ocean. Newly promoted Major Bob Kirtley later described what happened:

> I was sipping tomato juice from a canteen and eating crackers. I had my radio volume high on "D" Channel and hadn't heard a sound for two hours. The call "A-20 on fire!" woke me up. I dropped my crackers and spilled my tomato juice in a mad scramble to charge my guns. I had 50 rounds per 0.50-cal, no 20mm. I firewalled the throttle until detonation set in as I broke toward the A-20 with my flight. By this time both the Havoc and the P-38 were in the water, and all but one of the Ju 88s had re-entered the cloud cover.

The pilot of the remaining German fighter had shot down the Lightning. When Kirtley's flight turned toward him, he pulled up into the overcast. Kirtley followed. "As I came out of the overcast I was dead astern of the Ju-88 and closing fast. At 100 yards I fired one burst – 50 rounds per gun. His left engine exploded, pieces came off and he leveled out right on top of the overcast. I throttled back and flew formation with the aircraft for a minute or so, having exhausted my ammo. He re-entered the overcast, straight and level, and I followed him down." They came out of the clouds and the Ju-88 continued down till it hit the sea. Kirtley had just scored the 82nd's first combat victory and they were not yet in North Africa. Minutes later, his element leader spotted another of the Ju-88s and shot it down to give the group their second victory.

The group had originally planned to fly direct to Tafaroui, but with the poor weather over the Bay of Biscay, the P-38s all stopped at Gibraltar before heading on. The first Lightnings arrived at Tafaroui on December 26, and all were there by December 28. The group leaders found they had to turn over half of their airplanes to the 1st and 14th Groups to replace combat losses. On New Year's Day 1943, the group transferred to Telergma, another Algerian airfield closer to the front that was originally a Foreign Legion outpost, which pilots later remembered as being "worse than Tafaroui, if that was possible." The remaining P-38s were pooled, with pilots flying them as assigned on missions, until the 82nd received replacements from the 78th Group's P-38s when they were flown to North Africa in February.

The 52nd Fighter Group also saw action in the waning days of 1942. On Christmas Day, Lieutenant Jack de Rush Ludlow and Lieutenant Luis Zendegui were patrolling over Bône harbor when they were vectored onto a formation of five enemy aircraft five miles north of Cap De Fer and 40 miles from the harbor. They spotted two Regia Aeronautica Macchi C.202 fighters and attacked them. Ludlow reported, "We were above them and I was using deflection at a range of 100 yards." Ludlow was turning so tight and using such deflection that he couldn't see the target as he fired. "I turned over and looked down and saw the enemy aircraft going straight down." It disappeared into cloud but an Arab later reported it crashed into the sea. Lieutenant Zendegui shot down the second C.202. The day after Christmas, 2nd Squadron and RAF 242 Squadron escorted Hurricane fighter-bombers from 225 Squadron on a strafing mission to Medjez el Bab, where one 242 Squadron Spitfire was lost when hit in the engine by ground fire. When they returned to Bône, they found the airfield under attack by Fw-190s and Bf-109s. Wading into the enemy attackers, they damaged two and chased the others away.

The squadron's last victories of 1942 were scored on December 29, when it was scrambled to intercept inbound enemy aircraft that it found 25 miles northeast of the airfield. A brief engagement followed, in which Lieutenant Edwin N. Broughton destroyed one Bf-109 and damaged another, while Captain Harold R. Warren also damaged a 109.

The 33rd Group had been split up on December 7. The 60th Squadron stayed at Youks-les-Bains, while the 58th Squadron moved to the new field at Thélepte, and the 59th remained at Maison Blanche. The ground crews were transported to the distant field by C-47s. Truck convoys to keep the group resupplied would face a long overland journey, where they were subject to enemy air attack at any time. On arriving at Thélepte, 58th Squadron had to do almost everything at the base themselves. They maintained their planes, flew missions, and dug bunkers to protect them from German attacks. In the meantime, the 59th Squadron was ordered to hand over their airplanes to the French Air Force; the pilots of GC II/5 were now part of the Free French Air Force. Lieutenant Reed recalled in his diary that the Americans considered the French pilots "pretty damn good" as they transitioned from their old Curtiss Hawk 75s to the P-40 descendants. On December 18, the 59th Squadron received five reconditioned P-40s that Reed and the others discovered were the ones from the 17 that had crashed at Port Lyautey and gotten repaired. At the end of the month, 29 of the 34 pilots in the squadron flew to Thélepte in C-47s that were escorted by their five "retreads."

It didn't take long once the men of the 58th Squadron arrived at Thélepte for them to discover that life on the plateau was difficult, due to the weather and the enemy. The constant wind drove sand into every piece of machinery; ground crews were constantly cleaning the Merlin engines of the P-40s. There were no buildings and no one lived above ground. The new arrivals dug more holes in the surrounding plain of the plateau with their tents above to protect them from the ever-present rain; sleeping below ground level protected them from bomb explosions and subsequent shrapnel from the German air raids that were a feature of life at Thélepte any time the weather allowed the enemy to fly.

December 23 saw rain so bad throughout all of Algeria that Twelfth Air Force did not mount any operations. On Christmas Day, the 307th Squadron's Spitfires escorted C-47s to Biskra, Bône, Youks-les-Bains and Thélepte. By New Year's Eve, rain and mud had brought operations in Algeria and Tunisia to a crawl.

By the end of December, though Tunis and Bizerte were still under Axis control, Allied troops were now established in the Eastern Dorsale, the line of mountains facing the Tunisian plain; forces and supplies would be built up during the remainder of the rainy season for an offensive in the spring. Effort was spent on improving airfields while more air units arrived in the theater.

8

BOMBER BOYS

North Africa was the other theater besides the Southwest Pacific where the B-25 Mitchell saw widespread combat service with the USAAF.

The 57th Fighter Group was actually the second USAAF unit to arrive in the Middle East for service with the Western Desert Air Force. The first was the 12th Bomb Group (Medium), which was created in January 1941 with cadre personnel from the 17th Bomb Group – the first Group to equip with the new B-25 Mitchell in the summer of 1941 – and became the source for most of the crews who formed the Doolittle Raiders for the April 18, 1942 raid on Tokyo. The 12th re-equipped with the B-25 in February 1942 after operating for nearly a year with the obsolescent B-18 "Bolo." It was the first medium bomber group to be designated for service in the Middle East in April, as part of the USAAF commitment to send bombers to operate with the WDAF. The group received orders for transfer to the Middle East following the British defeat at the Battle of Gazala on June 21, and commenced deployment over the southern route on July 14. The 81st, 82nd, 83rd, and 434th Bomb Squadrons arrived in Egypt by August 12.

The 12th Bomb Group, along with the 57th Fighter Group, found themselves thrust into the ongoing battles in the Western Desert that had raged since earlier in the summer when the British Eighth Army had suffered defeat at the hands of Generalleutnant Erwin Rommel's Afrika Korps at Gazala, which followed the British loss of the surrounded port of Tobruk the day before. With British forces reeling, Rommel advanced into Egypt, threatening British control of the Suez Canal and the whole

"Regina IV," flown by 57th Fighter Group CO Major Frank H. Mears, was the first plane to take off from USS *Ranger* (CV-4) off the coast of Africa on July 19, 1942. The 57th was the first USAAF unit to enter combat in Europe, flying across Sub-Saharan Africa and up the Nile Valley to reinforce the British WDAF at El Alamein. (USAF Official)

A "Fighting-9" F4F-4 Wildcat prepares to take off from USS *Ranger* (CV-4) on Operation *Torch* D-Day, November 8, 1942. (USN Official)

Brigadier General Jimmy Doolittle, America's most famous aviator, was named commander of Twelfth Air Force following his return from China and the Doolittle Raid on Japan. His fame and acknowledged skill as a pilot kept morale high through the difficult early months of the campaign. (Corbis via Getty Images)

33rd Fighter Group P-40Fs take off from escort carrier USS *Chenango* (ACV-28) off the North African coast on Operation *Torch* D-Day, November 8, 1942. (USN Official)

SBD-4 Dauntless dive bombers and F4F-4 Wildcats of VF-9 and VF-41 on board USS *Ranger* (CV-4) during Operation *Torch*. (USN Official)

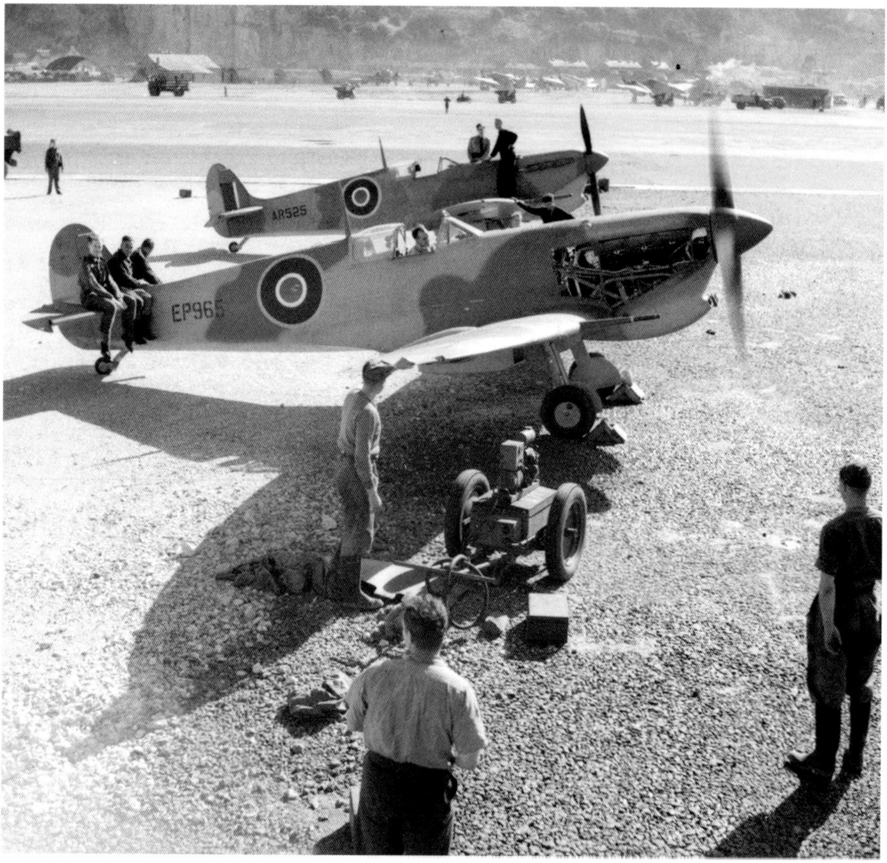

Over 100 Spitfire V fighters were assembled at Gibraltar for use by the 31st and 52nd Fighter Groups in Operation *Torch*. (© IWM CM 6699)

66th Fighter Squadron P-40F Warhawks take off on a fighter-bomber mission against the Afrika Korps from an advanced landing ground in the Western Desert in the weeks following Erwin Rommel's defeat at El Alamein. (USAF Official)

Following the change of allegiance of French forces in North Africa after the *Torch* invasion, fighter squadron GC II/5 of the Armée de l'Air was re-equipped with ex-USAAF P-40F Warhawks and took part in the Tunisian campaign, flying from Thélepte during the Battle of Kasserine Pass. (Library of Congress)

A pilot of the 31st Fighter Group's 309th Fighter Squadron stands in the cockpit of his Spitfire Vc, named "Steve," at Maison Blanche airfield in Algeria. (USAF Official)

A "Black Scorpions" P-40F loaded with a British 250lb bomb for a fighter-bomber strike. (USAF Official)

Captain Art Exon, commander of the 57th Fighter Group's 64th "Black Scorpions" Fighter Squadron until he was captured in Sicily, was one of the most popular of the group's "Wheels." (USAF Official)

All maintenance was done in the open on the advanced landing grounds in North Africa. The 57th Fighter Group's ground crewmen became so adept they could perform an engine change in 3–4 hours despite the conditions. (USAF Official)

Ground crewmen perform maintenance on a 12th Bomb Group B-25C at an advanced landing ground in Egypt. (USAF Official)

A 309th Squadron Spitfire Vb comes to grief standing on its nose after going off the dirt runway at the advanced landing ground at Thélepte in Tunisia. (USAF Official)

B-25C Mitchell medium bombers of the 12th Bomb Group over the Western Desert in January 1943. (USAF Official)

Douglas A-20B "Havoc" light bombers of the 47th Bomb Group fly at low level over the Tunisian desert in January 1943. (USAF Official)

A wrecked P-48G of the 82nd Fighter Group after a Luftwaffe attack on the group's airfield at Biskra in February 1943. P-38 losses during the initial months of *Torch* forced the USAAF to strip pilots and planes from the 78th Fighter Group in England to make up losses. (USAF Official)

A 33rd Fighter Group P-40F at the remote Thélepte advanced landing ground, only 20km from Kasserine Pass in Tunisia, in February 1943 shortly before Rommel's attack against the US Army's II Corps. (USAF Official)

P-38F Lightning "Spud" of the 1st Fighter Group's 96th Fighter Squadron with squadron pilots at Bône airfield in Tunisia, March 1943. (USAF Official)

Ground crew perform an engine change on a P-38G Lightning of the 82nd Fighter Group's 95th Fighter Squadron at an advanced landing ground in Tunisia in March 1943. (USAF Official)

A Ju-52/3m "Tante Ju" trimotor transport in flight over the Mediterranean en route from Sicily to Tunisia to bring supplies to the trapped Afrika Korps and their Italian allies in April 1942. Allied fighters intercepted the large Ju-52 formations and wreaked havoc with the vulnerable transports in battles such as the Palm Sunday Massacre, where the 57th Fighter Group claimed 25 Ju-52s shot down on April 18, 1943. (USAF Official)

Members of the 57th Fighter Group's 64th Fighter Squadron with a P-40K-5 Warhawk at their Tunisian airfield in April 1943. By this time, the Merlin-powered P-40Fs were war weary and out of production, resulting in re-equipment with Allison-powered P-40s. (Stocktrek Images, Inc./Alamy Stock Photo)

P-40Fs of the 64th "Black Scorpions" Fighter Squadron at an advanced airfield in Sicily in July 1943. (USAF Official)

P-40F-15-CU "Carole" of the 65th "Fighting Cocks" Squadron in Sicily, July 1943. (USAF Official)

A veteran P-38F of the 1st Fighter Group's 27th Fighter Squadron during the Sicilian campaign in July 1943. (USAF Official)

The Macchi C.202 Folgore (Lightning) of the 4° Stormo "Baracca." The C.202 was powered by a German DB 601 engine since the Italian aviation industry had failed to develop a reliable high-powered engine, and was the best Regia Aeronautica fighter during the North African and Sicilian campaigns. (USAF Official)

Lieutenant Colonel Benjamin O. Davis, graduate of the West Point class of 1934, was the first commander of the 99th Fighter Squadron, a unit manned by African American pilots trained in the Tuskegee Program, which entered combat during the Pantelleria campaign in June 1943. (USAF Official)

Curtiss P-40L Warhawks of the 99th Fighter Squadron taxi for takeoff at an airfield in Tunisia for a mission over Pantelleria in June 1943. (USAF Official)

An A-46 Mustang of the 27th Fighter Bomber Group at Maison Blanche airfield in Algeria, June 1943. (USAF Official)

An A-36 Mustang of the 86th Fighter Bomber Group over Mount Vesuvius near Naples during the Sicilian campaign, August 1943. The Mustang's long range allowed it to cover southern Italy, once it was based on Sicily at the end of July 1943. (USAF Official)

Middle East. There was real fear in the Allied leadership through the summer that if the Germans took Egypt there was nothing to stop their advance to meet the Japanese in India.

The 12th Bomb Group was the first Mitchell-equipped unit to see action in the MTO, initially flying both Inglewood-built B-25Cs and Kansas City-built B-25Ds. After an extremely long ferry flight from Florida by way of the southern route across the Atlantic and the African continent, with numerous refueling stops, the group arrived at its first base in Egypt (Deversoir) in August 1942.

After training with the South Africans, the 12th Bomb Group flew its first mission to bomb Mersa Matruh on the night of August 31–September 1, following up with more night attacks between September 1 and 4. Lacking flame dampers, the B-25s were easily targeted by German air defenses at night due to the brightness of their exhausts, so they were withdrawn from night operations after September 4 until the aircraft could be fitted with flame-damping exhausts.

Captain Douglas W. "Doug" Spawn, one of the first pilots assigned to the 82nd Bomb Squadron, remembered:

> I checked out as first pilot in the B-25 in January 1942 at McChord Field, where the group had 12–14 B-25s assigned to it. We flew these to Esler Field, in Louisiana, in February 1942 with no mishaps. At Esler our group was fully equipped with 64 B-25s, 16 per squadron. They were all painted Desert Pink, and with that, we knew our destination – Africa!
>
> In late July 1942 we left Esler and ended up in Deversoir, Egypt, in early August. Two of our squadrons were stationed some 15 miles north of us in Ismailia. Every airplane in our group arrived safely in Egypt, a record that I doubt many other groups could claim. We flew overloaded airplanes through tropical weather fronts and landed on short runways, sometimes in severe weather.
>
> In combat, the B-25 proved its worth many, many times over. We flew through desert dust storms and even mountain snowstorms in northern Algeria. The airplane was also capable of withstanding severe punishment from enemy flak bursts and fighter gunfire. In most cases the B-25s were able to return to home base. On one mission in particular my airplane, Battle Number 33, received more than 100 flak holes, both in the fuselage and wings. It was patched

up, and two days later it was in the air again dropping bombs on the enemy.

The first problem I encountered operating in combat conditions was that desert sand and dust clogged up the carburetor air filters. The sand and dust took its toll on the engines, especially if we removed the air filters for high altitude operations.

The second problem was caused by the B-25's original engine exhaust pipes. Each engine had only one large diameter stack, which was good for performance but awful when flying on a clear night. Flak gunners and fighter pilots could clearly see the exhaust gases at 8,000 to 10,000ft, which were our normal operating altitudes. We complained to higher authority about this deadly vulnerability. After we lost four of ten B-25s on the night of September 14, 1942, including the aircraft flown by Colonel Charles G. Goodrich, our group commander, we were ordered to fly no more night missions until the exhaust pipe problem was solved. North American Aviation engineers came up with the idea of "finger-type" exhaust stacks, one for each of the 14 cylinders. Then we resumed nighttime operations.

All in all, I feel that there was no purer combat plane than the B-25 Mitchell. It operated in all theaters – even over heavily defended enemy positions – and returned its crew home with a very low accident rate that was second to none during World War II.

Most of the tactics used by the other B-25 groups in the MTO were pioneered by the 12th Bomb Group.

At first, the 12th Group's B-25s flew night missions almost exclusively. Between 24 and 48 aircraft were assigned. There was no formation flying, with the aircraft taking off individually at five-minute intervals, with each on its own. The mission was flown to within 50 miles of the target under 1,000 feet, and never over 3,000 feet, to stay below enemy radar as long as possible. The aircraft climbed to 8,000–9,000 feet before making the approach. The B-25s used RAF 250lb and 300lb general-purpose (GP) bombs, with some fitted with nose-rods to explode above the ground and increase the blast area. RAF Albacores and Wellingtons went in first to drop flares over the target. The usual procedure was for the B-25s to swing out over the Nile Delta, then fly over the Mediterranean, before turning in to the target from the sea.

Target times were prearranged for each B-25, with each pilot briefed to release the bombs on the target within a specific time frame; individual aircraft could make as many as four runs over the target, with the exact number of runs prearranged.

After the initial run, the B-25 flew away from the target on a certain heading, for a certain length of time, then doubled back and hit the target again within another time bracket. Between the first and second runs, another B-25 made its first run and flew away from the target on another course. After the first bomber completed its second attack, at about the time the second was turning for its second pass, a third B-25 initiated its first attack. After it completed its initial run, the second followed with its second pass. This attack plan, which could involve as many as 48 bombers over the same target making multiple individual passes, required strict adherence to split-second timing.

Because the antiaircraft (AA) artillery fire varied from night to night and target to target, pilots were governed by the flak conditions encountered, to use their own judgement on the altitudes to fly over defended areas. This was why the system of exact target times and definite compass headings was adopted. Most enemy night opposition was AA; very few night fighters were encountered. Enemy AA was accurate and intense at important targets such as Mersa Matruh, El Daba, and Tobruk. The searchlights and AA were coordinated and controlled by radio. The basic evasive tactics against AA and searchlights were gradual turns right and left and gradual climbing and diving maneuvers.

Following the breakthrough at El Alamein, when it became possible to examine the landing fields and dispersal areas bombed by B-25s, there were few undamaged aircraft shelters, and many burned-out aircraft were discovered in wrecked shelters. B-25s and other aircraft destroyed several hundred enemy aircraft on the ground while providing air support for the El Alamein breakthrough.

Following the breakthrough, 12th Group's B-25s switched over from night to day bombing. On daylight missions the B-25s operated in formations of three six-ship boxes of two elements of three, flying in tight, shallow V-formation, maintaining position 15–25 feet apart. The rear element flew 25–50 feet above or below the lead element to stay out of the propeller-wash. Each flight maintained position not more than 50 yards apart. The lead flight was lowest, with the other two above the leader. Whether the left or right flight was highest was determined by the direction the formation would turn away from the target, with the flight making the greatest turn positioned highest.

The B-25s flew their initial daylight missions with formations of RAF Douglas A-20 Havoc and Martin A-30 Baltimore bombers in the lead flight. By late October, the B-25 pilots had perfected formation flying; during the advance across Cyrenaica and Libya, they operated in 18-bomber formations.

The type of attack most frequently used was pattern bombing, since the targets were mainly airfields, dispersal areas, or troop concentrations, which did not present an individual target needing precision bombing. The pattern of destruction was always worked out in advance with geometric precision. Approach to the target was made at low level, climbing gradually to the initial point between 6,500–8,500 feet, depending on the weather. Immediately prior to approach, the formation leader ordered the formation to space itself according to a prearranged plan based on the target's size and nature. The point was for the bombs to hit not more than 50 feet apart. Following aircraft "bombed on the leader," toggling their bombs when the lead bombardier dropped his. Setting the pattern according to the target, the B-25s hit troops, tanks, and trucks that otherwise would have escaped. Rommel's columns were well protected by mobile light and heavy AA; the 15. and 21. Panzerdivisions were especially feared.

During the pursuit of the German forces across Libya, the B-25s received protective cover from the 57th Group's P-40s. The 82nd Bomb Squadron's Captain Spawn recalled:

> The enemy fighters that were encountered were of the best the Axis had at the time. These included Me-109s, Fw-190s and Italian Macchi 202s; the Me 109s were the most prevalent. The most typical initial fighter attack was frontal – from above and out of the sun. Many missions were flown in the late afternoon when they were forced to fly westward into the sun. Enemy aircraft often dived out of the sun in elements of three from 12 o'clock, fanning out and making individual attacks from the 12 o'clock, 2 o'clock and 10 o'clock positions. Usually, then, the number one aircraft pulls up a little while the number two aircraft swings out to the left, does a wingover, and makes a pass at the number two aircraft in the lead element of B-25s from 2 o'clock.

The number three enemy aircraft dives under the formation and away after making its pass. Just as the number three enemy fighter begins its pass from the side at 2 o'clock, the number one enemy aircraft makes a direct diving pass at the lead B-25. The number one enemy fighter zooms over the formation, away and up again after another pass when it's out of range. In the meantime, the number three enemy fighter, acting simultaneously with enemy fighter number two, has crossed over to the right and above number two going the other way, and has made the same type of attack as number two, but from 10 o'clock and on B-25 number three. Enemy fighter number three also dives away under the bomber formation.

During a precision bombing mission, the tactics were the same as for pattern bombing, except each bomber made an individual run over the target, returning to the formation immediately after the attack. Precision targets included communication centers, fuel dumps, coastal defense gun emplacements at Pantelleria, and enemy naval vessels.

Perhaps the most outstanding example of precision bombing by the B-25 in the MTO was the destruction of Rommel's main El Alamein communications center, which was first located in an underground position just behind the German lines, early in the morning before dawn on October 24 by an RAF Wellington equipped with a magnetic ring-link detection system. The B-25s attacked at dawn in three formations of six, at 15-minute intervals. They scored four or five direct hits on the 150 × 150 foot target; all radio traffic immediately ceased. After the Eighth Army had broken the German line, examination of the communications center showed it had been completely destroyed. This was very important to the Allied effort, since it denied Rommel his quickest means of communicating with his units just at the time he needed to most.

Three other B-25-equipped groups – the 310th, 321st, and 340th Bomb Groups – followed the 12th Bomb Group and participated in the North African campaign with the Twelfth Air Force.

All B-25 groups received their training as a unit at Columbia Army Airfield, South Carolina. The B-25 Operational Training Unit was commanded by Colonel Robert D. Knapp, who first became involved in aviation when he met the Wright brothers during their stay with his family in Alabama for several weeks in 1910. Commissioned a second lieutenant in the US Army Air Service in March 1918 as a bomber pilot, he held US Pilot License Number 187 and had been an Army aviator longer than most of the young aircrews he trained had been alive. He served with future USAAF leaders Hap Arnold and Ira Eaker on the US–Mexico border in 1919 and pioneered the southern air mail route from Montgomery, Alabama, to New Orleans in 1923. Promoted to Chief of Primary Flight Training at Randolph and Kelly Fields in 1929, he controlled all Air Corps flight training, later leading a 98-plane formation of Advanced Flight Training graduates on a national tour to recruit ROTC students at land-grant colleges into the Air Corps in 1937.

The first B-25 group after the 12th to go to Europe was the 310th Bomb Group, which departed for England in early September 1942 when the advanced ground echelons of all four squadrons went aboard the *Queen Mary* in New York Harbor on September 4, arriving in the Firth of Clyde on September 11. Unlike the 12th Group, the 310th would deploy over the North Atlantic route. The air echelons reported to Westover Field, Massachusetts, on September 6 to train for their transatlantic flights. The B-25s of the 379th and 380th Squadrons were the first to leave Presque Isle, Maine, on September 25; they crossed in good weather, but the North Atlantic winter soon set in during October, and the 381st and 428th Squadrons had difficult and lengthy transfer flights that turned their crossings into epic adventures.

It was planned the 310th would operate from RAF Hardwick in Norfolk, near Norwich. A week after the 379th and 380th Squadrons arrived, they received their introduction to war on October 12 at 1127 hours, when the airfield was bombed by a single Ju-88 that made a low-altitude attack, dropping four 250kg (550lb) bombs that damaged one hangar and two small buildings while destroying two other small buildings as well as strafing one B-25. The third of the four bombs was a dud, which bounced to a stop under the tail of a B-25, while the fourth exploded in the woods beyond the airfield. No personnel injuries were reported. This was the first attack on an American air base in Britain.

The 381st Squadron left Maine on September 28; the flight to Goose Bay took 13 and a half hours. The next day the weather closed in; the first attempt to fly on to Greenland was made on October 9, when it had to turn back after two hours in the air due to weather. A second attempt was made October 12. Second Lieutenant Frank B. "Pancho" Hawkins, 21-year-old co-pilot for squadron commander Lieutenant

Colonel Anthony G. Hunter in the B-25C named "Green Eyes," wrote extensively in his personal diary about the month-long attempt to fly the Atlantic. The night of October 12, he wrote, "Well, we traveled 7 hours and 15 minutes today (1400 miles approx.) which was 45 minutes from Bluie West-l (Greenland) and then had to turn back to Goose Bay when we got into heavy rain storms. All ten A-20s and the two B-25s made a safe return. Of another flight, an A-20 was lost, making five ships lost en route to Greenland since our arrival here. Plenty tired tonight."

On October 13, the 381st flew to Bluie-West-One. Hawkins recorded, "What a runway – it heads right into a mountain. It is land right or land in a grave!" Once there, the weather closed in. After sitting in Greenland for a week, Hawkins wrote:

> I am beginning to wonder if I am going to spend the rest of the war here. I don't get up for breakfast anymore because it isn't worth the effort, and the more time one spends sleeping – the shorter the day. I have finally read every magazine and book in the library on aviation. Now I am really stuck with more spare time than ever. Most of the gang is getting on edge and very nervous due to this lack of things to do. The moon is really beautiful tonight – but no gals here so to bed I go!

Hawkins and their navigator, 20-year-old Second Lieutenant Nicholas deBelleville "Katz" Katzenbach (who would become Attorney General of the United States in 1965), went hiking that afternoon out of sheer boredom.

In England the same day, the 310th received orders assigning the group to Twelfth Air Force for service in North Africa.

The bad weather continued. On October 29, Hawkins wrote:

> The wind bellowed, and blew so hard I thought the barracks would flatten itself to the earth. Then we had a sea of mud around here. I spent most of the day reading tech orders on our bomber. Then the usual amount of time at the library. When they start to serve good meals at that session known as breakfast, I will get up at a decent hour instead of noon. Most of our crew had to pull KP today. I pity the boys cause it wasn't fun when I had to pull it as an enlisted man.

TURNING THE TIDE

On November 2, the weather finally allowed some of the 381st's planes to fly to Iceland. Unfortunately, the left engine of Hawkins' bomber would not start. He wrote, "Am beginning to wonder if we are ever going to get paid; or get to England. As yet, I haven't put any time in for my flight pay this month. Now to bed." The next day was worse. "Bad weather again so we didn't even get out of bed. Slept 13 hours! Played solitaire for three hours and made $8.00. Buy the deck for fifty cents and get a nickel for every card turned up. I have read every book of any value in the library." The weather finally cleared on November 9, the engine started, and eight hours later they landed in Iceland, where they learned about the landings in Morocco the day before.

Wind and rain closed in the next morning. On November 12 they headed for Scotland; after an hour the radio failed and they returned to Iceland. Finally, on November 16 they took off after an early breakfast at 0430 hours and landed in Prestwick, Scotland, in time for dinner. That night, Hawkins recorded his first impressions of Britain:

> And now before a roaring fire in the officers' quarters I add a few words for the day. The trip was grand except the fog made it impossible to see the ground or water. Women drive the trucks, cars, and everything over here. This place is really at war. There isn't any kidding around. These people take their war seriously. They treat us nice, so we can't complain. I know that I will be glad to help get this war over with, and then get back to the good old States again.

On November 5, the "first priority" ground echelons for the 379th and 380th Squadrons had loaded aboard a train for transport to Hurn airfield in Cornwall; they flew to North Africa on November 15, landing at Gabes airfield outside Oran. The rest of the ground echelon traveled to North Africa on board HMT *Derbyshire*, of which the group's war diarist wrote, "By comparison with *Queen Mary*, *Derbyshire* seemed hardly larger than a medium-sized life boat." The convoy departed Liverpool at 1200 hours on November 27. The diarist wrote of the voyage, "The ship was crowded to a point approaching extreme discomfort, and the sea was very rough. The beds were hammocks which swung wildly in tiers above the mess tables. The most optimistic description of the food was 'lousy.' There was little to do to pass the time, save shiver while standing on the windswept deck, watching the other ships pitching up and down in the water, or searching the surface of the sea for U-boats."

The A-20s of the 85th, 86th, and 97th Bomb Squadrons of the 47th Bomb Group, along with the first B-25s of the 380th Bomb Squadron of the 310th Bomb Group, arrived at Médiouna on November 17. The first B-25s of the 381st Squadron arrived the next day.

On November 18, B-25C 41-13041, flown by First Lieutenant S.J. Brennan, took off with Brigadier General Cannon, commander of XII Air Support Command, to check landing fields at Meknes, Fes, Taza, and Oujda; they found Meknes and Oujda were large enough to allow operations by B-25s. The ground echelon arrived on board the transport USS *Monticello* in Oran that evening; the next day they were transported to Tafaroui, where the war diary recorded, "mud is deep." A later entry noted:

> We were orphans at Tafaroui, not knowing where we were supposed to go from there, and finding no one who knew anything about the location of the 310th Bomb Group. We got along fine, however, sleeping in an old barracks building on top of a pile of camouflage netting during the nights, and eating good food in the Headquarters Mess.
>
> After three or four days, with a few air raid alerts scattered along to keep us from becoming too bored, we found the 310th was at Mediouna, and on the day before Thanksgiving, we flew down to join them.

The first major mission came on December 2, when the 310th's 379th Squadron bombed enemy antiaircraft positions near Gabes airfield. That same day, the final stragglers of the 381st Squadron, which had been stuck in Iceland due to weather, finally touched down at RAF Hardwick, after six weeks in transit from the United States.

On December 5, the 379th bombed Sidi Ahmed airfield, suffering the group's first combat loss when B-25C 41-13051, flown by First Lieutenant James W. Bishop, was hit by antiaircraft fire and all on board were killed.

That same day, two days of rain back at Hardwick finally came to an end. Hawkins wrote they were able to take off at 1430 hours and fly the 400 miles to RAF Portreath in Cornwall, from where they would leave for North Africa. The next day the weather closed in; the flight to North Africa was canceled after two aircraft crashed on takeoff.

Second Lieutenant Joseph F. Szczygiel, co-pilot of one of the last 381st Squadron B-25s to arrive at Hardwick, wrote that they were informed at a briefing the same evening they arrived that they were headed to North Africa.

> This flight will take place in the daytime, a distance of 1,300 miles. We are to fly just above the water along the coast of France and Spain and Portugal into the continent of Africa. We will leave here and fly to somewhere in Southern England and from there to Africa. On this trip we expect to encounter enemy fighters. Let them come, as they are due for a helluva surprise. At this briefing we were told the art of escape and where to head to. We are to be given large sums of money of all lands we are to fly over or near. We were told how to act during an escape. Very interesting.

On December 7, Hawkins' group of B-25s departed Portreath at 0830 hours and arrived at Oran just before nightfall. He complained in his diary that dinner was C-rations heated over an open fire and that the crews slept under the planes on a cold night, during which it rained around 0300 hours and awakened everyone.

Back at Hardwick, Lieutenant Szczygiel recorded they were informed they would leave for the first leg of their flight in the morning. At 2230 hours that night, he and navigator Captain William B. Green and bombardier Second Lieutenant Raymond E. Schick went down to the mess hall and swiped some cake, one gallon of hot chocolate, some cups, spoons, and a large cup of sugar. "We had a wonderful time eating all this." He closed with the comment, "I'll probably freeze all night as I only have two blankets, and three cushions for a mattress."

A week of rain began in North Africa on December 9. Hawkins wrote, "Slept in the plane as it isn't any fun sleeping in the rain. The temperatures here are swell; cool in the evening and warm in the day. It rained all day. Of course, it is expected to rain because it is the raining season."

On December 11, the weather cleared sufficiently for the 379th to fly their third mission, bombing the bridge at La Hencha. The weather was bad the next day when the 380th Squadron moved from Médiouna to Telergma. Four days later the weather cleared, and another mission hit El Aouina airfield; two 380th B-25s joined the 379th for the squadron's first mission. The mission was aborted when the fighter escort failed to rendezvous.

On December 18, Lieutenant Hawkins finally flew his first combat mission when the 381st bombed the marshaling yards at Sousse. The round house and tracks in the marshaling yards were hit with post-strike photos showing good results; they finished by landing at Telergma. Hawkins wrote of the mission and the new base:

> Not a bad trip. We had plenty of work to do when we got here. The plane was completely stripped to be the lightest possible. Even took the radio equipment out. A couple of B-26s got shot down today. All of our B-25s returned okay. Our plane had the left rudder shot off. Some fun. Living conditions here aren't bad. We sleep on the floor and still eat out of mess kits, but it has to be lousy, so why kick. I wish that we would have some mail here.

On December 20, Lieutenant Szczygiel's group of Mitchells flew to RAF St Eval, their last stop in Britain. The next day, Hawkins celebrated the final arrival of the ground echelon, and the fact that they would finally stop living on K-rations with the squadron mess finally opened. Hawkins noted, "This field is really getting to have plenty of planes from B-17s down to P-40s." They were finally allowed hot showers, which Hawkins described as "a real event, I'd forgotten how much I liked a hot shower." The rains continued; on December 22 Hawkins wrote, "It seems as though it is going to rain forever and ever. The raid for today was called off as to be expected. The Officer's Club opened today. Only one drink per day."

By Christmas, Telergma was filling up with aircraft and crews. Hawkins noted:

> Friday. Not bad weather but still not good enough for a raid. Plenty of activity here as lots of transport planes are going up to the front with much needed equipment. The Xmas dinner was swell. Really a good meal. We had bread, coffee, white meat of turkey, spuds, candied spuds, crackers, gravy, peas, and jelly. I would give a hundred

dollars to be home today. Captain Ferguson and two others have been sick for the last couple days. Better now. A P-40 was shot down today here by a B-26 it was escorting.

The next day, Lieutenant Szczygiel's group of 12 B-25s – each leading a flight of P-38s – flew from St Eval to North Africa. The 310th Bomb Group was all finally in North Africa. The continuing rain kept missions to a minimum.

On December 30, the weather cleared sufficiently for three B-25s from the 380th and five from the 381st to bomb the railyards at Sfax. Escorted by P-38s from the 1st Fighter Group, the 310th's war diary reported:

> Twelve P-38s of the First Fighter Group offered the boys protection and with weather clear and visibility unlimited, prospecting was good. The boys were tail end Charlies and for the first time they pushed their B-25s to the limit, as they climbed on the target. Surprise proved one of the main elements for the afternoon and the result was a good show. Three hundred pound bombs, eight to a plane, did the damage and the round house was seen to tremble and shake and finally fall. The turn table, which was proving useful in aiding Rommel's retreat, became useless, as a gift from American Industry hit it dead center. As the target run neared its close, heavy flak began to dot the sky. It was of medium intensity, the range was good, but the deflection was poor. No damage was done and all the boys arrived home safely.

The 381st's First Lieutenant Elwin F. Schrup later recalled the mission: "After 'sweating out' several briefings and 'dry runs,' the 381st Squadron for the first time in its history climbed into their own planes and prepared to start on a bombing mission in North Africa. It was the Group's 8th mission and the target was the Sfax Railroad Yard and Round House." The mission was flown at low altitude to maintain surprise, with the bombers climbing to bombing altitude just before they arrived at the target. Schrup continued:

> At 9,000 feet we leveled out and maneuvered into position for the bombing run. Bomb bay doors opened. Puffs of smoke appeared all

about us. This was it – the Flak. Finally, the bombardier's voice came over the interphone, "Bombs away, doors closed." We started for the deck, twisting, turning, diving and climbing. Still the puffs of smoke were around us. "Couldn't we go faster?" I asked. I had been too busy to notice that the air speed indicator was registering 380 mph! Soon we were back on the deck and the flight assembled, heading for home. Every ship had gotten off the target safely and our spirits were high. But as we were flying along on the deck, a flock of birds decided to take wing, directly in front of Lieutenant Alexander's plane. Birds splattered all over, and the plane looked as if Jerry had made several direct hits. The windshield was broken, navigator dome and gunner's dome were knocked off, wings were dented and engine cowlings wrinkled. All in all, the plane looked like it had been through the mill, but the able pilot and co-pilot landed it safely and were none the worse for it. Later, aerial photos showed that the round house was split wide open and that many bombs had made direct hits on the R.R. yards and torn up hundreds of feet of track. So, the 381st's first mission was a success and Jerry knew he had an enemy that was out for business.

On New Year's Eve, Hawkins wrote, "Thursday. Last day in the year of 1942. Had one drink to celebrate. Only B-26s went on the raids today. Their raid yesterday was a failure, whereas ours wasn't. We had a day of rest. Only one B-26 got shot down today over the target. We are getting ready to move tomorrow. Our new field is six miles east of here. Only the 310th B.G. will be there. We should go on a big mission today."

The 310th had one final move to make before entering serious combat when it moved from Telergma to Berteaux in Algeria. The weather on New Year's Day 1943 was as problematic as it had been throughout December. Three B-25s of the 380th, 11 from the 381st, and five from the 428th assigned to hit the La Goulette Docks in Tunis harbor broke out of the clouds right over the city when the lead ship missed the climb to bombing altitude point due to flying through a rainstorm that obscured the ground. They were too low to drop their bombs, and too far from the target to continue on with all hope of surprise now gone. They were able to get away from Tunis without damage. On the way back to Berteaux, they finally connected with the 121st Group P-38s that were supposed to have escorted them.

Lieutenant Hawkins wrote that Berteaux did not look like a bomber base from the air, having at one time been a farming school. The college consisted of a large, two-story tile and stucco building surrounded by a walled courtyard, which was actually surrounding outbuildings for the cattle. The stable opposite the administration building had been cleaned out as much as possible; the group's enlisted crewmen were installed in half of it, with farm stock still using the other half, which meant the stable odors and lowing of the cattle kept them awake at night. However, the building did protect from the frosty nights better than their previous quarters at Telergma. Officers' quarters for the combat crews were in the administration building's second story. With no cots, the men built beds from bomb storage boxes.

Another mission on January 2 was aborted when the fighter escort failed to show up in the cloudy skies over Thélepte. By the end of the day, half of the remainder of the flight crews in North Africa had arrived at Berteaux.

On January 4, the 310th flew their first really "hot" mission – to bomb the Kairouan marshaling yards. The nearby airfield was the main base for the Fw-190s of II./JG 2. Eighteen B-25s from all four squadrons were led by Hawkins' "Green Eyes." They were supposed to coordinate with B-26s from the 17th Bomb Group that turned back when they were intercepted over Thélepte by Ju-88 long-range fighters they mistook at first in the inclement weather for the P-38s they expected. The bad weather saved the Mitchells, preventing the II./JG 2 *Experten* intercepting the bombers. However, the ground was partially obscured by rain and fog, and only four bombs actually hit the marshaling yards. Several B-25s were hit by flak, and two pilots were wounded by flak, but all returned safely. Flying "on the deck" during the return trip, the formation received its only opposition when antiaircraft crews at Thélepte opened fire. The 379th's First Lieutenant J.R. Holstead received a scalp wound over his left eye, knocking him unconscious. Co-pilot Second Lieutenant John Wilvert successfully made his first B-25 landing back at Berteaux.

The 310th went back to the Kairouan marshaling yards on January 6, with A-20s from the 47th Bomb Group attacking a nearby Wehrmacht camp south of the city as a diversion. Escorted by 18 P-38s from the 14th Group, the 18 Mitchells came in "on the deck;" climbing to bombing altitude, this time they left the marshaling yard in flames and scored a direct hit on the round house as they dove back to low level and sped away. Hawkins wrote:

> "A bombing" we did go today. We threw eight 300 pounders at the rail road yards. Bombed at 8,800 feet. And when we came down, we were doing better than 360 mph. A couple Germans followed us back to the field (two 109s and one 190 were seen). The weather was beautiful today. The only disappointment today was "No Mail." If everything goes okay, I will get a medal in two more bombing raids. But better yet, I will go home in three months. Sure miss my honey.

Two days later, 12 Mitchells escorted by eight Lightnings hit the Graiba railroad bridges in a low-level attack, claiming all bridges destroyed. Hawkins described the mission:

> A bombing of bridges we went. And three R.R. bridges we hit with a total force of 18 tons – from 2,600 feet! We blew them sky high. Our P-38 escort was lost on the way. No B-25s were lost but minor damage was done by the low attitude of the bombing. This made my fourth mission. We didn't get any mail today. It looks as though it will be sometime before we get any. I hope we don't fly tomorrow as I like a day of rest between raids.

Six Mitchells from the 428th Squadron bombed the rail yard at Kalaa Srira. Four hit the primary target and two the secondary target, a rail station at Ben Zinn. The squadron war diary reported, "Intense heavy flak emitted from the Sousse area east of the target. No vital damage was sustained by our aircraft. One of the escorting P-38s went down near the target for causes unknown. The planes returned, substantially holed. In fact, after the bomb run, the evasive action was so violent that Sergeant Donald E. McDonald was cut by the jagged metal around a flak hole in the nose."

On January 9, the 310th flew their first maritime strike. Despite rainstorms that compromised visibility, they spotted an Italian freighter off the coast of Tunisia; the attempted attack demonstrated bombs with instantaneous fuses were useless for low-level shipping attacks. Rain squalls and a heavy overcast forced the formation back south. Headed for the bridge at Hammamet, they hit the coast at the right spot and attempted to follow the railroad to the bridge, but the rain was driving so hard pilots were forced to look out their side windows to see their way. With visibility at a minimum, they missed the bridge. Searching for a place to land since the weather was too bad to fly back to Berteaux, they landed at Bône, where they were forced to wait for two days till the muddy field dried out.

A second shipping search on January 11 saw five B-25s escorted by eight 82nd Group P-38s search for shipping headed to Bizerte. They did not find anything until they started back on the last search leg, when a medium-sized freighter was spotted and attacked; it was set afire by several hits. Turning for home, they spotted a formation of Ju-52s and what was identified as an enormous Blohm und Voss BV-222 six-engined flying boat. It is more likely this was one of the first six-engined Me-323s to be seen in the Mediterranean; they had arrived in Sicily in December 1942, and none of the 15 BV-222s was lost in 1943. The P-38s shot down two Ju-52s, while the bombers made passes on the "BV-222;" gunners Staff Sergeants Parker and Kirkland set it on fire to crash into the sea.

After several fruitless searches, five 380th B-25s and six 82nd Group P-38s found another Luftwaffe transport formation on January 15. This formation included what was identified as another BV-222 but was most likely a Me-323 since the combat report stated it did not try to maneuver defensively, something beyond the capability of the heavily laden and underpowered transport. This "BV-222" was shot down by a P-38 after the B-25s strafed it.

Six 379th B-25s found a tanker headed toward Tunisia, which they set on fire with five solid hits on January 20. The tanker, apparently full of avgas, blew up and sank. They ran into eight Bf-109s on the way home, and in a 20-minute running fight, one was claimed shot down by Staff Sergeant Duke Windham.

An attack against El Aouina airfield on January 22 saw 18 B-25s escorted by 16 1st Group P-38s bomb the airfield one mile east of Tunis. Turning toward the target, they were suddenly bracketed by flak so heavy returning crews reported seeing aircraft fly through the explosions. The flak was heavy enough to obscure the lead bombardier's view of the target on the bomb run. Fragmentation bombs damaged parked aircraft. Six JG 53 Bf-109s and six II./JG 2 Fw-190s intercepted but were driven off by the P-38s. The B-25 flown by First Lieutenant

Robert D. McDougall was hit and set afire. He held it level long enough for the crew to bail out, but it went out of control when he attempted to get out, and he died in the crash. Gunner Staff Sergeant Billy M. Duncan was fatally wounded by flak. Post-strike photos showed 20 enemy aircraft destroyed on the ground.

After another period of bad weather, six B-25s on sea search spotted two Italian destroyers south of Sicily on January 27 and attacked from 200 feet. The lead destroyer was hit with three bombs and was emitting steam when the third B-25s bomb hit the stern, setting off the depth charges, mangling the stern, and leaving the ship sinking. The second destroyer maneuvered well enough to avoid being hit by the attacking B-25s.

The next day, bombers went after the marshaling yards at Sfax. Several intercepting German fighters were blocked by the escorting P-38s, with one Bf-109 was shot down. The 428th's gunner Staff Sergeant Robert O. Kirkland was credited with destroying his second Bf-109, which exploded in midair, while the 380th's Staff Sergeant Fred Lindsay was credited with a probable when the Bf-109 he hit in the engine was last seen diving toward the ground.

After aborting a mission to Al Aouina on January 29 for bad weather, improving weather on January 30 allowed another all-squadron 18-plane formation to bomb effectively. Ten Bf-109s and two Fw-190s were spotted on the way in, and three Bf-109s were credited to the 1st Group P-38s escorting the mission, while Staff Sergeant Norris D. "Pop" Dickey of the 428th was credited with a Bf-109 shot down and another probable, and the 379th's Staff Sergeant Robert M. Brunner was credited with a Bf-109 shot down in a running fight with four Bf-109s that followed the bombers as they sped away at low altitude. The 381st's Staff Sergeant Duke G. Windham was credited with a Bf-109 probable in the fight.

Hawkins wrote of the mission:

> What a day! Bombed RR only nine miles from Gabes. We had a rough time of it. We lost 3 P-38s and got two 109s plus some probables. Eddy and I changed seats on the way back and I took command of the ship. Not a bad landing either. We had turkey and beer during the evening. Our squadron CO Captain Pell made Major today. I wish mine would come through. Old "Green Eyes" (41-13102) is

the lady of the squadron as she has 16 raids to her credit – most in the group too.

Poor weather made this the last successful mission of January.

February 1943 saw two important developments. The first was the extension of USAAF bombing attacks to Italy, with missions flown to Sardinia, then Sicily, and finally southern Italy. The second was the arrival in North Africa of the 321st Bomb Group, which had been formed while the 310th underwent final training and preparation for overseas movement in August and September 1942.

Colonel Robert D. Knapp, commander of the B-25 Operational Training Unit at Columbia Army airfield, became the 321st's commander after it was alerted for overseas assignment in November 1942. Despite being considered "too old for direct combat duty," Knapp convinced his old friend Hap Arnold – now commander of the US Army Air Forces – that he should be given command of one of the groups he had trained. General Doolittle, who had worked with Knapp to form the Doolittle Raiders the year before, also approved of his taking an active combat command. Knapp convinced several surviving pilots and crews of the Doolittle Raid to join the group, providing the newly hatched aircrews with experienced role models as they trained for combat.

During his time in command of the group through the North African, Sicilian, and early days of the Italian campaigns, Knapp flew lead on 40 missions, particularly every "hot" mission, including the Athens mission, for which the 321st was awarded the Presidential Unit Citation, and the first bombing of Rome, before he became commander of the 57th Bomb Wing when the 310th, 321st, and 340th Groups were finally brought together in early 1944.

While the 321st spent the first half of February in the States preparing for overseas movement, the 310th saw quite a bit of action. On February 2, six B-25s on a sea search mission came across a convoy of 11 merchant vessels, of which three were considered "large." They were escorted by what was identified as four destroyers and a cruiser. One Ju-88 and four Bf-109s were seen over the convoy, with ten other Bf-109s flying high cover. When they could not contact their base to report the convoy and get reinforcements due to enemy jamming, they determined the convoy's defenses were too strong and the B-25s turned away. At the same time, 18 other Mitchells bombed Sfax; one bomber went down when hit by defending flak.

The group met stiff resistance when 18 B-25s, escorted by 18 P-38s from the 1st Group, bombed the major Luftwaffe base at Gabes on February 8. Just before arrival over the target, 25–30 Bf-109s were spotted. They attacked the formation, shooting down two B-25s each from the 380th and 381st Squadrons. Group gunners claimed four 109s. Three others were shot down by the P-38s. Back at base, the surviving aircrews reported the enemy fighters were "the most aggressive" they had met in combat. Flak over the target was "heavy and intense." Lieutenant Szczygiel's bomber was strafed after it crash-landed, and all five crewmen were killed.

During February, General Doolittle flew missions twice with the 310th. He was unique among senior USAAF commanders for taking such a hands-on approach to his command. Knowing their commander might show up any day and tell the unit leader he was taking right seat on the lead ship kept all the bomber groups on their toes as word spread. Doolittle also flew at least one mission in a P-40 and another in a P-38 as he oversaw the operations of Twelfth Air Force. On February 9, Doolittle flew as co-pilot with the 379th's Captain John Allan on a sea search. They found four Siebel ferries south of Sicily headed toward Tunisia. After sinking three for certain and claiming the fourth a probable, they headed back to base but ran into rain squalls, snow, and a lowering ceiling over the mountains that forced six of the B-25s to land at Biskra before the weather completely closed in.

After four days of bad weather a sea strike patrol found a formation of 30 Ju-52s and Me-323 transports. The 379th's Sergeant Albert Dallaire was credited with an Me-323 shot down, while Staff Sergeants Donald Daly and John Thomas from the 381st were credited with one Ju-52 shot down each. The rest escaped by flying so low over the sea the B-25s could not attack at that level.

Doolittle flew a second mission with the group on February 16, again flying co-pilot for the 379th's Captain Allan. This time, the rain squalls over the Sicilian strait were so bad that no targets were found and the Mitchells returned early.

On February 17, 12 B-25s bombed Villacidro airdrome in western Sardinia, the first mission outside Africa. Heavy 7/10th cloud cover thickened over the target, leaving zero visibility that forced the bombers to drop through a hole in the clouds they were fortunate to find.

The 321st's B-25s differed from those flown by the 310th, with modifications resulting from combat reports made in the United States before deployment. The lower turret, which had proven virtually useless on operations, was removed, while the tail was modified to allow for a gunner with a single .50-caliber weapon there; the waist windows just ahead of the horizontal stabilizers were opened and a .50-caliber machine gun mounted in each.

The 321st had been alerted for overseas movement in January 1943. The ground echelon departed on January 21, traveling by train to Camp Kilmer, New Jersey, arriving on September 23. After processing for overseas movement, they departed at 0530 hours on February 7, arriving at the New York port of embarkation and boarding the transport USS *Elizabeth Stanton* at 1739 hours. The ship weighed anchor at 0600 hours on February 8, departing in a 22-ship convoy. Sergeant Barnard Seegmiller, an armorer in the 445th Squadron and dedicated diarist, wrote of the voyage to North Africa:

> The first three days of the voyage were rather rough and most of the men were ill. Weather now calm and fair. Sailing smooth. Most of the men have recovered from seasickness and appear each day on deck where the sun is warm and the sea breeze cool. I was not at ease for two days, but managed to retain all but one meal. Our conditions are such that the men are not favorably impressed with the life of a sailor. The general opinion is that only under extreme necessity would any of them go to sea again. The food situation is the most common cause of complaint. We eat oatmeal and grapefruit for breakfast and beans and stew for supper. The only variation from this I can recall is one time when we had scrambled eggs for supper and beans and ketchup for breakfast the following day. There is little appetite for eating and one does it more as an essential ordeal than as a source of pleasure. One is not likely to become seasick if the stomach is kept filled with proper food. I knew one fellow to go through the chow line for dinner three times in an hour before he could keep anything down. It requires courage to force oneself to eat when he is almost too sick to stand and it is the men who lack the stamina to do it repeatedly that remain sick the longest.

February 10 surprised everyone in the 310th. The weather had noticeably cooled over the previous few days, but when it got progressively colder that morning and snow flurries arrived, fliers were reduced to children as they ran out into the storm and several snowball fights erupted. As the snowfall ended, the wind came up and it was cold enough to drive everyone back into their unheated tents. The poor weather hung around for the next three days as men used to desert warmth shivered and pulled on extra clothing. When the sun finally came out on February 13, the men looked forward to flying missions.

On February 14, the four squadrons of the 321st flew to Morrison Army airfield outside West Palm Beach, Florida. Rather than fly the North Atlantic route, they flew the southern route, departing on February 15, crossing the Caribbean to Borinquen Field in Puerto Rico. It was cold and partly cloudy for the first half of the trip, flown at 2,000 feet. They crossed a cold front 200 miles out from Borinquen; two squadrons went down to water level to get through, while the others climbed to 13,000 feet and went over it. The next day, they flew across the Caribbean to Atkinson Field outside Georgetown in British Guinea.

On February 17, Sergeant Seegmiller wrote further about the voyage: "Nine days at sea. The chow is very bad. I passed by the officers' mess and saw the thick fat steaks being prepared for them. The old noise about fighting the war for principles of freedom and equality will sound better when the officers eat the same kind of food as the enlisted men."

That same day, the 445th and 446th Squadrons left Atkinson Field on the next stage of their African odyssey, taking off at 0645 hours headed to Belém, Brazil, hoping to arrive no later than 1400 hours to avoid the afternoon Amazonian thunderstorms. At 1020 hours, two flying hours from Belém, they ran into heavy thunderstorms that lasted more than an hour. The 446th climbed to 10,000 feet trying to find clear visibility. Once at altitude, the clouds extended up to 15,000 feet and the formation became separated. The 445th dropped to sea level, with Colonel Knapp leading one flight of seven planes and Captain MacFarlane the other seven. They were under the storm and only had to put up with patchy rain. Landing at Belém at 1646 hours, the crews reported this was the worst weather they had ever flown in.

The next day the 447th and 448th Squadrons departed Atkinson. The 448th's Second Lieutenant Ervin W. Sinclair, co-pilot of B-25C 41-29998, later wrote in his diary: "Got up at 0330 this morning in order to take off at 0630. Stationary front near Belém was pretty active so we cleared for Zandery Field, Surinam, Dutch Guiana. Enroute we hit a few cumulus at 1500–2000, visibility 10–12 miles. Zandery Field was not prepared for us. Some of the crews had to sleep on the ships. Plans for the next day are for another 0600 take off for Belém hoping to be able to get through the stationary front." The next day they made it through to Belém, flying at 500 feet under the stationary front. There, they joined the other two squadrons, which had been forced to remain due to bad weather between Belém and Natal. Rain arrived at 1300 hours and was steady throughout the rest of the day.

The next day the weather cleared and all squadrons left Belém, starting at 0445 hours; the last touched down at Natal's Parnamirim Field at 1445 hours. The bombers flew the first half of the leg at 500 feet to stay below the clouds, climbing to 1,500 feet for the remainder to get above ground fog in the jungle.

The convoy carrying the ground echelon split that day, with the *Stanton* heading to Oran, while the rest of the convoy went on to Casablanca. They arrived at Oran at 0900 hours on February 20. Once off the ship they were ordered to shoulder packs and marched six hours in a heavy downpour to their bivouac. They arrived at dusk and were then directed to pitch tents on ground all later recalled as the muddiest field they found in North Africa.

That day, six B-25s from the 310th came across a 10,000-ton tanker with a cruiser and two destroyers for escort after Ultra provided information that the convoy would put out from Sicily for Bizerte, with the tanker full of aviation gasoline disguised as a merchantman. The Axis fleet was exactly where it had been predicted, and the Mitchells immediately attacked; bombs dropped by the first three attackers set the tanker afire. The last three bombers then attacked the cruiser, with the first two getting close near-misses, heeling the warship over, while a bomb from the third hit the stern. As they flew off, the cruiser appeared to be sinking by the stern, with black smoke pouring from amidships. Sinking the tanker left the Afrika Korps with little fuel for either the support aircraft they so desperately needed or the armored vehicles that carried the war to the enemy.

At Natal on February 22, scattered showers began at 0320 hours, with occasional showers and drizzle until shortly before takeoff. The 447th departed at 0610 hours following a squadron of B-24s; the 448th and

446th took off at 0635, followed ten minutes later by the 445th. The distance to Ascension Island was 1,448 miles across the South Atlantic. Finding cumulus clouds with a ceiling at 1,400 feet, the bombers flew the entire trip at 1,300 feet just below the clouds, in occasional rain. Three hours into the eight-hour flight, the clouds became scattered stratocumulus. The Ascension Island radio beacon was picked up four hours after leaving Natal. Overall, the flight was uneventful, and all 54 Mitchells arrived in good order. The next day, the weather held, and they began taking off from Ascension at 0900 hours. All arrived at Robertson Field outside Monrovia, Liberia, by 1430 hours.

The next day, B-25s from the 310th sent out to intercept a convoy of barges headed for Tunisia found their target, but in the attack on the 13 barges, the group paid for sinking five of them with three B-25s shot down by murderous 20mm antiaircraft defenses that crashed into the sea. When air-sea rescue later arrived, no trace of any of the crews was found. One of the shot-down B-25s was "Green Eyes." A week later word was received that Lieutenant Hawkins and the rest of her crew were captured by the Germans when their raft was discovered at 1400 hours, and an E-boat had proceeded to pick them up; they were now POWs. Hawkins and his friend Nick Katzenbach were later in Stalag Luft III at the time of The Great Escape, which they did not take part in.

On February 24, the weather in Tunisia cleared enough for bombers to attack German positions following the retreat of the Afrika Korps from Kasserine Pass. Previously, all air support missions were flown by fighter-bombers. The 310th flew a mission to attack an Afrika Korps detachment spotted on a highway near Sbeitla. They flew no more missions the last four days of February due to bad weather. The group flew 18 missions during the month, their most active to date.

The four squadrons of the 321st left Robertson Field at 1030 hours on the 24th, headed to Dakar. Heavy clouds gave a ceiling a bit over 500 feet; the entire flight was made at low level. On February 25, the 445th led the way from Dakar to Marrakech, Morocco, flying across the Sahara and over the snow-covered Atlas Mountains, arriving at 1430 hours. This was the first time a complete group had flown together from the US to North Africa. The trip had taken a total of 50 flying hours from their departure in Florida. They flew on to Oujda in Morocco on March 7, where they were reunited with the ground echelon, then spent several days flying training missions to acquaint the crews with North African conditions.

The same day the 321st arrived in Morocco, the 310th engaged in a fight against an 11-ship enemy convoy when 18 B-25s spotted the ships headed for Bizerte and attacked. Lieutenant Robert M. "Ham" Hamilton, in the 379th Squadron's "June Bug," attacked the largest merchantman and set it afire with two direct hits. Defending flak was heavy, and "June Bug" was hit pulling off the target. Three escorting Bf-109s then closed on the wounded bomber. Top turret gunner Staff Sergeant Robert M. Brunner hit one that exploded in midair, and set a second on fire that crashed into the sea. The third managed to shoot up the area around Brunner's turret, knocking it out of commission and wounding him. Several other crew members were also hit and wounded by the flak and fighters. Co-pilot Second Lieutenant Isaac Grant and radioman Staff Sergeant Harris Haskell administered first aid to the other wounded, then each bandaged the other's wounds. "June Bug" was also hit in one engine and fell behind the rest of the formation as they headed for home. Lieutenant Hamilton kept the bomber in the air and brought it back to Berteaux. Despite the fact the bomb bay doors would not close, he managed to land successfully. Ground crews later counted 115 holes in "June Bug." The large merchantman and a second smaller ship were sunk, while six others were set on fire.

A six-plane sea search mission from the 381st and 428th Squadrons also found a convoy with one large and one smaller cargo ship escorted by a cruiser and two destroyers. As the bombers bore down on the ships, they raised two barrage balloons. The B-25s bombed them, but one bomber managed to hit one of the balloons. Two of the Bf-109s covering the ships attacked the B-25; their fire knocked the lower turret loose, lowering it, while one engine damaged by flak was also hit by the fighters. When the bomber returned to Berteaux, the crew had been unable to raise the turret and were not sure the landing gear would lock down. With two wounded on board, abandoning the B-25 was not an option. Pilot First Lieutenant Archibald Kearns managed to set down, and the gear did not collapse until he brought the bomber to a halt.

On March 12, 15 B-25s from the 310th escorted by 32 P-38s from the 1st Group sighted a Tunisia-bound convoy composed of 11 Siebel ferries. While the bombers sank three of the ferries and left six of the others on fire, the escorts shot down three escorting III./JG 53

Bf-109Gs. Flak over the ships got the B-25 flown by First Lieutenant Shrupp, which went down before reaching the coast in the bad weather without any survivors.

In 55 missions flown by the 310th Bomb Group during the first three months of 1943, the B-25 had proven itself in action, and the 310th had demonstrated its ability in anti-shipping strikes.

After undergoing training, the 321st moved to Ain M'Lila on March 14, near the 310th's base at Berteaux. The group flew their first mission on March 15 to bomb the airdrome at Mezzouna, where it reported destroying 12 enemy aircraft on the field. Two B-25s were damaged by flak but returned safely. The rest of March saw bad weather that prevented missions.

The final unit of what would become the 57th Bomb Wing came to North Africa "the long way 'round," as was written in the 340th Bomb Group's war diaries. The unit had originally been alerted in January 1943 for service in the Pacific, which began in early February with the ground echelon going aboard the transport USS *West Point* at Pittsburg, California, for a transpacific voyage by way of New Zealand to Bombay, India, where they would join the Tenth Air Force. While en route shortly before arrival in Wellington, new orders came: they would travel via Melbourne, Australia, to Bombay, where they would continue on to Cairo, Egypt. Stopping in Wellington for only a matter of hours, they were rewarded with a week in Melbourne to sample Australian hospitality before returning to the *West Point* for the voyage to Bombay, where they arrived on March 18, 1943. Departing Bombay on March 23, they finally arrived in Port Suez, Egypt, on March 29. From there they took a train to Kabrit, 50 miles south of Cairo, where the ground echelon and the air echelon were finally reunited.

The flight echelon had delayed departure from Columbia, South Carolina, after the ground echelon had loaded on a train for the west coast and were still there when the orders were changed. The 486th, 487th, 488th, and 489th Bomb Squadrons flew to Africa via the southern route like the 321st Group. However, they experienced stormy conditions flying the South Atlantic; the 486th and 489th Squadrons each lost one B-25, while the 487th lost three planes and two crews. The 340th Group's combat assignment was to Ninth Air Force operating with the RAF Western Desert Air Force, where they would fly with the veteran 12th Bomb Group. They joined the 12th at Medenine airfield outside Tripoli on April 13, 1943. The war diary noted, "We were in The Blue, as the RAF calls the desert." The 486th Squadron had already been operating with the 12th Bomb Group for several weeks when the group as a whole began flying missions on April 24, participating in the final weeks of war in North Africa. The group suffered its first loss on April 29, when 18 bombers from the 486th flew a mission to Tunis. Flak hit the right engine of squadron commander Captain Keller's B-25, and the crew bailed out during the return flight when it caught fire. All five got out successfully and were back with the unit that afternoon after they were spotted walking on the beach and later picked up by RAF air-sea rescue.

The other medium bomber that saw combat in North Africa was the Martin B-26 Marauder. The bomber was initially seen as "intimidating" to its crews due to the fact it had to be flown at precise speeds with one engine out or during landing approaches; the 150mph landing speed was much higher than that of other bombers, and if speed fell below that, it would stall quickly and crash. Until Jimmy Doolittle worked with the training unit at MacDill Army airfield, Florida, to institute proper training in engine-out procedures, and a larger battery for the Curtiss Electric propeller was installed to change prop pitch faster, the Marauder had a reputation for "one a day in Tampa Bay," as trainees unfamiliar with what needed to be done quickly upon loss of an engine on takeoff crashed, many fatally. The B-26B-10 that appeared in squadrons in February 1943 had an additional six feet of wingspan, which greatly improved flying characteristics by lowering the wing loading. With proper crew training and the improved wing, the B-26 eventually had the lowest operational loss rate of any USAAF bomber used during World War II.

The Marauder was roughly similar in overall size to the Mitchell, with a fatter fuselage. It had more power, with two R-2800 radials putting out 2,000hp as compared with the 1,600hp of the Mitchell's R-2600 engines, allowing it to carry a maximum bomb load of 5,800lb compared with the B-25's 4,000lb. Pilots who flew both types compared the Mitchell to the Marauder as "a Model-T versus a Packard Limousine."

Three B-26 bomb groups were assigned to Twelfth Air Force and initially flew low-level attacks against heavily defended targets, leading to heavy losses and poor results; by early 1943 they changed to medium-level attacks. By the end of the North African campaign, the B-26 groups had flown 1,587 sorties, losing 80 bombers; this was double the B-25's loss rate, and the Mitchell-equipped groups flew 70 percent more sorties with fewer aircraft.

Following the assignment of the 22nd Bomb Group – the first equipped with the Marauder – to the Southwest Pacific Theater in April 1942, the veteran B-25-equipped 17th Group re-equipped with the Marauder to become one of the B-26 Operational Training Units. The 320th Group was formed at MacDill on June 23, followed by the 319th at Barksdale Field, Louisiana, on June 26. The two groups only completed training in September; the 17th Group was relieved of training duties and joined the 319th and 320th Groups that had been assigned in July to Twelfth Air Force for the North African invasion.

The 319th was first to depart on September 25, flying their B-26s via the North Atlantic route to Britain while their ground echelon departed by sea a week later. Bad weather resulted in the loss of two bombers during the Atlantic crossing. Lieutenant Clarence Wall's B-26B 41-17790 was led astray between Iceland and Scotland by a false German radio beacon and eventually crash-landed at Noord Beveland in Holland, providing the Luftwaffe with a flyable example of the previously unknown bomber.

Once all four squadrons were in Britain by late October, the 319th set off for Algeria on November 12. One crashed on takeoff, and two others became lost and ended up over the Cotentin peninsula where they were shot down, taking Group commander Lieutenant Colonel Alvin G. Rutherford with them. By the time the 319th arrived at Maison Blanche, Algeria, where they were reunited with the ground echelon, the group had only 17 Marauders left of the 57 that had originally departed the United States six weeks earlier.

Despite these difficulties, the 319th flew its first combat mission on November 28 under the leadership of Doolittle Raider Major David M. Jones, bombing the port of Sfax after finding no targets at Kairouan airfield, dropping 69 300lb bombs from 1,000 feet and strafing the port. Only one tail gunner was wounded by flak and all aircraft returned safely. Losses began with the next mission on November 30, when nine B-26s escorted by 1st Group P-38s attacked Gabes airdrome; the flak was accurate, and the B-26 flown by the 439th Squadron's First Lieutenant David L. Floeter crash-landed in the desert. The B-26 flown by First Lieutenant Ashley Woolridge returned with a severely wounded tail gunner; Sergeant Robert L. Christman died on December 5, the first combat death.

On December 2, Major Jones led six Marauders in a low-level shipping attack on Bizerte harbor. Intense flak resulted in the loss of two B-26s, including that flown by Jones; new group CO Lieutenant Colonel Sam Agee, who had arrived at Maison Blanche the previous night and was flying co-pilot to Jones, was among those made POWs by the Germans after surviving the crash. After three more missions, the 319th was transferred to Telergma field following Luftwaffe attacks on Maison Blanche. They flew their first mission from Telergma on December 15, to bomb Sousse. Captain Ellis Arnold's "Horsefeathers" was hit by flak and crashed in the Gulf of Tunis; XII Bomber Command leader Colonel Charles T. Philipps was on board and lost with the rest of the crew. On December 18 six B-26s joined six 310th Group B-25s to bomb the Sousse marshaling yard. The B-26s went in first at low level, and the Marauders flown by First Lieutenants Edward H. Gibbs and Charles J. Leonard were both shot down, with Gibbs' bomber exploding over the target. By the end of December, the 319th had an 8 percent loss rate and was taken off operations to train as medium-altitude bombers.

Due to bad weather over the North Atlantic in October 1942, both the 17th and 320th Groups flew to Algeria via the South Atlantic route. The 17th's Marauders left first, and all were safely at Telergma by December 23. The 320th made the crossing over the course of December, with the last bomber arriving on January 3, 1943. The 17th flew its first mission on December 30, bombing Gabes airdrome. Flak and Bf-109s from I./JG 53 damaged all but one B-26; two were shot up so badly by fighters they crash-landed back at Telergma. Twelve Marauders bombed Gabes again on December 31, escorted by ten P-40Fs from the 33rd "Nomads." First Lieutenant Phillip W. Bailey's B-26 was hit by flak over the target; lagging behind, they were shot down by Bf-109s with all on board lost.

Over January 1943, the 17th and 319th Groups engaged in shipping strikes. By the end of the month, the 319th had only six Marauders left. The 320th Bomb Group was forced to transfer 18 B-26s to the 319th so the group could maintain operations and stayed off operations while it trained for medium-altitude missions.

The 17th participated in XII Bomber Command's first European mission when 19 Marauders bombed the Cagliari–Elmas airfield complex on Sardinia. Six days later, the 17th and 319th sent 25 B-26s to bomb El Aouina airdrome. Bad weather forced 12 Marauders to return early; the rest lost their fighter escort and were found and attacked by II./JG 2's Fw-190s. One B-26 was shot down over the target, and a second damaged bomber crash-landed in Allied territory.

The 319th was withdrawn from combat on February 15 to retrain and re-equip, handing over their last 17 B-26s to the 17th Group, now the only operational B-26 group in Twelfth Air Force. On February 17, the 17th's 17 B-26s joined B-17s and B-25s to bomb Decimomannu airfield on Sardinia. The B-26s flown by Captain Frank K. Walsh of the 95th Bomb Squadron and Second Lieutenant Ernest F. Case of the 432nd Bomb Squadron collided over the target.

On February 24, the 17th went back to El Aouina. Despite escort by 52nd Group Spitfire Vbs, II./JG 53 Bf-109Gs shot down the Marauders flown by First Lieutenants Henry C. Schmelig, Jr., Harry T. Martin, and Lester D. Rowher. Ten others were damaged by flak, including Captain Garnet Dilworth's "New York Central," which crash-landed back at Telergma with mortally wounded turret gunner Staff Sergeant Albert L. Dalton on board.

Five days later, the group flew their first mission against the well-defended bridges at La Hencha, between Gabes and Sfax. Eight Bf-109Gs from II./JG 77 penetrated the 82nd's P-38 fighter screen and quickly shot down the 95th's "Barrel House Bessie," flown by First Lieutenant Hiram F. Appleget, northwest of Kasserine Pass. Minutes later, the fighters sent the 432nd's "Terrible Terrapin," flown by Captain Allan E. Karstens, down in flames over the target. Attacking the bridges from an altitude of just 60 feet, Captain William R. Pritchard's "Coughin' Coffin" actually scraped the ground and only just avoided crashing when it was rocked by the concussion of nearby bomb blasts. The crew dropped bombs on the railway bridge and flew 100 miles across enemy territory at treetop height; Pritchard was awarded a Distinguished Flying Cross.

On March 11 and 24, the 17th flew anti-shipping missions, skip-bombing Axis shipping and losing one Marauder on each mission. On the first mission, Second Lieutenant Daniel C. Logan's "Defiant" from the 432nd Squadron was shot down by an Me-210 from III./ZG 1, while the 37th Squadron's Second Lieutenant Robert W. Grey was hit by flak and crashed with a wing on fire near Cap Bizerte on the second.

On March 12, 15 B-26s attacked the road and railway bridge east of Enfidaville. "Glory Bound," flown by the 432nd Squadron's Second Lieutenant Harry F. Pardee, was shot down by a II./JG 53 Bf-109G on the run-in to the target; the other 14 bombers scored near-misses on the bridge and a nearby supply dump exploded. On March 24, the 37th's "Earthquake McGoon," flown by First Lieutenant Frank P. Bedford, was hit by an 88mm shell that tore into the left engine nacelle and exploded while the bomber was on its bomb run over La Smala airdrome on the east coast of Tunisia. Despite this, Bedford pressed on and unloaded; the Marauder limped back to base as slowly as possible due to the severe vibration caused by the damage while the crew jettisoned as much equipment as possible so it could make a belly landing at Telergma, since the hydraulic system had been destroyed. Two weeks of poor weather then brought a halt to missions until April 10.

The 320th Bomb Group had been assigned to anti-submarine patrols in February but was re-assigned to bombing missions in mid-April. Their first mission on April 22 saw 18 Marauders led by Captain Theodore M. Dorman in the 444th Bomb Squadron's "Miss Fortune," escorted by P-40s of the 325th Fighter Group, bomb Carloforte harbor on Sardinia. They encountered only inaccurate flak and all returned safely.

As Axis forces retreated into the Cap Bon peninsula, the 17th and 320th Groups attacked ports and airfields on the Tunisian coast. A mission to Sardinia on April 23 saw 18 320th Marauders escorted by 22 82nd Group P-38s bomb the port of Arbatax. Bf-109Gs of II./JG 77 got through the fighters and attacked the bombers, shooting up the 442nd's "Fuzzy Baby," flown by squadron CO Captain Gordon F. Friday, who crash-landed on Cap Rosa to become the group's first combat loss. The 441st's First Lieutenant Carl E. Hoy was awarded a Distinguished Flying Cross for bringing "Most Likely" back to base despite heavy damage. The 441st's Staff Sergeant Martin E. Furrer, bombardier on board First Lieutenant Marshall W. Doxse's "Dorothy II," scored the group's first aerial victory when he shot down a Bf-109.

On April 28, the 320th flew an anti-shipping mission off Cap Bon. Attacking a convoy headed to Tunisia, intense and accurate defending flak claimed the 444th's B-26 flown by Captain Richard L. Chick, which ditched in the sea off Sousse, while the 443rd's First Lieutenant Thomas Summers, and Captain James H. Luttrell, crash-landed behind Allied lines.

After flying several unsuccessful sea sweeps between May 1 and 8, the group sent 37 Marauders along with 18 from the 17th Group in a large raid against Palermo, Sicily, on May 9. The 320th lost Captain Davis B. Elliott's B-26B when it caught fire after being hit by flak and crashed into the sea near St Vith.

The final mission of the North African campaign on May 11 saw seven waves of B-25s and B-26s devastate the port of Marsala on Sicily. Gunners from the 320th claimed three fighters destroyed while the Marauders bombed railway marshaling yards, warehouses, and shipping in the harbor. Several days later, on May 13, the last German and Italian units in North Africa surrendered.

9

KASSERINE PASS

The day after New Year's 1943, a large force of Ju-87s, escorted by Bf-109s and Fw-190s, attacked Bône harbor; RAF and USAAF Spitfires were scrambled in response. "Vince" Vinson caught one of the Stukas and hit it solidly; the dive bomber exploded and broke up before it crashed into the sea. Vinson's wingman, Second Lieutenant John Pope, also got one, and reported:

> Vinson and I went after two 87s that were just off the water and trailing the others. He fired a short burst at one and I fired at the other. Then we had to break because two 190s were diving on us. I saw tracers going by my head and the 190 went past just over my left wing, and close enough for me to see the color of the pilot's eyes, if that had been of interest to me. Just after the 190s went past, we saw the 87s that we had shot at go into the water.

Other squadron members engaged the escorts. Jimmie Peck shot down an Fw-190 for his fifth victory, to become the first USAAF pilot to "make ace" in a Spitfire. Two days later, the 2nd Squadron moved to Biskra after that port was attacked by Ju-88s. The 2nd was replaced at Bône by Major Robert Levine's 4th Squadron. The 5th Squadron was frustrated when it received orders to provide air cover for the port of Algiers, flying from the backwater of Maison Blanche.

Bône continued to be the hot spot for air combat, with the Germans continuing their attacks from Sicily. The 4th Squadron claimed its first successes on January 6, when Captain Donald E. Williams shot down an Fw-190 for his, and the squadron's, first victory; the victory was tempered moments later when another Fw-190 latched onto Williams' tail and shot him down, killing him in the process. Two days later, 4th Squadron CO Major Levine shot down an Fw-190 ten miles from Bône. Five days later, in a scrap over Cap Rosa, First Lieutenant Norman Bolle, Jr., sent a Bf-109 into the sea. On January 14, First Lieutenant Moss Fletcher, who had come to the squadron with a shared victory from his RCAF service, scored the first of four kills, a Bf-109G that went down between Cap Rosa and Bône, in the middle of a fight that saw Fletcher's Spitfire damaged by another 109, forcing him to bail out into the water. He was picked up and soon returned to the squadron. The next day, the rains came and Bône was soon too muddy for flight operations.

In early January, airpower was building up at Thélepte. The 59th and 60th Squadrons joined the 58th Squadron on January 4 and 5 respectively. So did the French GC/II-5 flying the 59th's P-40s, as well as a squadron of A-20 light bombers and 25 P-39s from the 350th Fighter Group. As of January 7, the entire 33rd Group was finally at Thélepte. Their assignment was to provide air support to the troops of US II Corps in southern Tunisia. The P-40s provided escort to A-20 light bombers and P-39 fighter-bombers, ranging over the southern front and searching for targets whenever the weather permitted. Thélepte was the site of the most intense fighting the 33rd experienced in North Africa. It faced an assortment of German aircraft: Ju-88 bombers; Ju-87 Stuka dive bombers; Bf-109 fighters; and soon new Fw-190 fighters when II./JG 2 moved into the region. The Stukas and Ju-88s proved relatively easy targets, but the fighters outperformed the P-40s in all ways; additionally, the pilots flying the fighters were far more experienced aerial warriors than were the Americans.

On January 8, the 31st Group's 308th Squadron was ordered to fly to Casablanca. After three days there, it found out the reason for its move was to provide air cover for the arrival of President Roosevelt and Prime Minister Churchill for the Casablanca Conference. At the same time, 309th CO Major Harrison Thyng convinced Colonel Dean to let him go to the front, and led a flight of Spitfires to Thélepte where the 33rd Group was under near-constant attack from the Luftwaffe. When the squadron returned to La Senia ten days later, the men were full of stories of how the P-40 pilots were living in dugouts and being strafed daily by Bf-109s and Fw-190s.

At this time, the USAAF units were not well organized for battle. At this point in the campaign, the air organization in North Africa paralleled the ground forces' division in separate American, British, and French contingents. Major General Carl Spaatz, who was nominally in command of the Allied air force, split the force, with Eastern Air Command under Air Marshal William Welsh supporting the British First Army while Twelfth Air Force under Brigadier General Jimmy Doolittle supported all US Army land forces. The XII Air Support Command (ASC) supported the US land forces, which were consolidated under General Lloyd Fredendall's II Corps.

The majority of the available USAAF fighters and light and medium bombers assigned to XII ASC suffered a number of operational handicaps. Many airfields had been turned to mud by the winter rains. Sortie rates were reduced due to shortfalls in logistics support and ground crews' inexperience. Lacking radar coverage at the front, XII ASC was forced to use fighter sweeps for counter-air operations that were easily avoided by their Germans opponents.

However, all this paled in comparison with the most crippling obstacle XII ASC faced: poor air support doctrine. Field Manual 31-35, "Aviation in Support of Ground Forces," held that the air support force must be subordinated to ground force needs, though it did not call for air units to be either assigned or attached to specific ground units. Ground force officers, who ignored the disastrous 1940 French experience in which the Armée de l'Air was broken into individual units controlled by different ground commanders, making them unable to respond quickly to changing battlefield conditions, objected to centralized control of air assets. They did, however, see the value in the manual's statement that "the most important target at a particular time will usually be that target which constitutes the most serious threat to the operations of the supported ground force. The final decision as to priority of targets rests with the commander of the supported unit." This gave them grounds to argue for direct assignment to specific units. General Eisenhower – who at this point did not have experience working with air support units due to the fact that, when the air support doctrine was being worked out before the war, he was in the Philippines serving as chief of staff to General MacArthur – came down on the side of subordination of the air units, writing in January 1943 that "we have a published doctrine that has not been proved faulty." A headquarters memo issued in October 1942, stating a policy that aircraft should not be "frittered away" on unimportant targets but rather "reserved for concentration in overwhelming attack upon important objectives," had not solved the problem.

The effects of this were exacerbated, following the landings in North Africa, by inexperience and inadequate training on all levels, which led to higher USAAF loss rates than expected once the Luftwaffe entered the battle, the fluid situation on the ground, and frequent command changes. Most importantly, the Americans paid no attention to the British experience with the Western Desert Air Force over the year before Operation *Torch*. Neither Air Vice Marshal Arthur Coningham nor Air Chief Marshal Arthur Tedder – the commanders who had been responsible for the success of the Western Desert Air Force – had been consulted during planning for Operation *Torch*.

The essential problem of this faulty doctrine was that it blurred lines of authority and encouraged conflict in setting priorities. The result was an event in which USAAF units sat idle during a fierce German attack on French lines in late January, with General Fredendall ordering XII ASC to refuse an urgent French request for an air reconnaissance mission on the grounds II Corps had no responsibilities in the affected area. The reported actions of the fighter groups in Tunisia bear out this analysis.

The new year of 1943 saw the 82nd start flying escort missions and getting into scraps with the Luftwaffe. The first such escort mission on January 7 saw the group provide cover for the 319th Bomb Group's B-26 Marauders that were also based at Telergma. As it happened, the 96th Squadron's Second Lieutenant William J. Sloan – a prewar enlisted pilot nicknamed "Dixie" for his pronounced drawl who would become the group's top ace – was the first pilot in the group to score in a fight with the enemy when six Bf-109s attacked the formation near their target, Gabes airdrome. Sloan turned into the attackers and latched onto the trailing 109, which he hit solidly. Sloan later explained away his success by saying how extremely frightened he was, and that the enemy fighter was in his way flying back to base. He was later remembered by other members of the squadron as a maverick who went after enemy aircraft while the other pilots in the unit adhered to strict aerial discipline.

Second Lieutenant Claude Kinsey, another of the 96th's former sergeant pilots on the same mission, also admitted to being scared, and reported:

> Frankly, I was frightened. Looking back, I could see a ship with the whole leading edge of his wing blinking flame at me. It was not a very nice thing to look at and, I'm telling you, I didn't look at it for long! Everything went forward in the cockpit and I was indicating well over 400 mph. I lost him and zoomed up and over and back to where the fight was. I picked out a ship but I couldn't get my sight on him for long enough to do any good. I made another pass at him and then rejoined the bombers. I was escorting them and had to stick to them.

Combat came regularly. The next day, Second Lieutenant Tom White, who would become one of the leading aces of the 97th Squadron, scored his first victory when he turned the tables on an Fw-190 that hit the formation of B-26s near Kairouan, Tunisia. Weather then closed in for a week. The next mission saw the 96th Squadron suffer its first combat losses, when two Lightnings were lost while escorting Marauders to the bridges at Oued El Akarit, in a fight with Bf-109Gs of II./JG 51 that saw squadron leader Major Harley Vaughn score his first confirmed victory; three other 109s ended up in the "probable" column, including one to Second Lieutenant Fred Wolfe that had shot down one of his best friends in flames.

The 14th Fighter Group's losses on January 8 were later recorded in the group's war diary as "catastrophic." Eight P-38s were flying an "armed recce," looking for "targets of opportunity" east of Gabes and south of Tunis when they were attacked by a mixed formation of Bf-109Gs from JG 77 and Fw-190s of JG 2, again led by the redoubtable Leutnant Bühligen. The P-38s had just spotted enemy tanks and made a strafing run when they were caught by the enemy fighters at low altitude. Second Lieutenant Bill Hoelle later remembered the fight:

> We were attacked from above by sixteen German fighters. The first thing I knew of the attack was when the fellow on my left was shot down. I immediately pulled the ship up into an Immelman. When I rolled the plane over and out of the Immelman, I found myself amidst another enemy flight. There was a Me-109 in my sights, and I immediately shot it down with one quick burst.

Hoelle then realised three fighters were on his tail:

> I put the maneuvering flaps down in an effort to get away, only to get hit in the flaps, which jammed them that way and left me with insufficient speed to get away. Finally, I got hit in the left engine and it burst into flames. I was only 50 feet above the ground. I pulled up because I knew I had to get out – a crash landing here would be fatal. When the ship stalled at 500 feet, I went out between the booms and immediately opened my chute.

Newly promoted Lieutenant Colonel Troy Keith managed to shoot down another attacker, but Bühligen claimed three P-38s, including the "Tail-end Charlie" that had been pulling up from strafing the tanks when the Germans showed up. Two other P-38s were also shot down, leaving only three to return to Youks and tell the tale. A fourth, badly shot-up Lightning limped back to the airfield and crash-landed.

The next day, the 14th Group said good-bye to Youks-les-Bains and transferred to Berteaux, south of Constantine. The pilots of the 16 surviving P-38s gave Youks a "buzz job" as they departed. Construction of the new airfield at Berteaux had just been completed: there was an all-weather runway that was properly drained, as were the dispersal areas. They shared the field with the B-25 Mitchell bombers of the 310th Bomb Group, and both pilots and ground crews were glad to find themselves welcome at the 310th's chow hall, since they were serving American food. Bill Schottelkorb confided to his diary that "We ate at the expense of the B-25 unit, and it was our first taste of American food in a long time. Boy, the food was good – especially the coffee and fruit."

The 14th was still "on call" for escort missions. On January 11, the group flew two low-level escort missions over the northern Tunisian coast. On the second, the eight P-38s led by Colonel Olds ran across a large formation of German Ju-52s and enormous six-engined Messerschmitt Me-323 Gigant transports that had just crossed the Mediterranean from Sicily. Olds immediately turned his flight away from the B-25s, quickly shooting down a Ju-52. Olds' element leader, First Lieutenant William Workman, shot down another, while Second Lieutenant William Moore set one of the gigantic Me-323s on fire as it dove into the sea below.

Enemy transports were found on two different missions flown on January 15. The 49th Squadron found another mixed formation of Ju-52s and Me-323s while escorting B-25s on an anti-shipping strike south of Sardinia. First Lieutenant Mark Shipman came out of the sharp fight with credit for an Me-323, while Lieutenants John Singleton, Wallace Sorrenson, and Elmer Warren claimed a Ju-52 each. The surviving transports managed to find refuge in a nearby rain cloud.

That afternoon, another formation from the 49th Squadron found more than it was expecting when it ran across a formation of transports over the Sicilian strait that turned out to have an escort of Bf 110s. Lieutenants Oscar Blueher and Robert Carlton each claimed a Ju-52, while Second Lieutenant Soren Anton damaged a Ju-52 and an Me-323. At that point, the previously unseen escorting Bf 110s made their presence known when they dove on the Americans and shot down Captain William Fulmer, whose Lightning other pilots witnessed hitting the sea and explode; Second Lieutenant Lawrence Driver was missing when the P-38s returned to Berteaux. Blueher got to Bône on one engine, where he walked away from a crash-landing. Carlton brought his damaged P-38 back to Berteaux successfully with one engine shot up. Captain Herbert Johnson was credited with a Bf 110 damaged. The next day the 14th received replacement pilots. The most experienced of them had 50 hours in P-38s.

The end for the 14th Group came on January 23, when 16 P-38s of the 48th Squadron on a hunt for enemy road traffic found 25 enemy vehicles between Gabes and Medenine. As the Lightnings swept down to strafe the road convoy, they were jumped by "more than twenty" Bf-109Gs of JG 51. Fighting their way out of the trap, Ralph Watson shot down a Bf-109 and Second Lieutenant Alfonso Seagraves damaged one, but the enemy fighters had all the advantages. Losses included Lieutenants Schottelkorb, Stuteville, Harley, Soliday, and Yates, all killed in action. Mark Shipman, who was wounded but survived a crash-landing, was robbed of his clothing by Bedouins who left him for dead; he managed to survive a 100-mile trek across the Sahara to be rescued by US ground forces.

The fact was that Twelfth Air Force was running out of P-38s. Eight squadrons, each with too few aircraft and pilots in need of relief, was too much of a strain. After the losses on January 23, XII Fighter Command was forced to withdraw the 14th Group from further operations until it could rebuild; of the 54 pilots who had arrived from England 70 days earlier, there were 38 left; they were sent back to the United States to bring their experience to new pilots. The undermanned 1st and 82nd Groups were left to fight on in the North African campaign's final months. The new pilots that had reported to the 14th in January were transferred along with the surviving P-38s to the 82nd Fighter Group.

With the reinforcement of pilots and planes from the 14th Group, the 82nd quickly moved into first place among XII Fighter Command units. Escorting B-17s on the first mission to Sardinia on February 7, the group returned with claims for two Bf-109s. On another Gabes "meat run" the next day, the 97th Squadron had its most successful mission since arriving in North Africa. Escorting B-25s and B-26s, the Lightning pilots saw 24 Bf-109s of JG 51 and JG 77 rise to meet them. When the fight was over, the Lightning pilots claimed eight destroyed and two damaged. Second Lieutenant Gerry Rounds recalled:

> In any direction one looked, there were P-38s and Me 109s diving straight down or going straight up – many in vertical banks, leaving two silver vapor trails from their wingtips. We fought for approximately 20 minutes from 10,000 ft down to zero. There would be a flicker of a '109 – you led him, fired a short burst, and you would see another out of the corner of your eye doing the same thing with you. You'd twist toward him to shorten his firing period, get a burst in if you could, break off your attack and then start in on another that was coming your way. It wasn't at all unusual to see a P-38 firing at a '109, with another '109 on the P-38's tail, as well as a P-38 on that '109's tail. But the train would only last a second or two, before breaking up as soon as the situation was realized by those in it.

The secret of the success that day was that the pilots had previously decided among themselves that they would take the initiative, leaving the bombers and engaging enemy fighters as soon as they were spotted. Unfortunately, four 310th Group Mitchells were shot down while the Lightnings were so engaged, with two more crash-landing due to battle damage when they got back to base.

There was no clear strategy for taking the fight to the enemy. Instead, the American units engaged in what the 33rd Group's Phil Cochran called "guerrilla warfare" – swift, frequent strikes to keep the enemy off balance. The 33rd's squadrons strafed airfields, accompanied the P-39s in attacks on German tanks, and escorted the A-20s on their missions. The technique failed to provide either the satisfying aerial combat the pilots wanted, or the level of cover the ground troops needed.

On January 10, Major Cochran, newly promoted from commanding the "Joker Squadron" replacement pilots group to commander of the 58th Squadron, made the first of the kind of spectacular raids he would become renowned for as the leader of the First Air Commandos in the China–Burma–India Theater. Taking off in the pre-dawn darkness and flying alone at low level, he arrived over Kairouan at dawn, and his 500lb bomb demolished the Hotel Splendida, site of German HQ for the region. Staying at low level on his return, he was not spotted by the Bf-109s sent to intercept him and returned safely to Thélepte.

Writing in his diary of his time at Thélepte, James Reed observed that the nights were as cold as any winter he had experienced back home the entire time the group was on the field, with white frost on the airplanes at dawn on several mornings. By January 14, less than half the P-40s were operational, due as much to the damage caused by the blowing sand as by enemy action; in the air, they were holding their own. By the end of January, group flight surgeon Major John A. Woodworth became worried about the effects of stress on the pilots and ground crews who had been in constant action in the air and on the ground.

Fortunately, a German ground attack was stopped on January 15 and the enemy was forced back. A major German air raid to knock out Thélepte as part of the offensive resulted in the biggest air battle to date. Nine Ju-88s escorted by four Regia Aeronautica C.202 "Folgore" fighters attacked the airfield. A motley group of P-40s from all three squadrons managed to get airborne to join the French P-40s that happened to be on patrol over the field. Major Hubbard and Lieutenant Beggs of the 59th Squadron were in the lead of the scrambled fighters, with Captain Boone and Lieutenant Smith not far behind. In the fight that developed, eight of the Ju-88s were shot down by P-40s, with Hubbard shooting down two and Beggs one, while Captain Boone shot down four; the defending antiaircraft gunners took out the ninth bomber. In exchange, one of the French P-40s was shot down, crashing near the airfield. The 58th Squadron's Lieutenant Watkins was also shot down; after he had bailed out, the tenacious wind collapsed his parachute just before he touched down, slamming him into the ground and killing him. Through their bold efforts, the 33rd were winning in the air. Such losses forced the Germans to dramatically reduce attacks on Thélepte. The group was later awarded the Presidential Unit Citation for its performance in this fight.

In response to its experience fighting the Luftwaffe, the group's tactics changed. The 58th Squadron's newly promoted Captain Levi R. Chase took a leading role in this. He had learned from a British aviator he had met in Casablanca about the Western Desert Air Force placing pilots with ground units equipped with radios, to call in close air support they could direct by explaining the target in terms pilots could understand. Chase argued with Lieutenant Colonel Momyer about setting up a similar operation. Momyer was reluctant to put pilots for whom replacements were difficult to obtain at risk on the front lines. Chase was able to convince him to try the system in the fighting after the Battle of Kasserine Pass in early March, when the Allied ground forces began their offensive.

In the meantime, Chase changed the tactics used in strafing German supply columns. In the beginning, the Americans would first make a low pass over the columns, giving the soldiers below a chance to get out of the vehicles before they came back and attacked. Chase realized this put his pilots at risk of being shot from the ground, while they were only destroying replaceable equipment and not the men who operated them. The pilots soon learned to make their attacks at low level without warning, with a second pass only if the defending flak was not heavy.

Following Levi Chase's death in 1996, his son Tom wrote of his father:

Levi Chase took his roles as an Air Force officer, commander and fighter pilot quite seriously and did not seek publicity. He did not want to see the serious business of war and military service glamorized or trivialized. In short, he did not seek the limelight. Unfortunately, this means that despite his combat record and accomplishments, he was not as well known to the public as many other fighter pilots who may have been covered a bit more by the press.

He would emerge from the North African fighting as the leading American ace, with ten victories – eight Bf-109s, one Ju-88, and one Macchi C.202.

After a January 31 attack by Stukas against an American truck convoy near Maknassy, Tunisia, which resulted in numerous casualties, ground commanders were convinced they needed the air force to provide "aerial umbrellas," despite the fact the attack was successful due to the inexperience of the American troops, who also had virtually no antiaircraft support. First Army commander Lieutenant General Anderson, who was unfamiliar with the Eighth Army's air–ground experiences in the Western Desert, wanted available aircraft assigned as "flying artillery"; according to his chief of staff, the general was uninterested "in the bombing of enemy airdromes," which would have ended the German air threat. General Fredendall stated that he wanted his men to see bombs dropped on the position immediately in front of them, as well as see enemy dive bombers shot down. Due to poor ground attack tactics, the A-20 and P-40 groups had already suffered heavy losses to German fighters and ground fire during air support missions, for which the replacement rate for both pilots and aircraft was unable to keep pace.

General Spaatz argued the air forces should be attacking airfields, tank parks, and unarmored convoys – all targets whose destruction would have greater long-term consequences. In one meeting he told Fredendall that were he to maintain a constant "umbrella" over the one section of the front involving II Corps, his available force "would be dissipated without any lasting effect." Ironically, the meeting was being held in Fredendall's elaborate bombproof headquarters 150 miles from the front. Fredendall conceded Spaatz's argument but would not agree to any change in ground support tactics or strategy proposed.

The results of this impasse were predictable. With no radar coverage alerting them to the presence of enemy air units, XII ASC was overwhelmed by trying to both provide "umbrellas" to ground force units and escorting attack aircraft on missions behind the front lines to destroy the enemy's bases. On February 2, 1943, six P-40s and four P-39s encountered a force of 20–30 Stukas escorted by 10 Bf-109s. Five P-40s were lost while claiming only one Stuka. This was the result of an air support doctrine that permitted the enemy to maintain air operations with virtual impunity.

Following the end of the Casablanca Conference, the 308th Squadron returned to La Senia, and at the end of the month the group received orders to transfer all three squadrons to Thélepte. The 70 pilots who flew in to the 33rd's base on February 5 soon discovered they had finally found almost more action than they could handle. At Thélepte, they joined the 52nd Group's 4th and 5th Squadrons who had flown in two days earlier. The first six Spitfires from the 307th Squadron arrived at Thélepte to find the field under attack from a formation of Bf-109s. When they attempted to intervene, the Germans broke off the attack, turned tail, and disappeared to the east.

On February 10, the exhausted pilots and ground crew of the 33rd were evacuated from Thélepte; by this time, there were only 13 P-40Fs that could be flown out, with the rest among the wreckage on the plateau. A group of pilots from the 325th Group arrived in one of the C-47s to see if there were any surviving P-40Fs of those that their group had donated a few weeks earlier; in fact, there were four, which the 317th Squadron's Herky Green later recalled had been "ridden hard" and were in terrible shape, though they were flown out by the pilots who had come to retrieve them. After transferring back to Youks-les-Bains, the 59th and 60th Squadrons had followed the 58th Squadron to Telergma, Algeria, where they could be proud of all they had learned and all they had achieved in just three months.

The constantly blowing sand at Thélepte soon proved to be an enemy worse than the Germans, as it got into the gun bays and caused gun stoppages that seriously reduced the Spitfire's combat effectiveness. All living was underground in bunkers or in caves in the sides of the hills that had been dug out by the 33rd; the group's 59th Squadron and GC II/5 remained on the field after the rest of the 33rd departed, with the P-40s flying fighter-bomber missions along with the 350th Group's P-39s in support of the Allied armies as they pushed into Tunisia.

Because of the relentless German raids, which could not be spotted from the ground until the enemy appeared over the hills, a constant four-Spitfire patrol was maintained overhead during daylight hours. The Germans were used to the P-40s, which the Messerschmitts and Focke-Wulfs outperformed, so the arrival of the Spitfires changed things; so, when an enemy flight was spotted inbound to attack, the sight of the Spitfires diving to attack them was enough to send them scattering.

February 1943 saw the American ground and air forces in North Africa face their greatest test. The Battle of Kasserine Pass, which was actually several battles, marked the first time the US Army went head-to-head with the Wehrmacht. It was a hard test, but the lessons learned and the operational changes made would bring victory on the battlefields of northwestern Europe in the last year of the war.

Following the successful Allied landings in French North Africa and the success of the British at El Alamein, the Allies hoped the days of the Afrika Korps were now numbered. The hope that the enemy was in its death-throes was premature. In fact, Rommel was consolidating his force. Frequently, battles are decided long before troops meet on the field; thus it was at Kasserine Pass. While the Afrika Korps appeared to be at a disadvantage due to the German inability to provide adequate supplies, every man there knew who was running things: Generalleutnant Rommel was there. That was not the case with the Allies. General Eisenhower, the Supreme Allied Commander, was 400 miles distant in Algiers. His field representative, Major General Lucien Truscott, Jr., was in Constantine, 200 miles behind the front. The field commander was Lieutenant General Sir Kenneth Anderson, leading the British First Army, while US II Corps commander Major General Lloyd Fredendall personally disliked Anderson, considering him cold and aloof, and he had no confidence in the French. Indeed, the front-line forces were hobbled by the fact the XIX French Corps took orders solely from General Alphonse Juin, commanding French ground forces, who only took his orders from General Henri Giraud. Divided command in the face of unified command was a recipe for disaster.

The battles began on January 3, 1943, when General Jürgen von Arnim, German commander in Tunisia, attacked the French with 5. Panzerarmee in an effort to link up with the Afrika Korps, which was at that point withdrawing into southern Tunisia. Eisenhower responded with an order to replace the French with fresh American troops. However, before this change happened, von Arnim successfully forced the French back, securing the German position in Tunisia, which created a safe enclave for Rommel. With the two German armies now consolidated, von Arnim's 100,000 troops and Rommel's 70,000 faced an Allied force of 150,000, scattered throughout the region.

Taking advantage of the confused situation in Tunisia at the end of January, Rommel determined to launch an offensive that would instill in the Americans "an inferiority complex of no mean order." He moved to force the Allies from their positions in the Eastern Dorsale, the mountain range extending south from Tunis, forcing the Allies to use Kasserine, further south. Thus, the Allies would be further from their supply lines, while the forces of von Arnim and Rommel would combine. Rommel planned to break through these American-defended passes, drive across the wide plain to the west, then force his way through the passes of the Western Dorsale running east of the border with Algeria, which would allow the Afrika Korps to overrun Allied airfields and supply depots as they pivoted and advanced northward to the Algerian coast.

The first half of February saw Allied intelligence scrambling to find out what the Germans were planning. On February 12, General Anderson was informed the Germans were planning a major attack against the French, following up with an attack on the British. Anderson ordered a French withdrawal, further damaging Anglo-French military relations.

The 308th Squadron experienced a near disaster on February 10, when 12 Spitfires and the P-39s it was escorting were led astray by German jamming of the Thélepte radio beacon, as they returned from a strike at Kairouan. They ended up over the desert 50 miles from base, with ten of the Spitfires so low on gas they were forced to land in the desert. Mission leader Major Avery and Lieutenant Corrigan were unlucky enough to turn their fighters over on landing and were injured, while the others set down safely. They soon found they were near the Arab village of Soukies, in friendly territory. The Arabs took Avery and Corrigan into their homes overnight. Lieutenants Taylor and Overend, who managed to reach Thélepte on the very last of their fuel, informed Colonel Dean of what had happened. A four-Spitfire rescue party took off and found the downed aircraft quickly. They informed the base of the position, and a rescue party in trucks set off driving through the desert at night, reaching the downed airplanes at dawn the next day. The rescuers fueled five of the Spitfires, which soon flew out; the remaining three flyable planes were repaired with parts from the two overturned Spitfires, which managed to return to Thélepte by dark.

For the next two days, the sirocco blew so strongly that planes that were not tied down rolled across the field, blown by the wind. With the winds calmer on February 13, Colonel Dean led 11 other Spitfires to escort P-39s in an attack on a German column of 100 trucks, ten miles south of Faid.

The Germans attacked out of a sandstorm on February 14 into the American positions around Faid Pass in the Eastern Dorsale; 44 American tanks, 26 artillery pieces, and 22 trucks were destroyed. The M3 Grant tanks that were the backbone of American armor proved they were no match for Panzer IVs and Tiger Is, and were even outfought by Panzer IIIs. The Americans, green and untested, suffered heavy casualties, retreating over 50 miles in a humiliating rout from their positions west of Faid Pass. Anderson, who thought this was a diversion to disguise an attack further north, did not send reinforcements until too late.

That afternoon, 200 German tanks were spotted in Sbeitla. The 31st Group flew several more patrols and ground attacks. By evening, the Germans were reported to be only 35 miles away. During the night, US Army units evacuated Gafsa and set up a defensive line only 15 miles from Thélepte.

The next day, II Corps' counterattack was beaten back with two battalions each of American armor, artillery, and infantry destroyed. With no defenses left, the Americans pulled back in poor order, destroying supplies; however, the Germans managed to capture a vital 5,000 gallons of aviation gas, allowing them to fuel the panzers. Retreating, the 1st Infantry and 1st Armored Divisions established more defensible positions in Kasserine Pass, which led to the vital Algerian crossroads town of Tebessa. Allied losses at this point were 2,546 men, 103 tanks, 280 vehicles, 18 field guns, three antitank guns, and a complete antiaircraft battery.

XII ASC was compelled to hastily evacuate forward airfields; bad weather hampered effective intervention over the battlefield, resulting in a disorderly retreat to the Western Dorsale by II Corps as the ground forces endured German air attacks.

The morning of February 15, the 307th Squadron took off at 0710 hours and circled overhead before being informed the P-39s had been delayed. The Spitfires landed to refuel. Minutes later, eight Bf-109s and ten Fw-190s appeared over the hills. Six of the Spitfires were shot up in an instant as the attackers strafed the field. The 309th Squadron arrived back from its morning mission in time to chase the Germans; Major Thyng and Captain Kenworthy each downed a 109. The others suffered gun stoppages from sand getting into the gun bays of their fighters. During a lunchtime mission led by Colonel Dean, the formation was attacked by Fw-190s and Bf-109s; First Lieutenant Jerry

Collinsworth of the 307th shot down an Fw-190 for his first victory, while Lieutenants Mitchell, Roche, and White each got a 109.

Collinsworth later recalled the mission and the fight:

> That day, twelve of us took off from Thélepte and went out to look for trouble. One of the pilots from my flight left early because of engine trouble, so I was the number three man in an oddball flight, the tail-end Charlie. I was thinking that if we were attacked that day, those so and so's would attack our oddball flight; it was just like them. Sure enough, a little bit later, I saw some bogies at 4 o'clock high. I was wearing glasses at the time; my vision was corrected to 20/10. I called out the bogies.
>
> We kept an eye on the bogies until, finally, when they got fairly close, I told the flight leader to break right. But the leader started to make what seemed to be a gentle Training Command turn. I knew his tail was in trouble, and that turn sure wouldn't hack it for me. My tail was in the most trouble! I made a tight, quick turn inside the other two Spitfires in my flight and faced the lead Focke-Wulf FW-190 alone.
>
> By the time I got around, I could see the sparklers flying from the German airplane. That made me mad. This guy was really trying to kill me! The Focke-Wulfs had jumped our oddball flight, just like I knew they would. But I wasn't scared; I was angry. I thought, You so and so!
>
> If you can dish it out, I can, too. With that, I pushed the firing button and squeezed the cannon trigger. I almost released them because nothing happened out there. The guns fired, but nothing seemed to happen. I was so green that I forgot it took a bullet time to go from Point A to Point B. Anyway, I shot him and he belly-landed into the desert.
>
> I was excited. I yelled, "I got him! I got him!" But when I got off the mike, this calm voice told me to shut up. There was a very good reason for that, and I did shut up. That was the 307th Fighter Squadron's first confirmed victory of the war, and other pilots on the mission damaged four other German fighters.

By February 16, German tanks were advancing from Sbeitla on the Fériana road, and it became clear that US Army units around Thélepte were evacuating their positions. By dusk, the fliers on the field could see the flashes of artillery, and the enemy was said to be only ten miles away. The A-20s on the field cranked up and took off in the last light of day, headed west.

At 0230 hours on February 17, word came to evacuate Thélepte. By 0300 hours the first trucks had pulled out with ground personnel. Spitfires managed to get off in the dark and head for Tebessa. By 0500 hours enemy shells began landing on the Thélepte plateau. Men were rounded up from their bunkers and caves around the plateau, and by 0700 hours trucks loaded with equipment began moving out. No sooner had the first trucks pulled out when orders came to load personnel in the remaining trucks and save themselves. By 0800 hours the last vehicles were leaving. The base was in flames set by the Americans, and six Spitfires that could not start had to be left behind. They were destroyed by throwing Molotov cocktails in their cockpits. The rest of the fighters circled overhead, ready to attack the enemy when they were spotted.

Lieutenants Callender, Corrigan, and Miller landed at Tebessa and commandeered ten trucks they sent back to Thélepte. The trucks arrived in time to take out the last of the 308th's ground personnel and all of their equipment. This was a lucky break, since the 307th and 309th Squadrons had lost so much of their gear the group could not have operated without this last-minute rescue. Captain Frank Hill recalled: "We were successful in getting out of Thélepte, even though we had very little warning. I was one of the last flights to depart the base, and as we were taking off, shells were landing in the mess area in the ravine on the side of the hill."

As the evacuation was happening, "Vince" Vinson led 12 Spitfires and 12 P-39s from the 350th Fighter Group on an armed reconnaissance at dawn, discovering and hitting enemy armor and troops headed west, in a desperate attempt to stop the Afrika Korps advancing beyond Kasserine and on to Thélepte.

Fortunately for the Allies, the Germans were plagued by command and control problems of their own, which delayed the assault on the pass by two days. The exhausted Americans used the time to regroup and receive reinforcements. Crucially, the 9th Infantry Division's artillery, which had moved 735 miles in four days, arrived on February 18. This would prove crucial.

After launching several probes on February 19, Rommel decided to attack Kasserine Pass the next day; he personally led 10. Panzerdivision while 21. Panzerdivision continued attacking northward. The US lines broke within minutes of contact with the Germans in the pass; light guns and tanks had no chance against the heavier German equipment, while their inexperience in armored warfare led the Americans to attempt tank-versus-tank fights while the enemy gathered overwhelming multi-tank firepower against weak points. American morale fell precipitously; the infantry and armor had been routed by evening. On February 20, the Germans broke through at Kasserine, and the Americans left their equipment on the field in the worst battlefield defeat and rout of the US Army since the First Battle of Bull Run 82 years earlier.

With Kasserine Pass now completely open, the ammo and fuel dump at Tebessa was threatened. Desperate defense by isolated groups left behind seriously slowed the German advance. General George S. Patton, Jr., with orders to hold regardless, replaced General Fredendall in command of II Corps. Following the Kasserine defeat, General Sir Harold Alexander, British Middle East commander, took command of the 18th Army Group, which included both Anderson's First and Montgomery's Eighth Armies; staggered by the confusion he saw, he ordered there would be no withdrawal anywhere.

The 10. Panzerdivision was outside Thala by nightfall on February 21. If Thala fell and the Germans advanced on the southern road, it would cut off the 9th Infantry Division from their supplies at Tebessa, while the 1st Armored Division's Combat Command B would be trapped between 10. Panzerdivision and their supporting units. Allied defeat loomed.

That night, British, French, and American infantry were sent piecemeal into the lines at Thala, with the 9th Infantry's entire 48-gun divisional artillery positioned just behind the line. When fighting began again the next day, British infantry largely held, strongly backed by 9th Division's artillery. Seemingly on the verge of victory, but unable to achieve a breakthrough and running out of fuel supplies and ammunition, Rommel suddenly became cautious. Impressed by the abundance of American equipment and supplies the Afrika Korps had found, and the speed with which reinforcements had been rushed into the Kasserine area, Rommel ceased the attack at the end of the day, withdrawing back through the pass overnight as he withdrew his forces to the Eastern Dorsale to prepare for an expected Allied counteroffensive.

The Allies, failing over the next three days to realize Rommel had withdrawn, did not pursue the retreating enemy, though XII Bomber Command did make a belated attack on Kasserine Pass on February 23. Once the German withdrawal was understood and freed from the constraints of being tied to units on the ground, RAF and USAAF units punished the retreating enemy through the next day. Although the effect of these missions was not apparent to the Allied commanders at the time, Rommel later wrote that his forces "were subjected to hammer-blow air attacks by the US air force in the Fériana–Kasserine area, of weight and concentration hardly surpassed by those we had suffered at Alamein."

By February 25, Rommel's forces had returned to the Eastern Dorsale, then moved into the reinforced Mareth Line; they would hold the position until they surrendered in Africa in May. Several days later, Rommel was relieved of command (officially to take "sick leave") after unsuccessfully arguing with Hitler that North Africa should be abandoned. The action in the Kasserine Pass cost the Germans 2,000 casualties and the Allies approximately 10,000, of which 6,500 were American. Despite the American demonstration of their ability to improvise in the face of defeat, Rommel remained convinced that the Americans posed little threat, while British and Commonwealth troops were the equals of his forces. He held this opinion for far too long, and it would prove very costly when the Axis commanders remaining in North Africa after his departure would continue to operate on the advice of their revered leader.

In the midst of the Kasserine crisis, the Allies made several command changes previously proposed at the Casablanca Conference. The most important was placing Air Vice Marshal Coningham in command of the Northwest African Tactical Air Force (NATAF), a new command under the newly created Northwest African Air Force commanded by Spaatz, who would participate in Allied conferences as an equal to the ground and naval commanders. Coningham's first action was to suspend "umbrella" missions unless they were specifically authorized by NATAF. When ground commanders complained, he pointed out that there were never enough aircraft to meet demand. He directed a halt to tank-busting missions by the P-39 groups and directed that all future missions would be against airfields, infantry concentrations, and soft-skinned vehicles.

Eisenhower eventually embraced the new philosophy, in part because he had lost confidence in Fredendall, who had been the main proponent of tying the air forces to specific ground forces. Nevertheless, it would take time for these new arrangements to affect the battlefield. While there were many changes made, the Americans did not adopt every British idea on the use of airpower. There was disagreement as to whether XII ASC should follow the RAF practice of directing all air support requests to the headquarters level. The Americans preferred using air support parties, where USAAF liaison teams operating independently of higher command traveled with the forward ground elements and communicated directly with aircraft assigned to the unit to provide close air support. This was so successful that the RAF would adopt it into their practice, developing what became known as the "cab rank" of fighter-bombers overhead an advancing unit, called in as needed by aviation personnel on the ground who could more accurately direct the attack by giving the pilots directions that made use of ground features pilots could recognize.

The pragmatic Americans immediately started a thorough housecleaning. Commanders who had failed the test of combat were sacked; their replacements were henceforth given permission to make on-the-spot decisions without having to ask higher command; communications were unified. As rapidly as possible, the M4 Sherman replaced the M3 Grant throughout the armored units.

There were many reasons for the American debacle at Kasserine Pass. The most significant in terms of lessons for the future was that poor handling of the combat air assets available to the Allies prior to the battle, as a result of inferior doctrine, had nearly resulted in the complete loss of the American position in Tunisia. Field Manual 31-35 was largely thrown away, replaced in July 1943 by Field Manual 100-20. The new manual stated: "Land power and air power are co-equal and interdependent forces. Control of available air power must be centralized and command must be exercised through the air force commander if this inherent flexibility and ability to deliver a decisive blow are to be fully exploited." The truth of this doctrine would be proven in northwestern Europe in the war's final year.

In the aftermath of Kasserine Pass, the 82nd Fighter Group hit its stride by the end of February. On February 28, after battles on nearly every mission flown, the 82nd took top honors as the most successful fighter group in North Africa when Tom White became its second ace three days after Dixie Sloan became the first; unlike many fighter groups, the group leaders encouraged element leaders as well as flight leaders to be the "shooter," and wingmen were not penalized for abandoning their job of watching a leader's tail if they managed to score. Thus, victories were spread among many pilots, which contributed to high group morale and underpinned further success.

March saw the run of air battles continue for the 82nd. On March 20, the 96th and 97th Squadrons escorted B-25s of the newly arrived 321st Bomb Group on an anti-shipping mission. While the 97th got separated from the others when it chased after enemy aircraft that were impossible to catch, the Mitchells found a convoy and set a large freighter on fire. The bombers stayed over the convoy long enough for an estimated 50 enemy fighters to show up. The 96th claimed 11 destroyed, one probable, and one damaged, for no loss. Top scorer was Second Lieutenant Ricky Zubarik with a Bf-109 and Ju-88. Four other pilots scored one Bf-109 each, including Lieutenants Wayne Jorda, Ward Kuentzel, Bill "Hut-sut" Rawson, and P.D. Rodgers. Squadron commander Major Harley Vaughn shot down the other of the two Ju-88s claimed, while Second Lieutenant Claude Kinsey claimed an unidentified Italian fighter for his fifth victory to become the group's third ace. Although no Lightnings were lost, two B-25s were seen to go in.

At the same time, the Spitfires of the 31st and 52nd Groups resumed their escort activities over the front; this time it was the 31st's 307th Squadron which enjoyed the most success as the Allies prepared for the final offensives in North Africa. Increased combat meant increased casualties. On March 8, two 307th Squadron pilots were lost south of Pichon in a battle with Fw-190s flown by experienced Channel Front veterans from II./JG 2. First Lieutenant Jerry Collinsworth became involved a fight for his life with *Experte* Unteroffizier Erich Engelbrecht, who had just shot down the Spitfire flown by Collinsworth's friend, First Lieutenant Woodlief "Woody" Thomas.

Collinsworth later explained the entire fight:

March 8, 1943, was one year and two days after I had graduated flying school. It was the day of my scariest mission. Lieutenant Merlin Mitchell was leading the mission, which consisted of just one flight of four Spitfires. A fellow from the 309th Fighter Squadron was flying as Mitchell's wingman, and I was leading the second element with "Woody" Thomas on my wing. We were supposed to just go out and find Rommel and the German Army. I guess we were to find out by being shot at.

We took off at 0915 hours. The weather was miserable. The ceiling ran between 800 and 1,200 feet, and we were flying along at about 600 feet above the terrain, in a box. That is, Mitchell and I were up even with one another, and our wingmen were behind us. Somewhere along the way, at around 0945 hours, while we were flying in a generally easterly direction, I could see machine-gun tracers coming up just in front of us. Mitch made a tight left break to get away from it. I was on Mitch's right. I rationalized that if I broke to my left, I would fly right through the wall of fire. I hesitated just a little bit, so I would pass the gunfire before I made my turn. Then, when we rolled to the left, Woody Thomas inadvertently pulled in front of me. He had cut inside me. When we rolled back into our box formation, Woody was now number three, and I was number four.

The accidental arrangement was fine with me. Woody and I had the same amount of experience. In fact, he had earned his wings one or two classes ahead of me. But Woody, being the good guy that he was, must have decided that his job was to be number four for the entire mission. He began to slip back. When he eased out to make way for me – I knew he'd chopped his throttle – I advanced my throttle. Just as I got past Woody, I heard guns. I looked back. Woody's Spitfire had already rolled over on its back, and flames were coming out of it. Woody went in from 500 feet. His Spitfire just blew up. It exploded on impact.

I looked up and saw the Focke-Wulf that had shot Woody down. It was directly above me, trying to slow down. It had been on an overtake course when it had hit Woody. The pilot was rocking his wings, trying to keep me in sight. It is my belief that a fighter pilot needs three things to be a good fighter pilot: He needs to believe in himself, be a good pilot, and possess good luck. That was my day for luck. That fellow had been coming up on me. If Woody Thomas hadn't decided that he was still number four, it would have been Woody telling you the story.

I hollered a warning to Merlin Mitchell. I had no idea how many German fighters there were, so I told Mitch, "Get into the clouds." But he answered, "Hell, no! I'm going to fight these so-and-sos." I tried to get under the Focke-Wulf, but I couldn't. I finally made up my mind to fly into the clouds even though I didn't know how to fly instruments. When the Focke-Wulf pulled to the left to try to dump some of his overtaking speed and get behind me again, I flew into the clouds.

We were about even when I went into the clouds. The good old Spitfire was very stable. I took my hands off the controls and gently eased the left rudder – the downside rudder. Just gently. I came back out of the clouds after only five or six seconds. As soon as I did, I saw two things, and I'm not sure which I saw first. Down below me, three airplanes were flying in a Lufbery circle, right on the deck. I figured that Mitch and his wingman from the 309th Fighter Squadron were chasing the tail of a Focke-Wulf – or that two Focke-Wulfs were chasing Mitch or his wingman. But I didn't have time to look harder. I also saw a Focke-Wulf off to the side. It was below me but higher than the three fighters in the Lufbery. I assumed it was the same airplane that had just shot Woody Thomas down. It was heading toward the Lufbery.

Just as I saw the Focke-Wulf, its pilot saw me. I know he did because I could see black smoke pouring out of his engine. He had firewalled that plane. I made up my mind quickly that I was going after the guy who had gotten Woody. That was the only time I ever shot at an airplane with the intention of killing the pilot. I always shot at airplanes, not pilots – except in this one instance.

The Focke-Wulf proceeded to the deck from about 500 or 600 feet, and I went after him. The Spitfire had an emergency boost, which was activated by a little red knob on the left side of the cockpit, just in front of the throttle lever. You could run for about five minutes at emergency power before you would have to replace the engine. You had to break a little wire to activate the emergency boost. I broke the wire. I had to hold the throttle and the red knob at the same time. I had everything pushed to the firewall. We were headed in a generally southerly direction. I had no idea where we were, only that we were somewhere in Tunisia.

I had a little altitude on the German, and I was gaining on him. The German got nervous and racked that Focke-Wulf into a tight left turn. Friend, I thought, you ain't about to out-turn this Spitfire. I knew he couldn't. I cut inside of him and fired. One of my 20mm cannon jammed and the other cannon, in the other wing, gave my

Spitfire a see-saw action. I don't know if I hit him or not, but he snapped over on his back. I thought that if I passed over him, he'd do a split-S and come up behind me. I rocked the other way to keep him in sight. And then I saw him hit the ground and explode. He was doing about 350 or 375 miles per hour when he hit the ground. I was so scared that I'd forgotten we were only twenty or thirty feet above the ground. When he snapped, he rolled his airplane right into the ground. I don't know if I even hit him, but it doesn't really matter.

The adrenalin was flowing through this twenty-three-year old. I had just seen my buddy hit the ground and explode a couple of minutes earlier. And now that German fellow had exploded and was on fire. I didn't know where I was. I was still at full throttle, but I knew enough to turn in a westerly direction, because that's where the Allies were – somewhere out there. At least I had to get away from German territory. I calmed down, dropped down to about ten feet or so, and pulled the throttle, fuel mixture, and RPM back.

All of a sudden, from my 10 o'clock to my 12 o'clock, I saw this airplane flying along at about 600–800 feet. There were clouds above me, and I was in a light rain. I thought the other airplane looked like a Spitfire, that maybe it was Merlin Mitchell or Mitch's wingman. But I didn't say anything on the radio, and I stayed right where I was. By the time the other airplane got to my 12 o'clock, I was close enough to see a swastika on the tail. It was an Me-109. I thought I could stay down where I was and stay directly underneath him. I could advance the throttle, mixture, and RPM, pull up, and just let him slide right in front of me. He'd never know what hit him. And that's what I proceeded to do – or to start to do.

As I turned underneath him and advanced the throttle, he still hadn't seen me. I knew that by the time I pulled up to 500 feet I would be behind him and probably close enough not to miss. And that's when a Britisher back in England saved my life. You can call it luck if you want. But I remembered this Britisher saying, "Chaps, remember this always: Where there's one, there's quite often two." I didn't look back; I just did a 180-degree turn, while I was still on the deck. As I got turned around, the German's number two man passed right over me. Neither one of the Germans ever saw me. If I had pulled up on number one, number two would have had me as a beautiful sitting target.

The adrenalin was flowing again. I headed west. I was going to fly west until I ran out of fuel or found an airfield. I came across Thélepte. We didn't have it – Rommel had kicked us out – but I knew where I was. I picked up a northwesterly heading, flew back to Kalaa Djerda, and landed. Merlin Mitchell never made it back. He was shot down and spent the rest of the war as a prisoner in Germany.

By March 2, the Allied forces had not only stopped the German advance through the Kasserine Pass but were throwing the enemy back. The 33rd's three squadrons transferred from Telergma to Berteaux, also in Algeria. By March 20, as the Germans continued to retreat, a detachment of the 59th Squadron, now equipped with replacement P-40L fighters in place of the lost P-40Fs, landed back at Thélepte to resume providing support to the ground forces. Like other units that re-equipped with the "lightweight" P-40L, they soon found that its reduced armament of only four .50-caliber machine guns provided an insufficient weight of fire for the combat they were engaged in. The "conversion" to this armament had involved merely removing the outer gun of the previous six-gun armament in the wings, so squadron armorers restored the earlier armament, since the "weight reduction" had not been sufficient to improve performance such that it justified the lighter weapons suite. By the end of March, the entire 59th Squadron was back at Thélepte.

Through the month of March, I. and II./JG 53 rarely had more than 50 Bf-109Gs serviceable at any one time, but the pilots managed to shoot down ten Spitfires and 11 P-38s. In mid-March convoy protection duties over the Sicilian strait became even more important, as the two JG 53 *Gruppen* in Tunisia and III./JG 53 in Sicily, along with the surviving fighters of JG 77, became the main Luftwaffe fighter force in the region, while yet more troops were poured into Tunisia in preparation for the coming showdown with the Anglo-American armies.

As the Afrika Korps was increasingly threatened by the Americans from the west and the British from the east and in increasingly desperate straits, the Luftwaffe threw in as much air support as it could. The 309th Squadron encountered a formation of Ju-87Ds from III./StG 3 on the afternoon of March 21. During the action, recently promoted First Lieutenant Carl Payne scored his second victory, and described it in his combat report:

> Our unit was flying middle position in a three-squadron escort to A-20s bombing Mezzouna airfield. The top cover was flown by the 307th, and was attacked by ME 109s just beyond the target, before the bombs were dropped. Shortly thereafter we sighted a formation of about 16 Ju-87s flying south at 4–5,000 feet. After securing permission from the bombers, I led Blue Flight down to attack from 8,000 feet. I fired at one Ju-87 and saw strikes on the wings and pieces flying off. The Stuka went into a steep downward spiral, finally getting out of control at 800 ft and going straight on in. Blue 2, Lieutenant McCarthy, also fired on the same aircraft and saw it crash.

Two other Stukas were also claimed destroyed and several others damaged.

That same afternoon, the 52nd engaged Bf-109Gs from JG 53, losing two Spitfires shot down. The next day, the 4th Squadron engaged more Bf-109s over Mezzouna. First Lieutenant Robert E. Armstrong scored his first victory as did First Lieutenant Sylvan Feld, who would emerge as the leading USAAF Spitfire ace at the end of the campaign. First Lieutenant Victor Cabas scored his third victory, as did First Lieutenant Moss Fletcher. Later that afternoon, "Vince" Vinson, now commanding the 2nd Squadron, spotted and engaged a formation of Ju-88s. Captain Norman McDonald shot down two of the bombers, the first of his eventual 11.5 victories, and later reported:

> I saw the enemy aircraft at about 1,000 feet above us, and I climbed directly up at them. They were flying a two-ship formation slightly echeloned to the right. I leveled off behind and slightly below their Number Two ship. I opened up with cannon and machine guns from 50 yards, with five degrees deflection to the right. My first cannon shells knocked his right motor out and the engine caught fire. Then the cannon shells exploded in the cockpit and along the fuselage, and the whole ship seemed to explode in midair. It went down burning. In all, I gave him about four seconds of cannons and machine guns. I then closed on the leader, who apparently had not seen me yet, and from a range of 25 yards I opened up with a four-second burst of cannons and machine guns. I set his right motor on fire, his right wing dropped and my cannon fire hit his left motor, setting it on fire also. Then I saw several other strikes of cannon fire along his fuselage. The airplane went into a spin towards the ground. I then looked round and saw the first Ju-88 hit the ground in flames.

During a very successful day in two fights, the 52nd claimed nine destroyed, and McDonald established himself on the path to "acedom." However, the main priority was support to US ground forces. The next day, March 23, was particularly busy. In a fight that happened shortly before 1000 hours, Captain Theodore Sweetland collided with a Bf-109G and both crashed. The 109 was flown by 135-victory *Experte* Major Joachim Müncheberg, *Geschwader Kommodore* of JG 77, who, a moment earlier, had shot down a Spitfire for his final victory. The loss of the charismatic Müncheberg, who was considered by his pilots to be unbeatable, led to a severe loss of morale in the *Geschwader*.

Ground support missions continued on March 24. Spitfires of the 2nd Squadron found a formation of Ju 88s, escorted by Fw-190s, over the Maknassy basin that afternoon. Squadron CO, Vinson, closed on an Fw-190 and opened fire from close range. He later reported, "The enemy aircraft lost speed very quickly and caught fire, emitting a volume of black smoke out of the exhausts. I pulled away after almost colliding with it." Vinson had just scored his fifth victory, making him the USAAF's third Spitfire ace and first to make all his claims with an American unit.

On March 25, 31st Group CO Lieutenant Colonel Fred Dean led a sweep of the area around La Fauconnerie. Flying at 7,000 feet over the Faid Pass, he spotted a solitary Fw-190 below and down sun of the formation; Captain Frank Hill of the 308th was ordered to engage it. Diving on the enemy fighter unseen from out of the sun, he opened fire and shot it down in flames in front of the whole group, scoring his second victory. On March 29, the 309th was attacked by nine enemy fighters near Gafsa; in the subsequent fight Major Thyng scored his third victory when he shot down an Fw-190 while his element leader got a Bf-109G.

Shortly after noon, the 52nd's Staff Sergeant James E. Butler – one of few USAAF NCO fighter pilots – who was part of a patrol covering troops near Djebel Hamad, looked up and spotted an Fw-190. As Butler raised his nose, the German pilot quickly dove to ground level; Butler chased the enemy fighter through the hills, scoring hits and seeing it pour smoke. However, he did not witness the crash, and was credited with a probable.

Later that afternoon, a 52nd Group patrol spotted a formation of Ju-88s escorted by Bf-109s over El Guettar and shot down five. The

4th Squadron's Sylvan Feld got one, while the 2nd Squadron's Norman McDonald shared another with George Williams. Staff Sergeant Butler was again involved, attacking the same bomber as Lieutenant Sanborn, who later reported, "I saw Butler go into clouds after him. Then the enemy aircraft came out of clouds in a dive, with its right engine and the right side of the fuselage in flames. The enemy aircraft went into a spin and crashed into a mountain and exploded just south of Djebel Hamadt." Unfortunately, several Spitfires were also shot down by the JG 77 109s.

The 52nd experienced even greater success two days later, a source of satisfaction since the Army had criticized the level of air support being provided. Captain Vinson led the 2nd Squadron on a patrol of the front line, taking off late in the afternoon. The Spitfires soon spotted a formation of 14 Ju-87s escorted by Bf-109s; the Stukas jettisoned their bombs when they spotted the attacking Spitfires and scattered before the escorts could intervene. The Americans claimed 13 Ju-87s destroyed, a significant success. Norman McDonald made a graphic report:

> As my flight was nearest the Stukas, we went after the farthest formation. They were very slow, so we caught them easily. I closed to within 25–30 yards of the trailing Ju-87 and opened up with both cannons and machine guns, using about five degrees of deflection. A two or three second burst was sufficient. The motor belched black smoke and slight flame. The aircraft dove down to the left and flew straight into the ground from about 1,000 feet. I closed on the next Stuka, and opened up with both cannons and machine guns in three-second bursts. The aircraft erupted in flames and broke into pieces in the air. This combat also took place at 1,000 feet. The third was about 500 yards ahead. I closed on him easily. He was in a slight climb. Again, my range was no more than 35 yards, with very slight right deflection from slightly below. The rear gunner was firing at me. I opened up with cannon and machine guns, again firing three-second bursts. Just as we entered a cloud, great chunks of his propeller and parts of the airplane just missed me. When I came out of the cloud, the Stuka was spinning into the ground, emitting much smoke and with pieces still flying off.

Staff Sergeant Butler, element lead in McDonald's Blue Flight, claimed two other Stukas destroyed. Squadron CO Vinson also shot down a

Ju-87, but when he turned on a Bf-109 headed toward McDonald, the enemy fighter's wingman intervened; Vinson was shot down and killed. The others in the squadron took this terrible blow hard, since Vinson had been a charismatic, successful leader. His wingman, Second Lieutenant Miles Lynn, described the last fight: "I was with Vinson when we were jumped by 109s. He had already shot down one Stuka. I called 'Break!' but he was hit as we turned." McDonald later said, "To those who flew with him as their leader, he was the best." Major George Williams took command of the squadron.

On March 28, former Staff Sergeant Herman Visscher of the 82nd Group's 97th Squadron flew a mission escorting B-26s to bomb Gabes. Visscher had been commissioned a second lieutenant shortly before the 82nd had transferred overseas. He had shot down a Ju-52 over the Mediterranean on only his second mission, on January 17, following that with a Bf-109 destroyed on the group's first mission to Gabes on February 8.

Visscher described how the "bombers and fighters had been screwing up bad at Gabes" in March 1943. In each mission, the bombers had been unable to line up and hit the airfield on the first pass, resulting in heavy German attacks on the second run. After multiple failed attempts, General Jimmy Doolittle visited Telergma, in Visscher's words, "to find out what the hell the problem was."

> The bomber people said the P-38s were always wandering off, trying to be heroes... And the fighter pilots complained that the bombers couldn't get lined up on the target the first time, and that they invited the Germans to attack or shoot them up on the second go-around. Finally, after listening to us go on and on about each other, General Doolittle said, "We're going to go there one more time, tomorrow. I want the fighters to stop trying to win the war alone. Your job is to protect the bombers! There'll be some massive personnel changes in both groups if that target's still there when you get home."

The mission of March 28 involved 24 B-26s and 20 P-38s – 16 P-38s from the 97th Fighter Squadron, plus a flight of four from one of the other squadrons. Visscher was named as the mission leader.

> That morning, at the briefing, I told the other pilots that if any of them got into a dogfight just to try to improve his personal score,

I'd do what I could to get him an interview with General Doolittle. Our job was to stick with the bombers because that's what General Doolittle said it was.

Visscher continued to describe the mission:

> We had two strokes of luck. That's all combat is – luck. Good and bad… The night before we flew, the Germans moved a lot of their stuff out of Gabes and up into the Tunis area, to the Cap Bon peninsula. That meant that the nearest German fighters to Gabes were 90–100 miles away. And that meant that any fighters they sent to get us couldn't fight very long because they had only a limited fuel supply and no auxiliary tanks. If the bombers damaged the runway at Gabes, there would be no place close for them to land, and they'd have to break off early to return to Tunis. The second stroke of luck was that, for once, the bombers hit the target on the first pass.

The flight time from Telergma was around 75 minutes, and German fighters appeared around 10 minutes before the group reached Gabes:

> 12–15 Me-109s came down from the north – our left – to intercept us. They were in a loose formation. When they started in after the bombers the first time, the nearest P-38 flights barreled right in after them, and the Germans pulled up and flew away from the bombers. As soon as the Germans broke off their attack, I called the P-38s back to the bombers. I wouldn't let them leave and chase the Germans until they caught them; I wanted them back scissoring over the bombers. Then the Germans returned and tried to get at the bombers again, but we chased them away again. And then we returned to guard the B-26s…
>
> I chased the Me-109s a few times, but I never got close enough to shoot. I don't think any of us did; the Germans withdrew every time.

Visscher remembered the amount of flak, mainly 88mm, over Gabes that day:

> No one in the B-26s or P-38s was wounded, and there was no damage to any of the airplanes. The Germans stood off when we went into

the flak. Coming out over the sea, the bombers turned right – south – and then continued on back to the west, straight toward Telergma.

The German fighters tried to get at them. Maybe they were hoping to pick off a cripple that had been damaged by the flak, but there were no cripples, and the P-38s kept challenging the Me-109s, forcing them to break off their approaches. The Germans never got up the nerve to press home an attack. After about another 15 minutes, the Me-109s had to leave. They couldn't land at Gabes, and they were down on fuel.

General Doolittle was waiting for the men when they returned, as Visscher recalled:

> He talked to the major who had led the bombers, wanting to know how it went. The major said they'd demolished Gabes Airdrome, and I agreed with him; I said there wasn't much left. The general reached in his pocket and pulled out a couple of Air Medals, which he pinned right on our flight suits.
>
> This was my most gratifying mission of the war... We didn't shoot down any Germans that day, but we had no losses among the fighters or the bombers.

By the time he finished his combat tour with the 82nd in the fall of 1943, former "Flying Sergeant" Herman Visscher was Captain Visscher, a seven-victory P-38 ace.

The first two months of 1943 were relatively calm for the 57th and 79th Fighter Groups operating with the Western Desert Air Force. March saw the WDAF begin softening up the Mareth Line. During one of these missions, First Lieutenant "Duke" Ellington of the 65th Squadron had a frightening experience:

> We were on the deck strafing in the Medinine area when my P-40 took a 20mm round in the wing, which resulted in a huge hole. I broke for the coast and stayed on the deck until I was certain I was behind friendly lines. When I cut in I was well behind our own landing strip and came upon a British P-40 re-supply unit. When I landed the RAF sergeant took a look at my bird and said, "Damn, Yank. You've got a problem there." I can't remember his exact words,

but the paraphrase is pretty close. My airplane was gushing fuel from its ruptured tanks, and you might say that I had a lucky day since I was damned fortunate not to have run out of fuel over the sea. The amusing thing about this incident was that the sergeant then said, "Yank, do you want another airplane?" I hadn't realized this was a re-supply outfit, but naturally I was eager to get back to my strip. So I jumped at the chance, even though this P-40's cockpit was set up for British use and was somewhat different from ours.

Ellington took off in the RAF-marked P-40 and flew to the 57th's landing ground. "By now it had been several hours since I had left my revetment at my home strip. They all knew I was missing. My appearance, taxiing into my own revetment with a new P-40 with British markings after taking off on a mission in my old one, was hard to explain." By the next morning, the RAF Kittyhawk had been inducted into the USAAF with fresh markings.

Early 1943 saw the 79th Fighter Group move forward from Landing Ground 174, where they had spent several months training since the situation on the British front was no longer as dire as it had been when the 57th had arrived. By now, the group's personnel were happy to move anywhere. As one wrote home regarding life in the desert, "We were in the land where Christ was born, and we wished to Christ we were back in the land where we were born!" While the group had remained in the war's backwater, many of the individual pilots had gained experience flying with the 57th. Captain Fred Borsodi of the 85th "Flying Skulls" Squadron had scored the group's first victory on December 15, 1942, when he shot down a Bf-109. The group began departing Landing Ground 174 on January 20, 1943, moving up to Tobruk where they remained in reserve. In mid-February they moved up to Castel Benito in Libya, where they remained until March 11, when they moved up to the Causeway Landing Ground across the border in Tunisia. The newly arrived 324th Group's 316th Fighter Squadron was assigned to operate with them there.

On March 13, the 57th engaged in its biggest fight with enemy fighters since earlier in the year. The 57th put up 36 P-40s of all three squadrons on a fighter sweep to the Gabes area. Several pilots from the 314th Squadron of the newly arrived 324th Fighter Group, the third

American P-40 unit assigned to the WDAF, had been assigned to gain experience and were flying in the 64th Squadron's formation.

They flew out over the sea after taking off from their base at Ben Gardane, turning in across the coastline just north of Gabes. The 64th, flying at low altitude, was suddenly bracketed by flak. In moments, the P-40s were attacked by Bf-109s from JG 51, and a huge dogfight broke out. One P-40 was hit immediately, diving from the formation toward the shoreline. This was likely Captain John Simpson, a flight leader in the 314th Squadron who survived to be taken prisoner and spent the rest of the war as a POW in Italy and later Germany.

Second Lieutenant John E. Teichrow was flying high cover in P-40 "75" with the 66th Squadron and later recalled, "On my 22nd mission, 13 March 1943, our squadron was attacked by approximately 25 Me 109s. The total flight lasted about 1 hour and 45 minutes and was a free-for-all melee. I fired instinctively at a Me 109 as he flew in front of me, and I was surprised to see pieces of his rudder and elevator flying off. He never saw me – I couldn't hit the side of a barn with a handful of sand."

First Lieutenant Dale Deniston, who was flying P-40 "27" in the same squadron, recorded the events in his diary:

> The 64th led with 12 aircraft, followed by the 65th with 12 as middle cover and we in the 66th providing top cover. I was in Jim Curl's section, him leading. I led the element, with Charlie Leaf as my wingman. We were near Gabes at 18,000 feet when we were attacked by 15-plus Me-109s and Macchi 202s. God! What a fight followed. I got in a fair firing burst on one then got lost from my formation and I flew all over the place – airplanes swirling thick as flies.

Teichrow and Deniston both received credit for a Bf-109 damaged in the fight that "lasted at least 20 minutes." The 64th Squadron's First Lieutenant William S. "Tommy" Beck, the 66th's Lieutenants Thomas Boulware, John Gilbertson, and Thomas T. William, and 57th Group's operations officer Major Archie Knight, were each credited with shooting down a Bf-109. Knight was shot down just behind German lines and managed to swim back to the British lines. From the 64th Squadron, Lieutenant Robert Douglas was taken prisoner when he bailed out, and Lieutenant William E. Jenks was shot down and killed. Deniston described it as "the longest and fiercest fight I've ever been in."

The 79th finally flew its first combat mission on March 14, 1943, when 23 Warhawks escorted the B-25s of the 12th Bomb Group on a mission against positions in the Mareth Line. Enemy flak defenses near Zarat saw some of the P-40s return with damage. The next day the group flew a sweep over the coast road between Toujane and Zelten northwest of Medenine. On March 16, the 85th Squadron escorted B-25s on a mission to Gabes that was intercepted by enemy fighters; Lieutenant Carl Simpson damaged one Bf-109 he tacked onto that came through the formation.

March 17 saw the beginning of a series of missions escorting bombers on repeated attacks against enemy positions in the Mareth Line, softening up the enemy in anticipation of the Eighth Army's coming assault. On March 22, the 79th engaged in its first big fight, against the battle-hardened veterans of JG 77 and their Italian allies. Twelve P-40s of the 86th "Skeeter" Squadron were flying escort at 10,000 feet for 12 RAF Baltimores and six Havocs as they unloaded over front-line enemy positions. Suddenly, a mixed gaggle of Bf-109s and Macchi C.202s attacked the escorts. Lieutenant Fred Wright damaged a C.202 that fell away smoking, while Lieutenant Asa A. "Ace" Adair caught a Bf-109 low over the coast road that went down with a single well-aimed burst. He then put shots into another, damaging it. Lieutenants Bob Liggett and Paul McArthur shared another 109. An hour later, 12 P-40s of the 86th and 87th Squadrons were again over the front escorting B-25s. Fifteen JG 77 Bf-109s jumped the 87th's top cover and a melee quickly developed. Lieutenant Kensley Miller was credited with a probable, while Lieutenant Frank Huff's hydraulic system was shot up; he managed a successful crash-landing near Castel Benito. The next day, Lieutenant Maxwell scored a Bf-109 that attacked the Mitchell formation they were escorting, but the 316th Squadron's CO, Major Delaney, was hit in the wing; he managed to get home safe.

10

TUNISGRAD

By the latter part of March, the German forces in Tunisia were in desperate straits, lacking food, fuel, and ammunition. Supply convoys were not getting through from Sicily or the Italian mainland, due to the British submarines operating from Malta as well as the anti-shipping squadrons on the island. The US medium bombers had also become proficient in anti-shipping attack, particularly the 310th Bomb Group.

The next eight weeks would in retrospect be called "Tunisgrad," as the Axis forces in North Africa suffered a defeat as thorough as that administered by the Red Army in January at Stalingrad. It would mark the second major surrender of a significant German military force after the survivors of the Sixth Army marched out of the ruins of Stalingrad into Soviet captivity.

The Eighth Army launched its assault on the Mareth Line frontier defense guarding the Gabes Gap, gateway to southern Tunisia, on March 21. This was followed by the First Army striking in northern Tunisia from the west.

General Oliver Leese's XXX Corps failed to punch through the Mareth Line, and Montgomery ordered a night attack by the New Zealand division to go through the Tebaga Gap on March 21–22 that made good progress until it ran into solid resistance in front of El Hamma. General Brian Horrocks sent the 160 tanks of the 1st Armored Division to its aid, along with the 4th Indian Division.

The Tebaga Gap was defended by a large number of German "88s" that threatened to block the advance. Western Desert Air Force commander Air Marshal Harry Broadhurst ordered a mass attack on the gap to support Operation *Supercharge II* on March 25. The 79th Group drew the assignment to make strafing attacks during the middle of the morning assault. At 0405 hours, Captain Fred Borsodi led 24 P-40s from the 85th and 87th Squadrons, with a second formation of 23 P-40s of the 86th and 316th Squadrons following. Nearing the gap, billows of smoke rose in the dawn light from burning vehicles below as Borsodi led the formation down to deck level from 6,000 feet at 0437 hours. Each pilot dropped the six 40-pound fragmentation bombs he carried over the front line onto the enemy's forward positions as they flew on toward El Hamma.

Borsodi flew over a low rise and saw before him the road was filled with enemy vehicles. Light flak filled the sky around the Warhawks, and Borsodi was suddenly hit. Clawing for altitude to bail out, with smoke filling the cockpit, he reached 600 feet, rolled inverted, and fell out, pulling the ripcord almost immediately; he soon found himself in the middle of no man's land. The other P-40s roared overhead as they opened fire on the enemy below, which turned out to be the 21. Panzerdivision. Flak was quickly silenced and several passes were made. The valley was filled with smoke from the burning vehicles as the P-40s pulled up from their final runs with the German unit smashed. Borsodi managed to walk back and was picked up by New Zealand troops and returned to the group the next day. His formation took the heaviest casualties; five were missing, with four later reported as POWs, while six badly damaged P-40s bellied in back at the Causeway airfield. Despite the cost, the attack was a success, as the New Zealanders broke through to El Hamma by nightfall. El Hamma was remembered by the survivors as the toughest mission the group flew in North Africa. Within a week, the Commonwealth forces had punched their way through the Axis defenses.

On March 28, Fondouk fell to American troops, and the Eighth Army advanced past Gabes on the 31st. The Axis forces were in retreat, but the fighting was far from over in Tunisia. The First Italian Army had managed to escape being cut off in their Mareth Line positions when the Allies took El Hamma and moved behind Wadi Akarit 18 miles above Gabes, which had perhaps the most-defensible terrain in North Africa, with rugged mountains and salt marshes to the west, making it impossible to outflank since the coastal strip was extensively mined.

Had Rommel been allowed to withdraw to this location in February, the end in North Africa would have been much prolonged.

The 79th Group suffered one of its worst days on March 29. Twelve P-40s from the 87th Squadron were low over the coastal road when they spotted a truck convoy south of Mahares. As they swooped to attack, the deadly JG 77 55-victory *Experte* Leutnant Reinert's four Bf-109Gs fell on them. With no altitude to maneuver, Lieutenant George Harris was hammered badly, barely making it back to base to crash-land. Group operations officer Captain Kenneth Boggs had his tail completely shot off and died in the explosion when the Warhawk hit the ground.

With aircraft from both the USAAF and RAF operating together, mistakes in identification were made. On March 31, Fred Wright and his wingman Lieutenant Jesse Dory were escorting a shot-up B-25 across the Gulf of Gabes after the formation had been shredded by JG 77's 109s, when four unidentified aircraft dove on them. Wright skidded left to get out of their way and thought he managed to put a burst in the tail of number four. An instant later, the sky was empty but for himself, Dory, and the limping B-25. Back at base, Wright was cursing himself for his poor shooting when a phone call came to group HQ from 244 Wing, RAF. Their operations officer was calling to apologize for the mistake made by a flight of four Spitfires that had mistaken the P-40s for C.202s attacking the B-25. He also mentioned that one of the Spitfires had a "well-peppered" tail.

Prior to the onset of the Allied offensive on March 21, I., II. and II./ JG 53 had been operating primarily on the northern front against the Allied air units supporting the First Army. In the midst of the battle, *Kommodore* Oberleutnant von Maltzahn sent part of Hauptmann Michalski's II./JG 53 to the southern sector, while the Eighth Army was still battering its way through the Mareth Line defenses. Shortly after, the *Kommodore* visited the Gabes area; it was immediately apparent that Tunisia could not be held. Rightly fearing the Axis forces faced another Stalingrad, and not wishing the *Geschwader* to be needlessly sacrificed to a "hold at all costs" order from Hitler, Maltzahn began to quietly send groups of nonessential personnel to the relative safety offered in Sicily. The first Group left before the Eighth Army breached the Mareth Line. On April 2, I./JG 53 retreated from Bizerte to Protville, north of Tunis. On April 5, Allied air forces began the systematic destruction of

Axis lines of communication. During March, JG 53 lost seven pilots killed in action. April would see a loss of 21.

Captain Lyman Middleditch of the 64th Squadron was confirmed as the 57th Group's first ace in a fight that occurred during the early afternoon of April 2. Middleditch was leading eight P-40Ks on an armed reconnaissance of the highway running along the Gulf of Gabes. Flying P-40K "11," Middleditch spotted over 20 Bf-109s headed northward from Gabes as he crossed the "bomb line" at 10,000 feet. The Germans climbed and turned left into the sun, attacking the Americans from 11,000 feet. Middleditch later described the fight:

> We spotted 20-plus Me 109s, which came in to attack, rather hesitantly, I thought. Things didn't look too good at first, but their hesitation gave us time to get set. They probably thought we were baiting them with a small formation, since we'd had things so much our way during the past few days. After a few minutes of maneuvering, one of the Jerries made a pass at me. He was a little late in pulling out and got in front of me. I saw my tracers go into his wing root and some pieces flew off the right wing. Then a few "golf balls" floated past my prop and I knew some of his friends were on my tail. I broke off my attack and went into a spin to evade, which worked, but I missed the opportunity to see the 109 I'd hit go into the deck. The ground forces later confirmed the crash.

While Middleditch only claimed a damaged, six days later Ninth Air Force credited him with his fifth victory. In July 1943, after the Sicilian invasion, he finished his combat tour and went home to spend the rest of the war in Training Command.

That same day, the 87th "Skeeters" Squadron from the 79th Group flew an escort mission for Baltimores and Bostons attacking the Italian positions, with top cover provided by four Spitfire IXs of the Polish Fighting Team attached to the RAF's 145 Squadron, known as "Skalski's Circus" for their leader, Squadron Leader Stanislaw Skalski, the top Polish ace of the war. Shortly after "bombs away," the formation was attacked by a large gaggle of JG 77 Bf-109s. Skalski and the other Poles turned on them as they dove through the top cover, and he sent one down in flames with a short burst of fire. His wingman, Flight Lieutenant Eugeniuz Horbaczewski, chased another 109 for 30 miles before he exploded it. The other two members of the Polish team destroyed a third Bf-109 and damaged two others.

By this point, the Germans were among the P-40s as they headed for the bombers. Lieutenant Charlie Jaslow pulled his fighter around in a tight turn and hit one 109 that went straight into the sea below. Lieutenant Morris Watkins damaged another, while Lieutenant Frank Huff damaged a second. However, 40-victory *Experte* Heinz-Edgar Berres hit Lieutenant Ed McDaniel's P-40; he bailed out but drowned when his parachute came down on top of him in the water.

The Eighth Army didn't allow the Germans and Italians enough time to consolidate their positions in "the best defensive terrain in North Africa." Tanks of the 1st Armored Division supported by the New Zealanders and Indians attacked on April 7. Unfortunately, the time taken to set up the attack allowed the bulk of the Italians to escape to Enfidaville, 150 miles above Wadi Akarit. Even moving to La Fauconnerie airfield, the 79th was suddenly out of range of the battle.

Over the next ten days the Tunisian battle was, in effect, a two-front war, with the Afrika Korps and Italian First Army facing major assaults in the northern and southern sectors. The First and Eighth Armies linked up on April 7, creating a single front, and began pushing their Axis opponents into a shrinking perimeter in Cap Bon, the northeastern tip of Tunisia. The area was soon referred to by the Axis forces as the "Tunis bridgehead." The now-combined Mediterranean Air Command gained air superiority over the Sicilian strait, the body of water separating Sicily from Cap Bon. In response, the Germans relied more and more on re-supply by air, with Ju-52 and Me-323 transports making the run from Sicily to Cap Bon. Adolf Galland, commander of the German fighter force, wrote after the war of the ordeal these crews faced in *The First And The Last*: "The performance of the transport crews is beyond praise. Even though they had succeeded in getting their planes with the urgently required load safely into the cauldron, while refueling, unloading and reloading, they were exposed to uninterrupted bombing and low-level attacks. If they survived these, they had to face the return journey, which was no less dangerous than the fly-in. Landing at last in Sicily, they were often raided on their airfields."

Air Marshal Tedder intended that Tunis would be Nazi Germany's Dunkirk, the difference being that he did not intend that the Germans and Italians would meet the success the British had in 1940 in successfully extricating themselves.

Tedder's staff created Operation *Flax* to deal with the German air supply missions. Under this plan, Allied bombers and escorts would target Axis airfields in Sicily and Tunisia, while fighter aircraft based in Malta and Tunisia would patrol the Sicilian strait to intercept German and Italian transport aircraft. Ultra intelligence from Luftwaffe radio traffic gave advanced notice of flights, which would allow Allied fighters to patrol at times when there were good chances of interception.

The first mission of Operation *Flax* began at 0630 hours on April 5, when 26 P-38s of the 1st Fighter Group took off to conduct a sweep over the Sicilian strait, while 18 B-25Ds of the 321st Bomb Group, escorted by 32 P-38s of the 82nd Fighter Group, took off on a maritime interdiction operation. The B-25s claimed two ferries damaged and a destroyer sunk. One B-25 was shot down.

The 1st Group arrived over Cap Bon at 0800 hours and quickly reported contact with several enemy formations, estimating 50–70 Ju-52s, 20 Bf-109s, four Fw-190s, six Ju-87s, and an Fw-189. Actually, the German formation was composed of only 31 Ju-52s, ten Bf-109Gs, seven Bf 110Es, four Ju-87s, and one Fw-190. The Lightnings attacked, and a large air battle began. The P-38s from the 82nd also engaged. The 1st Group's pilots claimed 11 Ju-52s, two Ju-87s, two Bf-109s, and the Fw-189, for two P-38s lost. The 82nd claimed seven Ju-52s, three Ju-87s, three Bf-109s, one Bf 110, and one Me-210, for loss of four P-38s. Actual German losses were 14 Ju-52s and three fighters, two of them Bf-109s from 5.II./JG 27's 5.Staffel.

That afternoon, Spitfires of the 52nd Group escorted 18 97th Bomb Group B-17s to bomb airfields at El Aouina. Two Me-323s, two Ju-52s, and five SM.82s were claimed destroyed. A second B-17 mission escorted by 31st Group Spitfires attacked Sidi Ahmed, where a few enemy fighters attempted to intercept without success. At 1500 hours, 35 B-25s from the 310th Bomb Group, escorted by 18 P-38s from the 82nd Group, bombed airfields in Sicily near Borizzo, where they counted 80–90 Axis aircraft poorly camouflaged and vulnerable, which they successfully damaged or destroyed, many with fragmentation bombs. They were intercepted by 15 Bf-109s and lost two B-25s. The bomber gunners claimed three Bf-109s, while the P-38s claimed two. A formation of B-17s from the 301st Bomb Group attacked Milo airfield and claimed 52 destroyed. Actual losses were 13 German and eight Italian aircraft destroyed and 11 German and 30 Italian aircraft damaged. The 99th Bomb Group sent 72 B-17s to attack Bocca di Falco airfield. While the bombers claimed to have spotted 100–150 aircraft there, the raid only destroyed four aircraft and damaged several others. Two sweeps by the 1st and 82nd Groups over Sicily at the end of the day found nothing further. The Northwest African Strategic Air Force (NASAF) claimed 201 destroyed, including 40 in the air. German records reported the loss of 14 Ju-52s in air combat and 11 Ju-52s and Me-323s on the ground, with 67 damaged.

Five days later, 27 P-38s from the 95th and 97th Squadrons, again escorting B-25s on a sweep between Cap Rosa and Cap Bizerte, spotted a formation of approximately 30 Ju-52s. The 95th's pilots piled into them and claimed seven destroyed and two damaged for the loss of one. The 97th claimed five more, including two by Ray Crawford, making him an ace.

The battle was not over. Twenty minutes later, 15 Me 109s appeared from Bizerte and attempted to attack the Mitchells. Bill Schildt downed one that was seen to crash into the sea off Bizerte; three others were damaged.

The 82nd's best day of the North African campaign was on April 11. The 95th Squadron took off on a *Flax* patrol shortly after 0600 hours. An hour later, they were 10 miles off the west coast of Sicily near Marsala, when 20 Ju-52s, escorted by Bf-109s, Bf 110s, and Ju-88s, were spotted heading south. Flight leader First Lieutenant Alex Hamric sent a Ju-52 down spouting bright orange flames and black smoke on his first pass. When a second exploded similarly, it was obvious the planes were carrying gasoline. Hamric turned and shot down another, while flight leader Bill Schildt flamed three more to become the group's fifth ace. Lieutenant "Manny" Moore came up on the tail of another low over the sea, which banked to get away and caught a wingtip in the wash, crashing into the sea without him firing a shot; he then turned and shot down a Bf-109. Second Lieutenant John R. Meyer also scored three Ju-52s. The pilots of the first flight claimed 18 Ju-52s shot down.

While the slaughter was taking place, the second and third flights provided cover and had a hard fight with the German escorts. Second Lieutenant Danny Sharp damaged a Bf 110 whose gunner managed to shoot out one of his engines. Despite this, Sharp turned behind a Bf-109 and shot it down before he got out of the fight. Second Lieutenant Will Hattendorf scored a Ju-88 and a Bf 110 destroyed, while Second Lieutenant Thomas D. Hodgson claimed one Ju-88 destroyed and one probable.

Overall, the 95th Squadron claimed a total of 27 destroyed, six probables, and one damaged. Seven pilots scored multiple victories. However, three pilots were killed, including Hamric. The pilots of III./ZG 26 claimed seven P-38s had fallen victim to the Bf 110s, including four to Leutnant Paul Bley, for the loss of two Bf 110s.

Later that morning, the 96th flew a similar mission, led by First Lieutenant Bill "Hut-sut" Rawson, whose flight shot down five more Ju-52s. Unfortunately, "Hut-sut" was killed when one of the gunners in a Ju-52 got lucky and hit his Lightning in the cockpit as he pulled up from shooting down the one he had attacked.

The afternoon of April 6, the 86th and 316th Squadrons spotted trucks on the coastal road and attacked. They ran into a blizzard of flak coming from a blockhouse that took out four P-40s almost simultaneously. George Harris attempted to ditch in the sea but was unable to get out before the Warhawk sank. Don McKay bellied on the shoreline and was last seen running for cover, though his body was never found. Lieutenant Ober Leatherman's P-40 crashed and exploded on impact, while the 316th's Lieutenant George Gilpin was last seen over the ocean with his P-40 on fire.

Five days later, on April 10, 75 1st Fighter Group P-38s intercepted a Regia Aeronautica formation of 20 SM.82s escorted by six C.200 Saetta fighters. In the resulting fight, ten SM.82s and two C.200s were shot down. In late morning, 27 82nd Group Lightnings were escorting 18 310th Group B-25s over Cap Bon when they spotted 30 Ju-52s, escorted by two Bf 110s, two Ju-87s, and three Ju-88s. Eleven P-38s stayed with the B-25s while the rest of the P-38s went after the enemy formation, but then the bombers flew past the transports with their turret gunners firing on them. A formation of 15 JG 51 Bf-109s scrambled from Tunisia to rescue the transports; they destroyed one P-38, whose pilot was killed when he flew into a Bf 110 and some B-25s were shot up. The P-38s claimed 25 victories, while the Germans reported losing ten Ju-52s, one Ju-88, one Bf-109, and one Bf 110 with several of the Ju-52s managing to ditch and their crews survived. A Spitfire patrol from the 31st Group later shot down four more Ju-52s.

Two Fw-190F fighter-bombers – one from SG 2, the other from SKG 210 – and an Hs-129 from SG 2, were intercepted and shot down on a ferry flight from Sicily to Tunisia.

On April 11, P-38s from the 82nd ran across a formation of 20 Ju-52s, four Ju-88s, four Bf 110s, and seven Bf-109s, claiming all the Ju-52s and seven escorts shot down. That afternoon, 20 82nd Group P-38s spotted 30 unescorted Ju-52s. The transports fought back, shooting down one P-38 and killing its pilot, for a loss of only five. The RAF also joined in, with 24 Spitfires from 152 Squadron intercepting 12 Ju-52s escorted by a few Bf-109s. Three Ju-52s were claimed shot down though the Germans reported no losses, while *Experte* Wolfgang Tonne of I./JG 53 shot down two Spitfires. Total reported Luftwaffe losses for the day were 18 Ju-52s – four from III./KG.z.b.V 1.

The Allied advance in Tunisia continued to gain momentum as spring weather dried up the muddy conditions following the end of the winter rains. The 33rd Group's 58th and 60th Squadrons moved from Berteaux, Algeria, to Ebba Ksour, Tunisia, on April 12, putting them back in range of the battlefield.

On April 13, B-17s from the 97th and 301st Bomb Groups bombed Castelvetrano and Trapani airfields in Sicily. The Regia Aeronautica reported the loss of 11 SM.82s destroyed and 16 damaged on the ground. At Trapani the Luftwaffe reported losing eight aircraft and 40 damaged, while two B-17s were shot down by Bf-109s of JG 27.

On April 16, 13 Spitfires from 145 Squadron led by 14-victory Battle of Britain ace Wing Commander Ian "Widge" Gleed ran into a large formation of enemy transports. The Spitfires shot down seven SM.82s and a Bf 109 for the loss of two, one of the two confirmed victims being Wing Commander Gleed, who was possibly the victim of the deadly Leutnant Reinert. After he was hit, Gleed headed for the Tunisian coast. His Spitfire, AB502, was found on sand dunes near the sea on the western coastline of Cap Bon. His body was not found there but was found buried at Tazoghrane. He was reburied in the Military Cemetery at Enfidaville on April 25, 1944.

Later that day eight SKG 210 Fw-190F fighter-bombers, escorted by 16 Bf-109Gs of JG 27, attacked Allied airfields near Souk el Khemis, destroying six A-20 Havocs. On April 17, five II./ZG 26 Bf 110s were shot down by 260 Squadron Kittyhawks. The 97th Bomb Group sent seven B-17s, covered by 40 82nd Group P-38s, to bomb airfields around

Palermo on Sicily. They were intercepted by 30 Bf 110s and Bf-109s from ZG 26 and JG 27. The Bf 110s attacked the Fortresses while the Bf-109s tackled the escorts, claiming five bombers and one fighter for the loss of one Bf-109.

At its base at El Djem, the 57th Fighter Group began receiving intelligence reports at first light that the Germans planned a large airlift of key personnel from Tunis to Sicily. Group commander Colonel Art Salisbury sent out patrols throughout the day, but each returned with nothing to report. The 79th had managed to move the day before to Hani West airfield, putting it back in the battle. They too had put out patrols and found nothing. As hope of a big score faded, Salisbury laid on the final mission in coordination with the RAF's No. 244 Wing. All four squadrons, including the "under instruction" 314th Fighter Squadron of the 324th Fighter Group, operating with the 57th, took off at 1705 hours for a final patrol after the completed refueling from an earlier unsuccessful patrol, led by the 66th Squadron's Captain James G. "Big Jim" Curl. The 66th flew in the low position at 3,500 feet, with the 65th and 314th Squadrons at 4,000 feet and the 64th at 4,500 feet. The 47 P-40s were escorted by 12 Spitfires of 92 Squadron RAF flying high cover at 15,000 feet. Curl led the formation on a route that skirted the coast from Sousse to Nabeul before he turned northwest and crossed Cap Bon, then headed out over the Gulf of Tunis under an overcast sky. The other pilots of the "Exterminators" searched the sky between them and the sea below.

The P-40s were six miles offshore when Curl led a wide turn and headed south toward the Tunisian coast. The sun was low when he spotted a "V-of-Vs" formation of Ju-52s – later estimated at 100 aircraft – emerge from the haze low over the water. Confirming the Spitfires were in position above, he ordered the "Exterminators" and the 314th Squadron, which were flying low cover, to attack, followed by the medium-cover 65th. The high-cover Spitfires and the 64th Squadron were attacked by escorting Bf-109s before they could dive on the formation. Curl described the flight later:

> When I first saw the Jerry aeroplanes they were right beneath us... Camouflaged as they were, it was rather difficult to distinguish them against the sea. When we got near they looked like a huge gaggle of geese, traveling in perfect V formation, tightly packed. The boys

simply cut loose and shot the daylights out of them. What concerned our pilots most was the danger of hitting our own aircraft, for the concentration of fire was terrific and the air was filled with whistling and turning planes. There were cases of pilots missing the transport they aimed at and hitting the one behind. It was as fantastic as that – you just could not miss. There was no real fighter opposition because the British Spitfires flying our top cover did a grand job in keeping the Messerschmitts so busy that they could not interfere with our attack to any extent.

Curl was credited with two Ju-52s and one Bf-109 destroyed and two Ju-52s damaged.

The fight saw three pilots become "aces in a day." The 66th Squadron's Second Lieutenant Arthur B. "AB" Cleaveland scored five Ju-52s. He was so excited when he got back to El Djem he wrecked his P-40 on landing by digging in the wingtip. The other two high-scoring pilots were in the 314th Squadron.

The 65th Squadron's Captain Roy Whittaker, now a highly experienced flight leader with three victories, added four to his score. Now with seven victories, Whittaker was the 57th's top-scoring pilot, as well as the Ninth Air Force's top scoring ace. He later described the fight for a reporter:

I attacked the Ju-52s from astern at high speed and fired at two in the leading formation. The bursts were short and the only effect I saw was pieces flying off the cabin of the second ship. I pulled away and circled to the right and made my second attack. I fired two bursts into two more Ju-52s, again in the leading formation. They both burst into flames. The second flew a little distance and then crashed into the water. I lost sight of the first and didn't see it hit. I then made a third pass and sent a good burst into the left of the formation, at another. As I pulled away, it crashed into the water. By that time, the Me-109s were among us. As I pulled up to the left, I saw a Me-109 dive through a flight of four Warhawks, and I tagged on his tail from below and gave him a long burst in the belly. He crashed into the sea from 1,000 feet. I then joined up with some Warhawks that were in a Lufbery with six Me-109s. I met one of these with a quartering attack and hit him with a short burst. Pieces flew off and he started smoking, but climbed out of the fight. It was a pilot's dream. I'd never seen such a complete massacre of the enemy in my life. I was afraid someone would wake me up.

The 65th's Second Lieutenant Richard O. Hunziker was on his second combat mission. Flying as wingman for squadron commander Major Gordon F. Thomas, Hunziker later described his experience for *Desert Campaign*, the official history of the Ninth Air Force:

> The enemy formation looked like a thousand black beetles crawling over the water. I was flying wing on Major Thomas, who was leading our squadron. On our first pass I was so excited I started firing early. I could see the shots kicking up the water. Then they hit the tail section of a Ju-52 and crawled up the fuselage. This one was near the front of the first V. As I went after it I realized I was being shot at from Ju-52s on both sides. It looked as though they were blinking red flashlights at me from the windows – Tommyguns, probably.

Inside the transports, the troops took desperate action to defend themselves:

> The ship I was firing at hit the water with a great sheet of spray and then exploded. As I pulled up, I could see figures struggling away from what was left of the plane in the water. I lost Major Thomas. There were so many P-40s diving, climbing and attacking that it was difficult to keep out of the way of your own side. I made a circle and then heard someone say over the radio "There's Me-109s up here – come up and help us," so I climbed to 5,000 feet and flubbed around among the dogfights, not knowing just what to do. Finally, I got on the tail of a Me-109. As I was closing, I noticed flaming red golf balls streaming past me on both sides. That meant there was another enemy fighter directly behind me, firing with his 20 mm cannon. I took evasive action. That brought me over the shoreline, where I hooked onto another enemy fighter. My first squirt hit near the nose of the Messerschmitt. Pieces flew off, and he went into a steep dive. I followed him closely, still firing, until he crashed in a green field with a big splash of smoke and flame. Then I heard them giving instructions to reform.

Second Lieutenant Alfred Froning was another 65th Squadron replacement who tasted success on the mission, shooting down two Ju-52s. He later "made ace" flying P-47 Thunderbolts with the squadron in December 1943.

Flying top cover, the 64th Squadron scored six Bf-109s for no loss. First Lieutenant Robert J. "Rocky" Byrne recalled, "The Messerschmitts were all messed up. I got three of them, but that isn't anything. I had a ringside seat for the whole show. All you could see were those big ships coming apart in the air, plunging into the sea and crashing in flames on the beach. Their fighters couldn't get in to bother our ball carriers at all."

In the final victory tally, the 64th Squadron was credited with six Bf-109s and half of a Ju-52; the 65th Squadron was credited with three Bf-109s, two Bf-110s (although German sources state there were no Bf-110s in the area at that time), and 12 Ju-52s. The 66th Squadron received credit for three Bf-109s and 23.5 Ju-52s, while the new 314th Squadron got two Bf-109s and no fewer than 22 Ju-52s. The 324th's CO, Lieutenant Colonel W.K. "Sandy" McNown received credit for destroying two Ju-52s. Actual German losses were reported as 24 Ju-52s, nine Bf-109s, and one Bf 110. Some Italian fighters may also have been shot down. In addition to the 24 Ju-52s destroyed, 35 were damaged and managed to crash-land along the Sicilian coastline. Since they did not return to their base, they can confidently be claimed in the battle.

7.Staffel of III./JG 53 was flying as part of the escort for the Ju-52s. Two *Staffeln* of II./JG 53 rushed from its base in Tunisia to try to respond to the cries for help over the radio and protect the transports. Between all three units, they claimed seven P-40s destroyed for the loss of one. The *Geschwader*'s final claim for the day was ten. But April 18, 1943, went down in popular aviation history, known to both sides by the same name: "Palmsonntag Massaker" or "Palm Sunday Massacre," for the slaughter of the hapless transports, with the Germans admitting to 24 Ju-52s shot down, with another 35 damaged.

The 57th's pilots had inflicted such a stunning blow to the Luftwaffe that it was not a surprise when German bombers pounded their field at El Djem on the night of April 19–20 in retaliation. Unfortunately, First Lieutenant Alan H. Smith, who had scored 1.5 victories in the Palm Sunday Massacre, was killed by a bomb fragment, and seven others were injured. Four P-40s were also destroyed.

Additionally, a flight of P-40s from the 33rd Wing on patrol caught a group of straggling survivors in the last light of day and shot down four Ju-52s.

Early the next morning, Kittyhawks of the SAAF's 7 Wing spotted and pounced on an Italian formation of SM.82s and their C.202 escorts near the island of Pantelleria, and shot down 12 of the transports. Later in the day, JG 53 caught Spitfires escorting B-25s that were attacking Luftwaffe bases in Cap Bon. In a furious battle the Germans claimed 11 Spitfires shot down, including two by Hauptmann Gerhard Michalski, II./JG 53's *Gruppenkommandeur*. The next day, B-25s attacked II./JG 53's Tunisian base at La Marsa, wrecking 12 Bf-109Gs that had been flown in as replacements two days earlier. April 20 saw Lieutenant James Reed fly as a spare and take the position of wingman for 33rd Group CO Colonel Momyer when his wingman had engine trouble and was unable to take off. Their target was a German airfield near Tunis. Arriving over the target, Momyer led the P-40s in a dive for a low-level bomb run. Suddenly flak opened up and Reed took a hit in his left wing that left a large hole, knocking out the three machine guns in that wing. Reed immediately toggled his bomb; the other 34 pilots on the mission saw a bomb fall from the leading flight and assumed it was Momyer's, which they were all supposed to bomb on. A mile short of their target, all 34 bombs dropped in what Reed later described in his diary as "some Arab's cornfield."

JG 53 claimed only six kills on April 20, all of which were scored by I./JG 53. The victories were overshadowed by the loss of Hauptmann Wolfgang Tonne, *Staffelkapitän* of 3.Staffel. Tonne had just claimed three Spitfires for victories 120–122. When he returned to the *Gruppe*'s base at Protville on Cap Bon, he set up to land with his usual flamboyant sideslip. This time, he misjudged his height and "Yellow 1" crashed near the edge of the field, bursting into flame on impact. Tonne's death left only one "centurion" in the *Geschwader*: Hauptmann Friedrich-Karl "Tutti" Müller, *Kommandeur* of I./JG 53.

Following the end of the German air bridge, the Axis forces pressed every type of surface vessel into running what the crews called "the death route" from Naples to Tunisia. The Allied air forces flew maximum effort patrols from April 19 to go after this shipping.

The 79th Group flew 42 missions over the Sicilian strait between April 19 and 30, and ran into defending German fighters on several. On

April 20, the group flew a patrol between Pantelleria and Cap Bon; it was attacked by four Bf-109s 20 minutes after it took up station, which hit the top cover 85th Squadron. Lieutenant William Abbott sent one cartwheeling into the sea, while his wingman Lieutenant Carl Simpson damaged another that was last seen streaming glycol as it headed toward Tunisia. Minutes later, the 86th Squadron spotted four Ju-88s escorted by six Bf-109s. Fred Borsodi and his wingman Lieutenant Pete Bedford hit two 109s as they were punching off their belly tanks; Borsodi's target exploded while the pilot of the second helpfully bailed out just as Bedford opened fire. They then went after the Ju-88s, and each sent one bomber into the water below.

Shortly before midday on April 21, the group was on anti-shipping patrol; the 85th and 86th Squadrons were carrying one 500lb bomb each for shipping attacks, with the 87th providing cover backed up by the four Spitfire IXs of the Polish Fighting Team. They found two 100-foot motor barges and attacked unsuccessfully. As they were pulling out, a lone Bf-109 lurking in the low clouds hit Lieutenant John Anderson, who bailed out of his burning Warhawk but was never seen again. Suddenly, many other 109s appeared out of the clouds and a running dogfight quickly developed. The Poles downed three in quick succession, setting them on fire. The 86th's Leo Berinati exploded another, while Ed Fitzgerald became involved with three that nearly had him until he flamed one and the other two broke off. John Kelly caught one running for Sicily at low altitude that dug a wingtip and disappeared into the spray when he hit it with two bursts. The group made no other aerial contacts until April 29.

On April 23, the SAAF 7 Wing came across a formation of 20 of the giant Me-323s and shot down 16. This event ended the Axis attempt to maintain an air bridge to Tunisia.

The 64th Squadron added two final names to its ace list during the last of the 57th Group's North African victories on April 26. Second Lieutenants Robert J. "Rocky" Byrne and R.J. "Jay" Overcash each destroyed two Bf-109s while escorting RAF Baltimore bombers. The squadron's war diary recorded what happened when the formation was attacked by upwards of 20 Bf-109s over the target:

> 2nd Lieutenant Byrne got on an Me-109's tail and gave it a burst. The Me 109 started down and then turned back up, and Byrne gave him

a second good burst. Immediately following, Byrne attacked another Me-109. Flying Officer Marcum saw the Me-109 Byrne had been shooting in flames and going toward the deck. Marcum duly claims an Me-109 destroyed for 2nd Lieutenant Byrne. Byrne continued after his second Me-109, got in two good bursts and saw the enemy fighter go over on its back and the engine explode. 2nd Lieutenant Byrne claims a destroyed Me-109. He got in some shots at a third Me-109 but makes no claim from that engagement.

2nd Lieutenant R.J. Overcash spotted a pair of Me-109s coming across just above himself and Capt Mobbs. Then six Me-109s came in from three o'clock, and 2nd Lieutenant Overcash got in a long burst on the leading enemy fighter. It started down toward the deck but turned back up, so Overcash went down and got in a good 30-degree deflection shot on the enemy aeroplane. The Me-109 started for the deck trailing smoke. When it was at 2,000 feet 2nd Lieutenant Overcash was engaged by another Me-109. He turned back up, spun out and upon recovering saw the Me-109, which he had been following, crashed and burning on the deck. He claims an Me-109 destroyed.

Lieutenant Overcash then formed up with four friendly aircraft and started home. Just prior to crossing the bomb line area, two Me-109s attacked from nine o'clock. Lieutenant Overcash got a good shot at the leading enemy fighter, saw it roll over on its back and explode, going toward the deck in flames. Lieutenant Overcash claims a second 109 destroyed.

These claims brought Byrne's total to six and Overcash's to five.

Since its arrival as the first American fighter group in the Middle East, the 57th had flown 350 missions in 4,730 sorties, claiming 130 confirmed aerial victories during the campaign. Of 72 pilots who had flown their P-40s from *Ranger* off the coast of Africa ten months earlier, five were dead and four were prisoners of war.

The 79th's Warhawks ran into 15 Bf-109s and C.202s over Cap Bon the afternoon of April 29 as they pulled out of their bomb runs. Bill Hanson turned on a C.202 and hit it with the pilot bailing out quickly. Major Jack Watkins was bounced by an aggressive Bf-109; turning so tight he almost spun out, Watkins got inside the 109's turn and hit its wing, after which it tumbled into the sea. Jack Kauffman got into a turning fight with a 109 that seemed to last an eternity until, on the edge of a stall, he hit his opponent in the wing root; it flipped on its back and the pilot fell out. Kauffman was amazed to look over his shoulder and find wingman Bill "Tiger" Taylor still in position. Captain Barney Turner and Lieutenant Conly each shot down a Macchi. All four squadrons returned without loss.

The next day, the group was again airborne as a complete unit when it spotted an Italian destroyer below. Making masthead attacks, it hit it with four bombs and it stopped dead in the water. Just as it was about to administer the coup de grace, 15 Bf-109s slammed into the formation and a wild fight quickly ensued. Barney Turner and Lieutenant Rhynard each scored a 109, while Bob Allard and John Hutt were credited with probables. Unfortunately, in all the wild maneuvering, Lieutenants Thomas McCarty and Bill Hanson collided. Amazingly, two chutes popped out of the twisted metal. Both were picked up by the Italians and became POWs. As they left, the destroyer was sinking. After refueling back at base, the 79th returned to the straits battlefield and ran across a second Italian destroyer, covered by ten new C.205 "Veltro" fighters. The Warhawks dove through the escorts and planted four hits that mortally wounded the ship as fires raged throughout; it capsized and sank near Sidi Daoud. Two of the C.205s were shot down, including that flown by the CO, Maggiore Luigi Caroli, hit by Lieutenant Sammy Say, while Charlie Bolack and Michael McNall shared the second. The two destroyers the group finally credited with were the only enemy men-of-war ever sunk by P-40s. This ended the Axis naval effort.

April 30 also saw I./JG 53's "Tutti" Müller score one of three P-40s his *Gruppe* claimed in fights that day. It marked Müller's 115th victory and the "official" end of the *Gruppe*'s part in the Tunisian campaign. The next day, I./JG 53's remaining Bf-109s were handed over to II./JG 53 at La Marsa, and the pilots and surviving ground crew were airlifted to Comiso, Sicily. The transports were escorted by the four Bf-109Gs of Oberleutnant von Maltzahn's *Geschwaderstab*.

Operation *Strike* – the final Allied assault against the Afrika Korps and their Italian allies – commenced on May 6, 1943, at 0300 hours, when the most intensive artillery barrage of the entire North African campaign opened, with more than 400 British and Commonwealth artillery batteries firing what were described by one young officer as "stunning rates of metal." At El Alamein, gunners had plotted one shell for every 30 feet of enemy frontage; here, they fired one shell for every six feet. The artillery buried 72 enemy batteries that had been identified, hammering each with three two-minute concentrations by 25–30 guns.

First light came at 0540 hours, and the Allied air units filled the sky over the front, with more than 2,000 sorties flown, hitting targets from Medjez el Bab to Tunis. RAF and USAAF fighter-bombers concentrated on a four-mile square between Massicault and St Cyprien, going after every enemy vehicle spotted. The 5. Panzerarmee was powerless in the face of the advance of Allied armor, being reduced to only 70 tanks, none with a full load of fuel or ammunition. The Allied armor was under orders to race to Tunis, not stopping for anything. When it stopped that night, the forward units were less than a day's travel from Tunis.

Ultra picked up a message from General von Arnim informing German headquarters on Sicily that they should cease flying fuel or ammunition to his forces because they had no way of moving it to the front-line units.

II./JG 53 held out in Tunisia until May 7, during which the *Gruppe* was joined by 7. and 8.Staffeln of III./JG 53, which flew in from Sicily to operate for three days. JG 53's final days in the Tunisian campaign involved several missions flown from Sicily to provide what support they could to the ground forces at the front. The loss of both Tunis and Bizerte on May 7 meant the end was now at hand. The pilots flew several shuttle flights to Sicily, with a member of the ground crew stowed uncomfortably, but uncomplaining, in each fighter's rear fuselage. Von Maltzahn had brought the *Geschwaderstab* back from Sicily to fly out the last of those who could be rescued.

JG 77's *Kommodore* Johannes Steinhoff was also able to evacuate many of his ground crews, sending Bf-109s with a single crewman crammed into the rear fuselage across the straits at night that week. He was still forced to leave the majority of the ground crews behind when he was ordered to fly the surviving fighters to Sicily in the last light of day on May 7.

The 79th's last battle of the North African campaign happened on May 8, when it ran into 30 Bf-109s on the last anti-shipping mission of the day. The 316th's Captain Robert Dempsey scored one, while Sammy Hay, Robert Hoagland, and Lieutenant Charles Hale each shot down one. On the way home, Hale ran across a Fieseler Storch and shot it down for the group's final North African victory. I./JG 77's Oberfeldwebel Karl Hosmann was flying the Storch to Tunisia in a final attempt to bring back some of the ground crew left behind.

The Allies had feared that von Arnim would turn the Cap Bon peninsula into a dug-in redoubt after the fall of Tunis and Bizerte, but the Wehrmacht's fuel shortage and the speed of the Allied ground advance prevented the Afrika Korps from regrouping. On May 8, 5. Panzerarmee recorded the last entry in its war diary at 1535 hours: "the mass of our tanks and artillery is destroyed. No ammunition, no fuel left. In loyal performance of duty, the last fighters of the 5. Panzerarmee greet the homeland and our Führer. Long live Germany."

US Army ground combat operations ceased on May 9. American correspondent Ernie Pyle, whose reputation had been made during the North African campaign for his stories about the common soldiers on the front lines, wrote that "Winning in battle is like winning at poker or catching lots of fish. It's damned pleasant and it sets a man up." US ground combat casualties in the final assault were in excess of 4,400 killed and wounded. Enemy dead in the American sector of the battlefield came to 3,000, with 41,000 others surrendered and made prisoner.

Over the next few days, more than 225,000 German and Italian troops surrendered, which surprised Eisenhower, who had assured General Marshall on May 5 that the enemy could not have more than 150,000 troops left in North Africa. Unlike Hitler, with his exhortation to General von Arnim to "fight to the last bullet," to which the general asked when the order was read to him, "What does the last bullet mean in a modern war?" Benito Mussolini cabled General Giovanni Messe, commander of the Italian First Army, "As the aims of your resistance can be considered achieved, Your Excellency is free to accept an honorable surrender." When the newly promoted field marshal attempted to negotiate, he was given the choice of unconditional surrender or annihilation.

As one German unit tried to March into captivity as an organized unit, GIs watching them broke into a song recently popularized by bandleader Spike Jones and his City Slickers, "Der Führer's Face": "Are ve not der Supermen? Ya, ve iss der Supermen, super-dooper Supermen! Und ve heil, ve heil, right in der Führer's face!"

At 1316 hours on May 13, General Sir Harold Alexander cabled Winston Churchill: "Sir, it is my duty to report that the Tunisian campaign is over. All enemy resistance has ceased. We are masters of the North African shores."

The 33rd Group was still at Ebba Ksour. Three days later it moved to Menzel Temime, on the east coast of the Cap Bon peninsula, where it would operate during the coming campaign against the island of Pantelleria.

While the "Nomads" of the 33rd Fighter Group were the first P-40 group of the Twelfth Air Force to enter combat in North Africa, the last unit to arrive before the campaign ended was the 325th Fighter Group.

Herschel Green graduated from Advanced Flight Training on April 29, 1942, pinning on his silver Army Aviator wings and gold bar of a second lieutenant, receiving orders to join the 57th Pursuit Group, which was based at Bradley Field, Connecticut. By the time he got there after two weeks' leave en route, it was the 57th Fighter Group, and he was assigned to the 66th Fighter Squadron. He soon felt at home in the P-40F, which was the most powerful airplane he had yet flown in his short flying career. Five weeks after arrival, he was among the pilots "hived off" from the 57th to form the 79th Fighter Group, becoming a member of the 86th Fighter Squadron, with which unit he continued building experience in the P-40 over the summer of 1942, until for a second time he joined the "cadre" taken from the 79th to form the 325th Fighter Group that September. The 325th's component units were the 317th, 318th, and 319th Fighter Squadrons; Green found himself assigned to the 317th, commanded by Major Leonard C. Lydon. Training continued, and by Christmas 1942, Green – who had been renamed "Herky" by the squadron's first sergeant, in honor of the cartoon character Herk the Jerk, star of aviation safety posters on the hangar walls, when he was promoted to first lieutenant in October – had over 200 hours in the P-40F and felt proficient in handling the fighter from all the mock combats he and his squadron mates had engaged in, jumping flights from the other two squadrons. He was also a leader in buzzing the fishing boats off Martha's Vineyard.

New Year's Day 1943 found the 325th with orders to proceed by rail to Langley Field, Virginia, where it found 72 P-40Fs in fresh desert camouflage paint waiting for them. After two days spent learning to take off in the shortest distance possible, the group went aboard the carrier *Ranger* for another of the ship's transatlantic voyages to Africa, departing the Norfolk naval base at 1130 hours on January 8, 1943.

The pilots were unsurprised when once at sea they were informed their destination was Casablanca. Green remembered they spent their days watching Navy training films about carrier operations that all seemed to feature planes crashing and being pushed over the side, which they all found not reassuring regarding their immediate future.

On January 19 at 0800 hours, *Ranger* turned into the Atlantic trade winds off North Africa, increased to maximum speed, and began launching the P-40s. Green was number six of the 317th to take off, pulling his P-40 off the deck just above stalling speed and immediately sinking toward the water below. He gained sufficient speed to turn away from the carrier, leaving a long wake on the ocean's surface from his propwash. An hour later, the sparkling white city of Casablanca hove into view; Green remembered they were flying high enough not to see the squalid conditions below that they would soon discover. The Casablanca Conference was in session, and the group's unannounced arrival created a problem of where to put them on the crowded airfield. After four nights sleeping on the concrete floor of a hangar, they were all glad to be ordered to Médiouna airfield on January 23, where they found their new quarters were former horse stables. After flying patrols protecting President Roosevelt on his departure on January 24, they flew on to Tafaroui on January 25, where they finally connected with the ground echelon, which had been brought separately by ship.

In late January, Green was one of 20 pilots who flew their P-40s to Thélepte, where they were handed over as replacements to the 33rd Fighter Group. After a night spent on the primitive base, with a can of Spam ceremonially opened to celebrate their arrival with the replacement aircraft, Green and the others were glad when the ration trucks arrived the next morning. They rode them back to Telergma, where they caught a ride in a C-47 that returned them to Tafaroui. After a night listening to the pilots talk about the heavy combat and losses they had experienced, Green found his enthusiasm for arriving in the war zone had evaporated.

The 325th continued to be held in reserve and committed to further training. Finally, on April 5, it received orders to move to Montesquieu airfield in Algeria, which would be its first operational base, only 75 miles from the front lines. The 317th Squadron remained behind since the unit was short of seven airplanes; it was able to rejoin the rest of the group the first week of May.

The 318th and 319th Squadrons flew their first mission on April 17, when 22 P-40s of the 318th and 14 from the 319th took off at 1645 hours to escort B-26s from the 321st Bomb Group on a mission to bomb Mateur. Over the target, two JG 77 Bf-109s dove through the formation, shooting down Flight Officer Howard T. Cook, who bailed out and was picked up by the British. Six more missions were flown before the group was assigned a mission to dive-bomb the docks at Cape el Melah and Cape el Drek on April 29. Hits were scored on vessels at both locations.

First blood was scored on May 6, 1943, during a sea sweep between Cap Bon and Cap Serrat. The flight – led by First Lieutenant Harmon Burns, with Second Lieutenant Frank J. "Spot" Collins and Flight Officers Richard L. Catlin and Edmund A. Parent – was separated from the rest after dropping their bombs along with the others on some small ships that were left burning. As Burns led his flight home, they came across 20 Ju-52s parked on a coastal landing strip and strafed them, leaving several on fire. Collins then spotted a Bf-109 with its wheels down in the landing pattern. Slipping in behind, he closed in to point-blank range and opened fire; the 109 exploded when it crashed on the runway. Leaving the airfield, Burns came across a solitary Ju-52 and shot it down in flames near Cap Bon. Parent and Catlin ran across a small formation of Ju-52s and damaged two before their fuel shortage forced them to break off and head home.

The next day, Flight Officer Paul M. Hesler, Jr., came across an airfield where an Me-323 had just landed; he set it afire with one pass, then exploded a Ju-90 transport. Lieutenant Edward B. Walton was hit by flak and crashed into the sea.

There was no further success before the German surrender. The 325th would find itself heavily involved in the coming events that followed the victory in North Africa.

During the North African campaign, the Axis armies suffered casualties of 290,000 to 362,000 men, including those surrendered at the end; losses are still unclear, but it is estimated the Wehrmacht lost 8,500 killed and the Italians 3,700; a further 40,000–50,000 Axis soldiers were wounded. Luftwaffe losses were approximately 2,422 between November 1942 and May 1943, 41 percent of the total Luftwaffe force at the time. These losses would never be made good during the remainder of the war; more important was the loss of experienced aircrew, most of whom were prewar-trained veterans who had honed their skills in three years of war. They would be sorely missed in the air campaign to come over the next year in northern Europe.

American military historian Williamson Murray wrote of the Tunisian campaign: "The decision to reinforce North Africa was one of the worst of Hitler's blunders: admittedly, it kept the Mediterranean closed for six more months, with a negative impact on the Allied shipping situation but it placed some of Germany's best troops in an indefensible position from which, like Stalingrad, there would be no escape. Moreover, Hitler committed the Luftwaffe to fight a battle of attrition under unfavorable conditions and it suffered losses that it could not afford."

The highest compliment was paid by the Luftwaffe's Generalfeldmarschall Albert Kesselring after the war: "It was in Tunisia that the superiority of your air force first became evident."

11

PANTELLERIA

The Allies' next objective in the Mediterranean left the Allied air forces with little time to catch their breath following the surrender of Axis forces in Tunisia on May 13. In fact, some of the first missions for the new campaign had already been flown by that time.

The Casablanca Conference, held January 14–24, 1943, in the glow of the success of the British victory at El Alamein and the *Torch* landings, was held to assess the progress of the war to date and set new goals. The decisions made there would shape how the war was won. For those in North Africa, the most important decision was the agreement that Sicily was the next goal following the Axis defeat in North Africa. Control of the island would secure the Mediterranean sea lanes and end the need to send shipping around the Cape of Good Hope since access to the Suez Canal would be restored. Invading Sicily would divert the Wehrmacht from the Eastern Front, intensify pressure on Italy to surrender, loosen Axis control of the Balkans, and perhaps induce Turkey to enter the war. This was a decision that was the result of an argument won by Churchill over Roosevelt's military advisors; the American Joint Chiefs were still committed to a cross-Channel invasion at the earliest moment and rightly saw Sicily as a further diversion of men and material from the buildup of forces in Britain to support such an invasion. Stalin's decision not to attend, citing the Battle of Stalingrad, meant that the Americans and the Soviets would not be able to promote the "Second Front" in France as a majority viewpoint.

The British arrived in Casablanca with a common purpose and immaculate preparation, while the American military leadership was relatively unprepared, having left their staff back in Washington, and had to cobble together a staff on the spot. HMS *Bulolo*, a 6,000-ton passenger and cargo liner converted into a combined operations HQ, was stationed in the port of Casablanca to provide communication with London, support staff, and extensive documentation supporting an invasion of Sicily.

Additionally, Sir John Dill, the previous Chief of the Imperial General Staff, who had been posted to Washington as the Chief of the British Joint Staff Mission a year before, where he became a trusted confidante of both General Marshall and Admiral King, despite the admiral's well-known Anglophobia, was present. Dill's knowledge of the American leaders' thinking allowed the British to prepare preemptively to respond to American counterarguments to their position. Most importantly, Dill understood that Admiral King's agreement with the "Europe First" strategy made him wary of having naval forces idle in Europe while Japan remained a threat in the Pacific; once the British made the argument that remaining in the Mediterranean would keep the enemy off-balance until the cross-Channel invasion King had come to think the British would never agree to could come about, he became an ally. Marshall wrote, "I think the Mediterranean is a kind of dark hole, into which one enters at one's peril."

Churchill made the presentation. He pointed to the fact that the German U-boats had yet to be defeated, a requirement for getting American troops and supplies to England to create the 40-division force that was seen as the minimum necessary for success; that the Luftwaffe still held air superiority over western Europe, which must be broken if an invasion was to succeed; that production of landing craft would be insufficient to allow an invasion large enough to offer a real chance of success before the spring of 1944; and finally that allowing the Wehrmacht a year "to catch their breath" would only make such a cross-Channel invasion more difficult. Churchill stressed how control of Sicily would open the Mediterranean, enabling shipping for the war in the Far East to go through the Suez Canal, allowing a more rapid buildup of forces. He also pointed to the loss of Sicily as a pressure point on the Italian government that could lead to an early Italian surrender, thus depriving Germany of its one major ally in Europe and forcing the

Wehrmacht to take forces from the Eastern Front or France to occupy Italy and replace Italian forces in the Balkans.

Once again, President Roosevelt agreed with Churchill's argument, particularly with regard to opening the Mediterranean. With his focus on the domestic political effect of military operations, Roosevelt also saw deposing Mussolini as an opportunity to strengthen political support for the war in the Italian-American community. Once again, General Marshall bowed to political and military reality, offering little opposition to the decision in favor of taking Sicily, which he now saw as logical if the Allies meant to remain active in the Mediterranean. The decision to invade Sicily in July 1943 was made following Churchill's public promise to support the cross-Channel invasion in 1944.

Many other decisions regarding operational strategy were made. The Combined Bomber Offensive from Britain was confirmed as the method to destroy the Luftwaffe's air superiority over western Europe to set the invasion. For those in the Mediterranean, the most important decision was a command restructuring among the Allied air forces to strengthen international cooperation. Air Marshal Arthur Tedder was given command of the Mediterranean Air Command (MAC), with effect on February 18, 1943. This united the RAF and Commonwealth Air Forces and the USAAF. American General Carl Spaatz commanded the Northwest African Air Forces (NAAF), which included the Northwest African Strategic Air Force (NASAF) under General Doolittle, and the Northwest African Tactical Air Force (NATAF) commanded by Air Marshal Sir Arthur Coningham, and the Northwest African Coastal Air Force (NACAF) under Air Vice Marshal Sir Hugh Lloyd.

Tedder worked constantly to make unity of command and purpose a reality. At a dinner in Spaatz's headquarters, he offered the following toast:

> You know, we British are intensely proud of our Air Force. We think that it is the very best in the world, and that it saved England and the world – all of us. We have our own ways of doing things and I suppose we feel we are justified in keeping those ways. But we also know that you Americans are equally proud of your splendid Air Force, and that you feel justified in doing things your way – as well you are. However, it will be the fusion of us, the British, with you,

the Americans that is going to make the very best Air Force in the world. From here on, I shall not speak of we, the British, and you, the Americans, but rather of we, the Allies.

Writing in his postwar memoirs, Tedder stated that when MAC was formed, he believed Mediterranean operations had to continue, since "that was the theater in which the enemy could be most effectively engaged in 1943." Strategically and operationally, he believed in the theater air power doctrine, which held that the air force was to focus on air superiority, battlefield interdiction, and close air support, in descending order of importance. His unified control of the unified air force insured that this order of priority would be applied by all units throughout the theater.

There are two schools of historical thought regarding the Mediterranean war from Sicily. One view has long held that the war the Allies fought at Sicily and later in Italy was poorly thought-out and opportunistic, with the Allies out-generaled and outfought, leading to a "dreadful slogging match" in a theater of little importance, a campaign sufficient to rival rather than complement the main effort to defeat Germany in northwestern Europe. Another, more recent view is that Allied Mediterranean policy and strategy was indeed opportunistic and adopted due to the recognition that it was not possible to engage the enemy quickly with a cross-Channel invasion. The Sicilian and Italian campaigns, however, created an "ulcer" in the Wehrmacht, as it became mired in a struggle that diverted forces that might have been useful in delaying, if not stopping, the Allied landings at Normandy and the subsequent offensive across northwestern Europe after it lost its major European ally.

While there are strong arguments to both, more than 80 years on it is important to look at what was actually attempted and accomplished.

On April 24, the transport *Mariposa* docked in Casablanca, and the officers and men of the 99th Fighter Squadron came ashore. They were a squadron unlike any other: independent, not attached to any fighter group. That was because the officers and men were African American, the first graduates of the Tuskegee Aviation Project, which inducted and trained the first non-white pilots and ground crew to be part of the then all-white USAAF. They were commanded by Lieutenant Colonel Benjamin O. Davis, a graduate of the West Point class of 1934 where he had been "silenced" by his white classmates for the entire four years. Davis later recalled that "It was apparent, not only to me, but to the people in the 99th, that they held the future of blacks in the Army Air Corps in their hands. This was something that everyone in the 99th understood as early as the autumn of 1942 – that their performance would create the future environment for blacks."

A day after their arrival, they boarded an ancient French train and traveled 150 miles across the desert to the former Luftwaffe air base at Oued Naj, near the town of Fez, Morocco. The grass field was ten miles from Meknes at the foot of the Atlas Mountains. At the field, they were met by the wrecked Bf-109s, and waited for a week for the arrival of their 27 P-40L Warhawks. Once the fighters arrived, Davis set them to a rapid training schedule. Transition training to the Warhawk was completed at the end of May. They had been fortunate to spend time with Phil Cochran, who filled them in on enemy capability and trained them on the latest tactics, including dive-bombing, which they would soon become intimately familiar with in combat.

Their training deemed complete, the squadron moved 1,000 miles east to Fardjouna, on Tunisia's Cap Bon peninsula, at the end of May. "The flying out of Cap Bon could be quite hazardous in that we flew off a dirt strip," Davis recalled. "We would take-off in a 12-plane formation. Although we never had a collision, it was a hairy operation, especially if you had to get back into the field soon after takeoff in case of an emergency – if there was no cross-wind to blow the dust away, the strip would be totally obscured."

The 99th Squadron was soon assigned to the 33rd "Nomads" Group, to make up the group's heavy losses in the Tunisian fighting over the previous four months. Group CO Lieutenant Colonel William Momyer was not happy about the assignment, making his antipathy obvious at the first meeting with the squadron's leaders. When squadron commander Davis and executive officer Major George S. "Spanky" Roberts reported to his office, Momyer did not return their salutes. On June 3, he scheduled a group briefing, then changed the time, moving it up an hour without telling the 99th, with the result the pilots arrived late. His efforts to embarrass the squadron affected its reputation negatively; only later would the full extent of Momyer's intentional damage be understood.

The Battle of Pantelleria quickly became the next phase of the war after the Axis surrender in Tunisia. An essential requirement for the Sicilian invasion was the ability of the Allies to provide air cover. Since there were no aircraft carriers available as there had been for the Moroccan invasion, such air cover would have to be land-based. With the nearest Allied airfields located on the Cap Bon peninsula, the 183 miles of the Sicilian strait between North Africa and Sicily made provision of such cover, which would have to be constant, very difficult, since only the limited number of P-38s remaining after the Tunisian battles had the range to fly to Sicily and remain over the beaches long enough to provide effective cover.

The only island base currently held by the Allies that was near Sicily was Malta. That much-bombed island's airfields were already at maximum use by defending fighter units and offensive strike fighter and torpedo bomber units. While the fighters could provide some cover for the invasion, the 138-mile distance separating the two islands was only some 40 miles less than the distance from Cap Bon and meant that the Spitfires based there would only have minutes over the invasion beaches before they would be forced to return for lack of fuel.

General Eisenhower had decided on May 6 to invade and occupy Pantelleria island. The island was eight miles long and five miles wide with sheer cliffs in its 42 square miles; its importance stemmed from its location: 53 miles east-northeast of Tunisia and 63 miles southwest of Sicily. Thus, Pantelleria lay astride the route from North Africa to Sicily. As many as 100 Axis aircraft had operated from the island's Marghana airfield during the Tunisian campaign. The airfield had a large underground hangar with repair and maintenance shops, while its 5,000-foot airstrip was large enough that damaged Allied bombers could land there if it was impossible for them to continue on across the Sicilian strait. The underground maintenance facilities could support up to five fighter squadrons, almost two complete fighter groups.

It was obvious that Pantelleria and the surrounding Pelagie islands of Lampedusa, Lampione, and Linosa should be taken as soon as possible. Eisenhower's planning staff created Operation *Corkscrew*, an invasion of the island to pave the way for the invasion of Sicily. The Allied Combined Chiefs of Staff approved the operation on May 13.

PANTELLERIA DURING OPERATION *CORKSCREW*, 1943

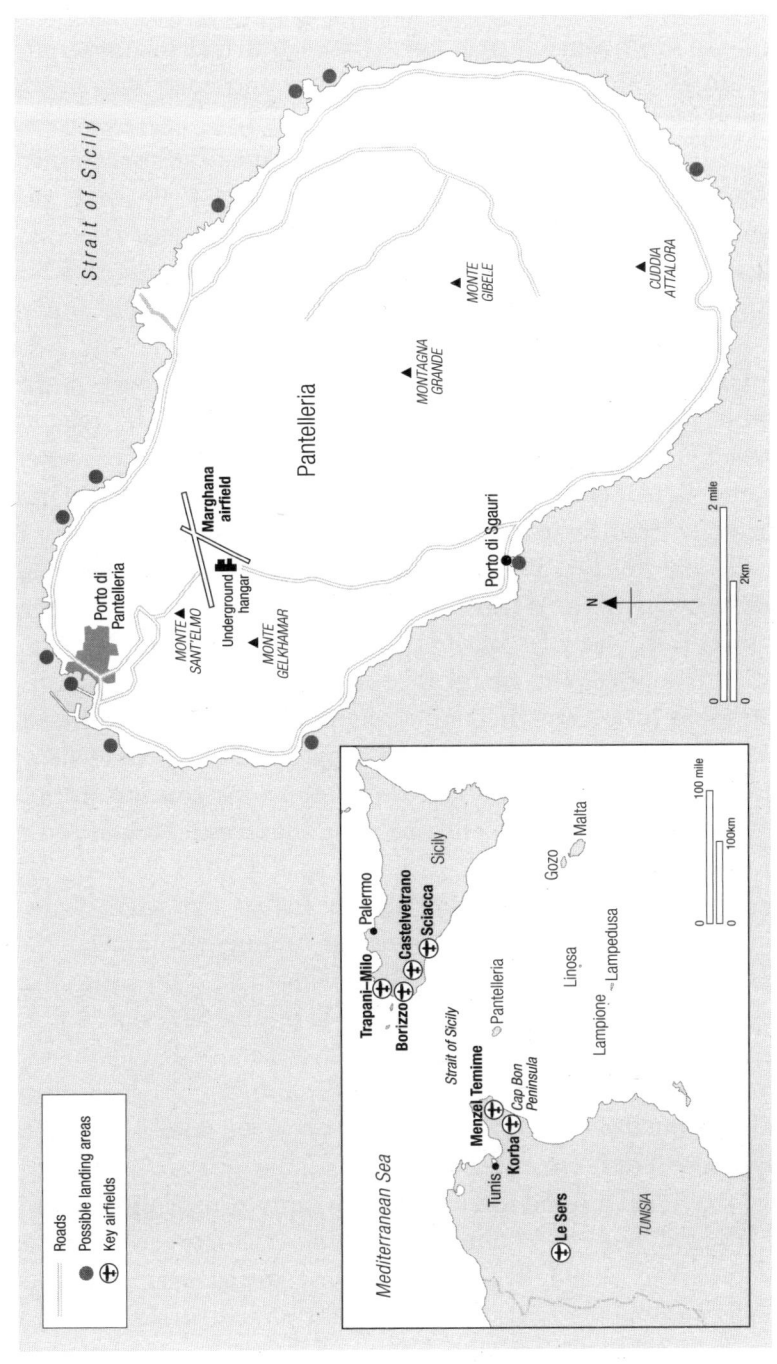

While Mussolini had proclaimed Pantelleria "the Italian Gibraltar" when he began fortifying the island in 1925, the fact was it could be cut off from outside support. The island had an underground water supply, and the electric power plant and ammunition supply dumps were also located underground. The 100 gun emplacements on all sides of the island had been carved out of the rocky cliffs and reinforced with concrete. Marghana airfield had an underground hangar capable of holding up to 50 fighters, with blast-proof doors. Additionally, the island was covered with stone fences and houses built of rock and masonry, each of which could be easily converted into a miniature fortress that would have to be taken individually by infantry in an invasion. The conditions would allow a stubborn garrison to make taking the island a drawn-out, bloody affair. However, the 12,000-man Italian garrison was not composed of stubborn defenders. By this point in the war, a majority of Italian soldiers had seen their comrades turned into cannon fodder by their fascist leaders for no gain; they had also watched the growth of Allied power over the previous two years, and most on the island understood that their role would be sacrificial. There were perhaps 1,000–1,500 German troops on the island who might offer a stiffer response to an invading force, but their numbers were insufficient to block the ultimate outcome. The Germans also operated Freya and Würzburg radar stations on the island. Allied planners took comfort in the fact that, during the Tunisian campaign, the island's antiaircraft gunners made a poor showing.

While Allied planners believed the Italian defenders were not committed first-rate troops, any sort of prolonged campaign would upset the timetable for invading Sicily, which was set for early July. A show of strength on Pantelleria could result in a morale boost for Sicily's defenders when the opposite was needed.

In the face of these questions and uncertainties, the Allied plans for invading Pantelleria called for a massive, sustained aerial bombardment campaign to crush enemy power on the island, thereby reducing the size of the Allied ground force needed to capture and hold it. Between May 18 and June 11, fighters and bombers of the Mediterranean Air Command would fly 5,285 bombing sorties against targets on Pantelleria, dropping 6,313 tons of bombs on the Italian and German forces there. Additionally, Royal Navy surface fleet units bombarded the island from the sea at night. By the time the campaign was completed, it would become a case study in the devastating use of airpower.

Once the Axis forces on the island had been sufficiently weakened, the British 1st Infantry Division, supported by naval forces, was to occupy the island along with the nearby Pelagic islands, giving the Allies absolute control of the Sicilian strait, and providing "unsinkable aircraft carriers" within close range of the Sicilian invasion beaches. D-Day was set for June 11, 1943.

The *Corkscrew* air offensive began May 18, led by 42 B-25s, 44 B-26s, and 91 P-38s and P-40s of Doolittle's NASAF. The Allied force was opposed by the Regia Aeronautica C.202 fighters of 151° Gruppo based at Marghana airfield that managed to get airborne before the P-38s dive-bombed the runway. One C.202 managed to make a few passes against the 310th Group's B-25s but was shot down by defending gunners on the third pass. The raid destroyed an S.79 Sparviero bomber and several C.202s, but most importantly set fire to 450 fuel drums. Gradually, the units assigned to NATAF also entered the fray, with almost all Allied air units taking part in the campaign by late May. RAF units also participated in the campaign.

Spaatz's NAAF intelligence experts relied on aerial reconnaissance to make target assignments. The initial photo-recon missions were flown by the legendary Wing Commander Adrian Warburton, commander of Malta's 683 Photo Recon Squadron. Warburton had established a reputation for derring-do in flying dangerous recon missions, and he lived up to that with the missions flown on May 18 and June 4, in which he flew his photo-recon Spitfire around and over Pantelleria at an altitude of 200 feet, photographing the coastal gun positions and all other defensive positions on the island. Defending flak chased him across the island, but he emerged from both missions undamaged. The photos returned from the June 4 mission confirmed Marghana airfield had been heavily damaged, with craters in the runway, while the main barracks and buildings near the underground hangar had been destroyed by direct hits and the supply dumps were heavily damaged. These photos were used to change the bombing campaign, and Warburton was awarded a US Distinguished Flying Cross for the result.

Eisenhower and Spaatz were convinced that the Pantelleria garrison could not hold up under a concentrated air bombardment such as was being flown. From late May through June 6, the heavy bombing by

Doolittle's NASAF was incrementally intensified. In a second phase, from June 7 to June 11, Pantelleria was attacked day and night, with the weight of attack increasing from 200 sorties a day to 1,500–2,000 sorties on the 11th. At the same time, targets were bombed in Sicily, Sardinia, and mainland Italy to confuse the enemy.

On May 19 six of the Bf-109Gs that had recently re-equipped 150° Gruppo and seven 153° Gruppo C.202s scrambled from Sciacca and Chinisia to engage B-17s escorted by 12 P-38s from the 14th Group's 49th Squadron heading for Trapani–Milo airfield on Sicily. The attackers were intercepted over Marsala. The Italians claimed one P-38 shot down with two probables while damaging 16 B-17s. The 14th Group admitted the loss of First Lieutenants Frank C. Hawk and John L. Wolford, one of the 1st Group veterans transferred to the 14th to refresh the group's leadership after it was withdrawn from combat due to high losses in the spring. Wolford was covering two damaged P-38s when he was jumped by the 150° Gruppo Bf-109Gs and turned back to engage the Messerschmitts and protect the damaged Lightnings when he was shot down.

On May 20, the 33rd "Nomads" Group moved from Ebba Ksour airfield to Menzel Temime airfield on the Cap Bon peninsula, where they were only some 20 minutes' flying time from Pantelleria. By now, they were quite experienced as dive bombers from their operations in the closing battles in Tunisia. Now equipped with a full complement of P-40Ls and replacement pilots, the group was no longer the ghost of its former self it had been after battling the Germans in January and February.

Lieutenant James Reed noted in his diary that once missions began to be flown against Pantelleria – with the first flown on May 21 – the group's squadrons flew two missions a day each as weather allowed. Reed was unable to fly until the end of the month, after cutting his hand when he attempted to grab a fish while swimming at the nearby beach. He wrote, "My hand swelled up that night nearly to my elbow. I spent the next day soaking my hand and arm in cold water. It hurt like hell." He finally returned to operations on May 29, assigned as a spare and making the mission when one of the other Warhawks wouldn't start up. The squadron dive-bombed shipping in the harbor, and strafed the piers. Reed recorded in his diary that night that "Our bombs missed the boats, but as we were leaving a P-38 made a direct hit on one and it blew up." Missions over the island continued as the operational tempo built up. Reed wrote, "That island is really catching hell. Every time we go out there, some group has just been there, another group is there, and there is another group following us."

While the Pantelleria campaign was consuming more and more Allied air force attention, the campaign to decimate Axis airpower on Sardinia that began in March continued, in order to deny the enemy the ability to mount any air defense of Pantelleria. By mid-May, the 325th Fighter Group was up to full strength when the 317th Squadron finally received replacements for the aircraft it had transferred to the 33rd Group that had been lost in the Kasserine Pass battles after a six-week wait, and joined the 318th and 319th Squadrons on May 15.

First Lieutenant Herschel Green recalled that when the 317th Squadron finally rejoined the group, they were told by the pilots of the other squadrons that they were fortunate to have been assigned to operations at this time, since the escort missions being flown had seen almost no response from the enemy, and the newcomers would have the chance to ease into combat slowly. The mission of May 19 was one Green would remember above all others to come.

> Group Mission Number 26, which would be our first at full group strength, was an escort for B-26s bombing the supply depot at Decimomannu Airdrome on Sardinia, just north of the port city of Cagliari. Our four-plane flights were distributed around the formation; we paralleled the west coast of Sardinia, then turned southeast toward the target and crossed the Gulf of Oristano at 13,000 feet.
>
> The flight behind mine was jumped by the enemy and broke into the attack. I heard "Mayfair Red, break left! Break left! Herky – they're coming in from eight o'clock high!" They were threatening our very lives before we even knew they were about. It was violent. I immediately flung the stick to the left, kicking hard rudder at the same time to whip into a left turn. The strain greyed-out my vision for a second or two and when the mist cleared a glance over my shoulder revealed two Me-109s coming in from my left rear. Machinegun fire ripped into my P-40. A part of my instrument panel dissolved in a hail of bullets.
>
> I became covered in sweat; it ran down my back; it streamed down my chest; my eyes burned from it. I knew the P-40 couldn't catch,

out-run, out-climb, or out-dive them. All I could do was out-turn them and that is what I tried. Another 109 was firing at me from my right. I threw the P-40 into a hard skid to the right and he overshot me, but pulled up sharply before I could bring my sights to bear on him. My heart was pumping like a sprinter's.

Me-109s were coming from every direction and my four P-40s were hopelessly scattered. I found myself alone and engaged by six Me-109s that proceeded to maul me like cats playing with a mouse. This continued for several minutes, which seemed like a lifetime, as they made multiple passes at me from each side. By slipping, skidding and racking my P-40 around in some impossible maneuvers, I kept managing to elude them. I continued taking hits! My radio was blown out. It was only a matter of time till one of them got me.

I glanced left – another 109 was coming in. I whipped the stick left and back into my gut as hard as I could, almost blacking out in the process. Suddenly, my P-40 staggered as something slammed into the armor plate behind my seat and I knew I had taken a cannon hit; a gaping hole appeared in the fuselage just behind my head. I whipped back to the right as he shot past me, just in time to meet another head-on with all guns blazing. Dust was swirling up from the floor. I headed right at him.

By the grace of God, I was getting hits all over him and pieces started to fly off. We missed a head-on collision by a hair's breadth. As he passed me, his plane exploded in a tremendous ball of fire. The two were coming at me from different sides. If I turned into one, the other would be on my tail in an instant. I fought my panic. My terror faded and I waited for my death. A swarm of tracers flashed past my cockpit. I reacted violently; in my terror I pulled the stick left and back too fast as I kicked the right rudder hard. The next thing I knew, I was in an over-the-top snap roll ending in a spin. I was headed straight down in a vicious power-on spin.

The Me-109 pilot figured he shot me down when I spun out because he abandoned me. I fell through the undercast and was able to recover from the spin at about 3,000 feet. I took cover in the clouds and headed for Africa.

Minutes later, Green spotted another aircraft in the distance that soon became one of the missing P-40s from his flight. Without a radio, he signaled by hand that he would follow. "When we finally arrived back at Montesquieu airfield, he led me in to landing because I didn't have an airspeed indicator." Green was later given a shell fragment that had clipped the top off a junction box and then embedded itself in one of the engine cylinders. The mechanic told him that if that fragment had been an inch lower, the engine would have stopped dead. Green's 109 was the first victory for the 317th, and the ninth for the 325th.

In addition to Green, Major Bob Baseler, First Lieutenants Joseph Bloomer, Jr., and Lawrence Ritter and Flight Officers John Smallsreed and Ebert W. Smith were credited with a 109 each, while two P-40s were lost – First Lieutenants Charles Housel bailed out and D.R. Brown crashed to his death. Decimomannu was obscured by heavy clouds, so that the bombing results were questionable.

Green's 109 was confirmed by Captain W.R. Reed, who witnessed the engagement. His P-40, side number "13," had been shot so full of holes it was consigned to the scrapyard; as far as Green was concerned, so was the number "13." After this hair-raising ordeal he switched to side number "11," which he used with all his remaining assigned aircraft.

The May 19 bombing had been so inaccurate that a second mission against Decimomannu was flown the next day; bombing results this time were excellent. Just as the 325th's Warhawks dove on the airfield to strafe the few remaining targets left, 16 enemy fighters dove on them and a dogfight quickly broke out. Frank "Spot" Collins claimed a second victory, reporting, "At 1155 hours I shot down one Me-109 from about 7,000 feet in a diving attack just west of Decimomannu airfield. The Me-109 came in from the east, and I saw it crash into the ground just west of Siligna. The pilot did not bail out." Six other victories were scored by Captain Everett Howe and First Lieutenants Harold Crossley, William Lott, and Arthur McDaniel, with Second Lieutenant Thomas Johnson hit in the fight and forced to ditch in the sea.

While this was going on, group commander Colonel Austin's flight spotted seven enormous Me-323 transports and shot them all down, with Austin, First Lieutenants John Tuchson and John Grove, and Flight Officers David McCampbell, Archie McKeithen, and John Smallsreed each claiming one.

On May 21, the 325th returned to Decimomannu and got involved in yet another battle. First Lieutenants Grove and Frank Hamilton each shot down one but were both shot down in turn by other enemy fighters. Captain William Reed and First Lieutenant John Palmer also shot down one Bf-109 each. These victories were the last scored by the 325th for a few days while the group spent the next seven days participating in the Pantelleria battle.

They dive-bombed the airfield and strafed gun emplacements on the first mission. The 325th flew two missions a day over the next several days, racking up eight missions to Pantelleria. Captain Robert W. Myers experimented with carrying a 1,000lb bomb. Once he demonstrated a P-40 could take off with such a load, the group flew three missions to Pantelleria with these bombs. Green remembered, "Our P-40s could barely stay with the bombers when we carried the thousand-pounders. We flew close escort, really formation with the bombers over the target, and toggled our bombs when they dropped theirs." Two pilots were lost to the heavy flak during these missions.

Every fighter pilot dealt with fear, both in combat and back at base, remembering a fight or thinking of those that might come. Few ever spoke about their fear and how they dealt with it; Herky Green was one of the few.

> After that first mission, I was so shook up that I couldn't sleep. We knew every day whether we had to fly a mission the next day. That way, I could lay awake all night and think about it. I continued to fly because there just wasn't any honorable way out of it. But it was hell.
>
> After I'd flown a few more missions, I began to calm down a little bit. And I got to the point that, once we were in the air, I felt okay and was really kind of hoping we would find some enemy aircraft, so we could have a go at them. From that low on May 19, 1943 – from being absolutely terrorized – I kept flying until I realized one day that everybody who fights a war can tell you about the time that, but for the grace of God, he would have been dead. I said to myself, "You've been through that a half dozen times." And a great light came on: *I wasn't going to get killed in the war!* So, from then on, I had no fear, no inhibitions. I could go tearing into a gaggle of enemy airplanes with just a wingman and not be worried at all about getting killed. My main concern was how many were going to get away before I could shoot them down.

May 25 saw the fighters of the Regia Aeronautica put up their best performance over Sicily. C.202s of 374ª Squadriglia were scrambled to engage a large formation of B-24s headed for Reggio Calabria, intercepting them over Messina. Tenente Vittorio Satta and wingman Sergente Ricotti shared in the destruction of a Liberator; Satta's Folgore was damaged by defensive fire from the bombers. Four Folgores of 151° Gruppo intercepted 14th Group P-38s near Palermo and claimed one. The 14th reported the loss of two Lightnings – one to flak and the other lost over Tunisia returning to its base. Additionally, C.202s from Asso di Bastoni were scrambled from Catania three times to intercept formations of bombers heading for Messina, during which the *Gruppo* pilots claimed 14 victories.

The 31st Fighter Group finally commenced operations over Pantelleria on May 26, when the Spitfires escorted six B-25s bombing Marghana airfield. In the time since the Axis surrender in Tunisia, the group had undergone several changes. They had moved to Korba airfield on the tip of Cap Bon, from where Pantelleria could be seen on the distant horizon on a clear day. The move on May 20 had not been met with happiness by anyone in the unit, since they were moving from Le Sers, a former French Air Force field where they had good accommodation, to a dusty, primitive forward strip with unfinished runways that were not even level; the hastily scraped surface undulated. The surrounding ground was rocky and barren, lacking trees or shade. At first, they had thought the airfield's location on the coast with its own beachfront was a good thing, until the first ones to venture in the water discovered the hard way that the water was full of stingrays lying just below the sandy bottom; their stings left agonizing welts on feet, legs, and hands. Additionally, the field had been most recently used by the Luftwaffe, and the engineers had quickly found that nearly every piece of wrecked gear on the field was booby-trapped; one did not venture anywhere that the engineers' safety flags were not fluttering. There was also the fact they were back to pup tents and sleeping bags without cots, while the food took several weeks to graduate from "cold C-rations" to "hot C-rations."

The one good thing was that the supply of Spitfire IX fighters in North Africa had finally increased to the point where the 307th and 309th Squadrons were fully equipped with the superior Spitfire, while the 308th benefitted from the arrival in theater of Spitfire VIIIs with which they were now equipped. The Merlin-60 series Spitfires finally put the group in a position of technological equality with their Bf-109G and Fw-190-equipped opponents.

The 325th escorted B-26s to Decimomannu on May 27, where it ran into 24 Bf-109s of JG 53 and the Regia Aeronautica's 150° Gruppo Autonomo, which had been the first Regia Aeronautica fighter unit to re-equip with the German fighter back in March. Ten C.202s of 53° Stormo were also in the Axis force that attacked the bombers. Bob Baseler's flight responded to the Axis fighters, and in a spirited dogfight over Cape Spartivento, Baseler and Major E.B. Howe each shot down a C.202, while four Bf-109s – of which three were Italian-flown, unknown to the Americans – were shot down by "Spot" Collins, John Smallsreed, Dick Catlin, and Mark Boone. Bill Hemphill was hit and had to ditch in the sea. Flight Officer Catlin dropped a life raft and radioed for air-sea rescue. Unfortunately, though Hemphill was picked up by an RAF Walrus, the amphibian crashed on takeoff after pickup, killing all on board.

The 325th flew its 44th mission on May 28, a bomber escort to Trapani–Milo airfield on Sicily. The defenders were the newly operational Bf-109Gs of 150° Gruppo that the Americans mis-identified as being German-flown, and C.202s of 153° Gruppo. Green, recently promoted to captain, recalled that Bf-109s first attacked the bombers east of the target, and the fight continued out to sea:

> I was ten miles off the coast at 9,000 feet when I saw a Me 109 far below me. I rolled over and went after him, opening fire on the way down. As the range shortened, he pulled up and I did likewise, firing into him. I then went over him and climbed, before rolling over and diving after him again, shooting on the way. To keep from hitting the water I pulled up and climbed to 9,000 feet again, blacking out for a moment. When I looked for the Me 109 again, I couldn't find a trace of him.

At the post-mission debrief, Major Howe confirmed Green's victory, stating he and several other pilots saw a Bf-109 plunge into the water at the point Green described; this was victory number two for Green. Two other pilots, First Lieutenant Rayburn Lancaster and Flight Officer Bruce Cunningham, were each credited with one Bf-109 destroyed.

Sadly, Flight Officer John Smallsreed, a talented pilot and potential ace who had scored his third victory only the day before, was listed missing in action; no one saw what had happened to him, a frequent fate for a fighter pilot.

Eight Bf-109Gs of 365ª Squadriglia, 150° Gruppo, took off from Sciacca at 1740 hours to intercept an attack on Castelvetrano airfield when radar spotted two other formations approaching Trapani. These were B-26s of the Northwest African Strategic Air Force on their way to attack Sciacca, Castelvetrano, Trapani–Milo, and Borizzo airfields. The eight Bf-109s engaged four 31st Group Spitfires and several 14th Group P-38s escorting nine bombers. Tenente Eugenio Lecchi and Tenente Giosuè Carillo claimed two Spitfires shot down and a P-38 damaged. The 14th claimed two Bf-109s shot down by the 48th Squadron's Captain Robert R. "Bob" McCord and First Lieutenant Sidney W. Weatherford, while Captains Charles J. "Charley" Crocker Campbell and Sam L. Palmer, and First Lieutenant Richard A. Campbell of the 37th Squadron, and Second Lieutenant Daniel D. Africa of the 48th, claimed four Bf-109s as probables.

On June 1, 19 B-17s, together with a force of six Wellingtons, pounded Pantelleria from end to end. By June 6, daily sorties had increased to more than 200, and the number doubled or tripled during the next five days. Bomb tonnage had greatly increased, with 231 tons dropped on June 5–6 and increasing to 600 tons on June 7. On June 8, B-17s, B-25s, B-26s, and A-20s dropped almost 700 tons of bombs, followed by more than 822 tons the next day. Surrender leaflets were also dropped.

The day before the infamous late briefing, the 99th flew its first combat sorties in the Pantelleria campaign. Lieutenants William Campbell and Clarence Jamison flew as wingmen to other 33rd Group Warhawks on an offensive sweep; that afternoon, Lieutenants James Wiley and Charlie Hall flew as wingmen on a second mission in which the group bombed and strafed Marghana airfield on Pantelleria, with Wiley assigned as group commander Momyer's wingman. Following the late briefing the next day, the four pilots who had flown as wingmen on the previous day's missions flew as element leaders on a third mission to the same target.

Over the next days, attacks on Axis forces occupying Pantelleria continued. The 99th rotated its pilots through the missions so it could gain combat experience. On June 4, First Lieutenant Charles Dryden got his initiation to war over Pantelleria. He later recalled, "Following my leader in a dive, I saw hundreds of red tracers streaking past my cockpit. I was concentrating on hitting the target, so I didn't have time to get scared. It wasn't till I pulled out of my dive that the thought hit me they were trying to kill me!"

The 99th Squadron flew its first mission as a unit on June 5, to bomb Marghana airfield on Pantelleria. The 99th finally encountered the Luftwaffe on June 9, when it was assigned to escort A-20s in another attack on Pantelleria. Flying as top cover for the mission, First Lieutenant Charles Dryden, leading five other Warhawks flown by Lieutenants Willie Ashley, Sidney Brooks, Lee Rayford, Leon Roberts, and Spann Watson, spotted four unidentified "bogies" at "five o'clock high." Several minutes later, the JG 77 Bf-109Gs dove on the Warhawks. The pilots turned into the attacking Germans and were quickly involved in a melee that thoroughly tested their flying skills.

Rayford soon had two enemy fighters on his tail; their bullets stitched across his right wing. Watson opened fire from long range on the 109s pursuing Rayford and convinced them to abandon their attack. Meanwhile, when Ashley's excited turn into the enemy put his fighter into an uncontrollable high-speed spin, he quickly lost several thousand feet of altitude directly over Pantelleria before he recovered. Remembering Cochran's injunction never to split up, he looked around for any other fighter to join up with. Spotting one, he turned to it, only to discover it was an Fw-190. He set his sights on the enemy fighter and opened fire; the Würger began to smoke, but ground fire forced him to abandon the chase and prevented him confirming that the Fw-190 had indeed crashed.

As that was happening, Dryden spotted a formation of 12 Ju 88s above him and set off after them. Unfortunately, the Warhawks were set up for low-level operations and lacked an oxygen system. Having climbed to 16,000 feet and finding himself still out of range of the Junkers bombers, Dryden passed out. The Warhawk's nose came up and the fighter stalled and fell into a shallow dive; Dryden regained consciousness at 12,000 feet and regained control.

The six returned safely, elated they had survived their first brush with the enemy. Momyer turned their eagerness for a fight into "panicky" and "undisciplined" behavior in his official report on the engagement. He continued to deliberately minimize and mischaracterize the squadron's achievements in his reports to XII Fighter Command.

While operations from Marghana airfield on the island were impossible, German and Italian fighter units on Sicily attempted to intervene between June 5 and 7 and again on June 10–11, though they failed to impede the Allied air offensive.

June 6 saw the 31st finally meet the Luftwaffe with its new Spitfires. While escorting a squadron of RAF Baltimore bombers to strike the Pantelleria harbor, the 308th Squadron that was flying high cover was hit by eight Bf-109s as the formation turned away for home, having completed the bomb run. First Lieutenant Trafton was flying one of the two Spitfires that became separated from the rest of the squadron by the enemy attack. He soon found himself alone, surrounded by the eight enemy fighters, which were taking turns diving on him in pairs, for which all he could do was break into them and try to fire a burst as they flashed past. Despite his frantic calls for help, the group could not come back to help without leaving the bombers unprotected. Finally, three 308th pilots were allowed to turn back and help. With their arrival, Trafton dodged underneath the formation and took off for Korba. The enemy, low on fuel after all the maximum-performance maneuvering, quickly departed when the three rescuers dove through their formation to announce their presence.

Reveille at Korba was held at 0615 the following morning – by the enemy. A Luftwaffe force of six Fw-190 fighter-bombers escorted by six Bf-109s made three passes over the field out of the light of the rising sun, strafing everything in sight while the Fw-190s also dropped 500kg bombs. There was no place to run or hide, and Group members hit the ground where they were when the enemy appeared. As fast as they could, men took protection in the slit trenches that had been hacked out of the rocky ground as the enemy fighters roared overhead. As the enemy made a second pass, one 40mm Bofors gun began firing at them. One of the Bf-109s was hit by the gun as it turned to make a third pass, and it crashed short of the runway. When the enemy flew off, ten Spitfires had been damaged to varying degrees, and 30 wounded were taken to the aid station.

Despite all this, the group flew two escort missions in the afternoon. Group commander Fred Dean later remarked to one of his ground crew when he returned that the sky over the island was so full of American and RAF airplanes that midair collisions seemed to be the biggest threat. The next day, June 9, was one of the 31st's most successful of the war. The 308th returned from its first mission of the day claiming five C.202s shot down. That afternoon, the squadron was attacked by 36 Bf-109s and C.202s; these were most likely all Italian-flown, though that was unknown to the Americans. In a wild free-for-all, the squadron's pilots claimed eight shot down, while two pilots were forced to bail out of shot-up Spitfires; they were both picked up by RAF air rescue Walrus amphibians and retuned to Korba by dusk. On June 10, the bomber formation the 307th Squadron was escorting was intercepted by "30-plus" Bf-109s. The pilots returned to Korba claiming seven shot down. The 309th was sent to patrol over the harbor and arrived just as 13 C.202s attacked a formation of B-25s that had just dropped their bombs. As the Spitfire IXs swept in on the Italians, six Bf-109s and six Fw-190s hit them. The 307th's pilots claimed four of the six Fw-190s, three C.202s, and three Bf-109s in the swirling dogfight. The 309th emerged from the battle with claims for six C.202s, a Bf-109, and an Fw-190. Best of all, both squadrons reported no losses.

Of the claims for 57 Axis aircraft destroyed and ten probably destroyed over the island in the June battles, 25 of these would be credited to the 79th as it engaged in a four-day aerial battle between June 7 and 10 that was its best air combat success of the war.

In addition to the P-40-equipped 325th and 33rd Groups, the 79th "Falcons" Group – which had been flying convoy escort missions as part of the Mediterranean Coastal Command following the surrender in Tunisia – moved to a dry lakebed near El Houaria on the tip of Cap Bon. It began flying dive-bombing missions on June 4, targeting the dug-in gun positions on Pantelleria. It first ran into aerial opposition the afternoon of June 7, when the 86th "Comanches" ran across two Bf-109s and shot them down. The next day, the "Comanches" scored four from a formation of ten 109s they came across east of Pantelleria. By the end of the day on June 9, the 85th and 86th Squadrons had scored ten victories between them, On May 10, the "Skeeters" of the 87th Squadron, who had trailed the other two squadrons since the group had entered combat over Tunisia, would see their finest hour.

The squadron flew several escort and dive-bombing missions through the day as the aerial assault approached its high point. At 1700 hours, the 85th Squadron was returning to Cap Bon shepherding an A-20 squadron when it ran across an air battle between P-40s, Spitfires, and 15 C.202s and Bf-109s. One of the Macchis flew in front of the "Flying Skulls" and was jumped by the leading P-40 flight, which shared destruction of the Italian fighter in the only air battle that had happened for the group all day.

Five minutes later, 16 "Skeeters" arrived over Pantelleria at 5,000 feet for their final patrol of the day. A lone C.202 was spotted by the top cover. It was quickly dispatched by flight leader Captain Paul McArthur. As the Macchi left a smoky trail to the waters below, squadron commander Lieutenant Colonel Charles Grogan spotted a German rescue plane low over the water surrounded by ten Bf-109s. He immediately arced over in a dive on the enemy formation, followed by the three P-40s of his flight. The pilot of the 109 he picked out turned left when he should have turned right, and the P-40's left wing sliced through the Messerschmitt's fuselage just ahead of the tail. The midair collision knocked off the P-40's wingtip outboard of the aileron, and Grogan had his hands full for a long moment as he managed to pull out of his dive a matter of feet above the water while the tailless 109 struck the water and sank immediately.

While Grogan was saving himself, his wingman, First Lieutenant Morris Watkins, shot down the wingman of the colonel's victory, shooting it into the sea as his guns tore off chunks of the enemy fighter. Element leader Captain Johnny Kirsch downed a third 109 while his wingman Lieutenant Kensley Miller got the fourth.

Captain Frank Huff, leading Yellow Section's Lieutenants Charlie Jaslow, Leo Berinati, and John Dzamba, spotted two Bf-109s orbiting over a downed pilot; the two 109s barely had time to realize Yellow Flight's P-40s were on their tails when Huff shot down the leader with a single burst of fire. Berinati chased the survivor almost to Sicily before he caught it and sent it into the water.

Lieutenant "Porky" Anderson spotted a C.202 engaged with the P-40s flown by George Lee and Ed Fitzgerald. When the Italian pilot managed to evade his opponents, Anderson dove on him and blew the Macchi apart with a well-placed burst into the cockpit and engine. As he pulled out, he spotted a Bf-109 low over the water and rolled onto its tail, setting the fighter on fire with his second burst.

Lieutenants "Goose" Gossett and Francis Hennin spotted another rescue plane in the distance with eight Messerschmitts giving cover.

The two dove on the enemy, and Gossett exploded the leading 109 while Hennin was frustrated when his guns would not fire. Gossett's victim exploded, and a piece penetrated the P-40's radiator, causing a coolant leak. Fortunately, Gossett was able to make it back over Tunisia before the engine seized, and he landed dead-stick back at El Haouaria. The fight was over as quickly as it had begun, and the "Skeeters" made claims for 15 Axis fighters shot down, doubling the squadron's previous score.

Paul McArthur was forced to bail out of his P-40 after shooting down his second claimed 109 when the wingman managed to shoot him up. The engine seized up with Cap Bon in sight and he went into the water. Climbing into his raft 30 miles off the coast of Tunisia, he awaited the arrival of RAF Air Rescue while two squadron mates orbited overhead. Rescue was delayed almost to sunset, with two other pairs of P-40s coming out in relays to keep him in sight. The Walrus amphibian arrived in the last light of day and managed to land and take him aboard, but the engine then died. McArthur and the RAF crew were forced to spend the night manning the Walrus' bilge pumps to stay afloat until a British destroyer sighted them shortly after dawn and took them aboard.

June 6, 1943, saw the introduction into combat of a new type when the 27th Bomb Group (Light) – which had arrived in North Africa the preceding December equipped with the A-20 and re-equipped in April with the North American A-36A Mustang dive bomber – flew its first mission, dive-bombing enemy shipping in Pantelleria harbor. Despite having heard rumors of stateside A-36 units wiring the dive brakes shut, the dive brakes worked as advertised, allowing the A-36s to execute near-vertical dives while holding diving speed to 290mph, which allowed great accuracy. The Mustangs arrived over the harbor at 8,000 feet, dropped their two underwing 500lb bombs at 3,000 feet, and pulled out of their dives at 1,500 feet. By June 11, they had flown five more successful missions, taking out artillery positions on the island that conventional bombing attacks had failed to destroy. Following the surrender of Pantelleria, Italian survivors of the A-36 attacks reported that the noise emitted by the bombers in their dives was as terrifying as the actual bombing.

The 27th Group's A-36As were not the only Mustangs that first saw combat during the Pantelleria campaign. The 111th Observation

Squadron, a former National Guard unit from Texas, had also arrived in North Africa in December 1942. In May, it exchanged its A-20s for 35 P-51-2NA (Tac Recon) Mustangs originally introduced in theater by the 154th Observation Squadron in March; the unit had been withdrawn from operations before it could fly these tactical-reconnaissance Mustangs operationally. The 111th soon became the 111th Tactical Reconnaissance Squadron, and the photos taken during low-level operations over the island were used for targeting enemy gun positions and pillboxes for attack. These Mustangs, which differed from other P-51 fighters in being armed with four 20mm cannon in addition to the camera mounted in the rear of the cockpit, were able to engage in ground attack of the positions they photographed.

Between June 7 and 10, the 325th escorted bombers on missions to Pantelleria. The fifth mission of June 10, escorting B-26s of the 320th Bomb Group and dive-bombing gun positions, took off at 1400 hours. Twenty-five German and Italian fighters intercepted the Marauders. Lieutenants Herbert Andridge, Lawrence Ritter, and Kenneth Rusher each shot down a Bf-109 during the subsequent dogfight, with another four Bf-109s claimed as damaged. Flight Officer Jim Dunlap was killed.

The sixth mission of the day took off at 1440 hours, escorting 319th Group B-26s with the P-40s dive-bombing assigned targets. Fourteen Bf-109s were spotted over the target; two were shot down by Captain Ralph "Zack" Taylor while a third was shot down by enemy ground fire. Taylor later remembered his dogfight:

> The group was dive-bombing gun positions on Pantelleria, and also escorting B-26s of the 319th BG that were level bombing the same targets. Flying rear cover, I was on the left when my flight was attacked simultaneously by three Me 109s from the side and two Me-109s diving from the rear. Lieutenant Crawford and his wingman turned to meet the three coming from the side while I turned into those diving from the rear. I shot at one of the Me-109s and saw him start smoking, then crash into the water at a point two miles due west of the island. After seeing the first Me 109 crash, I pulled behind another that did not see me coming. Firing from dead astern, I saw him roll over and start downward toward the water.

The onslaught had continued day and night during the last five days, with the air offensive reaching its crescendo on June 10, when wave after wave of bombers swept over the island. There was a three-hour lull during the middle of the day, when there was another surrender call. By dusk, more than 1,760 sorties had been flown by heavy, medium, light, and fighter-bombers, with 1,571 tons of bombs dropped, making the final day at Pantelleria one of the heaviest air attacks of the war up to that time.

Among the Allied fighters providing cover for the Pantelleria invasion on June 11 was the 52nd Group's 4th Squadron. The 52nd had been surprised at the end of the Tunisian campaign when it was taken from XII Fighter Command to take up duties with the Coastal Command responsible for providing air cover over convoys. Thus, it had largely missed out on the air battles over Pantelleria, though it had caught enemy fighters nearby while on convoy escort. The 4th Squadron considered itself lucky to be assigned to cover the invasion, when it was put in the line of battle in order to provide as many fighters overhead as possible. The Luftwaffe tried hard to put up a battle with the invaders, and during the day the Germans lost 17 fighters shot down by Allied fighter pilots. Lieutenants Robert Armstrong and Dale Anderson managed to latch onto two of these enemy fighters, with Armstrong claiming an Fw-190 shot down north-northeast of Pantelleria, and Anderson got a Bf-109 north of the island.

When there was no response to the second surrender call, the British 1st Infantry Division was embarked the night of June 10/11 to assault and capture the island. As landing craft headed toward the island shortly after 0900 hours, 40 B-17s delivered a final pounding to the harbor area over 12 minutes that resulted in simultaneous flashes and a great roar. The USAAF official history stated that "Suddenly the whole harbor area appeared to rise and hang in midair, while smoke and dust billowed high, dwarfing Montagna Grande, Pantelleria's tallest peak."

At approximately 1100 hours on June 11, a white cross was spotted on the airfield, just before the first British assault wave landed on the beach. Pantelleria's military governor, Vice Admiral Gino Pavesi, surrendered the island and the garrison of 78 Germans and 11,121 Italians to the landing force commander.

Allied troops found that the harbor facilities had been badly damaged and the town itself practically destroyed. Communications were a

KEY AAF TARGETS IN SICILY, SARDINIA, AND ITALY, JUNE 15–JULY 9, 1943

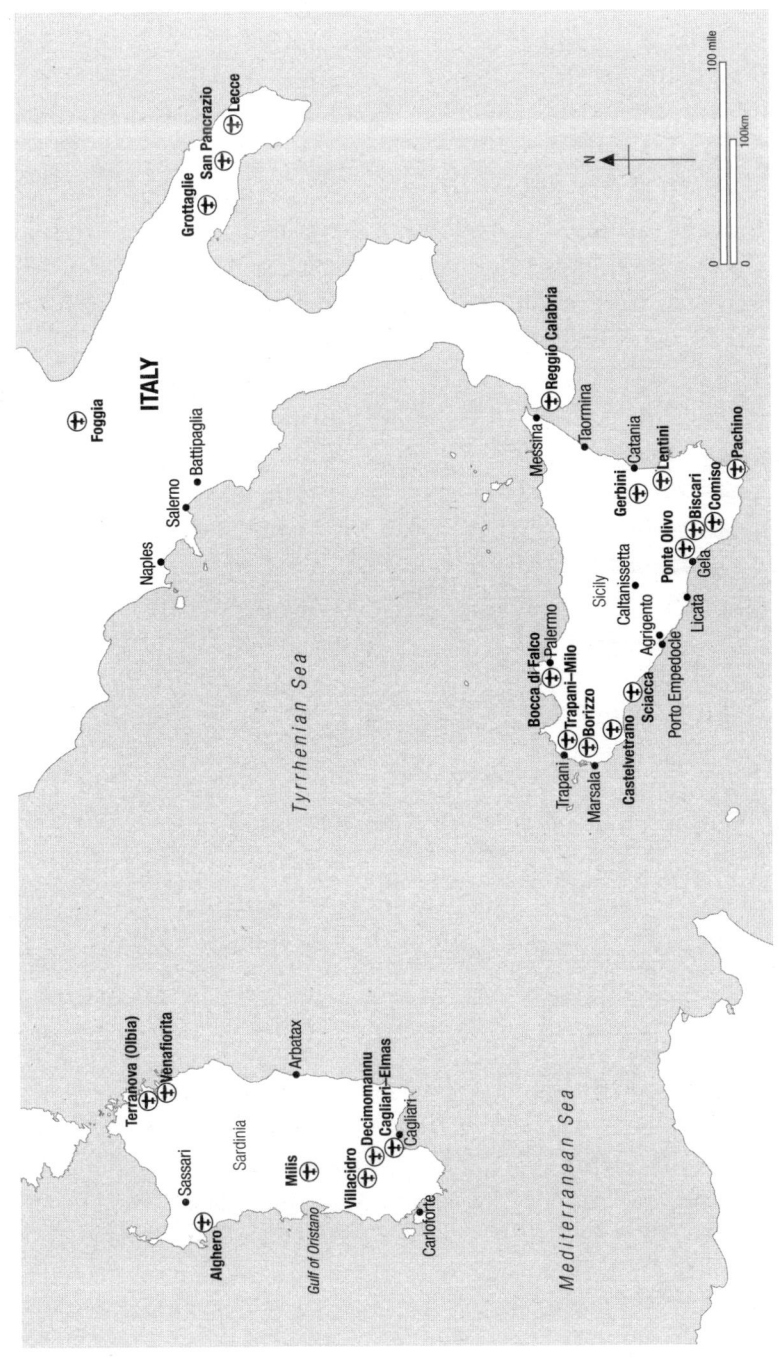

shambles, roads were obliterated, electric power destroyed, and the water mains broken. The underground hangar at Marghana airdrome had withstood a number of direct hits, but all of the 80-plus enemy airplanes had been either destroyed or damaged except for two.

The next day, when the first Allied aircraft arrived over nearby Lampedusa island following the surrender of Pantelleria, they were met with white flags fluttering in the breeze. The Italian commander of the island managed to establish contact with the Allied forces and negotiate a surrender before any bombing happened; he informed those he negotiated with that he had wished to surrender the island from the first day of the Pantelleria campaign.

The day saw Luftwaffe fighters again try to interfere with Allied operations. The 52nd's 2nd and 4th Squadrons were providing air cover over the invasion fleet when a formation of Fw-190s flew into the 4th Squadron's patrol zone. Robert Armstrong was lucky a second day, claiming one of the Fw-190s, along with Lieutenants Robert Burnett III and James O. Tyler, who also scored an Fw-190 each.

Operation *Corkscrew* had succeeded dramatically, marking the first time that an enemy land force was compelled to surrender in the absence of an accompanying ground invasion. Saturation bombing, plus limited shelling by the Royal Navy, had broken the defenses and the enemy's will to resist.

In mid-June, the 325th became the most distinctively marked fighter group of all the USAAF front-line fighter groups at the time. No USAAF fighter group was allowed to use markings that would identify it individually from any others. Captain John A. Watkins recalled his role in the creation of the Checkertail Clan several years after the war:

> I was recruited into making this possible because I was the son of a regular Air Force Colonel and had known most of the senior leaders in the Mediterranean since childhood. I had also been on General Arnold's staff before going to flying school, which gave a low-ranking officer such as myself greater opportunities to wend my way through the usual channels than someone unfamiliar with headquarters bureaucracy. I did not conceive of the checkertail, or design it; I used friendship and politics to get the idea past the lower echelons who were opposed to it.

At the time, the argument against specific group markings was that it would allow the enemy a certain advantage from an intelligence point of view. After being turned down at lower levels, we argued successfully to General Spaatz that the enemy already knew the 325th because we were operating almost alone in Sardinia and argued that because of our successes some kind of identification might strike terror into the hearts of enemy pilots encountering us, just like some enemy units which were respected, if not feared, for their successes.

In any case, General Spaatz, who was a highly imaginative and open-minded officer, bought our argument and that, to my knowledge, is the first time any group in the air force was identified by airplane markings.

The original force behind the idea of group markings had come from Bob Baseler, who was soon to take command of the group on July 5. After some experiments on one of the group's P-40s, the marking was standardized as black 12-inch square checkers over a yellow background, giving squares the same size, with checkerboard carried on the vertical fin and rudder and the upper and lower surfaces of the horizontal stabilizers and elevators. "Checkertail Clan" was adopted as the group name, with "clan" symbolizing the brotherhood of all members – pilots and ground personnel together.

With their distinctive markings, the Checkertail Clan continued its missions to Sardinia, focused on Decimomannu airfield. By the end of June, when it and all other units focused on Sicily, the group had flown 80 missions to the island and scored 59 victories for 20 losses in its battles with the Luftwaffe and Regia Aeronautica.

The three P-38 groups had been active in the Pantelleria campaign and the strikes against Axis airfields in Sardinia, Sicily, and southern Italy. The 14th Fighter Group – which had been withdrawn from combat in March due to losses – had been rebuilt by group commander Lieutenant Colonel Troy Keith, who managed to obtain experienced pilots from the 1st Group to replace leadership losses and new P-38Gs as replacements. At the end of May the group was finally brought to three-squadron strength when the 37th Fighter Squadron arrived. The 37th's commander was Major John G. "Gil" Bright, a former naval aviator who had flown with the American Volunteer Group in Burma and China, where he scored three victories, gaining a fourth when he remained in China with the AVG's successor 23rd Fighter Group. The 14th had rejoined combat in time to take part in the slaughter of German transports in April, and then in May had begun escorting B-17s on missions to Italian targets.

The 82nd Group's 96th Squadron had its best day on June 18, with the pilots claiming 16 victories for no American losses while escorting B-25s to strike Decimomannu airfield on Sardinia. Flight Officer Frank Hurlbut claimed a Bf-109 and a Reggiane Re.2001 destroyed, for his third and fourth air combat claims, while Second Lieutenant Larry Liebers increased his score from two to five Italian fighters shot down when he claimed two C.202 Folgores and a new C.205 Veltro. The Lightnings were at low altitude when the first six Italian fighters attacked them. Using the P-38's outstanding climb capability, the battle soon reached 10,000 feet as more Italian fighters showed up. First Lieutenant Ed Waters was credited with a Bf-109, while "Dixie" Sloan shot down a C.200 to bring his score to eight, making him the 82nd Group's top ace.

On June 20, the 14th Group escorted bombers over Sicily, and the formation was intercepted by a large mixed force of Bf-109s and Fw-190s. This time, the 49th Squadron scored, with Lieutenants Anthony Evans, Beryl Boatman, and Wayne Manlove scoring one each. Captain Richard Decker was shot down, waiting overnight in his dinghy to be picked up by a Walrus the next morning.

The escort mission flown by the 14th on June 24 saw the 37th Squadron's big day when five Bf-109s were shot down; First Lieutenant Carl Rudder claimed two, while Lieutenants George Wightman, Jim Hollingsworth, and John Garbett claimed one each. On June 28, both the 14th and 82nd Groups escorted B-17s to Sardinia, with the 14th claiming three and the 82nd four victories.

Allied bombers and their escorts opened the final pre-invasion air offensive against bases and transport facilities on Sicily on June 18, with particular attention paid to the city of Messina. By June 20, the airfield on Lampedusa Island was ready, and several RAF squadrons landed there. On June 26, the 33rd "Nomads" Group moved into Pantelleria's newly reopened airfield. June 30 saw the 31st Fighter Group move to the island of Gozo north of Malta, placing it within range of the Sicilian invasion beaches. On July 2, the intense Allied air attacks on Sicily shifted focus to destruction of enemy airplanes and the neutralization of enemy airfields on and within range of the island in the Italian peninsula. Axis air losses were 43 between then and July 9, the day before the invasion began.

With Pantelleria and the surrounding islands now in Allied hands, the much-bombed Marghana airfield was cleared of the wreckage from the Regia Aeronautica that was pushed to the side and the bomb craters filled in. The 33rd "Nomads" Group had been notified on June 9 that it would move onto Pantelleria once the island was taken. That day, the group headquarters and advance ground personnel left Menzel Temime airfield for Sousse. They were transported to Pantelleria on board LCIs on June 19, landing in the harbor during an attack by Luftwaffe Ju-87s, which let them know they were back on the front line as they had been at Thélepte. They moved to Marghana airfield, where they set up housekeeping in the bombproof underground hangar and made preparations to receive their aircraft. On June 23, the 33rd Fighter Group began its move from Menzel Temime airfield to Pantelleria. The first 15 planes to arrive in the morning found the island weathered in and were forced to return to Tunisia. Later that day, Lieutenant Reed recorded that they flew to the island and were able to land. The first ones to arrive were impressed by the numbers of wrecked Italian fighters in the airfield scrap pile. After he investigated the underground hangar, Reed wrote that it was "really something," with its bombproof doors.

An RAF Spitfire group found a new home on Lampedusa at the same time, where the airfield was relatively undamaged compared with Marghana on Pantelleria. On June 25, the "Nomads" flew their first dive-bombing attacks against Sicily, with the RAF Spitfires flying cover. Now that Allied fighter units were based only 65 miles from Sicily, it would be possible to mount effective air cover over the invasion beaches.

On June 26, over 100 Ju-88s and Fw-190 fighter-bombers attacked the Allied fleet that was gathering off Cap Bon in preparation for the coming Sicilian invasion. Patrolling RAF and USAAF fighters covering the fleet drove them off before they were able to inflict any serious damage. Among the victorious American pilots was First Lieutenant Albert Adams, Jr., of the 52nd's 2nd Squadron, who chased one of the Focke-Wulf fighter-bombers nearly to Pantelleria, shooting it into the sea south of the island and damaging the wingman.

The 52nd Group had its best day since the Tunisian fighting had ended on July 1 when the 5th Squadron's First Lieutenant John Carey, leading a convoy patrol of four Spitfires off Cap Bon, spotted enemy fighters approaching from the direction of Sicily. The flight turned into a mixed formation of Fw-190 fighter-bombers with Bf-109 escorts. Carey got on the tails of two Fw-190s in company with a Bf-109 and shot down both of the Focke-Wulfs while his wingman, Second Lieutenant Charles T. O'Connor, Jr., exploded the 109. An hour later, another flight of Spitfires covering the convoy – which was now approaching Bizerte – engaged a small formation of Fw-190s, and First Lieutenant Irwin Gottlieb shot down one of the "Butcher Birds," giving the 5th Squadron four victories in one day.

On July 2, the 99th Squadron, which was still operating with the "Nomads," escorted 16 B-25s on a mission to bomb a German airfield at Castelvetrano. They were part of a larger mission that involved 72 fighters from other groups and a similar number of Mitchells, Havocs, and Marauders. The lead bomber of the formation the 99th was covering missed the initial point for the run to the target, and the bombers were forced to circle the target directly overhead as they maneuvered to repeat the run.

The pilots of the 99th spotted plumes of dust on the airfield as enemy fighters hastily scrambled to intercept them. Once the B-25s dropped their bombs, they started a gentle descending left turn and headed toward their bases in Africa. As they did, the enemy Bf-109s, which had climbed above the escorts, made a slashing attack. The P-40s of Sherman White and James McCullen disappeared as the 109s ripped through the rest of the squadron; White and McCullen were the first members of the 99th killed in action.

Charlie "Seabuster" Hall spotted a pair of Fw-190s stalking the bombers. He gained position behind the wingman and fired a long burst; the Focke-Wulf lurched into an abrupt dive. Hall followed his victim until he saw it hit the ground in what he later described as "a big cloud of dust." Hall had just scored the 99th's first aerial victory.

At about the same time Hall was scoring, "Ghost" Lawson fired at another Fw-190, claiming it as a probable and then damaging a Bf-109 moments later. As this happened, two Bf-109s made a head-on pass at the elements led by Charles Dryden and Bill Campbell. Dryden called the break, but a radio malfunction prevented Campbell hearing him. Dryden threw his fighter into a tight turn and fired at the Germans as they climbed for another attack. Within seconds, he was alone, searching the sky for a friendly fighter. He spotted a P-40 about 500 feet below, flying straight and level. Diving to join up, Dryden spotted two Bf-109s stalking the other P-40. Latching onto their rear, he opened fire and damaged the trailing wingman. A spurt of tracer fire flew past his cockpit. He glanced to the rear and spotted a third 109 close behind him. Following Phil Cochran's directives, Dryden hauled "A Train II" into a tight turn but found the enemy pilot staying with him in the turn. "The first time around, I saw the top of his canopy. The next time around, I saw his nose, and the next time around I saw his belly. At that point I realized it was a Macchi 202!" While the P-40 could out-turn a Bf-109, the Italian fighter could out-turn the Warhawk.

Dryden watched, transfixed, as the enemy pilot opened fire with his wing-mounted 20mm cannon. One shell blew a chunk out of "A Train II's" left wing. Desperate, Dryden called for help. Jim Knighten heard him; spotting Dryden above, he climbed and then made a diving turn that put him behind the C.202. A burst from his guns saw the enemy pilot break off and dive away. Waving "thank you," Dryden joined Knighten and they turned back to Pantelleria. Moments later they were attacked from below by two other Bf-109s. The P-40s and the 109s "scissored" back and forth for what Dryden thought at the time was an hour but was only ten minutes when he glanced at his watch; neither side could gain an advantage. At one point, the two Americans thought they had lost their opponents. When they dove for the deck, Dryden spotted the two Bf-109s duplicating the maneuver. The turning duel resumed, with Dryden thinking they were not going to get away when he saw the lone C.202 rejoin the fight. Suddenly the enemy fighters broke off and turned north toward Sicily. "Fortunately for us, they ran low on fuel," Dryden recalled. They flew on back to Pantelleria.

Pantelleria was initially celebrated by airpower advocates as the proof of a new dawn in warfare. To senior leaders, the experience pointed the way toward the Allies' future strategy: intensive aerial bombardment, increasing in tempo, and naval bombardment would precede landing operations. The official USAAF history noted: "The surrender of the Italian-held islands furnished a spectacular illustration of the intense and violent force the Allies could bring to bear upon the enemy. The reduction of the islands furnished the first proof of the power of such bombardments to induce surrender. The pattern set here was probably one that would be followed in other island operations and perhaps in the invasion of the continent itself."

Eisenhower wrote to Marshall, pointing out that many had opposed *Corkscrew*, noting, "I am particularly pleased that the operation turned out as it did because I personally had to make the decision for its capture in the face of much contrary advice, but I predicted that the garrison would surrender before any infantry soldier got ashore."

However, as was shown later during the Italian campaign, this developing belief that dropping a large number of bombs on enemy strong points in advance of troop movements would "make land movements a matter of flitting from one dazed body of enemy troops to another" failed to deliver the expected results. In truth, the surrender only took place after the Italian commander realized an overwhelming amphibious assault was imminent. The day before, informed the assault was imminent, and realizing his position was hopeless, he cabled for permission to surrender.

Air Chief Marshal Tedder saw things more clearly than his fellow air commanders and disagreed with the initial optimism, writing "Pantelleria is becoming a perfect curse." The ancient Benedictine monastery at Monte Cassino would prove him right.

12

AIR WAR OVER SICILY

At 0415 hours on April 30, 1943, the submarine HMS *Seraph*, commanded by Lieutenant N.L.A. "Bill" Jewell, surfaced off the small Spanish fishing village of Huelva on the Atlantic coast. The crew quickly set to work bringing out a steel container on deck. It was opened to reveal the body of a Royal Marine whose papers identified him as Major William Martin, RM. Attached to the belt of the trench coat Major Martin wore, in a briefcase, was a letter of introduction from his commanding officer, Vice Admiral Louis Mountbatten, RN, chief of the Royal Navy's specialist Combined Operations to Admiral of the Fleet Sir Andrew Cunningham, commander-in-chief of the Mediterranean Fleet. The letter identified Major Martin as a specialist in amphibious warfare. Other papers in the briefcase outlined the Allied plan to shift operations to the eastern Mediterranean following the coming victory in Tunisia, with the main landing on Crete and a secondary on Sardinia, to take control of airfields to interdict Italian targets, with "cover" operations in Sicily and the Dodecanese to distract the Wehrmacht from the true targets.

As commanding officer, Lieutenant Jewell read the Service for the Burial of the Dead at Sea, and Major Martin was dispatched into the cold Atlantic on his mission, which was a product of the imagination of Lieutenant Commander Ian Fleming, RN, an officer who had been seconded from Naval Intelligence to MI6, the British Secret Service. Just before *Seraph* disappeared beneath the dark waters, Jewell sent a message to the Admiralty: "Mincemeat completed."

A local Spanish fisherman found Major Martin at around 0930 hours that morning in the sea just outside the port of Huelva. The fisherman turned back and handed the body over to the authorities. British vice-consul at Huelva Francis Haselden was notified of the discovery once it was determined the body was that of a British officer who must have been the victim of an air crash. Haselden, who knew of the operation, immediately cabled the Foreign Office regarding the discovery, making sure that several other messages were sent back and forth on the matter over the next several days to attract German attention. In the meantime, Spanish medical authorities signed a death certificate stating the major had died as a result of "asphyxiation through immersion in the sea." Major Martin was accorded a funeral with full military ceremony in the local cemetery on May 2.

On May 5, Major Martin's briefcase was sent to local naval HQ at San Fernando, outside Cadiz, for forwarding on to the Navy Ministry in Cadiz. While at San Fernando, the contents were photographed by Abwehr agent Adolf Clauss; though he was unable to open the letters, he inventoried the other items, including the stubs of two tickets to a theater performance in London two weeks earlier and a note from the Wren officer who attended the performance with her boyfriend, Martin. In Madrid, Karl-Erich Kühlenthal, head of the Abwehr in Spain, contacted Abwehr chief Admiral Wilhelm Canaris, who prevailed on the Spanish to allow examination of the letters. The Spanish removed the letters from their envelopes and photographed them, then returned them to the envelopes. The information in the letters was so important that Kühlenthal personally flew the photos to Berlin for examination. Major Martin's effects were returned to Haselden; it was not difficult to determine the letters had been opened.

The news the Allies intended not to invade Sicily – the obvious next target in the central Mediterranean – but planned to commence operations in the Balkans, was met with incredulity by senior Wehrmacht leaders. Adolf Hitler, however, was not incredulous. He had long held that the Balkans were an obvious Allied target due to the restiveness of the local populations.

On May 14, 1943, a German Ultra communication was decrypted at Bletchley Park. The message had been sent two days previously. It warned German commanders at Sicily, Sardinia, Crete, and Greece that the next Allied invasion was to be in the Balkans, with a feint to the Dodecanese and Sardinia, and that they should make preparations accordingly. The confusion generated by the "intelligence coup" of obtaining the contents of the briefcase carried by "Major Martin" would have a profound effect in the coming campaign, since the change in unit dispositions created confusion that was never properly resolved.

In June, Feldmarschall Wolfram Freiherr von Richthofen, nephew of World War I's Red Baron, arrived in Italy to take command of Luftflotte 2. He had read the reports based on examination of Major Martin's letters. His first act was to transfer the bulk of the fighter units in his command to Sardinia. By the end of June, days before the Sicilian invasion, only JG 53 and II./JG 77 were still based on Sicily.

For the Germans, the July 10, 1943 invasion of Sicily marked the war's turning point. The Wehrmacht – badly overextended on all fronts – was forced to confront the first Allied penetration into "Fortress Europe," an event which threatened to force Italy to surrender. Losing 40 Italian divisions serving as occupation forces in southern France, Greece, and Yugoslavia meant the Wehrmacht would be forced to replace them with German troops at a time when there were no "extras." Once it became clear the invasion would likely result in the collapse of Italy, Hitler was forced three days after the Allied landings to call off Operation *Zitadelle*, the German offensive against the Kursk salient on the Eastern Front. Losing *Zitadelle* meant the strategic initiative had passed from Germany to the Allies; Germany was now on the defensive permanently. The Sicilian invasion did not create this climactic turn in German fortunes, but it was the disasters at Stalingrad and Tunis that stopped German momentum and turned the war permanently in the Allies' favor.

For Allied planners, the main Axis threat to Operation *Husky* (the invasion of Sicily) was the use of airpower during the landings. Land-based bombers and torpedo aircraft had proven they were deadly against maritime targets at every opportunity during Mediterranean sea battles since 1941. Both British and American naval leaders expressed high anxiety regarding the vulnerability of the Allied invasion fleets as they approached Sicily. The admirals pointed to the April 1943 estimate by Allied intelligence that the enemy would be able to deploy 840 Luftwaffe and 1,100 Regia Aeronautica aircraft in the Sicily–Sardinia–Pantelleria region; naval losses were estimated at 300 ships likely to be sunk. This threat had been reduced in the taking of Pantelleria in June, but it was also believed that the enemy could base air units in southern Italy that would be in range of Sicily while their bases would be out of range to all but the Allied strategic bomber forces.

To meet this, an air campaign against Axis airfields in Sardinia and Sicily had been initiated in May, which increased in size and momentum following the taking of Pantelleria. Allied fighter units based on Pantelleria, Lampedusa, Malta, and Gozo islands would provide cover over the invasion beaches.

In mid-June, Generalmajor "Onkel Theo" Osterkamp, the well-liked World War I ace who was *Jagdfliegerführer Sicily* (fighter commander on Sicily) was replaced by General der Jagdflieger Adolf Galland.

The Allied bombing campaign used American heavy and medium bombers flying from North Africa in the daylight campaign and RAF Wellington bombers based on Malta at night. The Axis bomber forces so feared by Allied naval commanders were withdrawn from Sicily on June 22, when Fliegerkorps II commander Wolfram von Richthofen and the Regia Aeronautica Super Aereo (Air Force high command) agreed that they could not continue to base bombers on Sicily in the face of Allied air attacks. The available airfields in southern Italy were too small for the bombers to operate from, with the result that the Axis bombers were based on airfields near Naples, 200 miles from Sicily. Despite the fact that German bomber strength in Italy doubled during the first ten days of July, the distances involved complicated attempts by units from different bases to rendezvous over Sicily to make attacks with sufficient force to overwhelm the defenders.

General Galland later wrote in *The First and the Last* that "an air offensive of dimensions as yet unprecedented in the war" resulted in 80 raids against airfields in Sardinia and Sicily in the ten days before the invasion. Galland had come to the conclusion that the Luftwaffe's best chance of affecting the battle was a "Gross Schlag" (great blow) against the bombers, putting every available fighter in the air to deliver a crushing, hopefully decisive, blow against the enemy's bomber forces. His opportunity came on June 25, when the NASAF mounted its heaviest single raid of the month against Messina.

Messina was within JG 53's area of operations. Galland ordered the "Pik As" and all of JG 77 which was responsible for western Sicily to intercept, providing a force of fighters. The mission was a shambles due to the inability of the *Jagdgruppen* to maintain formation in the poor visibility. Additionally, German radar lost track of the bombers in the poor weather. With their fuel dangerously low, the leading Bf-109s eventually spotted a formation of B-17s nearly 100 miles off the northwest tip of Sicily, running hard for Africa low over the water. Attacking the formation, the 80 fighters achieved only five victories between them.

That evening, a message was received from an enraged Reichsmarschall Hermann Göring. He demanded that every *Jagdgruppe* that had participated in the operation was to put forward one pilot to be court-martialed for "cowardice in the face of the enemy." The courts were convened, but few, if any, of the accused were convicted. The order did nothing to lift morale.

On June 26, some 50 ground crew from the 31st Group's 307th Squadron arrived at "Banjo Field," a secret airfield built in 12 days on Gozo Island, only two miles north of Malta, by US Army engineers; the two runways met in a "V"; they were crooked and narrow, their surfaces uneven, with either a deep cut or a high fill to either side. On June 28, the group's "pioneers" were joined by the ground crews of the 308th and 309th Squadrons. Two days later, on June 30, the group's Spitfires arrived. Gozo was eight miles by five miles in size, with 300-foot cliffs all around rather than beaches; it was 80 miles from Sicily, allowing the short-ranged Spitfires to provide effective cover over the invasion beaches. The 31st's first mission over Sicily was flown on July 6. The second patrol of the day was jumped by 12 enemy fighters over Comiso airdrome. The Spitfire pilots scored no victories, but the 307th's new CO was shot down in flames and killed. The next day the group flew as escort for B-25s bombing Biscari airdrome. That night it was briefed on the coming invasion, in which the 31st would fly cover for the invasion fleet.

On July 2, the Allied air campaign against Sicily shifted focus to the destruction of enemy aircraft in the air and on the ground, and neutralization of enemy airfields on Sicily or within range of the island. The Luftwaffe's second attempt to carry out the *Gross Schlag* was made on July 4, when both *Gruppen* of JG 77, the three *Gruppen* of JG 53, and the single JG 51 *Gruppe* on Sicily made all-out assaults on Allied formations. The air battles did not live up to German hopes. The next day, Allied bombers went after the Gerbini airfield complex where the *Jagdflieger* were concentrated, with carpet-bombing missions. Allied records reported a total of 100 German fighters were encountered in the air, but the attacking bombers still hit the target. A second raid bombed the target without German fighter units making any attempt to intercept.

The day also saw two missions flown by 82nd Group P-38s that resulted in air combat with Regia Aeronautica units. The morning mission, flown by the 97th Squadron, saw B-25s bomb the Gerbini airfield complex. When enemy Bf-109s most likely from 150° Gruppo intercepted, the Lightnings engaged the interceptors in combat and came away with claims for three destroyed and seven damaged for the loss of one P-38. The early afternoon mission saw C.202s intercept the bombers. Second Lieutenants Jim Gant and Bob Muir were each credited with one, while a further three claimed by other pilots were confirmed as probables.

In response to the events of this day, Göring sent an order decreeing every *Schwarm* (flight of four aircraft) taking off on a mission was to return with at least one victory, or with every fighter damaged as proof they had engaged the enemy in combat; court-martials for cowardice were again threatened. JG 53 *Kommodore* Oberstleutnant von Maltzahn confessed after the war to being ashamed at having followed Göring's order to read this to his pilots.

JG 53 and JG 77 were joined by the Bf-109s of 150° Gruppo "Gigi Tre Osei" in the defense of Sicily. On July 2, 15 Bf-109Gs from 150° Gruppo's 363ᵃ Squadriglia intercepted B-25s bombing the Comiso airfield complex, while 364ᵃ Squadriglia took on the P-40s from the 99th Fighter Squadron escorting the bombers. Tenente Chiale and Tenente Fornoncini each claimed a P-40, while Sottotenente Camaioni claimed a B-25 probable. The 99th's First Lieutenant Charles B. Hall claimed one Bf-109 destroyed and one probable.

The next day, 14 Bf-109s from 150° Gruppo led by Tenente Colonello Vizzotto were scrambled from Sciacca airfield at 1035 hours to intercept A-20s of the 47th Bomb Group, accompanied by Baltimores from 3 Wing SAAF, escorted by P-40s from the 33rd and 324th Groups over Marsala headed for Sciacca and Trapani–Milo airfields. The Bf-109s from 364ᵃ Squadriglia went after the Baltimores, shooting down four, while the 363ᵃ Squadriglia attacked the A-20s and their escorts. Sottotenente Camaioni was credited with two P-40s, Tenente Fornoncini with one, and Capitano Bellagambi two severely damaged. The Italians claimed a total of seven P-40s and three bombers, plus another bomber and three

Warhawks probably destroyed. The Americans admitted loss of an A-20 and a P-40, although pilots from I./JG 77 who also joined the fight claimed two A-20s. 364ª Squadriglia's Tenente Giovanni Dell'Innocenti, a "Gigi Tre Osei" top scorer, was lost along with another Bf-109 from I./JG 77.

On July 4, 11 150° Gruppo Bf-109s were scrambled at 1000 hours, returning an hour later with the pilots claiming two A-20s and four P-40s south of Cape Passero. In fact, the 47th Bomb Group lost one A-20, while the 324th Group's Second Lieutenant Roy L. Huser had been lost.

At 1400 hours, four Bf-109s intercepted Marauders escorted by 21 Spitfire IXs from 93 and 111 Squadrons bombing Gerbini airfield. The "Gigi Tre Osei" pilots claimed two Spitfires, though only one 111 Squadron Spitfire, JK924 flown by Pilot Officer R.K. Whitney, was damaged; Whitney was able to return to Malta.

The experience of JG 53 in the Sicilian campaign was representative of the battle waged by the rest of the *Jagdfliegern*. Despite the enormous increase in Allied air attacks starting on July 3, the final week of softening-up before the troops hit the Sicilian beaches proved to be the most successful period of the three months the *Geschwader* was on the island. In the end, though, their losses – the highest casualties experienced during the Mediterranean combat of the previous years – were the kind that permanently weakened the unit when four of the unit's nine *Staffelkapitäne* were shot down and killed in combat.

JG 53 engaged P-38s of the 97th Fighter Squadron escorting B-25s to bomb the airfield complex at Gerbini on July 4. The Lightnings claimed three Bf-109s destroyed, one probably destroyed, and seven damaged, against the loss of a P-38. Two hours later the 95th Squadron flew an identical mission but ran into C.202s over Gerbini, submitting claims for three destroyed, two probables, and one damaged, without loss.

July 4 saw the loss of Leutnant Herbert Broennle, recently appointed *Staffelkapitän* of 2.Staffel. Broennle, who had arrived in late June after his recovery from severe wounds suffered with JG 54 on the Eastern Front, already wore "the tin tie" – the Ritterkreuz – in recognition of 57 victories scored while serving with JG 54 on the Eastern Front. He had gotten off to a good start, shooting down a B-24 after taking command of the *Staffel*, but in a low-level combat with Spitfires south of Catania, his Bf-109 "Black 8" went straight in from 1,000 feet after he was hit; two other pilots in the *Staffel* were wounded. However, the day in total was JG 53's best since arriving in Sicily, with nine Allied aircraft claimed destroyed.

July 5 saw the same score, this time including six B-17s, on a day that saw widespread raids by American bombers against airfields and other targets over the length and breadth of the island, as JG 53 and 77 sent 100 fighters into combat. While the "Pik A" Geschwader was credited with six Boeings shot down attacking the airfield complex west of Catania, the USAAF admitted losing only three. JG 53 engaged the 31st's escorting Spitfires off Cape Passero in a fight that saw Oberleutnant Willi Klein, *Staffelkapitän* of 1.Staffel, and his wingman both crash into the sea. Leading *Experte* Hauptmann Friedrich-Karl Müller scored his 118th and last victory with JG 53 when he downed one of the Spitfires.

The USAAF fighters defending the B-17 force sent against Gerbini claimed 35 victories against two losses. Oberst Johannes Steinhoff, *Geschwader Kommodore* of JG 77, was among the German pilots shot down; this was the third Bf-109 he had lost in a week, with the other two having been lost on the ground at Trapani on July 25 and Comiso on June 27. Steinhoff later wrote in his memoir *Messerschmitts Over Sicily* his belief about the Luftwaffe's position in Sicily: "It was then that I realized that a turning point had come and that we were on the road to final defeat."

The Luftwaffe attempted to answer the Allied bombing campaign with a raid by 75 Ju-88s of KG 30 against Bizerte the night of July 6–7, in an attempt to destroy shipping for the Allied invasion fleet. The raid was unsuccessful; no ships were hit and only light damage was inflicted on the docks, while Allied antiaircraft fire and RAF night fighters shot down 12 of the attackers. One Luftwaffe crew revealed under interrogation after they were captured that their unit was based at Viterbo, 60 miles north of Rome, and that the other German bomber units were based further north in Italy and in southern France, which made coordinated attacks against Allied targets difficult. The fliers stated that of 43 crews in the *Kampfgeschwader* who had come south from Norway at the beginning of May, there were only nine left; replacement crews were unable to take part in operations since they were untrained in night flying.

July saw the Checkertail Clan's CO, Colonel Gordon H. Austin, leave the group to take command of the 319th Bomb Group. His place was taken by 319th Squadron commander Lieutenant Colonel Robert L. Baseler. The group was still at Mateur airfield near Bizerte in Tunisia, which meant it would fly escort missions for bombers in the coming campaign. It would continue to fly missions to Sardinia, to prevent air units on that island from reinforcing the enemy on Sicily.

The 82nd's P-38s staged a ground attack strafing mission on July 5 against Gerbini airfield. Once again, 150° Gruppo Bf-109s misidentified as German rose to oppose the attackers. Top-scoring 96th Squadron ace "Dixie" Sloan claimed a Reggiane Re.2001 and a Bf-109 for victories nine and ten, while the 97th Squadron's First Lieutenant Gerry Rounds claimed a Bf-109 as victory number four.

On July 6, six 150° Gruppo Bf-109Gs were scrambled from Comiso to intercept B-25s attacking San Pietro airfield, where 13 Bf-109s were destroyed on the ground. The Italian pilots claimed to have shot down one B-25 with another probable, in addition to two P-38s and two Spitfires. However, no P-38s were lost, while two Spitfires from 601 and 145 Squadrons were damaged but were able to return to Malta. SAAF Lieutenant H.E. Wells, flying Spitfire VIII EE790, reported he was attacked by five fighters, identified as Re.2001s and Bf-109s.

After flying several missions to Decimomannu, Sardinia, in early July, the Checkertail Clan flew as escorts for 25 RAF Baltimores from 223 Squadron to bomb Trapani–Milo airfield in Sicily. Over the target, the 23 P-40s were intercepted by 13 Bf-109s of 150° Gruppo, though the Clan identified their opponents as Germans. Lieutenants Hank Brundydge and Walter B. Walker, Jr., and Flight Officers Bill Brookbank and Bruce Cunningham were each credited with a Bf-109 destroyed. Lieutenant Donald Castleberry was shot down in flames. Another mission to the same target on July 10 saw Captain Zack Taylor and Lieutenants Collins and Reed shoot down a Bf-109 each, for the loss of Captain Bill Reed and Lieutenant Clark, who were both able to bail out over the sea and were picked up by landing craft.

A sharp increase in Allied sortie rates began on July 8, D-2; three-quarters of the total Allied air missions were flown against the main airfields on the island. With the exception of Sciacca and Trapani airfields, the other 19 developed airfields were severely damaged and abandoned.

Among the airfield attackers on July 8 was a formation of 12 RAF Baltimores, 12 47th Bomb Group A-20s, and 70 B-25s from the 12th and 340th Groups, escorted by 36 324th Fighter Group P-40s, which dropped 111 tons of bombs on Sciacca, Comiso, and Biscari airfields. 150° Gruppo was able to scramble six Bf-109Gs to intercept. While the pilots claimed to have attacked three P-40s, the badly damaged Bf-109 flown by Sottotenente Virgilio Pozzoli of 363ª Squadriglia hit a wall when he attempted to land, killing him in the crash. The 324th Group admitted the loss of Captain Don B.M. Wood and Second Lieutenant Warren McHenry, who were both posted as missing. A third P-40 crashed into the sea with its pilot bailing out while the P-40 flown by Second Lieutenant W.S. Buchanan from the 316th Squadron barely made it back to Tunisia, where the fighter was written off as a total loss.

Between July 2 and 9, USAAF fighter pilots claimed 43 German and Italian aircraft – nearly all fighters – destroyed over and around Sicily. On D-Day alone, USAAF fighters covering the invasion claimed 24 Luftwaffe and Regia Aeronautica aircraft destroyed.

The Sicilian invasion began with a near catastrophe for the paratroopers who were to lead the way. In part, this was due to the fact that half of the groups assigned to Northwest African Troop Carrier Command did not arrive in the theater until June and had only been able to participate in one training drop with the 82nd Airborne. The invasion fleet that had departed North Africa several days earlier arrived 40 miles west of Gozo, having taken a course that would lead any German aerial snoopers to think it was another Malta-bound convoy. In the event, the fleet was spotted by a Regia Aeronautica reconnaissance aircraft off Pantelleria in the pre-dawn hours of July 9; this was followed by three other sightings during the day. It was determined from these reports that this was the long-awaited invasion force, and the German garrison on Sicily was put on alert that evening at 1840 hours. A short time before, several Ju-88s from Sicily attempted to attack the convoy but were driven off by two flights of 31st Group Spitfires and the formidable antiaircraft defenses on board the ships.

The paratroopers were transported by 220 C-47s carrying the 505th Parachute Infantry Regiment and the third battalion of the 504th Parachute Infantry Regiment. Once over the island, their problems were exacerbated by the 30-knot headwind they found over the drop zone, which had not been forecast. Navigation errors due to the wind meant that the paratroopers were not dropped with any precision. The paratroopers were dropped all over southern Sicily in isolated groups. They managed to self-organize on the ground and carried out demolitions, cut communications, set up roadblocks, and ambushed German and Italian truck convoys bringing troops to the invasion area; so much confusion was caused over such an extensive area that initial radio reports estimated the number of parachutists dropped to be ten times the actual number. By dawn, only 400 of the 1,600 troops had managed to find their way to their original objectives, but the confusion sown among the enemy still managed to contribute to the success of the landings.

The first 31st Group Spitfires left Gozo at 0530 hours. The patrols met no enemy aerial resistance as Allied troops came ashore before dawn on July 10 along a 90-mile stretch of Sicilian coast between Licata and Syracuse. The 31st flew five missions over the beachhead over the course of July 10 without making contact with any enemy forces. Two pilots were shot down by flak from ships in the invasion fleet, but both pilots were able to bail out and were picked up.

Between 0800 and 2200 hours that day, JG 53 flew nine separate missions – reconnaissance, *Freie Jagd*, and *Jabo* ('fighter bomber') escort. The unit claimed 17 victories at a cost of two 5.Staffel NCOs wounded.

German records show that by D-Day on July 10, Luftwaffe fighters on the island had been reduced to 100. The Regia Aeronautica was in even worse shape; 150° Gruppo had 21 Bf-109Gs at San Pietro di Caltagirone airfield, but only six were airworthy, and two of those were lost that morning when they were caught by Spitfires of the RAF's 185 Squadron. Tenente Angelo Fornoncini, one of the *Gruppo*'s top scorers, was killed while Tenente Cavatore managed to return to Sciacca airfield, where he belly-landed successfully.

Later that afternoon three "Gigi Tre Osei" Bf-109Gs came across P-40s of the 324th Group over Capo San Mauro. Maresciallo Walter Bertocci claimed three P-40s shot down, while pilots from JG 53 and JG 77 claimed four other P-40s. The 324th admitted the deaths in action of 316th Squadron CO Major Robert G. "Bob" Dempsey and First Lieutenant Charles L. Chalker, with Captain David E. Carpenter shot down and captured, and First Lieutenant Emile Selig, Jr., missing. The 316th's First Lieutenant James T. Johnson claimed a Bf-109 destroyed; his P-40 was badly damaged by another Bf-109, but he made it back to Tunisia.

Twenty-four P-38s from the 82nd Group's 96th Squadron patrolled the beachhead in the late afternoon of D-Day. They spottted 16

Fw-190s, Bf-109s, and C.200s taking off from Castelvetrano and Carcitella airfields. As the Lightnings fell on the fighters, First Lieutenant Ward Kuentzel shot down a Ju-88 as it took off. In the fight, the Lightning pilots claimed ten destroyed, two probably destroyed, and eight damaged, for one loss. Flight Officer Frank Hurlbut raised his score to seven, claiming three Fw-190s destroyed and one damaged. He remembered how the enemy fighters:

> Quickly rose to our altitude, and the fight began. The first Focke-Wulf was banking in front of me – it was very close, and I hardly had to use my gunsight. I set it on fire and saw it circle down to the left, but didn't see it crash. Other enemy fighters were all over the place and I turned my attention to them. Suddenly, a Lufbery developed, made up of Focke-Wulfs and P-38s in singles and doubles – all in single-file and swinging in a banking turn to the left, first climbing, then descending.

Hurlbut described closing in on an Fw-190:

> Behind me was another P-38 with a Focke-Wulf on his tail, and a P-38 on the Fw-190's tail. We were all playing follow-the-leader. I was very close to the Fw-190 in front of me and hit him with three quick bursts. He went over on one wing and then fell into a spin, before crashing in Sicily.
>
> I recall I was very concerned about the P-38 on my tail, who was following my maneuvers and who was being pursued by the second Focke-Wulf. I would fire, then look back and yell over the radio for my friend to watch out for the enemy fighter on his tail. I was the luckiest, I guess, because the guy behind me was on my side. The other Nazi airplane in our game of crack-the-whip apparently was damaged, as he dropped out and left the area. Another Fw-190 cut across and in front of me from the right. I led him and fired, hitting him as he flew through my fire, but he kept on going and cut back to the right. I claimed him as a damaged.

Hurlbut continued:

> I found my third while descending. I looked down and saw him skipping along close to the water, heading for Sicily. He had a P-38

chasing him some distance back, but he was pulling away and leaving the Lightning behind. I had plenty of speed, so I dove down between them and started to shoot. My first burst got him and he looped over and crashed into the sea. I claimed the two I had seen crash, but also got credit for the first one because other pilots in our squadron had seen it go down.

Additionally, Lieutenants Larry Lieber, Ed Waters, and Fred Wolfe were credited with an Fw-190 destroyed and two damaged, a Bf-109 destroyed, and an Fw-190 destroyed respectively.

Leading 82nd Group ace "Dixie" Sloan's claim for a C.200 destroyed raised his score to 11, making him the top Twelfth Air Force ace. He later described the event:

> All of a sudden, I'm on the tail of a P-38 and he's firing away at an MC.200. I watched with admiration until suddenly he broke away. I thought, "Why did he pull away? The Macchi looks OK to me." I moved in on it and was just about to fire when its canopy flew off and the pilot bailed out. I almost hit him with my wing. I can still remember coming so close I could see the buttons on his flight suit.

The 14th Group's Lightnings maintained almost continuous patrols in two flights of four P-38s over the landings. The fighters were primarily engaged in dive-bombing and strafing of ground targets, and faced deadly defensive antiaircraft fire. The 37th Squadron's Lieutenant Harry Crim recalled that the fighters carried a 1,000lb bomb on one underwing pylon and a 165-gallon drop tank on the other. On one mission, Crim's flight caught four German tanks in the open at a crossroad. The fighter dive-bombed the enemy tanks and hit all four. One tank was knocked over on its side, and one of the crewmen continued to fire at the P-38s as they strafed the area, putting holes in seven of eight P-38s, though he failed to bring down any of them.

Captain Jim Stitt related that the missions were so frequent that there was not time for proper repair of battle damage. Instead, ground crews would slap a fabric patch over a bullet hole and fix it in position with dope. Since they were operating mostly at low level where they did not need the turbocharging, these patches held. When operations slowed, the sheet metal people were able to work on the planes and

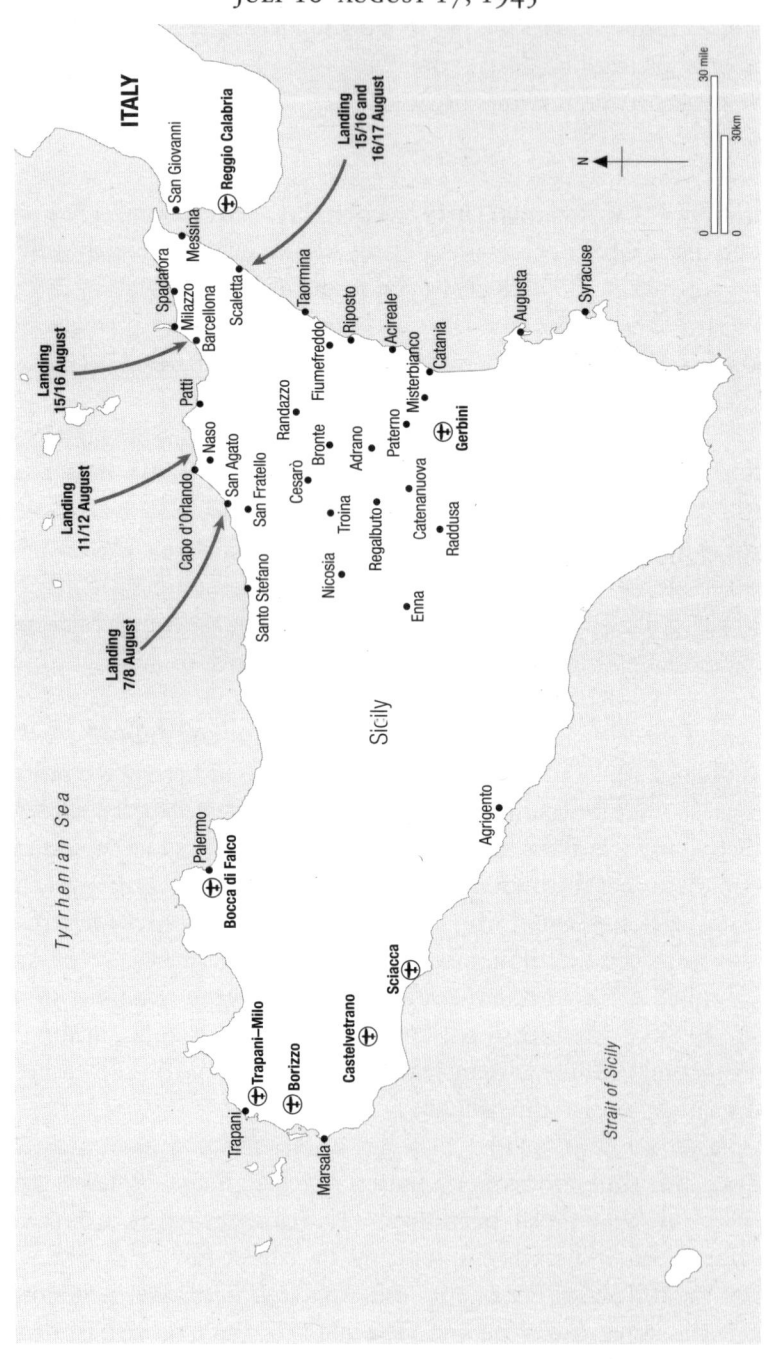

KEY AAF TARGETS IN SICILY DURING OPERATION *HUSKY*, JULY 10–AUGUST 17, 1943

replace the temporary patches with metal patches they fixed in place with flush rivets.

The next day, July 11 – D+1 – things changed; the 31st Group claimed seven aircraft destroyed. The 309th Squadron's Captain Carl Payne described one of the combats:

> I was leading a section of Spitfire IXs on a patrol over the Gela beachhead. At approximately 1615 hours, while over Pazzollo at 12,000 feet, we saw an Fw-190 about 2,000 feet above us. We climbed to engage, and as we came within range, he made a turn towards us and then entered a vertical dive. I followed and fired a three-second burst with cannons and machine guns at a range of 100 yards. I observed explosive shells striking in and behind the cockpit. The enemy aircraft immediately entered a violent spin from which it did not recover. As it crashed it exploded and burned.

A later flight from the 308th also ran across a formation of 20 Do-217s approaching the fleet. Captain Paulk and Lieutenants Callender and Watner each shot down one of the bombers, while Lieutenant Woodrich hit one he later claimed as "badly damaged."

The 309th's patrol – again led by Carl Payne – soon relieved the 308th and ran across a formation of ten Do-217s, an He-177, and two Ju-88s. Spotting the defending Spitfires, the German pilots immediately dove to sea level and headed toward the fleet, pursued by the Spitfires. Payne later reported that as the German attackers approached, the ships opened fire, with most of it missing the enemy and forcing his flight to break off its pursuit. The enemy bombers managed to bomb an ammunition ship which blew up with such force that nearby ships were damaged by flying debris. The Spitfires managed to catch the bombers as they headed away from the ships. Lieutenant Wright claimed one Do-217 as a probable, while Payne was only credited with a damaged.

In a later patrol that day, the 307th Squadron's Captain Jerry Collinsworth and his wingman managed to catch up with four Fw-190 *Jabos* and shoot down two of them; this was Collinsworth's fifth victory. He would repeat that battle the next day, shooting down another *Jabo* for his sixth and final victory.

The "Pik As" claimed six fighters and one B-26 Marauder on June 11, including a pair of P-38s that were victories 74 and 75 for Oberleutnant

Hans Röhrig, *Staffelkapitän* of 9./JG 53, and the second-highest scoring *Experte* after "Tutti" Müller in the *Geschwader*.

Despite this record, Reichsmarschall Göring, thoroughly rattled by events, fired off another telex the evening of July 11, which read, "Together with the fighter pilots in France, Norway and Russia, I look with scorn upon the pilots in the south. I want to see an immediate improvement, and expect all pilots to display more fighting spirit. Should this improvement not be forthcoming, all pilots – from *Kommodores* downwards – must expect to be reduced to the rank of aircraftman and sent to serve as infantry on the Eastern Front." For the *Jagdfliegern* who faced overwhelming Allied superiority in the air, Göring's increasingly empty and irrational threats counted for nothing.

By July 11, JG 53 was preparing to evacuate its still-airworthy fighters across the Strait of Messina to mainland Italy. Hauptmann Michalski's II./JG 53 was the first to go, sent north for re-equipment with a new Bf-109 complement of G-6s. 9.Staffel's Oberleutnant Röhrig became the third *Staffelkapitän* lost in action when he was shot down fighting Spitfires south of Catania. Late that afternoon, four unserviceable 9.Staffel fighters were blown up and III./JG 53 left Torrazzo to relocate at Lecce, on the heel of the Italian boot.

Given the success of the first night's drop, a second paratroop drop was laid on for the night of July 11/12. A total of 144 C-47s carried the remaining two battalions of the 504th PIR, along with artillery and engineer units, to reinforce the beachhead at Gela. Unfortunately, after they took off from Kairouan airfield in Tunisia in the late afternoon, several Ju-88s attempted to attack the invasion fleet at dusk, and the C-47s arrived over the fleet about an hour after the last German had been driven off. Nervous gunners on one ship opened fire on the formation in the mistaken belief they were Axis bombers. In moments, the rest of the fleet opened up on the transports, which were flying at an altitude of 1,200 feet preparatory to dropping their loads. In minutes, 23 C-47s were shot down; the troops on board had no chance to take to their parachutes, and 318 paratroopers died. The rest of the formation was broken up as the pilots sought to evade the friendly fire, which ended all possibility of dropping the troops as planned when they approached the drop zones at Gela. The ground units had not been informed the paratroopers were coming and took the descending parachutists as being enemy, which took some time to straighten out once they were on the ground. Overall, the paratroops suffered nearly 20 percent losses on the second mission.

On July 12, the 14th's 48th Squadron Lightnings ran across a mixed force of Luftwaffe and Regia Aeronautica aircraft. In the fight that followed, Lieutenants John Saum, Daniel Africa, and Sid Weatherford were each credited with a Bf-109 destroyed, for the loss of Second Lieutenant Robert Herman, whose P-38 was seen to crash into the sea. A similar mission the next day saw Flight Officer Jack Homan shoot down a Bf-109, while Lieutenants Yarbery and Robertson claimed one probable and one damaged, respectively. Again, there was a single loss, with Second Lieutenant Donald Lister failing to return.

July 12 saw 150° Gruppo pilots Tenenti Giosuè Carillo and Giovanni Chiale and leading ace Capitano Mario Bellagambi fly the last three surviving Bf-109Gs out of Sciacca to Palermo. Late that afternoon Tenente Gianelli, Sottotenente Camaioni, and an unnamed pilot flew the Gustavs on to Rome Ciampino airfield. The "Gigi Tres Osei" pilots had fought to the end with their Bf-109s, though they were mistaken for Luftwaffe pilots by the Americans they opposed.

The two Fw-190 *Jagdgeschwadern* were withdrawn to southern Italy after the satellite airfields they operated from were attacked and put out of commission; during the invasion, the units only used Sicilian airfields as advanced landing grounds. Axis records for the first ten days of July recorded losses of 227 aircraft destroyed and 183 damaged on Sicily and Sardinia, with 113 destroyed and 119 damaged on Sicily alone. Additionally, the Allies attacked the ports and ferry traffic in the Strait of Messina, isolating Sicily from mainland Italy.

A message from Hitler to Mussolini on July 13, intercepted by Ultra, revealed the Führer's displeasure over reports of the loss of 320 fighters on the ground by Allied air attack in the previous three weeks. Interviewed after the war, Luftwaffe Generalfeldmarschall Albert Kesselring, who commanded German forces on the Southern Front, stated that by the time the Allies landed on July 10, the Luftwaffe was unable to intervene effectively in the battle.

The Allies planned to put captured airfields to use as quickly as possible, to bring airpower to the front. July 13 saw the 31st Group begin operating its Spitfires from Ponte Olivo airfield, just inland from the Gela beaches. They were joined there by the 27th group's A-36 Mustangs. July 14 saw the North African Air Force's bomber offensive shift targets to close the Axis supply line across the narrow Strait of Messina. On June 23, the 31st Group moved ten miles west to Agrigento, where they operated in support of Allied forces advancing on Palermo; the Spitfires were again joined by the 27th's Mustangs, which were establishing themselves as the close air support the ground units liked best since their dive-bombing missions were so accurate they could attack targets 200 yards in front of the ground troops. Two days later, the 27th was joined by the newly operational 86th Group. During the rest of the campaign, the A-36s gained a reputation as the most accurate and effective Allied fighter-bombers in providing close air support to ground troops. Over the course of the campaign, by August 1 the A-36s of the 27th Group had flown 1,971 sorties, destroying 353 motor vehicles and seven tanks, one entire train, 12 locomotives, four ships, and numerous ammo dumps, fuel dumps, gun positions, and troop concentrations. In one mission flown on July 31 against four artillery pieces that could not be seen from the air, the pilots bombed the pinpoint position that had been given; all four guns were destroyed.

By July 14, Allied ground forces were advancing north, and former enemy airfields had been captured that allowed P-40 and Spitfire units to operate on the island. The P-38 groups were relieved of tactical missions over the invasion beaches and began to fly missions to the Italian mainland on fighter sweeps and in support of strategic bombing missions. The 1st and 14th Groups flew their deepest penetration yet, an escort mission on July 17 to Naples where the bombers hit a railroad yard. The enemy failed to put up any aerial opposition, an indication of the losses it had suffered over Sicily.

Two flights of 14th Group P-38s escorting an RAF Sunderland on a rescue mission caught a formation of Ju-52s over the Ligurian Sea headed for Sardinia on July 18. The 37th Squadron's First Lieutenant Lloyd shot down four of the lumbering transports while Second Lieutenant Paul Wilkins scored two. 48th Squadron pilots First Lieutenant Sidney Weatherford and Captain Herbert Ross each were credited with two Ju-52s destroyed.

JG 53's role in the Sicilian campaign ended rapidly, though, like the end in Tunisia, it was not a straightforward process. Since late June, "Tutti" Müller's I./JG 53 had shuttled between airfields in Sicily and southern Italy. Finally, on July 16, the *Gruppe* was at Vibo Valentia north of the Strait of Messina, when the field was attacked by 100

B-25 and B-26 bombers; when the Americans flew away, they left 21 I./JG 53 fighters blown up or damaged beyond repair among the 80 Bf-109s it and I./JG 77 were operating from the field, which was left with vehicles, hangars, and fuel dumps in flames. Müller's *Gruppe* was out of action for the next three weeks, waiting for replacements.

Adolf Galland's headquarters was also at Vibo Valentia. As soon as the bombers departed, he climbed in his car and headed for Naples. Several days later, "Onkel Theo" Osterkamp was returned to his position as *Jagdfliegerführer Sicily*, and Galland was back in Berlin in his role of *General der Jagdflieger*.

On July 19, over 500 XII Bomber Command bombers attacked military targets in and around Rome, dropping more than 1,000 tons of bombs. Axis aerial opposition to the Rome attack was negligible, with only one Italian fighter claimed shot down over the target.

On July 18, the 57th Fighter Group flew their P-40Fs from Malta to Catania airfield on Sicily. The three veteran squadrons began air support missions from Catania the next day. Pilots and ground crew shared the dangers. Several times, Luftwaffe night raiders attacked the airfield; fortunately, damage was limited to loss of sleep. In the first two weeks, group commander Colonel Art Salisbury and Squadron commanders Gil Wymond and Buck Bilby were shot down.

On July 20, the 65th Squadron's Gil Wymond, one of the group's originals, had just strafed a target when he flew through the debris thrown up by the explosion of an ammunition truck, which punctured his P-40's radiator. Fortunately, he was able to fly back to friendly territory before the engine overheated and failed. Wymond was able to make a successful forced landing near Syracuse. Salisbury was hit by flak on July 25 attacking a target 35 miles to the rear of the front lines in enemy territory, but managed to fly the damaged P-40F back to friendly territory before being forced to bail out when the engine caught fire. He was picked up by British troops and returned to the group two days later. On July 27, 64th Squadron CO Major Buck Bilby was flying off the east coast of Sicily when his engine failed. Bailing out, he landed in the water and drifted in his dinghy for 28 hours before an air-sea rescue launch picked him up. Bilby's combat expired two weeks later and he was on his way home.

That same day, the Checkertail Clan escorted B-25s to hit Decimomannu on Sardinia again. The 48 P-40s strafed the field thoroughly, blowing up five Bf-109s and three Ju-52s they found there with fragmentation bombs and gunfire. As they pulled off their run, 12 Regia Aeronautica fighters dove on the Warhawks. In the ensuing fight, the 317th Squadron's Captain Zack Taylor doubled his score with the group's first triple claim, shooting down two C.202s and a Bf-109, to increase his score to six and become the first Checkertail Clan ace. Captain Warden and Flight Officer Jones were credited with a Bf-109 each, and Lieutenants Novotny and Brundydge scored a C.202 each.

George Novotny remembered the fight in which he scored his first victory:

We were to hit Decimomanu with fragmentation bombs. I was Alzie Donovan's wingman. We came in just above the water. Just before we got to the airfield, our flight got hit by Italian fighters and we had to break off and take them on. Everybody was fighting just above ground level, really low. I was following Alzie, who was shooting at two of them, when a third guy came at us head-on. He missed Alzie and headed for me. I began firing at him and as he flashed past I turned and looked over my shoulder to see him catch fire and go right into the ground. We must have missed each other by less than fifty feet.

Dixie Sloan scored his 12th and final victory on July 22 while escorting 12th Group B-25s to bomb a railroad junction at Battipaglia in southern Italy. Three Bf-109s attempted to attack the bombers as they came off the target, but Sloan and fellow ace Ward Kuenzel's flights blocked them, and the two aces each shot down one Bf-109 within seconds of each other.

It fell to Hauptmann Michalski's newly returned and re-equipped II./JG 53 to undertake the "Pik-A" Geschwader's final operations over Sicily. Flying from secondary airfields around the Lecce region, Michalski's *Gruppe* flew *Freie Jagd* sweeps that nearly always resulted in mostly inconclusive contact with Allied fighters now based at Comiso and other former Luftwaffe airfields in southern Sicily. Between July 17 and 26, the *Gruppe* lost only a 4.Staffel pilot killed in action against B-17s over the Gulf of Taranto on July 23. During that time, it was credited with two fighters and three B-26 Marauders shot down on July 24. On July 26 it relocated to the airfield at Scalea on the west coast midway between Vibo Valentia and Naples. On July 27, nine of the new Bf-109s were destroyed or damaged when a mixed force of B-25 and B-26 bombers struck the field. The raid also saw the loss of JG 53's fourth *Staffelkapitän*. Oberleutnant Fritz Dinger, *Staffelkapitän* of 4./JG 53, had claimed a P-40 as his 67th victim while leading a *Freie Jagd* over Sicily that morning. His four Bf-109s were in the midst of being re-armed and refueled for a second mission when the first wave of bombers appeared overhead. Dinger was the only casualty, killed by a bomb splinter while taking cover in a slit trench.

Following the liberation of Palermo, the 307th Fighter Squadron moved to nearby Bocca di Falco airfield on July 27. The next day, Lieutenants Trafton and Muchler were bounced by a pair of Bf-109Gs that stayed in their dive after attacking the two Americans. The Spitfire VIIIs they were flying soon caught up with the enemy fighters, whose pilots increased their dives and flew straight into the sea. Neither pilot claimed a victory.

The 57th moved to the airfield at Scordia on July 28. The 64th Squadron managed one more scrap with Bf-109s on July 31. Captain Gerald Brandon was leading nine bombed-up Warhawks on an anti-shipping mission in the Milazzo area when he spotted six Bf-109s and attacked. Captain Art Exon and Lieutenant Mike McCarthy were credited with a shared probable when both hit a Bf-109 that dove away trailing smoke. Second Lieutenant Bill Nuding went after a Bf-109 that attacked his wingman, putting several bursts into the enemy fighter, which caught fire and crashed into a coastal mountain for Nuding's second confirmed victory.

The Checkertails fought their biggest air battle yet on July 30 during another fighter sweep to Sardinia. The 317th sent 20 P-40s and the 319th 16, taking off from Mateur at 0800 hours. They were over Alghero at 9,000 feet when the 317th was pounced on by 25–30 Bf-109s, quickly followed by 12 Bf-109s and C.202s that attacked the 319th. A fight broke out that lasted 20 minutes, at the end of which the checkertailed P-40 pilots claimed 21 Bf-109s destroyed, and three Bf-109s and a C.202 probably destroyed.

The two squadrons had gotten separated in the fight and the 317th arrived back at Mateur first. When the 319th's Warhawks failed to show up for several long minutes, those on the ground became concerned. Finally, the 319th's fighters showed up; they had lost one pilot. The 319th's Lieutenant Walter B. "Bud" Walker, Jr., had the group's second triple claim with three Bf-109s; overall the two squadrons claimed an additional 18. Captain D.E. Warden, Lieutenant H.E. Eyerly, and Flight Officer C. Huntingon claimed two each, with Captains Reed and Hearn, and Lieutenants Carroll, Mock, Staley, Sederberg, Dunkin, Hamilton, Novotny and Flight Officers Tudor, Dean, and Donovan credited with one Bf-109 each. The group was awarded the Presidential Distinguished Unit Citation for the mission.

USAAF fighter claims for combat over Sicily in July came to 175 Axis fighters shot down. Given that the continuing viability of Italy as an active Axis combatant was at stake, the overall reaction by the Luftwaffe and Regia Aeronautica was considered extremely disappointing by the Oberkommando der Luftwaffe (OKL).

JG 53 was little involved in the Sicilian campaign's last two weeks. By early August, I./JG 53 was at San Severo, part of the Foggia airfield complex, still waiting to make good recent losses, while II. and III./JG 53 were now based on two secondary landing grounds north and east of Naples.

The pilots of the 52nd Group were finally able to say good-bye to their posting to Coastal Command at the end of July. The 2nd and 4th Squadrons flew to Sicily on July 31 to take up residence at Bocca di Falco airfield with the 31st Group. The Luftwaffe had flown regular nocturnal raids since the invasion. Taking off before dawn on August 1, two 2nd Squadron pilots exacted a toll on these raiders when Captain Norman McDonald and wingman First Lieutenant Dave Macmillan spotted two enemy bombers. McDonald later recalled, "Eureka! Dead ahead, two bombers were about 1,000 feet above us." Both Spitfire IXs climbed at full throttle but didn't seem to be catching up to the enemy, which they identified as Do-217s. Suddenly, the two bombers separated and dove toward the sea. McDonald took the one on the left while Macmillan went after the one on the right. Once the bomber filled his sighting ring, McDonald opened fire with a long burst into the belly, followed by a burst that set the right engine on fire. A third burst into the belly and left engine, which saw McDonald run out of 20mm ammo. By this time, the Do-217 was headed toward the dark sea below with both engines on fire and pouring black smoke in the pre-dawn grayness. McDonald's success was quickly followed by Macmillan's target catching fire and diving away. Both crashed into the sea off the volcanic island of Stromboli.

On August 2, the 14th Group escorted B-25s of the 310th Group to Sardinia. They were met by Regia Aeronautica Bf-109s and Macchi C.202s that turned into a swirling fight. The 48th Squadron's Captain Hanes was credited with a C.202 destroyed, while the 49th Squadron's First Lieutenant Carrol Knott was credited with two C.202s.

Two days later, on August 4, the group escorted B-26s to southern Italy and were met by another mixed force of German and Italian fighters. A major dogfight developed, and the Lightings were credited with eight destroyed or probable. The 37th Squadron's Major Forrest Barker and Second Lieutenants Richard Atkinson and Robert Highsmith were credited with a 109 each, while the 49th Squadron's First Lieutenants Anthony Evans and Carroll Knott were credited with two Bf-109s each. With a single shot down over Pantelleria, and the two C.202s scored over Sardinia on August 2, Knott's two Bf-109s shot down in this fight made him an ace.

There was no other enemy air activity day or night until August 8, when 12 31st Group Spitfires – six Spitfire Vbs and six Mk VIIIs – spotted a formation of 20 Fw-190 fighter-bombers headed toward the ships as they covered a landing at Cap Orlando. Diving into the formation, three *Jabos* were quickly set afire and headed into the sea. While two of them had been hit by multiple pilots, Second Lieutenant Richard Hurd was credited with a solo victory, the first of six he would eventually score. A fourth was damaged by flight leader Captain Royal Baker.

Following the Rome mission on July 19, XII Bomber Command's second large raid against military targets around Rome saw 106 B-17s and 168 B-25s and B-26s bomb targets in the city and surrounding area on August 13. While Regia Aeronautica fighter opposition was heavy, only two B-25s and three defending fighters were shot down. The 14th Group's Lightings provided high cover for this mission; First Lieutenant Russell Moomaw was credited with a C.202 destroyed, while Lieutenants Jim Hollingsworth and Bob Gardner were each credited with a C.202 damaged. On August 14, the Italian government declared Rome an open city.

As the air campaign heated up over mainland Italy, Hauptmann Franz Götz's III./JG 53 claimed the *Geschwader*'s first significant success when the *Gruppe* was credited with shooting down six B-24s in a raid on the Foggia airfield complex on August 16. On August 19, units of all three

Gruppen were in action against large formations of Flying Fortresses and Liberators that returned to the same target. JG 53 claimed ten and a single P-38, losing one pilot killed and two wounded. The 14th Group flew escort for this mission, and the 49th Squadron's Captain Richard Decker, First Lieutenant Harold Harper, and Second Lieutenant Walter Hoke were each credited with a Bf-109 destroyed; the 37th Squadron's First Lieutenant Jim Hollingsworth was credited with one Bf-109 destroyed, while Flight Officer Herbert Hickman shot down two.

On August 20, the JG 53 claimed 14 P-38s shot down in a huge battle over the coast near Naples – their opponents claiming 13 Axis fighters destroyed with many others claimed damaged. Over the course of August 21–22, II. and III.Gruppen were credited with shooting down 18 Marauders attacking marshaling yards in the Naples area, though Allied records indicate only three failed to return. The Allies' weight of numbers continued to make itself felt when Hauptmann Michalski's II./JG 53 lost 11 Bf-109Gs destroyed or damaged beyond repair during a raid by medium bombers on Cancello airfield near Naples on August 26. On August 30 the *Gruppe* claimed 11 P-38s for the loss of one pilot from 4.Staffel, but the 14th Fighter Group they fought only reported three losses while claiming 11 enemy fighters destroyed in the two missions of August 26 and 30.

However, the high rate of success experienced in August could not be maintained; JG 53 only claimed 18 enemy aircraft shot down in the whole month of September. Never again while the *Geschwader* was in Italy would any daily total of claims reach double figures.

On Sicily, the Allied offensive by the 15th Army Group came to a successful conclusion. Several German and Italian divisions fought a dogged delaying action around Messina, while the majority of their surviving forces were successfully evacuated to the Italian mainland. The Axis rearguard was successfully withdrawn over the night of August 16. The next morning, leading Allied ground units entered Messina.

The Checkertail Clan continued operations against Sardinia in late August and early September before the Italian surrender. Most missions involved strafing and frag-bombing targets on the island, but finally, on August 28, the 319th Squadron was attacked by 26 Bf-109s. Captain Herschel Green recalled that seven were shot down. Captain John Watkins was credited with two, making him an ace, while Lieutenants George Novotny, Frank Collins, Daniel Owen, and Hank Brundydge, and Flight Officer John Palmer scored one each. Green, Brundydge and Frank Hamilton were credited with a Bf-109 probable each.

During August, Twelfth Air Force fighter groups claimed 131 enemy aircraft shot down over Italy, Sicily, and Sardinia. All but a handful were fighters; nearly all were German. The largest aerial action of the entire campaign occurred on September 2, when 82nd Group P-38s claimed 25 Bf-109s and Fw-190s shot down over the island of Ischia during an escort mission to Naples.

When the Checkertails later landed at Decimomannu on September 22 following the island's surrender, they learned from the Italian commander that their claims for the fight on July 30 were too low. The newly arrived Luftwaffe unit they fought had lost 35 Bf-109s, most from trying to stay with the P-40s in turns. III./JG 77 was evacuated to Germany the next day. George Novotny later remembered that he got involved in a turning fight with a Bf-109 and turned so tight that the P-40 went into a high-speed stall, nosed up, made a complete 360-degree roll, and ended up back in the turn. "The '109 went right by me, and I got on his tail and shot him down."

The Sardinian campaign demonstrated that the fighter squadrons that had arrived in North Africa inexperienced and green had learned the art of air warfare successfully. However, the failure to interdict the successful German withdrawal from Sicily to Italy across the Strait of Messina would have major implications in the campaign to come in Italy. Unlike the evacuation of Tunisia, the distance from Messina to the mainland was only two miles. The Axis forces carried out their evacuation at night, between August 11 and 16, and were not detected until they had completed over half of the maneuver; over 38,000 troops and 15,000 tons of supplies were successfully carried across the narrow strait.

The withdrawal of all Ninth Air Force B-24s to participate in Operation *Tidal Wave*, the attack on Ploesti on August 1, removed the one aerial force that could have had a major effect in disrupting the German evacuation due to the heavy losses incurred in the raid. The medium bombers and fighter-bombers had to face the heaviest defensive antiaircraft fire they had come across, which reduced their effectiveness. The B-24s did not return to operations in Sicily and Italy until August 13, by which time the majority of the evacuation had been successfully accomplished. Those troops that successfully escaped Sicily made the landing at Salerno in September the closest the Allies came in World War II to a defeat in a major amphibious operation.

Overall, however, Twelfth Air Force demonstrated that the air units had learned the lessons of how to provide proper air support to ground troops, after prewar USAAF doctrine had been shown to be ineffective. The success of Twelfth Air Force in Sicily demonstrated what was possible and what was needed for Operation *Overlord* a year later.

The year between the introduction of USAAF units in North Africa, which gave the RAF the necessary margin to stave off the defeat in the Mediterranean that seemed inevitable in July 1942, had seen a true turning of the tide. The success of the Allied campaign in North Africa and Sicily reversed Axis fortunes in western and southern Europe as effectively as they had been reversed on the Eastern Front with the resounding Soviet victory at Stalingrad. The disastrous surrender of experienced troops at Stalingrad and in Tunisia was a blow from which the Wehrmacht would never recover. The Luftwaffe force that opposed the USAAF units in North Africa was more experienced, and had more experienced and successful pilots in its ranks, than the force the Eighth Air Force battled. The North African losses, combined with the losses in western Europe, sealed the fate of the Luftwaffe, which would be unable to oppose the cross-Channel invasion ten months later. The successful USAAF pilots of the North African campaign would provide many of the leaders of the Eighth and Ninth Air Forces that wrote finis to their Luftwaffe opponents over the year between D-Day in Normandy and VE Day.

At the conclusion of the Sicilian campaign, Air Marshal Tedder reported to the Chief of the Imperial General Staff in London, "The outstanding feature of the whole operation was the ability of two air forces – American and British – supported by certain French and Polish units, operating from mainland and island bases covering a front of some 2,000 miles, to integrate their operations and achieve the intense concentration of their effort which contributed vitally to the success of the whole operation."

The USAAF had indeed learned to walk and then to run. The success of Operation *Overlord* would not have been possible without the lessons learned in battle over the North African desert and Sicily during the 12 months when the tide turned in World War II.

BIBLIOGRAPHY

Atkinson, Rick, *An Army at Dawn* (Henry Holt and Company, 2002)
Atkinson, Rick, *The Day of Battle* (Henry Holt and Company, 2004)
Auphan, Paul and Jacques Mordal, *The French Navy in World War II* (Greenwood Press, 1976)
Bechtold, Mike, "A Question of Success: Tactical Air Doctrine and Practice in North Africa," *The Journal of Military History*, Vol. 68, No. 3, 2004
Blake, Steve with John Stanaway, *Up and At 'Em! A History of the 82nd Fighter Group in World War II* (Boise: 82nd Fighter Group History Inc., 1992)
Blake, Steve, *P-38 Lightning Aces of the 82nd Fighter Group* (Osprey Publishing, 2012)
Bucholz, Chris, *332nd Fighter Group: Tuskegee Airmen* (Osprey Publishing, 2007)
D'Este, Carlo, *Bitter Victory: The Battle for Sicily, 1943* (E.P. Dutton, 1988)
Deniston, Dale R., *Memories of a Combat Fighter Pilot* (1995)
Doolittle, James H. with Carroll V. Glines, *I Could Never Be So Lucky Again: An Autobiography* (Bantam Books, 1991)
Ehlers, Robert S., Jr., *The Mediterranean Air War: Airpower and Allied Victory in World War II* (University of Kansas Press, 2015)
Fitzgerald-Black, Alexander, *Eagles of Husky: The Allied Air Forces in the Sicilian Campaign 14 May to 17 August 1943* (Helion & Co. Ltd., 2017)
Galland, Adolf, *The First and the Last* (Ballantine Books, 1954)
Gladman, Brad W., *Intelligence and Anglo-American Air Support in World War II* (Palgrave, 2009)
Green, Herschel H., *Herky! The Memoirs of a Checkertail Ace* (Schiffer Military History, 1996)
Groom, Winston, *1942: The Year That Tried Men's Souls* (Grove Press, 2006)
Hammel, Eric, *Aces Against Germany: The American Aces Speak, Volume II* (Pacifica Military History, 1993)

Hooton, E.R., *Eagle in Flames: The Fall of the Luftwaffe* (Arms & Armour Press, 1999)
Ilfrey, Jack with Max Reynolds, *Happy Jack's Go-Buggy* (Exposition Press, 1979)
Ivie, Thomas G., *Aces of the 325th Fighter Group* (Osprey Publishing, 2014)
Ivie, Tom and Paul Ludwig, *Spitfires and Yellowtail Mustangs: The 52nd Fighter Group in World War II* (Hikoki Publications Ltd., 2005)
Kelly, Orr, *Meeting The Fox: The Allied Invasion of Africa* (John Wiley & Sons, 2002)
Ketley, Barry, *French Aces of World War 2* (Osprey Publishing, 1999)
Kucera, Dennis C., *In A Now Forgotten Sky: The 31st Fighter Group in World War 2* (Stratford: Flying Machines Press, 1997)
Lambert, John W., *The 14th Fighter Group in World War II* (Schiffer Military History, 2008)
Laslie, Brian D., *Architect of Air Power: General Laurence S. Kuter and the Birth of the U.S. Air Force* (University of Kentucky Press, 2017)
Luce, Steve W., *The 86th Fighter Group in World War II* (Eagle Editions Ltd., 2007)
MacCloskey, Monro, *Torch and the Twelfth Air Force* (Richard Rosen Press, 1971)
Massimello, Giovanni and Giorgio Apostolo, *Italian Aces of World War 2* (Osprey Publishing, 1999)
Matteoli, Marco, *530 Stormo* (Osprey Publishing, 2010)
McDowell, Ernest R. and William N. Hess, *Checkertail Clan: The 325th Fighter Group in North Africa and Italy* (Aero Publishers, 1969)
Molesworth, Carl, *57th Fighter Group: First in the Blue* (Osprey Publishing, 2011)
Molesworth, Carl, *P-40 Warhawk Aces of the MTO* (Osprey Publishing, 2002)
O'Hara, Vincent, *Torch: North Africa and the Allied Path to Victory* (Naval Institute Press, 2023)
Pace, Steve, *B-25 Mitchell Units of the MTO* (Osprey Publishing, 2002)
Perret, Geoffrey, *Winged Victory: The Army Air Forces in World War II* (Random House, 1993)
Persyn, Lionel, Kari Stenman and Andrew Thomas, *P-36 Hawk Aces of World War II* (Osprey Publishing, 2009)
Porch, Douglas, *The Path to Victory: The Mediterranean Theater in World War II* (Farrar, Strauss & Giroux, 2004)
Reed, James E., *The Fighting 33rd Nomads in World War II* (Reed Publishers, 1987)
Rein, Christopher, *The North African Air Campaign: U.S. Army Air Forces From El Alamein to Salerno* (University of Kansas Press, 2012)

Rife, Shawn P., "Kasserine Pass and the Proper Application of Air Power," *Joint Forces Quarterly*, Autumn/Winter 1998/1999

Scutts, Jerry, *Bf-109 Aces of North Africa and the Mediterranean* (Osprey Publishing, 1995)

Scutts, Jerry, *Mustang Aces of the Ninth & Fifteenth Air Forces & the RAF* (Osprey Publishing, 1995)

Stanaway, John, *P-38 Lightning Aces of the MTO/ETO* (Osprey Publishing, 1998)

Steinhoff, Johannes, *Messerschmitts Over Sicily* (Stackpole, 2004)

Styling, Mark, *B-26 Marauder Units of the MTO* (Osprey Publishing, 2008)

Sullivan, Brian R., "Downfall of the Regia Aeronautica 1933–43," in Robin Higham and Stephen J. Harris (eds.), *Why Air Forces Fail: The Anatomy of Defeat* (University of Kentucky Press, 2006)

Tedder, Arthur, *With Prejudice: The War Memoirs of Marshal of the Royal Air Force Sir Arthur Tedder* (Cassell & Co., 1966)

Thomas, Andrew, *American Spitfire Aces of World War 2* (Osprey Publishing, 2007)

Tillman, Barrett and Chris Davey, *Wildcat Aces of World War 2* (Osprey Publishing, 1995)

Weal, John, *Focke-Wulf Fw-190 Aces of the Western Front* (Osprey Publishing, 1996)

Weal, John, *Jagdgeschwader 53: Pik-As* (Osprey Publishing, 2004)

Williamson, Murray, *Strategy for Defeat: The Luftwaffe 1933–45* (Air University Press, 1983)

Woerpel, Don, *In A Hostile Sky: The Mediterranean Air War of the 79th Fighter Group* (The Andon Press, 1977)

Wolk, Herman S., "Pantelleria 1943," *Air and Space Forces Magazine*, June 1, 2002

Wordell, M.T. and E.N. Seiler, *"Wildcats" Over Casablanca: US Navy Fighters in Operation Torch* (Potomac Books, 2006)

Zaloga, Steven J., *Sicily 1943: The Debut of Allied Joint Operations* (Osprey Publishing, 2013)

Zaloga, Steven J., "War Diaries of the 310th Bomb Group: September 1942 – August 1943," www.57thbombwing.com

Zaloga, Steven J., "War Diaries of the 321st Bomb Group: November 1942 – August 1943," www.57thbombwing.com

Zaloga, Steven J., "War Diaries of the 340th Bomb Group: November 1942 – August 1943," www.57thbombwing.com

GLOSSARY

The list below contains acronyms and non-English terms used in the text.

ACRONYMS

ASC: Air Support Command
HALPRO: Halverson Provisional Detachment
MTO: Mediterranean Theater of Operations
NASAF: North African Strategic Air Force
NATAF: Northwest African Tactical Air Force
RAAF: Royal Australian Air Force
RAF: Royal Air Force
SAAF: South African Air Force
USAAF: United States Army Air Forces
WDAF: Western Desert Air Force
VF: Fighter Squadron (US Navy)
VGF: Escort Fighter Squadron (US Navy)
VGS: Escort Scouting Squadron (US Navy)
VS: Scouting Squadron (US Navy)

NON-ENGLISH TERMS

German
Experte(n): German term for "ace"
Fliegerkorps: air corps
Freie Jagd: free hunt patrol

GLOSSARY

Geschwader(n): wing(s)
Geschwaderkommodore: wing commander
Gruppe(n): group(s)
Gruppenkommandeur: group commander
Jabo: abbreviation for Jagdbomber, a German fighter-bomber
Jagdflieger: fighter pilot(s)
Jagdgeschwader(n): fighter wing
Luftflotte: air fleet
Luftwaffe: German Air Force
Staffel(n): squadron(s)
Staffelkapitän: squadron commander
Schwarm: flight of four aircraft
Würger: nickname for Fw-190

Italian
Gruppo/gruppi: group/groups
Squadriglia/Squadriglie: squadron/squadrons
Regia Aeronautica: Royal Italian Air Force
Stormo/stormi: wing/wings

INDEX

Note: page numbers in **bold** refer to illustrations.

Abbott, Lt William   69, 240
accidents   34, 46, 81, 91, 115, 162
Accra assembly depot, Gold Coast   49–50
ace pilots   63, 64, 87, 91–95, 116, 117, 119, 136, 138, 155, 192, 195, 196, 201, 212, 217, 218, 222, 229, 232, 238, 240, 276, 287, 293, 297, 300, 304; aces in a day   79, 81, 140, 236; German *Experten*   36, 65, 66, 67, 72, 74–75, 78, 79, 80, 81, 131, 134, 154, 155, 174, 212, 218, 228, 230, 234, 239, 284, 295
Africa, Second Lt Daniel D.   265, 297
African Americans in the USAAF   252–253
Afrika Korps, the   12, 13, 21, 23, 24, 26, 27, 52, 65, 71, 72, 76, 78, 85, 88, 89, 99, 160, 182, 183, 204, 205, 208, 216, 226, 230, 242; 5. Panzerarmee   204, 243, 244; 10.Panzerdivision   208–209; 15. Panzerdivision   164; 21.Panzerdivision   164, 209, 227; 621st Signal Battalion   51
air tactics   81–82, 84, 87, 131, 133, 135, 136, 140, 162, 163, 164–165, 199, 201
aircraft, France: Curtiss H-75 Hawk   105, 110, 111, 112, 114, 115, 116, 117, 119, 158; Dewoitine D.520   105, 112, 114, 117, 121–122; Lioré et Olivier LeO 45   115, 116; P-51B   86; Potez-630   118
aircraft, Germany: BV-222   176; Dornier Do-217   295, 302; Fieseler Storch   243–244; Focke-Wulf Fw-189   231; Fw-190   13, 35, 80, 81, 82, 138–139, 147, 153, 154, 158, 164, 174, 175, 176, 177, 192, 193, 194, 196, 203, 206–207, 212, 213, 214, 218, 231, 264, 266, 267, 268, 272, 274, 277, 278, 291–293, 295, 297, 303, 305; Fw-190 Jabo   295, 303; Fw-190A   36, 79–80, 128, 154; Fw-190F   234; Heinkel He-177   295; Henschel Hs-129   234; Junkers Ju-52   91, 128, 138, 140, 176, 179, 197, 198, 220, 230, 231, 232–234, 235–239, 247, 298, 299; Ju-87 "Stuka"   60, 73, 77, 78, 88, 89, 131, 192, 193, 202, 217, 219, 220, 231, 233, 277; Ju-87D   216; Ju-88   78, 130, 131, 136, 137–138, 139, 140, 141, 142, 154, 166, 174, 178, 192, 193, 200, 201, 212, 217, 218–219, 232, 233, 234, 240, 277, 290, 292, 295, 296; Ju-88C   156–157; Ju-90   247; Messerschmitt Bf-109   13, 26, 35, 48, 54, 55, 56, 57–59, 60–61, 62, 63, 64, 69–70, 74, 77, 79, 84, 87, 134, 137, 141, 144–145, 146, 147, 148, 149–152, 155, 158, 164, 175, 176, 177, 178, 179, 184, 192, 193, 194, 195, 199, 200, 201, 202, 203, 206, 207, 212, 215, 217, 218, 219, 220, 221–222, 223, 224, 225, 229–230, 231, 232–236, 237, 238, 240–242, 243, 247, 253, 259–260, 261, 264–265, 267, 268–269, 271, 272, 276, 278–279, 286, 287–288, 289, 290, 291, 292, 293, 297, 299, 300, 302–303, 304, 305; Bf-109E   66; Bf-109F   66; Bf-109G "Gustav"   66, 78, 80, 86–87, 138, 139, 146, 184–185, 189, 190, 193, 196, 198, 216, 217, 218, 228, 239, 258, 264, 265, 266, 286, 289, 290, 291, 296, 297, 301; Bf-110   142–143, 198; Bf-110E   231; Me-210   190; Me-323 Gigant   130, 176, 179, 197, 198, 230, 231, 240, 247, 261
aircraft, Italy: Fiat CR.32   87; Fiat CR.42 Falco   60, 64, 87, 93, 94; Fiat G.50 Freccia   87, 88, 89, 93; Fiat G.55 Centauro   86; Macchi C.200 Saetta   27, 86, 87, 88, 91, 93, 94, 233, 276, 292, 293; Macchi C.202 Folgore   27, 35, 48, 55, 63–64, 86, 88, 89, 90, 91, 92, 94–95, 157, 164, 200, 201, 224, 225, 228, 239, 241, 242, 257, 263, 264, 268, 269, 276, 279, 287, 300, 301, 302–303; Macchi C.205 Veltro   86, 91, 93, 242, 276; Reggiane Re.2000   94; Reggiane Re.2001 Falco II   86, 276, 289; Reggiane Re.2005 Saggitario   86; Savoia-Marchetti S.79 Sparviero Aerosiluranti   87–88, 94, 257; Savoia-Marchetti SM.81 Pipistrello   138; Savoia-Marchetti SM.82   231, 233, 234, 239; Savoia-Marchetti SM.84 Pipistrello   89–90

INDEX

aircraft, UK: Boston III 54, 55, 60, 78, 92, 93, 94, 229; Bristol Beaufighter 73, 94, 131; Bristol Beaufort 73; Bristol Bisley V 78, 80; Bristol Blenheim 90, 93; Fairey Albacore 162; Gladiator 91; Hawker Hurricane 59, 87, 90, 91, 92, 93, 121, 141, 157; "Kittyhawks" 42, 54–55, 59, 67, 73, 74, 83, 89, 91, 92, 93, 94, 95, 223, 234; Lockheed Hudson 46, 115; Martlet 79; Short Sunderland 91, 298; Spitfire V 11, 36, 67, 75, 76, 77, 78, 79, 80, 81, 82, 83, 86, 87, 90, 139, 189, 303; Spitfire VIII 263–264, 289, 301, 303; Spitfire IX 36, 86, 229, 240, 267–268, 285, 287, 295, 302; Supermarine Spitfire 91, 92, 95, 105, 115, 120–121, 123, 124, 128, 138, 140–141, 192, 193, 203, 205, 207, 208, 212–216, 217, 218, 219, 228, 231, 233–234, 235–236, 239, 254, 257, 263, 265, 269, 277, 278, 289, 290, 295, 296, 298; Supermarine Walrus 264, 268, 270, 276; Vickers Wellington 162, 165, 265, 284

aircraft, US: Bell P-39 Airacobra 11, 35, 81, 82, 91, 137, 193, 199–200, 202, 203, 205, 206, 208, 210; Boeing B-17 Flying Fortress 36, 78, 81, 82, 83, 91, 92, 93, 124, 131, 137, 143, 146, 147, 153, 154, 171, 199, 231–232, 234–235, 258, 265, 285, 288, 300; C-54 49; Consolidated B-24 Liberator 25, 26, 27, 182, 263, 287, 303, 305; B-24D 67, 76; Curtiss P-36 Hawk 44, 97, 111, 112; Curtiss P-40 "Warhawk" 49, 67, 78, 79, 81, 82, 117–118, 119, 137, 141, 158, 164, 171, 179, 190, 193, 194, 200, 202, 222–224, 225, 227, 228, 230, 233, 235, 236, 237, 238–239, 241, 242, 245, 246, 247, 257, 259–262, 268, 269–270, 279, 286, 287, 290, 291, 298, 299–300, 301, 305; P-40B 42, 97; P-40C 42; P-40E 39, 42, 44, 49; P-40F 35, 39–41, 44, 48, 50, 55, 56, 57, 59, 60–62, 64, 65, 68, 69, 83, 97, 98, 105, 188, 203, 216, 245, 299; P-40K 69, 229; P-40L 35, 216, 253, 258; Douglas A-20 Havoc 50, 54, 155, 156, 164, 167, 169, 174, 193, 200, 202, 208, 217, 225, 234, 265, 266, 268–269, 270, 271, 278, 286, 287, 289; Douglas B-18 "Bolo" 160; Douglas C-47 122, 127, 130, 137, 158, 203, 246, 290, 296; Douglas DB-7 114, 116, 117, 118; Douglas SBD-4 Dauntless 105, 108, 110, 118; Grumman F4F-4 Wildcat 105, 110, 111, 112–114, 115, 116, 117, 118; Grumman TBF-1 Avenger 105, 108; Grumman TFB-1 105; Lockheed P-38 Lightning 33, 35, 77, 78, 80–81, 82, 83, 86, 95, 128, 130, 131–135, 136–137, 139, 140, 142–145, 146, 147, 148–152, 153, 155–156, 172, 173, 174, 175, 176, 177, 179, 188, 189, 190, 196–197, 198, 199, 212, 216, 220, 221–222, 231, 232–234, 254, 257, 258, 263, 265, 275, 286, 287, 289, 291–293, 295, 297, 298, 303, 304, 305; Lockheed P-38F 13, 15, 16, 17–19, 33, 143–144, 153; Lockheed P-38G 275–276; Lockheed P-38J-25 34; Martin 167 Maryland 110, 116; Martin A-30 Baltimore 164, 225, 229, 240, 267, 286, 289; Martin B-26 Marauder 15, 16, 36, 93, 95, 156, 171, 173, 174, 186–191, 195, 196, 199, 220, 221, 247, 257, 259, 264, 265, 278, 287, 295, 298, 300, 303, 304; B-26B 186, 187, 191; North American A-36A Mustang 270, 297, 298; North American B-25 Mitchell 36, 78, 79, 160–165, 166, 169, 170, 171, 172, 173, 174–175, 176–177, 178–180, 183, 184–185, 186, 188, 189, 197, 198, 199, 212, 225, 228, 232, 233, 239, 257, 263, 265, 268, 278, 285, 286, 289, 298, 299, 300, 303; B-25C 161, 167, 169, 181; B-25D 161, 231; North American P-51 Mustang 86, 271; Republic P-43 44, 97; Republic P-47 Thunderbolt 30, 134, 238; Vought F4U Corsair 116; Vought OS2U Kingfisher 110–111; YP-38 132–133; aircraft, USSR: I-15 Chato 87; I-16 Mosca 87

airfields 127, 128, 130, 141, 159, 194, 231–232, 234–235, 284, 292; "Banjo Field," Gozo Island 285; Berteaux, Algeria 173, 174, 176, 184, 185, 197, 198, 216; Biscari, Sicily 285, 290; Biskra, Algeria 153, 159, 179, 192; Bizerte, Tunisia 140, 182, 184, 278; Bluie West-l, Greenland 167–168; Bocca di Falco 232, 301, 302; Bône, Algeria 99, 125, 127, 130, 138, 139, 140–141, 157, 159, 176, 192, 193, 198; Cazes 110–115; El Djem, Tunisia 235, 236, 238; Gabes, Tunisia 142, 148, 155, 168, 169, 179, 188, 195, 221–222, 228; Korba, Tunisia 263, 267, 268; Maison Blanche, Algeria 127, 131, 136, 139, 141, 158, 187, 188, 192; Marghana, Pantelleria 256, 257, 263, 265, 266, 267, 274, 277; Mateur, Tunisia 289, 301; Medenine, Libya 185–186; Médiouna, Morocco 118; Mitchell Field, New York 40, 41, 43, 44, 97; Montesquieu, Algeria 246, 261; Oued Naj, Morocco 253; Ponte Olivo, Sicily 297; Port Lyautey, Morocco 117, 118–119, 158; RAF Hardwick, England 166, 169, 170; Sidi Ahmed, Tunisia 169; Tafaroui, Algeria 102, 121–123, 128, 137, 139, 157, 169, 246; Telergma, Algeria 171–172, 173, 188, 189, 190, 195, 203, 216, 220, 221; Thélepte, Tunisia 141–142, 158, 193, 200–201, 202–203, 205, 207–208, 216, 246; Wideawake, Ascension Island 49; Youks-les-Bains, Algeria 130, 139–140, 142, 148, 153, 155, 158, 197, 203 *see also* bombing raids

Alexander, Gen Sir Harold 52, 209, 244–245
Allied strategy 28–30, 98–100, 104, 105, 106, 107, 126, 141, 162–163, 193, 210, 242–243, 249–252, 254–256, 276, 279–280, 281–284, 290, 297–298, 304, 305–306
Anderson, Lt Gen Sir Kenneth 202, 204, 205, 206
anti-shipping missions 26, 185, 189, 191, 240

313

antiaircraft fire 60, 62, 74, 110, 112, 115, 118, 137, 150, 151, 152, 161, 163, 164, 169, 172–173, 174, 176–177, 179, 183, 184, 185, 186, 187, 188, 189, 190, 191, 201, 221–222, 225, 227, 233, 239, 257, 262, 263, 288, 291, 293, 299, 305
Arcadia Conference, the 25, 98–99
Armée de l'Air, the 83, 104, 105, 158, 200; *Groupes de Chasse*: GC II/5 158, 193, 203 *see also* Free French forces, the; Vichy Armée de l'Air de l'Armistice, the
Armstrong, First Lt Robert E. 217, 272, 274
Arnim, General Hans-Jürgen von 83, 204, 205, 243, 244
Arnold, Gen Henry "Hap" 25, 178, 274
August, Lt Charles "Chuck" (j.g.) 111, 112–113
Austin, Col Gordon H. 261, 288
Avery, Maj 123, 124, 205

Bär, Major Heinz "Pritzl" 75, 83
Baseler, Lt Col Robert L. 261, 264, 289
Battle of Alam el Halfa, the 53
Battle of Britain, the 75, 80, 93
Battle of Ein el Gazala, the 73
Battle of Gazala, the 160
Battle of Kasserine Pass, the 13, 35, 36, 37, 201, 203–225, 259
Battle of Kursk, the 29
Battle of Normandy, the 30
Battle of Pantelleria, the 254–274, **255**, **273**, 275, 279, 283
Battle of the Coral Sea, the 116
Battle of the Mareth Line, the 78
Battle of Tunisia, the 76–85, 95, 130–131, 135, 242, 243, 248, 254, 256, 272
Bedford, First Lt Frank P. 190, 240
Berres, Leutnant Heinz-Edgar 67, 76, 78–79, 230
Berry, Sqn Ldr Ronald "Razz" 139, 141
Bilby, Cpt Glade "Buck" 45, 60, 299
Bisleri, Tenente Franco Bordoni 92–93
bomb loads 27, 110, 134, 162, 166, 172, 186, 187, 200, 227, 240, 256, 262, 265, 270, 272, 290, 293, 299
bombing raids 56, 59, 64, 69–70, 77, 89, 131, 142, 169, 175–176, 183, 190, 225, 288, 302; Benghazi port, Libya 26–27; Biskra, Algeria 153–154, 192; Bizerte, Tunisia 81, 143–145, 154–155, 188, 288; Bône, Algeria 77, 89–90, 125, 130, 141, 157–158, 192; Cagliari–Elmas, Sardinia 189; Cancello airfield, Naples 304; Castelvetrano, Sicily 234, 265, 278; Decimomannu airfield, Sardinia 189, 259, 261, 264, 275, 276, 289, 299–300; Dieppe, France 120; El Aouina airfield, Tunisia 171, 176–177, 189, 231; El Daba, Egypt 57–58; Enfidaville, Tunisia 190; Faid Pass, Tunisia 147–148; Foggia airfield, Italy 303–304; Fuka, Egypt 60; Gabes, Tunisia 149–150, 179, 188, 199, 220; Gerbini, Sicily 285–286, 287, 289; Graiba railroad bridges, Tunisia 175; Kairouan marshaling yards, Tunisia 174–175, 200, 205; Kalaa Srira rail yard, Tunisia 175; La Goulette docks, Tunis 173; Maison Blanche, Algiers 131, 136; Maknassy, Tunisia 202; Marsala, Sicily 191; Mateur, Tunisia 247; Mezzouna airdrome, Tunisia 185, 217; Palermo, Sicily 191; Ploesti oil fields, Romania 26, 67, 305; Rome, Italy 95, 178, 299, 303; San Pietro airfield, Italy 289; Sfax, Tunisia 172–173, 177, 179, 187; Sousse, Tunisia 171, 188, 277; Tobruk, Libya 27–28; Trapani–Milo airfield, Sicily 289; Tunis 147, 186; Vibo Valentia airfield, Italy 298–299; Villacidro airdrome, Sardinia 179–180
Boone, Cpt Mark 200, 264
Borsodi, Cpt Fred 70, 223, 227, 240
Boulware, Second Lt Thomas M. 64, 224
British Army, the; 1st Armored 226, 230; 1st Infantry 257, 272; 4th Indian 226, 230; 7th Armored 53; Australian 9th 51; Eighth Army 12, 13, 24, 27, 52, 53, 59, 65, 70, 73, 89, 99, 160, 165, 202, 209, 225, 226, 227, 228, 230; First Army 194, 204, 209, 226, 228, 230
British strategy 23, 24–25, 27, 28, 31, 51, 52, 53, 59, 73, 88, 103–104, 206, 222, 225, 226–227, 230–231, 272 *see also* Allied strategy
Broennle, Leutnant Herbert 287–288
Brundydge, Lt Hank 289, 300, 304
Brunner, S/Sgt Robert M. 177, 184
Bühligen, Leutnant Kurt 80, 81, 82, 134, 154, 155, 196, 197
Butler, S/Sgt James E. 218, 219
Byrne, First Lt Robert J. "Rocky" 61–63, 64, 238, 240–241

Campbell, Lt William 265, 278
Carey, First Lt John 277–278
Carillo, Tenente Giosuè 265, 297
Casablanca Conference, the 193, 202, 210, 246, 249–251
Casablanca landings, the 105–109, 119, 120
Castoldi, Mario 85–86
Catlin, Flt Off Richard L. 247, 264
Cazes airfield battle, the 110–115
CCS (Allied Combined Chiefs of S/Sgt), the 98, 100
Churchill, Winston 21, 22, 23, 24, 28, 30, 52, 102, 125, 193, 244–245, 249, 250–251
Clark, Gen Mark W. 103, 125
Cochran, Maj Philip G. 42, 43, 199, 200, 253, 266, 279
Collins, Second Lt Frank J. "Spot" 247, 264, 289, 304
Collinsworth, Cpt Jerry 206–207, 212–216, 295
combat reports 82, 176, 180, 216–217, 219 *see also* war diaries
Coningham, Air Vice Marshal Arthur 195, 210, 251

INDEX

crash-landings 26, 91, 95, 111, 114, 115, 143, 179, 187, 188, 189, 190, 191, 197, 198, 199, 225, 228, 238
crew morale 74, 200, 203, 212, 218, 285
Curl, Cpt James G. "Big Jim" 224, 235–236
Custer, Sgt Lyle 67–68

Darlan, Admiral François 107, 119, 125–126
Davis, Lt Col Benjamin O. 253
Dean, Lt Col Fred 124, 139, 193, 205, 206, 218, 267
Decker, Cpt Richard 276, 304
Democratic Party, the 23–24, 32
Dempsey, Maj Robert G. "Bob" 243, 291
Deniston, First Lt Dale 44, 45, 224, 225
Dickfeld, Oberleutnant Alfred 79, 80, 81, 82
Dinger, Oberleutnant Fritz 78, 301
dive-bombing missions 64, 108, 247, 253, 257, 258, 262, 268, 270, 271, 277, 293, 298
dive flaps 34, 133
dogfights 54–55, 60–61, 62, 81, 82, 111–112, 122, 131, 149–150, 151–152, 154, 155, 156–157, 176, 199, 207, 212–215, 220–221, 224, 229–230, 235–236, 237, 239, 240, 259–260, 264, 265, 266, 268, 269–270, 271, 278–279, 292, 295, 297, 301, 303
Doolittle, Gen Jimmy 37, 120, 121, 124, 127, 136, 155, 178, 179, 186, 194, 220–221, 222, 251
Doolittle Raid, the 23, 25, 160, 178
Dryden, First Lt Charles 266, 278–279
dust storms 54, 68, 71, 161, 205–206

Eastern Dorsale mountain range, the 159, 204–205, 206, 210
Eisenhower, Gen Dwight D. 32, 99–100, 103, 125, 126, 194–195, 204, 211, 244, 254, 257, 280
El Alamein, Egypt 13, 24, 27, 31, 51, 165, 204; First Battle 27, 51–52; Second Battle of 59–65, 76, 89, 91, 99, 249
El Hamma, Tunisia 226–227
Ellington, Second Lt Edward "Duke" 44, 45–47, 54, 56, 222–223
engines 17, 34, 87, 155, 162; Allison V-1710 44, 59, 69; Daimler-Benz DB 601 86; Daimler-Benz DB 605 66, 86; Merlin-60 264; Merlin 61 36; Merlin V-1650 35, 39, 44, 58, 59, 69, 158; Pratt and Whitney R-2800 86, 186; and turbo-superchargers 35, 134
Ethell, Second Lt Ervin 140, 142
evacuations 29, 67, 74, 78, 79, 82, 83, 92, 93, 95, 203, 206, 207–208, 243, 296, 304, 305 *see also* retreats and withdrawals
Evans, First Lt Anthony 276, 303
Exon, Captain Art 301

Faid Pass, Tunisia 147, 206, 218
fighter-bomber attacks 59, 60

fighter escorts 30, 36–37, 55, 57, 59, 60, 63, 72, 77, 78, 88, 92, 110, 117, 131, 136, 137, 143–144, 146–147, 153, 154–155, 157, 171, 173, 174, 175, 176, 177, 179, 184–185, 188, 189, 190, 192, 193, 195–196, 197, 198, 199, 202, 205, 212, 217, 218, 220, 225, 228, 229, 231, 233, 235, 247, 254, 259, 262, 264, 267, 268, 271, 276, 285, 287, 289, 290, 291, 298, 299, 300, 302–303, 304
fighter sweeps 138, 191, 194, 218, 223–224, 225, 231, 232, 247, 265, 298, 300, 301
flak *see* antiaircraft fire
Fletcher, First Lt Moss 193, 217
flight formations 163–164, 165
food rations 52, 128, 170, 171, 180, 181, 197, 263
Fredendall, Gen Lloyd 194, 195, 202, 204, 209, 211
Free French forces, the 104, 106, 125, 126; XIX French Corps 204 *see also* Armée de l'Air, the
French Air Force, the *see* Armée de l'Air, the
French colonies of North Africa, the 100, 102, 106
French Foreign Legion, the 123, 124, 157
French involvement in Operation *Torch* 100–104
French Navy, the 125; attack at Mers el-Kébir 103–104; ships: *Jean Bart* (battleship) 106, 108, 109–110; *Le Conquérant* (submarine) 109; *Primauguet* (light cruiser) 106, 108, 110
fuel supplies 52, 123, 182, 206, 209, 216, 221, 243

Galland, General der Jagdflieger Adolf 299, 230, 284
Garman, Lt Col Ralph 145, 146, 147
Gaulle, General Charles de 100, 102, 103, 104, 125, 126
German strategy 12–13, 21, 22, 23, 51, 53, 65, 71, 72–73, 76–77, 78, 89, 125, 127, 160–161, 200, 204–205, 208–210, 216, 228, 243, 248, 283, 284–285, 288, 291, 297, 300, 302
Giraud, General Henri 102–103, 125, 126, 204
Göring, Reichsmarschall Hermann 22, 83–84, 285, 286, 296
Green, Cpt Herschel "Herky" 203, 245–246, 259–261, 262, 264, 304
ground-attack missions 137
ground support 89, 202, 210, 211, 216, 218, 298

Hale, Lt Charles 243–244
Hall, Lt Charlie "Seabuster" 265, 278
HALPRO (Halverson Provisional Detachment), the 25, 26, 27, 67, 76
Halverson, Col Henry 25, 27
Hamilton, First Lt Frank 261–262, 304
Hanson, Lt Bill 241, 242
Harris, Lt George 228, 233
Hawkins, Col John R. 121, 122–123
Hawkins, Second Lt Frank B. "Pancho" 166–168, 169–170, 171–172, 173, 174, 175, 177–178, 183

315

Heer, the 29, 30; Army Group Centre 23; Sixth Army 226
Hennin, Lt Francis 269–270
high-G combat maneuvering 35, 87, 134
Hitler, Adolf 12–13, 22, 23, 65, 72, 76, 79, 125, 210, 228, 244, 248, 282, 283, 297
Hoelle, Second Lt Bill 196–197
Hollingsworth, Lt Jim 276, 303
Huff, Cpt Frank 225, 230, 269
Hunziker, Second Lt Richard O. 237
Hurlbut, Flt Off Frank 276, 292–293

IJN (Imperial Japanese Navy), the: *Shoho* (carrier) 116
Ilfrey, First Lt Jack 16–20, 130, 140, 142, 147, 148, 149–151, 152–155
intelligence 51, 57, 100–101, 205, 235, 243, 257, 281–283; and Ultra 52, 53, 182, 231, 243, 282–283, 297 *see also* reconnaissance
interdiction missions 99, 231, 252
Italian aircraft design 85–86
Italian Army, the 256; First Italian Army, the 227, 230, 244
Italian Navy, the 26, 177, 242; *Littorio* (battleship) 26
Italian strategy 88, 89, 127

Japanese actions in the Far East 21, 22, 23, 25
Jaqua, First Lt Arnold D. 59, 69
Jewell, Lt Cdr N.L.A. "Bill" 103, 281
Jones, Maj David M. 187, 188

Kasserine Pass 183, 203–211
Katzenbach, Second Lt Nicholas de Belleville "Katz" 167, 183
Kauffman, Jack 241–242
Keith, Lt Col Troy 197, 275
Kenworthy, Cpt Paul 121, 206
Kesselring, Generalfeldmarschall Albert 248, 297
King, Adm Ernest 98, 99, 250
Kirtley, Maj Bob 156–157
Knapp, Col Robert D. 165–166, 178, 181
Knight, Maj Archie J. 41, 224
Kuentzel, First Lt Ward 292, 300

Lancaster, First Lt Rayburn 61, 62, 264
landing grounds 53, 54, 56, 57, 60, 61, 64, 67, 68, 71, 223
Levine, Maj Robert 192, 193
Lieber, Second Lt Larry 276, 293
Linn, Second Lt Marcus "Junior" 143, 144, 145
living conditions 53, 54, 140, 141, 153, 158, 170, 174, 180, 203, 263
logistics and supplies 23, 24–25, 27, 31, 53, 65, 87, 128, 158, 182, 194, 204, 205, 206, 226, 230–231, 243
Lovell, Second Lt Robert 148, 150, 151, 152
low flying 145–146, 151, 156

Lucchini, Franco 91–92
Lufbery circle, the 81, 82, 214, 236, 292
Luftwaffe, the 13, 15, 18, 22, 29, 31, 36, 37, 57, 60, 63, 85, 87, 90, 104, 107, 125, 128, 131, 136, 141, 154, 187, 195, 216, 247, 248, 250, 251, 263, 272, 284, 302, 306; Condor Legion 83; JG (*Jagdgeschwader*): JG 2 196; II./JG 2 "Richthofen" 36, 79–81, 82, 128, 154, 174, 189, 193, 212; JG 26 66, 154; JG 27 "Afrika" Geschwader 65, 72, 74, 234–235; I./JG 27 65; II./JG 27 231; III./JG 27 65; JG 51 75, 128, 198, 199, 224, 233, 285; II./JG 51 79, 146, 196; IV./JG 51 75; JG 53 "Pik As" 80, 83, 155, 176, 216, 217, 228–229, 239, 264, 283, 284–285, 286, 287, 288, 291, 295, 296, 298–299, 302, 304; I./JG 53 26, 63, 77, 78, 84, 188, 228, 234, 239, 242, 298–299, 302; II./JG 53 65, 73–74, 77, 78, 80, 84, 189, 190, 216, 228, 238, 239, 242, 243, 296, 300, 302, 304; III./JG 53 65, 72–73, 77, 84, 146, 184–185, 216, 238, 243, 296, 302, 303–304; Stab./JG 53 84; JG 54 287; JG 76: I./JG 76 75; JG 77 66, 71, 74, 75, 78, 79, 83, 196, 199, 216, 218, 219, 225, 228, 229, 243–244, 247, 266, 284–285, 286, 288, 291; I./JG 77 65, 67, 75, 76, 79, 83, 84, 244, 287; II./JG 77 65, 74, 75, 76, 79, 189, 190, 283; III./JG 77 65, 74, 76, 305; KG (*Kampfgeschwader*): KG 30 288; LG (*Lehrgeschwader*): LG 2 76; Luftlotte 2 283; *Staffeln* 36; 1./JG 2 75; 1./JG 77 67, 79; 2./JG 2 77; 2./JG 53 287–288; 3./JG 53 239; 3./JG 77 76; 4./JG 2 80, 154; 4./JG 53 78, 300, 301, 304; 4./JG 77 76, 79; 5./JG 27 231; 5./JG 53 153, 155, 291; 6./JG 2 80; 7./JG 26 66, 74; 7./JG 53 24, 77, 238; 7./JG 77 74; 8./JG 53 243; 9./JG 53 73, 77, 295, 296; 14./KG 40 156; SG (*Schlachtgeschwader*): SG 2 234; I./SG 2 65; SKG (*Schnellkampfgeschwader*): SKG 210 234; StG (*Sturzkampfgeschwader*): StG 3: II./StG 3 77; III./StG 3 216–217; X Fliegerkorps 88; ZG (*Zerstörergeschwader*): ZG 1: III./ZG 1 190; ZG 26 235; II./ZG 26 234; III./ZG 26 233

MAC (Mediterranean Air Command), the 230, 251, 252, 256
MacArthur, Gen Douglas 29, 30, 99, 194
Maltzahn, *Kommodore* Oberstleutnant Günther Freiherr von 77, 78, 80, 84, 228, 242, 286
Mareth Line, the 70–71, 78, 210, 222–223, 225, 227, 228
Marin la Meslée, Capitaine Edmond 116, 117
markings and insignia 39, 43, 56–57, 84, 93, 111, 223, 274–275
Marshall, Gen George C. 24, 28, 30, 31, 32, 98–99, 244, 250, 251, 280
Martin, Maj William 281–282, 283
Martinoli, Sergente Teresio 90–91
McArthur, Cpt Paul 225, 269, 270

316

INDEX

McDonald, Cpt Norman   217–218, 219, 220, 302
McDougall, First Lt Robert D.   176–177
McGoldrick, Lt Col Peter   42, 49, 50, 68
McWherter, First Lt Richard   148, 150, 152, 154
Mears, Maj Frank H.   39–40, 42, 43
mechanical problems   17, 19, 34, 132–133, 162
medals and honors   16, 75, 76, 79; Air Medal   16, 222; Distinguished Flying Cross   155, 189, 190, 257; Navy Cross   116; Presidential Unit Citation   178, 201, 302; Ritterkreuz des Eisernen Kreuzes   75, 76, 79, 80, 287; Ritterkreuz mit Brillanten   83
Meimberg, Oberleutnant Julius   77, 78
Mendenhall, First Lt Harold "Mendy"   143, 144, 145
Mers el-Kébir and the French naval fleet   103–104
Messina   263, 276, 284, 304, 305
Michalski, Hauptmann Gerhard   84, 228, 239, 296, 300, 304
Michelier, Vice Adm   106, 110
midair collisions   152, 189, 218, 242, 260, 268, 269
Middleditch, Cpt Lyman, Jr.   60–61, 64, 229
military strength and complements   29, 36, 37, 41, 43–44, 66, 72, 78, 85, 89, 105, 135, 198, 204
Mitchell, Lt Merlin   212, 213–214, 215, 216
Mobbs, First Lt George D.   57–58, 59, 69–70
Momyer, Lt Col William   20, 118, 239, 253–254, 265, 266–267
Montgolfier, Lt Paul de   111, 114
Montgomery, Gen Bernard   31, 52, 53, 59, 226
Mount, First Lt Bill   40–41, 57
MTO (Mediterranean Theater of Operations), the   55, 161
Müller, Hauptmann Friedrich-Karl "Tutti"   78, 84, 239, 242, 295, 298
Müncheberg, Maj Joachim   65, 66, 67, 74, 79, 218
Murphy, Robert D.   100, 103, 107
Mussolini, Benito   12, 22, 69, 88, 244, 251, 256, 297

NAAF (Northwest African Air Force), the   251, 257; NACAF (Northwest African Coastal Air Force)   251; NASAF (Northwest African Strategic Air Force)   232, 251, 257, 265, 284; NATAF (Northwest African Tactical Air Force)   210, 251, 257
Naval Battle of Casablanca, the   108–110
NCOs (non-commissioned officers)   80, 218, 291
New Deal reforms, the   24, 32
night missions   26, 142, 162–163, 288, 299, 302
Noguès, General Charles   106, 119
North Africa landing proposals   28, 30
Novotny, Lt George   300, 304, 305

O'Neill, First Lt William W.   54–55
Operations: *Barbarossa* (June–December 1941)   76; *Blau* (June–November 1942)   84; *Corkscrew* (June 1943)   254–274, **255**, **273**, 280; *Crusader* (November 1941)   23; *Flax* (April 1943)   231–242; *Husky* (July–August 1943)   296, 283, 291, **294**, 297; *Pedestal* (August 1942)   73; *Strike* (May 1943)   242–243; *Tidal Wave* (August 1943)   305; *Torch* (November 1942)   30, 31, 32–33, 37, 50, 76, 77, 84, 89, 98, 99–100, 102–116, 127, 135, 195, 249; *Zitadelle* (July–August 1943)   283
Oran port, Algeria   **101**, 128, 130
Osterkamp, Generalmajor "Onkel Theo"   284, 299
Overcash, Second Lt R.J. "Jay"   64, 240, 241
Owens, Cpt Joe   143–147

paint and camouflage schemes   39, 44, 50, 161, 231, 235, 245
"Palm Sunday Massacre," the   238
Palmer, First Lt John   262, 304
Patton, Gen George S., Jr.   32, 100, 108, 121, 209
Payne, First Lt Carl   121–122, 216–217
Pearl Harbor attacks, the   22, 99
Peck, Cpt Jimmie   139, 192
performance and maneuverability   33, 35–36, 48, 66, 86, 87, 112, 115, 132–133, 140, 186, 193, 197, 203, 214, 216, 276, 279
Pétain, Marshal Philippe   100, 102
Ploesti oil fields, Romania   25, 26, 67, 305
Pope, Lt John F.   141, 192
POWs   12, 71, 74, 115, 183, 188, 216, 224, 227, 241, 242, 244
precision bombing missions   164, 165
production   23, 85, 87, 88
public opinion and political pressure in the US   23, 24, 28, 32, 33, 99, 125–126, 251

Qattara Depression, the   51, 59, 62–63

RA (Regia Aeronautica), the   57, 85, 87, 88, 89–90, 95, 234, 275, 277, 283, 290, 302–303; Asso di Bastoni XXIII Gruppo   91; Corpo Aereo Italiano   93, 94; *Gruppi*   63; 3° 89, 94; 8° 88; 9° 90; 10° 92; 13° 90; 18° 93, 95; 20° 88, 89; 32° 89; 101° Tuff 94; 150° "Gigi Tre Osei"   27, 89, 258, 264, 265, 286–287, 289, 290, 291, 297; 151° 257, 263; 153° 88, 264; 157° 90; *Squadriglia*: 73ᵃ 91; 74ᵃ 94; 78ᵃ 90; 84ᵃ 91; 95ᵃ 93, 95; 278ᵃ 94; 363ᵃ 286, 290; 364ᵃ 286, 287; 365ᵃ 265; 374ᵃ 263; 377ᵃ Autonoma 94; 384ᵃ 90; *Stormi*: 2° 90; 3° 93, 95; 4° 90, 91, 92; 10° 94; 30° 94; 53° 264; 54° 94; Super Aereo   284
RAAF (Royal Australian Air Force), the   52, 83; Squadrons: 3 Sqn 59; 450 Sqn 59, 83, 94
Raby, Lt Cdr Jack   110, 117, 118
radar systems   15, 156, 162, 194, 202, 256, 265, 285
RAF (Royal Air Force), the   25, 26–27, 35, 36, 39, 44, 47, 52, 56, 57, 72, 83, 84, 87, 90, 121, 186, 192, 210, 211, 251, 306; Air Rescue   270;

Bomber Groups: 211 Group 56, 59; Fighter Wings: 233 Wing 64; 239 Wing 59; 244 Wing 228, 235; 322 Wing 141; Long Range Desert Group 88–89; Polish Fighting Team 229–230, 240; Squadrons 276; 6 Sqn 59; 18 Sqn 80; 81 Sqn 80, 141; 92 Sqn 235; 112 "Shark" Sqn 59, 68, 83; 145 Sqn 229, 234, 289; 152 Sqn 234; 185 Sqn 291; 223 Sqn 289; 225 Sqn 157; 242 Sqn 157; 250 Sqn 59, 63, 89; 260 Sqn 53, 54, 95, 234; 272 Sqn 94; 601 Sqn 289; 614 Sqn 80; 683 Photo Recon Sqn 257 *see also* WDAF (Western Desert Air Force), the

ranges 26, 31, 134, 137, 141, 285

Rawson, First Lt Bill "Hut-sut" 212, 233

reconnaissance 65, 115, 124, 125, 140, 147–148, 195, 196, 208, 257, 271, 290, 291 *see also* intelligence

Red Army, the 21, 23, 29, 226

redeployments 67, 73, 82, 84, 97, 125, 128, 160, 173, 188–189, 193, 197, 202–203, 216, 220, 234, 235, 242, 245, 246, 253, 258, 263, 268, 276, 277, 288, 297, 300, 304, 305

Reed, Cpt W.R. 261, 262, 289, 302

Reed, Second Lt James E. 96–98, 117, 118, 158, 200, 239, 258–259, 277

Reinert, Leutnant Ernst-Wilhelm 76, 79, 228, 234

reinforcements 13, 30, 39, 65, 72–73, 76, 79, 117, 141, 155, 157, 199, 206, 208, 209

repairs and maintenance 26, 59, 69, 78, 119, 135, 158, 161–162, 293

replacements 36, 53, 65, 69, 78, 84–85, 157, 198, 200, 201, 202, 239, 246, 258, 259, 275, 288, 299

Republican Party, the 23–24

retreats and withdrawals 13, 27, 36, 65, 67, 73, 78, 84, 85, 89, 90, 99, 123, 161, 172, 183, 189, 190, 198, 204, 205, 206, 209–210, 216, 227, 228, 271, 275, 284, 297, 304, 305 *see also* evacuations

Richthofen, Feldmarschall Wolfram Freiherr von 283, 284

Ritter, First Lt Lawrence 261, 271

Roberts, Cpt Newell 132–133, 135, 142–143, 147–148, 150, 151–152

Röhrig, Oberleutnant Hans 295, 296

Rommel, Generalleutnant Erwin 12, 13, 23, 27, 51, 52, 53, 65, 71, 89, 92, 160, 165, 172, 204–205, 208, 209–210, 216, 227

Roosevelt, Franklin D. 21, 23, 24, 28–29, 30, 31, 39, 98–99, 102, 125, 126, 193, 246, 249, 251

Rounds, Second Lt Gerry 199, 289

Royal Navy, the 100, 103–104, 256–257, 270, 274; Fleet Air Arm 105, 119; ships: HMS *Firedrake* (destroyer) 94; HMS *Leinster* (transport) 120; HMS *Seraph* (submarine) 103, 281; HMT *Derbyshire* 168

Rudorffer, Oberleutnant Erich 80, 81–82

Ryerson, First Lt Gordon 64–65

SAAF (South African Air Force), the 53, 54, 56, 239, 289; 3 Wing 286; 7 Wing 240; Squadrons: 7 Sqn 59

Salisbury, Col Art 43, 44, 48, 235, 299

Say, First Lt Sammy 69, 242

Schottelkorb, First Lt Bill 128, 137–138, 197, 198

Schrup, First Lt Elwin F. 172–173

sea rescues 116, 183, 186, 264, 268, 270, 276, 289, 299

sea search missions 177, 178–179, 184

Seegmiller, Sgt Barnard 180, 181

Sfax, Tunisia 147–149

Sharp, Second Lt Danny 232–233

Shields, Lt Charles "Windy" (j.g.) 111–113

Shipman, First Lt Mark 130, 198

Sicily as Allied objective 250–251, 252, 254, 276–278, 281, 282, 283, 287–291, **294**, 297, 302

Simpson, Lt Carl 225, 240

Sloan, Cpt William J. "Dixie" 136, 195, 212, 276, 293, 300

Smallsreed, Flt Off John 261, 264, 265

Smith, First Lt Virgil 140, 155

Solaroli, Capitano Giorgio 93–95

sorties 63, 71, 187, 194, 241, 243, 256, 265, 272, 289, 298

Soviet strategy 21, 22–23

Spaatz, Gen Carl 194, 202, 210, 251, 257, 275

Spanish Civil War, the 87–88, 91, 100

Spawn, Cpt Douglas W. "Doug" 161–162, 164–165

speeds 33, 69, 115, 118, 132, 186, 270

split-S maneuver, the 46, 57, 215

Stalin, Joseph 23, 28, 249

Steinhoff, Oberst Johannes "Macky" 74–75, 83, 243, 288

strafing runs 57–58, 62, 68, 71, 89, 110, 115, 116, 117, 118, 124, 137, 142, 147–149, 157, 198, 201, 222, 247, 261, 265, 267, 289, 293, 299

Strait of Gibraltar, the 100, 106, 120

Strait of Messina, the 296, 297, 298, 305

Stumpf, Oberfeldwebel Werner 73, 74

supply convoys 178–179, 182, 183, 184–185, 191, 212, 226

surrenders: of Axis forces in North Africa 13, 37, 191, 210, 226, 244–245, 247, 249, 254, 263; of Axis forces on Pantelleria 270, 272–274, 279–280; of British forces in Tobruk 89; of Italian forces in Sicily 12, 91, 283, 305; of Vichy French forces 13, 106, 125, 130

Szczygiel, Second Lt Joseph F. 170, 171, 172, 179

tanks 124; M3 Grant (US) 77, 206, 211; M4 Sherman (US) 53, 211; Panzer III (Germany) 206; Panzer IV (Germany) 53, 206; Tiger I (Germany) 206

Task Forces: Force 34 104; TG 34.8 105, 106; TG 34.9 (Center) 105, 107; TG 34.10 105, 106; Force H 104; Force O 104

Taylor, Cpt Ralph "Zack" 271, 289, 300

INDEX

Tedder, Air Marshal Sir Arthur   13, 25, 195, 230–231, 251–252, 280, 306
terrain   51, 54, 62–63, 77, 128, 204–205, 227–228
testing   132–133, 146
Thomas, First Lt Woodlief "Woody"   212, 213
Thyng, Maj Harrison   121, 193, 206, 218
Tobruk, Libya   27, 89
Tollen, Second Lt Jim   137, 138
Tonne, Hauptmann Wolfgang   78, 234, 239
Trafton, First Lt   267, 301
training   23, 34, 36, 42, 43, 44, 47, 48, 49, 71, 75, 79, 87, 94, 96–97, 104, 115, 135, 140, 161, 165, 166, 178, 184, 185, 186, 187, 188, 189, 195, 223, 245, 246, 253, 290; carrier takeoff instruction   39, 40–41, 45
transatlantic crossings   16–17, 25, 45, 49–50, 98, 161, 166–168, 169, 180–182, 183, 185–186, 187, 188, 245–246
Tricaud, Commandant Georges   111, 114
Tuskegee Aviation Project, the   252–253

U-boats   50, 104, 250
Ultra code-breaking machine, the   52, 53, 182, 231, 243, 282–283, 297
US Army, the   13, 29, 30, 37, 194, 203–204, 207, 209, 244, 285; Corps: II Corps   193, 194, 195, 202, 204, 206, 209; Divisions: 1st Armored   206, 209, 226, 230; 1st Infantry   206; 3rd Infantry   107; 9th Infantry   208, 209; 82nd Airborne   122, 130, 290; First Army   77, 202; Regiments: 47th Infantry   106–107; 504th Parachute Infantry   290–291, 296; 505th Parachute Infantry   290–291; 509th Parachute Infantry   127, 130
US Congressional elections (1942), the   23–24, 30, 31, 32, 99
US Navy, the   22, 98, 105; ACV (auxiliary aircraft carriers)   104; Fighter Squadrons: VF-9   105, 110, 115, 116–118; VF-41   105, 111–114; Escort Fighter Squadrons: VGF-26   105, 116; VGF-27   105; VGF-28   105; VGF-29   105, 116; VGF-30   105; Escort Scouting Squadrons: VGS-26   105; VGS-27   105, 108; VGS-29   105; Scouting Squadrons: VS-41   105, 108; ships: *Augusta* (heavy cruiser)   108, 109; *Brooklyn* (light cruiser)   108; *Chenango* (escort carrier)   98, 105, 117, 118; *Elizabeth Stanton* (transport)   180, 182; *Juneau* (light cruiser)   45; *Leonard Wood* (attack transport)   107; *Ludlow* (destroyer)   108; *Mariposa* (transport)   252; *Massachusetts* (battleship)   108, 109, 111; *Monticello* (transport)   169; *Murphy* (destroyer)   108; *New York* (battleship)   106; *Philadelphia* (light cruiser)   106; *Ranger* (carrier)   13, 38–39, 45, 104, 105, 108, 109, 111, 116, 118, 241, 245–246; *Sangamon* (carrier)   105, 116; *Santee* (carrier)   105, 115, 116; *Savannah* (light cruiser)   106; *Suwannee* (carrier)   105, 108; *Texas* (battleship)   106; *Tuscaloosa* (heavy cruiser)   108; *Wasp* (carrier)   38, 42; *West Point* (transport)   185; *Wichita* (heavy cruiser)   108; *Wilkes* (destroyer)   107 see also Task Forces
US strategy   13, 23, 24, 25, 26, 28–29, 30–31, 32–33, 36–37, 165, 178, 194–195, 199–200, 202, 204, 206, 208, 210–211, 218
USAAC (US Army Air Corps), the   16, 40, 41, 96, 166, 253
USAAF (US Army Air Force), the   13, 26, 27, 36, 72, 84, 87, 90, 104, 178, 210, 211, 251, 272, 279–280, 288, 306; 33rd Fighter Wing   239; 57th Bomb Wing   178, 185; Air Forces: Eighth   30–31, 34, 37, 72, 120, 131; Ninth   229, 236, 237, 305; Seventh   31; Tenth   185; Twelfth   30, 34, 36–37, 97, 120, 127, 139, 155, 159, 165, 167, 179, 187, 189, 194, 198, 245, 305, 306; Bomb Groups: 1st Provisional   27; 7th   27; 12th   57, 160, 161–163, 166, 185–186, 225, 289–290; 17th   160, 174, 187, 188–191; 27th (Light)   270; 47th   169, 174, 286, 287, 289–290; 97th   83, 143, 144, 231, 234–235; 98th   27; 99th   92, 232; 301st   83, 231–232, 234; 310th   165, 166, 167, 169, 172–176, 178, 179–185, 188–189, 197, 199, 226, 231, 233, 257, 302–303; 319th   187–189, 195, 271, 288; 320th   187, 188–189, 190–191, 271; 321st   79, 165, 178–179, 180, 181, 183–184, 185, 212, 231, 247; 340th   165, 178, 185–186, 290; Bomb Squadrons: 15th   155; 37th   190, 293; 81st   160; 82nd   160, 161, 164–165; 83rd   160; 85th   169; 86th   169; 95th   189; 97th   169; 379th   166, 168, 169, 170–171, 174, 176, 177, 179, 184; 380th   166, 168, 169, 171, 172, 176, 177, 179; 381st   166–167, 168, 169, 170, 171, 172, 173, 177–178, 179, 184; 428th   166, 173, 175, 177, 184; 432nd   190; 434th   160; 439th   188; 441st   190, 191; 443rd   191; 444th   190; 445th   180, 181, 183; 446th   181, 183; 447th   181, 182; 448th   181–183; 486th   185, 186; 487th   185; 488th   185; 489th   185; Fighter Groups   35; 1st   15, 16, 82, 83, 128, 130, 132, 135, 136, 139, 142, 143, 146, 147, 157, 172, 176, 177, 179, 184, 188, 199, 231, 232, 233, 258, 275, 298; 14th   34–35, 128, 136–137, 139, 140, 142, 155, 157, 174–175, 196–199, 258, 263, 265, 275–276, 293, 297, 298, 302–303, 304; 23rd   276; 31st   36, 79, 82, 83, 105, 120–121, 122–123, 128, 130, 139, 193, 206, 212, 218, 231, 233–234, 263, 265, 267–268, 276, 285, 288, 290, 291, 295, 297–298, 302; 33rd "Nomads"   42, 43, 44, 81, 83, 97–98, 105, 117, 119, 158, 188, 193–194, 199–200, 201, 203, 216, 234, 239, 245, 246, 253–254, 258–259, 265, 268, 276, 277, 278, 286; 51st   39, 42; 52nd   36, 79, 120–121,

124, 125, 130, 138, 140, 157–158, 189, 203, 212, 217, 218–219, 231, 272, 274, 277–278, 302; 56th 44; 57th 13, 39, 41, 42–45, 49, 53, 54, 55, 56, 59–63, 65, 67, 68, 71, 79, 83, 89, 97, 160, 222–224, 229, 235–236, 238, 240, 241, 245, 299, 301; 78th 13, 157; 79th "Falcons" 48–50, 68, 69, 70, 71, 222, 223, 225, 227, 228, 229–230, 235, 239–240, 241–242, 243–244, 245, 268; 81st 82; 82nd 82, 135, 155–157, 176, 190, 195, 199, 211–212, 220, 222, 231, 232–235, 276, 286, 289, 291–292, 293; 86th 298; 121st 173; 324th 71, 223, 235, 238, 286, 287, 290, 291; 325th "Checkertail Clan" 49, 190, 203, 245–247, 259, 261–262, 264, 268, 274–275, 288–289, 299–300, 301–302, 304, 305; 350th 193, 203, 208; Fighter Squadrons: 2nd 124–125, 138–139, 140–141, 157–158, 192, 217–218, 219, 274, 302; 4th 124–125, 192–193, 203, 217, 219, 272, 274, 302; 5th 125, 192, 203, 277–278, 27th 136, 143–144, 298; 37th 265, 275–276, 303; 48th 128, 136, 137–138, 140, 198, 265, 297, 303; 49th 128, 136–137, 138, 140, 197–198, 258, 276, 303, 304; 58th 158, 193, 200–201, 203, 234; 59th 81, 97, 158, 193, 200, 203, 216; 60th 81, 158, 193, 203, 234; 61st 44; 64th "Black Scorpions" 39, 40–41, 42, 43, 47, 56–57, 60, 61–62, 64, 67–68, 69–70, 224–225, 229, 235–236, 238, 240–241, 299, 301; 65th "Fighting Cocks" 39, 40, 42, 43, 44, 46, 47, 48, 54–55, 56, 59, 60–61, 63–64, 69, 83, 222, 224, 235–238, 299; 66th "Exterminators" 39, 41, 47, 54, 55, 57, 59, 64, 68, 69, 83, 224–225, 235–236, 238, 245; 71st 136; 85th "Flying Skulls" 48, 49, 69, 223, 225, 227, 240, 268–269; 86th "Comanches" 48, 49, 70, 225, 227, 233, 240, 245, 268; 87th "Skeeters" 48, 49, 225, 227, 228, 229, 240, 268, 270; 94th "Hat in the Ring" 16, 82, 130, 136, 142–143; 95th 156, 232–233; 96th 195–197, 212, 233, 276, 289, 291–292; 97th 196, 199, 212, 220–221, 232, 286, 287, 289; 99th 252–254, 265–266, 278, 286; 126th 139; 307th 124, 159, 203, 206–207, 208, 212–216, 217, 263, 268, 285, 295, 301; 308th 121, 123–124, 193, 202, 205, 208, 218, 263–264, 267–268, 285, 295; 309th 121, 193–194, 206–207, 208, 212–214, 216–217, 218, 263, 268, 285, 295; 314th 223–224, 235–236, 238; 316th 223, 225–226, 227, 233, 243, 290, 291; 317th 203, 245–246, 259, 261, 301; 318th 245, 247, 259; 319th 245, 247, 259, 289, 301

Vaughn, Maj Harley 196, 212
Veterans' recollections 40–41, 44, 45, 46–48, 54, 56, 57–58, 61–63, 67–68, 69–70, 81–82, 92, 94, 111–113, 115, 116, 122, 132–133, 137–139, 140, 142, 143–152, 153–154, 156, 161–162, 164–165, 171–173, 175, 177–178, 196–197, 199, 203, 207, 208, 212–216, 222–223, 229, 235–237, 259–260, 262, 264, 271, 274–275, 292–293, 295, 300
Vichy Armée de l'Air de l'Armistice, the 105, 111–114, 118, 194; *Groupes de Bombardement*: GB I/22 116; GB I/32 114; *Groupes de Chasse*: GC I/5 "Champagne" 105, 116, 117, 119; GC II/3 105; GC II/5 "Lafayette" 82, 105, 110, 111, 114–115, 116, 117, 119; GC II/7 105; GC III/3 105; GC III/6 105 *see also* Armée de l'Air, the
Vichy France 12, 13, 28, 32, 76, 102, 105–106, 128; and German occupation of 125
Vichy French Armistice Army, the 100, 102
Villacèque, Lt Pierre 110, 111, 114
Vinson, Cpt "Vince" 138–139, 192, 208, 217, 218, 219–220
Visscher, Cpt Herman 220–222

Wadi Akarit 227–228, 230
Walker, Lt Walter B. "Bud," Jr. 289, 301
war diaries 82, 98, 114, 137–138, 167–168, 169, 170, 172, 175, 180, 181–182, 185, 186, 196, 200, 240–241, 244, 258–259
Warren, Cpt Harold "Ray" 138, 158
Waters, First Lt Ed 276, 293
Watkins, Cpt John A. 274–275, 304
Watkins, First Lt Morris 230, 269
Watkins, Maj Tarleton "Jack" 70, 241
WDAF (Western Desert Air Force), the 13, 48, 52–53, 59, 65, 67, 89, 160, 185, 195, 201, 222–223, 224, 226–227
weaponry 39, 66, 86, 106, 109, 114, 123, 133–134, 214, 267, 271; 0.50-caliber machine gun (US) 62, 111, 112, 115, 156, 180, 216; 0.303-caliber machine gun (US) 124; 12.7mm machine gun (Italy) 27; 20mm cannon (Germany) 56, 62; 37mm cannon (US) 35; Modèle 1935 138mm gun (France) 106
Weatherford, First Lt Sidney W. 265, 297, 298
Wehrmacht, the 21–23, 29–30, 37, 75, 76, 85, 174, 204, 244, 247, 249, 250–251, 252, 281, 282, 283, 306 *see also* Afrika Korps, the; Heer, the; Luftwaffe, the
West, Lt Col Graham 138, 140
Wheeler, Maj Clermont "Pudge" 57, 61, 62, 63, 64
White, Second Lt Tom 196, 207, 212
Whittaker, Cpt Roy E. 40, 63, 64, 236–237
Williams, Maj George 219, 220
Windham, S/Sgt Duke G. 176, 177
Wolfe, Second Lt Fred 136, 196, 293
Wright, Lt Fred 225, 228